CHILD WELFARE:
A UNIFYING MODEL OF PRACTICE

Jannah Hurn Mather
Wilfrid Laurier University

Patricia B. Lager
Florida State University

Brooks/Cole
Thomson Learning

Australia • Canada • Mexico • Singapore • Spain • United Kingdom • United States

Social Work Editor: Lisa Gebo
Assistant Editor: Susan Wilson
Editorial Assistant: JoAnne von Zastrow
Marketing Manager: Caroline Concilla
Project Editor: Marlene Vasilieff
Print Buyer: Stacey Weinberger
Permissions Editor: Joohee Lee
Photo Researcher: Progressive Publishing
Alternatives

Copy Editor: Progressive Publishing Alternatives
Cover Designer: Bill Stanton
Cover Images: PhotoDisc, The Image Bank
Signing Representative: Mark Francisco
Compositor: Progressive Information Technologies
Printer/Binder: R. R. Donnelley & Sons Co.

For more information, contact
Wadsworth/Thomson Learning
10 Davis Drive
Belmont, CA 94002-3098
USA
http://www.wadsworth.com

International Headquarters
Thomson Learning, International Division
290 Harbor Drive, 2nd Floor
Stamford, CT 06902-7477
USA

UK/Europe/Middle East/South Africa
Thomson Learning
Berkshire House
168-173 High Holborn
London WC1V 7AA
United Kingdom

Asia
Thomson Learning
60 Albert Street, #15-01
Albert Complex
Singapore 189969

Canada
Nelson Thomson Learning
1120 Birchmount Road
Toronto, Ontario M1K 5G4
Canada

Library of Congress
Cataloging-in-Publication Data
Child welfare: a unifying model of practice/by Jannah Hurn Mather and Patricia B. Lager.
    p. cm.
Includes bibliographical references and index.
ISBN 0-534-26376-3
    1. Child welfare — United States. 2. Social work with children — United States. I. Lager,
Patricia B. II. Title.

HV741 .C499 1999
362.7'0973 — dc21

Contents

This book is dedicated to the people we love for their support and patience: Grafton, Tom, Sean, R.J., Jake and Tiffany; and to our editor, Lisa Gebo, who always believed in us and was there to make things happen.

Preface

This text has been developed in response to the learning needs of both social work students and current child welfare social workers. The premise of the text is to present a fundamental model of social work practice that addresses both the issues of residual and universal (preventive) types of intervention. By focusing on an approach that has a multi-systemic view, child welfare social workers can move beyond a protective focus and help place an emphasis on prevention. The preventive modes of intervention introduced in this book are reflective of "out of the box" thinking. This term refers to those methods of intervention that do not fit neatly into the framework of the public child welfare system but rather are more innovative and blend both policy changes and practice applications into the entire domain of the child welfare practitioner.

Chapter 1 describes the relationship of the profession to the development of the field of child welfare. It also addresses those factors that have affected the welfare of families and children within our society. An overview of current social welfare changes and their impact on families and children is also discussed. Chapter 2 provides a brief review of the foundation of social work practice and how it relates to the model of Social Work Protocols in Practice (SWPIP). The best practice protocols are presented and the phases of the model are reviewed. Chapter 3 describes and gives examples of the protocols in action in child welfare practice, while chapter 4 addresses both formal and informal services that can be provided to families and children. Particular attention is paid to those preventive types of service that can be initiated by the child welfare social worker or welfare team in an effort to change the conditions in which families and children live.

The second section of the book, from chapter 5 through chapter 11, examines common child welfare situations in which social workers provide aid. The model is introduced in each chapter through a case study of a particular child welfare situation. Each phase of the model is discussed and attention brought to protocols in practice for each case. Neglect, abuse, sexual abuse, teenage pregnancies, delinquencies, divorce/loss, and special needs are all addressed in this section through the application of the model.

The final chapter of the text discusses the leadership and learning environment needed within child welfare agencies to promote the use of models that bridge the gaps between prevention and intervention. This chapter discusses the importance of the social worker's involvement in changing policies and implementing interventions that bring equality to all families and provide greater prevention for all children.

Acknowledgements

This book would not have been completed without the tireless efforts of Jane Kirkpatrick, Helen Bingeman, Susan Hardie, and Marie Morrison. We would also like to acknowledge Debra McPhee and Claudia Trische for their visions and knowledge.

List of Reviewers

The editors, authors, and publisher thank the reviewers of the manuscript for their helpful comments and suggestions:

Diane Alperin
Florida Atlantic University

Christy Baker
University of Southern Indiana

Thomas Collins
University of Scranton

Patricia Dempsey
Hunter College

Christie Reed
San Jose State University

Joan R. Rycraft
University of Texas at Arlington

Elizabeth Timberlake
Catholic University of America

Claudia Triche
Northwestern State University

Vernon Wiehe
University of Kentucky

Biographies

Jannah Hurn Mather is Dean of the Faculty of Social Work at Wilfrid Laurier University. Dr. Mather has written numerous articles on families and children. She has practiced in the field of child welfare, family service agencies, in-patient adolescent units and private practice. She received her BSW from Bowling Green State University, her MSW from the University of Michigan, and her PhD from the University of Illinois.

Patricia Lager is a field coordinator and Assistant Practicum Professor at Florida State University. She received her MSW from Florida State and has extensive practice experience in child welfare and private practice. Ms. Lager's work includes numerous articles and presentations which concentrate on child welfare and liability issues in social work practice.

1

■

Child Welfare, Poverty, and the Profession

Child welfare is not just about the welfare of children, it is about the welfare and future of humankind. As we touch a child in any way, we influence tomorrow and the tomorrows to come. In a society that can afford to love and value their children, we must ask ourselves what the reasons are that we seem unable to love all children.

INTRODUCTION

This chapter provides the context for understanding the relationships between the social work profession, child welfare, and poverty. The text examines those societal factors that affect social work practice in child welfare agencies and concludes by identifying ways in which child welfare practice may be enhanced through the use of a bridging model of practice that intervenes from both a residual and preventive perspective of social work. The model, Social Work Protocols in Practice (SWPIP), is introduced as a model of social work practice that can be utilized within the context of a child welfare agency and yet provide "out of the box" types of methods that advance societal change as well as bridge with the resolution of individual case situations.

THE HISTORICAL ROLE OF SOCIAL WORK
IN THE DEVELOPMENT OF CHILD WELFARE

Issues surrounding child welfare in the United States have been a major focus of the social work profession since its North American beginnings in the mid-nineteenth century. Early social workers, who were primarily concerned with the child and family, worked through two different paradigms to rectify the poverty conditions in which children lived. These paradigms included social workers who worked from the philosophy of Charity Organization Societies and social workers who worked from the philosophy of Settlement House workers. Those social workers within Charity Organization Societies believed that difficulties within families could best be treated though personal rehabilitation (Popple & Leighninger, 1996). Focus from this perspective was on a medical model of casework and the treatment of individuals and their disorders. Mary Richmond was a key supporter of this philosophy and a leader in the development of casework in Charity Organization Societies. It is important to also note that this casework philosophy fit very well with the fundamental ideologies upon which the United States itself developed. Individuals were and are seen as the source of their own accomplishments, therefore their difficulties are viewed as their own doing.

The Settlement House Philosophy, in direct contrast, maintained that problems for people could be defined environmentally and change could occur as a result of concentrating intervention efforts on the environment and societies in which families lived. Jane Addams and Hull House are an example of this philosophy and movement. Highlight 1.1 explains this philosophy through a speech by Jane Addams. Settlement houses reflected a more liberal conceptualization of social problems and placed the focus of needed change on the institutions within societies (Popple & Leighninger, 1996).

In addition to struggling with these internal philosophical differences, social workers during the early 1900s were becoming more focused on the development of social work as a profession. In an effort to legitimize the profession, social workers began to concentrate more on the medical or "scientific" model to explain their work. Training schools began to be developed across North America in the early 1900s where a social service degree could be obtained. Focus on the "scientific" within the profession resulted in an emphasis on studying systematic techniques. This seemed to justify more of a movement toward "social casework" (p. 59) (1996). By the time psychiatry

> ❖ **HIGHLIGHT 1.1   Jane Addams's Speech**
>
> This site for a Settlement was selected in the first instance because of its diversity and the variety of activity for which it presented an opportunity. It has been the aim of the residents to respond to all sides of the neighborhood life: not to the poor people alone, not to the well-to-do, nor to the young in contradistinction to the old, but to the neighborhood as a whole, "men, women, and children taken in families as the Lord mixes them." The activities of Hull House divide themselves into four, possibly more lines. They are not formally or consciously thus divided, but broadly separate according to the receptivity of the neighbors. They might be designated as the social, educational, and humanitarian, I have added civic—if indeed a Settlement of women can be said to perform civic duties. These activities spring from no preconceived notion of what a Social Settlement should be, but have increased gradually on demand. In describing these activities and their value to the neighborhood, I shall attempt to identify those people who respond to each form. (p. 12)

was embraced around 1919, a majority of social workers had moved toward individual treatment as a preferred method of intervention with less emphasis on social reform issues. This is not to imply that there were no continuing proponents of the environmental change philosophy. However, post–World War I and the sense of patriotism had led many away from more liberal or radical ideas of social change (Popple & Leighninger, 1996). Although the profession of social work has moved back and forth in its emphasis on the individual, group, or environment, it is easy to recognize within early public social welfare agencies the impact the changing profession of social work had on intervention with families and children.

In child welfare agencies in particular, the casework method and the treatment of individuals within the family were seen as the major components of intervention. In many ways this approach fit well with welfare as public agencies developed in the United States in response to "residual" needs or issues already affecting individuals rather than on a preventive basis. Because the family was seen by both the state and profession as the foundation of society, it became common practice to bring about change from within this familial institution. However, with the onset of the Depression in the 1930s, social workers once again began to broaden their philosophy and look for ways in which to bring about change for impoverished families and children through the environment and society. The recognition during the Depression that no individual or family, regardless of their background, was immune to economic effects helped the profession see the need for both paradigms during this period.

The emphasis on societal changes needing to be made in order to support children and their families continued into the 1960s as programs such as the "war on poverty" began to make significant differences in moving "residual" welfare services into "universal" welfare services. Although much of the focus of the war on poverty was to affect change for children and their families, those that were primarily affected were the elderly and the disabled (Lindsey, 1994). In fact, child welfare services remained for the most part a tax supported endeavor and therefore limited in the types of services it could provide. Although the Family Assistance Act in 1972 would have provided the beginnings of a "universal" type program for child welfare through a guaranteed minimal income for each family rather than a means tested system, it did not pass through Congress and was therefore not provided to children and their families (Lindsey, 1994).

As you may have gathered from reviewing this brief historical account, the current practice of professional social work in the field of child welfare has not experienced the early success social workers sought. There are numerous factors that continue to hamper this progress in public child welfare agencies, although child welfare services were seen as one of the main domains of professional social workers. The agencies themselves became systems through which internal and external factors created not only limits to solving child welfare problems but complicated them. These factors continue to affect the profession's work today. Among these factors, shifting societal ideologies, economics, and political agendas have created a major impact and will be examined in more detail later in this chapter. Other factors include issues within the profession itself, primarily based on training in residual treatments through counseling and case management rather than from a societal method of change. Additionally, the field of child welfare has become very interdisciplinary, and while this is good in many ways, it does create issues among professionals as to how to handle programs, interventions, and services.

While these factors are significant to an examination of the field of child welfare practice and how it is affected, the most critical component affecting child welfare today is the increase of poverty that exists within the United States. This factor more than any other appears to have been a major deciding issue in whether families become involved in the child welfare system. Before moving ahead to examining other issues, a child welfare worker must become aware of how poverty affects the families worked with and how their poverty may affect the worker's decisions.

THE ROLE OF
POVERTY IN CHILD WELFARE

The importance of understanding the role of poverty in child welfare cannot be overemphasized. Many researchers believe strongly that poverty is the underlying base of all issues in the child welfare field (Lindsey, 1994; Gil, 1981). Although we as social workers are quick to recognize that child welfare issues do not only exist in or as a result of poverty conditions, it is certainly significant that the majority of neglect situations dealt with are associated with poverty and a lack of resources and education. Gil's (1981) research studies have suggested that the typical profile of the abuser in the United States is likely to be a mother in a single parent headed household who is living below the poverty level. However, these statistics can often be deceiving, as it is more likely that single mother headed families living below the poverty line are in frequent contact with public social service agencies and are more often noticed. While characteristics of at-risk families need to be identified, it is important to understand that the issues behind neglect and maltreatment are not solely limited to the victims of society's inequality.

However, many problems in the child welfare field are closely tied to economic and family support resources. The stresses that poverty places on most families increases the likelihood of abuse and neglect. According to Pelton (1989), the majority of child welfare cases related to abuse and neglect are clearly associated with poverty, as indicated by the inordinate proportion of low-income families who become part of the child welfare system.

Poverty conditions in a family can bring about a demoralizing and debilitating focus in and about individuals living in the family. The need to ensure there is a place to sleep each night and food to eat can consume parents to the degree that little else can be given to their children. Living in a society that emphasizes material worth increases the likelihood that individuals without material goods will have low self-esteem and view themselves as worthless. The economic hardships of the low-income family additionally places more stress on the relationship between the parent and the child. Chilman (1991) found that low-income single mothers experienced so much stress overload that they often developed negative and rejecting attitudes toward their young children. The economic conditions in which a family and child live in this society therefore significantly reflects whether or not they will need child welfare services. Even if the family has a greater sense of worth and self-esteem, the fact that they are living below the poverty line creates a situation in which they are more likely to be noticed by child welfare services simply because they come into contact with other welfare supports. To best understand how a child welfare social worker can begin to counter the effects of poverty, it is important to recognize what conditions create and maintain poverty situations.

Factors Linked to Poverty in the United States

The fact that the numbers of single-parent families has dramatically increased over the last 20 years has had a significant impact on the poverty level of families with children. The 1997 U.S. Census Bureau stated that in families with an adult male present, 9 percent of white children, 20 percent of African-American children, and 26 percent of Hispanic children were poor in 1996. In families with female heads and no adult male present, the child poverty rates were much higher: 25.7 percent for whites, 39.8 percent for African-Americans, and 46.2 percent for Hispanics. The number of children living in poverty in the United States has increased at a steady rate over the last two decades. Statistics from the 1997 U.S. Census Bureau suggest that one in every five children in the United States currently lives in poverty whether they are in a single or two-parent household. The rising cost of inflation has also added to poverty levels. Because inflation has not held steady with the low increase in wages, young families with young wage earners are worse off economically today than their counterparts 20 years ago.

According to Kamerman and Kahn (1990), the United States clearly has not modeled the standards of good living conditions for children, with such a high number living in poverty relative to other developed countries. The United States ranks second for the highest percentage of children living in poverty, with only Australia being higher among industrialized nations. Even our methods of dealing with this poverty have been limited in comparison to other governments—especially as these programs affect children. Many other industrialized nations support families in their venture to raise their children through providing funds for each child in a family regardless of the families' income. For example, in Sweden, every family receives a specific monetary amount a year for each child under the age of 18 in each family (Lindsey, 1994).

The family support benefits in this country, however, have been tied to other factors affecting child welfare, such as shifting ideologies, the economic environment, and political agendas set through the last 50 years. In 1935, the Social Security Act enacted additional resources for families with children; yet in the late 1990s, the United States is once again moving backward in its endeavors to help children as the current Social Welfare Reform Act is implemented. This Act, signed in 1996, has had far-reaching consequences for children living in poverty. To begin to understand how poverty and the policies in this Act affect child welfare programs, it is important to first understand how other poverty policies, programs, and services have historically affected families and children.

Poverty Policies

To give an historical account of poverty as it relates to children makes little sense without acknowledging that the initial impact of poverty is on families. Adult individuals without children may make decisions and take steps in their lives to change their financial situation that families with children may not have the freedom to make. Financial decisions you might make for yourself may not be the same ones you make for your children to ensure their development. The living conditions of the family take on a different meaning when children are involved.

It was during the Depression that the field of child welfare services began to take on a formal national approach with regard to families with children. With the Social Security Act of 1935, Title IV was initiated to aid children and families with the creation of Aid to Needy Families. This Act was the forerunner of the Aid to Families with Dependent Children (AFDC). AFDC was designed as the principal income transfer program affecting dependent children. This program, unlike other income supportive programs, was not indexed. This meant the amount of money families could receive under this program differed from state to state.

As public support for children in poverty continued to develop from the Social Security Act of 1935, many states set up child welfare units. From the beginning, the majority of the services provided in these units focused on placing children in substitute care. In part, this trend was the result of the beginning structure of the child welfare field in which abandoned children were placed in institutions or homes. Although the early general assistance programs, such as Mother's Pensions in 1911 and AFDC, attempted to support children and families, the case loads were so heavy and the resources so limited, that many children were placed out of home instead of being supported within their families (Kadushin & Martin, 1988).

Two amendments to the Social Security Act were added in 1956 and 1962 related to families and children. The first amendment emphasized the restoration of families and children and the second amendment attempted to provide support services through the AFDC Program and granted additional funds to states to help the child welfare field do this. This latter amendment led to services being provided to children in their homes and supported the theory that children remaining in their families with support services was the least restrictive environment and therefore the best. As can be noted today, the debate of supporting the child within the family or placing the child in substitute care continues to be argued within the child welfare field. The emphasis now is toward the continued maintenance of children in their families with intensive support.

The field of child welfare services continued to expand in the 1960s. Social workers were active in supporting the policies tied to the expansion, explaining that by expanding services, poverty and issues related to child welfare would begin to diminish. However, the expansion created an increase in the budget as the new programs were set up to serve more people. As part of this expansion, the focus on residual services took a forefront and those more universal services, such as income supplements and childcare incentives, took a backseat. This broadening of need as a result of supplying more residual services is what is referred to as "needs elasticity." It was during this period that Congress acted to separate the service provisions from general assistance to children and families. This meant that two separate divisions of the child welfare field would be dealing with the child and family. Often these services were not closely coordinated and the aid provided to clients became inconsistent (Kadushin & Martin, 1988).

In 1972, Congress began setting limits on the services that could be provided in order to reduce the increasing costs. The resulting effect of this was a reintegration of services between social services and general assistance. This increased integration led to an increased use of substitute care for children in families at-risk due to a further decrease in resources as a result of combining the programs. Because the costs of providing substitute care were often initially less than the costs of intensive supportive services, child welfare policymakers sought this direction. In addition, as the integration of services continued, the specialization of providing some type of social support/direct practice to the family was being consumed by the time taken with large numbers of case loads, and priority began to be given to income maintenance programs.

It was during the 1960s that Kempe (1962) first published an article on the battered child syndrome. This article brought the plight of the abused child to the public through the media. The response, however, created an increase and a refocusing in child protective work of child welfare services and a loss of the more holistic issues, such as reducing poverty and developing welfare for the healthy development of the child. The significance of this shift surfaced as the numbers of abused and poor children increased. At the same time the child welfare system was affected by the rising awareness of abuse issues, the numbers of single-parent families was increasing along with drastic economic changes. The result was spiraling numbers of single-parent families falling below the poverty line, while the public service agencies providing them aid were moving toward another focus. The programs and services that were currently being provided could not keep up or aid these increasing numbers of families falling below the poverty line.

Programs and Services Related to Poverty

The programs and services that developed for families and children in poverty were varied. Many addressed the financial needs of the family (Mother's Pension, AFDC, Child Support Services, Supplemental Security Income), the abuse and/or neglect risks (Family Preservation, Protective Services, Child Protection Teams), and the educational and care needs of the children (Head Start, governmentally supported day care spaces, Child Support Programs).

There were also many programs developed that were believed to focus on both intervention and prevention. For example, programs that have focused on residual cases have sometimes included the financial supports given to families with children living below the poverty line. The most well-known of these, AFDC, is a program that ended with the current welfare reform initiatives. Initially, AFDC provided funding to families deprived of parental support, meaning the family was missing the support of one or more parents due to death, absence from home, or incapacity of the parent. In 1961, unemployment of the father was added as a reason to provide AFDC. However, each state had control of this program and could decide whether assistance for families would be provided or not. As of 1990, all states were required to provide money for families with either parent unemployed, dependent upon the income level of the family, and the reason for the unemployment.

The AFDC program was never highly supported by many Americans as it was believed that it created an environment in which low-income single-parent families would purposely have children in order to obtain more money on a monthly basis. What many Americans did not understand, however, was that the amount of AFDC a family received was dependent upon the state in which the family lived. Families with children who lived in one state, for example, could receive up to $950 a month for a family of four (one parent and three children) while the same family in another state might receive only $250 per month. The differences in large part were the result of each state being allowed to set their own guidelines for AFDC. The argument that individuals had more children in order to make money does not hold up in light of the small amount of funds and the requirements to obtain the funds. For example, in many states individuals were required to go to their caseworker's office on a monthly basis in order to obtain ongoing funding. Often these visits required the family without transportation or childcare to bring their small children from long distances on public transportation and wait in waiting rooms for hours to see their caseworker for a few minutes in order to receive their monthly funding.

Along with AFDC, families could receive food stamps, limited childcare, and social services to support the family in moving upward out of poverty. The amount of food stamps and social services the family received was again often determined by the state in which they lived. Based on the amount of money the state identified as a minimal standard of living and taking into account the funds and resources the family had, the difference was what the family received. These amounts often kept families below the poverty line and did very little to enable them to move beyond this condition. Many single mothers found that by the time they obtained a minimum wage job and were required to pay for childcare or reimburse the programs for certain amounts of the childcare, they made more by staying home and caring for their own children.

Medicaid, another in-kind program closely associated with AFDC, was added to the services provided to families with children living below the poverty line. Medicaid was a program that established medical care for all children without the financial means of receiving care. Although Medicaid standards also differ from state to state, the availability of poor families to receive medical attention has brought better health for many children.

Many of these funding programs do have what are called "means tests" which determine whether or not a family is qualified for the program. At times, these means tests serve as catch-22s for families attempting to remove themselves from the welfare roles. Some means tests would not allow families to qualify if they owned a car worth over a certain amount of money, such as $1500. So in order for a family to receive any aid they were often forced to give up their means of transportation which could have enabled them to seek jobs or to take their children to day care so they could work. In many ways the programs set up by the welfare system have not promoted a means for families to move beyond their present status, but instead have held them back. Because of these barriers, many families do not stay on these programs. Like many myths perpetuated in welfare, the average length of time for a family to have received AFDC is 3 years, not for generations of families (Kadushin & Martin, 1988).

Other types of income assistance, such as SSI (Supplemental Security Income), designed to help needy aged persons as well as blind and disabled

individuals, including children under the age of 18, are more equably distributed and provide for monthly cash benefits which are equivalent across the
states. These types of funds, along with such federally guided programs as
Women, Infants, and Children (WIC) and Nutrition Programs for Children,
have served as supplemental "in-kind" services for families.

Social services to families are also tied to federal legislation but more often
determined by the state which receives the federal funds. As the Social Welfare
Reform Act has been implemented, the majority of the preceding income
support programs have become consumed under Federal Block Grants. Under
the block grants, each individual state makes discretionary decisions about
how the monies will be divided and spent. For example, how much support
will go for roads and how much for child welfare? This distribution of funds
by state has created many inconsistencies across the country.

SOCIETAL IMPACT ON
POVERTY POLICIES AND SERVICES

It is important to recognize how policies and services impact families. These
policies and services as noted represent an underlying belief system within this
society. This belief system is composed of three significant societal factors that
impact all our lives: shifting ideologies, economic conditions, and political
agendas. In order to provide a positive impact on child welfare policies and
services, social workers need to be educated in understanding these factors
and how they can be utilized in positive ways for families and children. Following is a brief discussion of these three factors and the impacts they have
had on the field of child welfare.

Ideologies

The prevailing ideologies that underlie a society are created by many different
aspects, both internally and externally. One of the major ideologies within the
United States is the focus on individualistic success and competition. This ideology has done much to place the United States in its powerful position, but
does not lend itself to child or family-oriented policies (Garbarino, 1992). Its
constant reminder of the value of the individual does little to support or com-
plement the development of the family or a collective view of the value of
children as the future of the country. Until the Great Depression in 1935,
when every person in the United States was affected, programs to aid children
and families were only initiated by private individuals and organizations.
As previously noted, it was during the Depression that the success of the individual first became seen not only as a result of their own inner character, but
also as a result of the environment in which the individual lived and the
opportunities open to them. The idea that external factors played a role in the
success of an individual led to federal and state programs to aid all families and

children. Although some of these programs continue today, their reasons for beginning have become misunderstood by a society which continues to support them. Now more than ever, the majority of people view the success or failure of an individual based on their inner character. Survival of the fittest continues to underlie our basic belief system. While this ideology does move the society away from collective thinking, it also increases the incentive of individuals to self-actualize to their fullest extent. This positive aspect of individualism could be used by the social worker to empower family members to bring about change if environmental resources are available.

A second ideology that has had a significant impact in this society is the belief that accomplishment is measured by the amount of money or material goods you can obtain. This ideology is counter to the profession's belief in the value of all beings regardless of wealth. Social workers' ability to understand and take steps to counter this ideology by placing value on areas other than money, such as education or family relationships, can enable a family or community of families to move forward in mutual support of themselves.

Economic Influences

In the United States, the economy has great control over the prevailing policies developed in social programs and social welfare. Although the economy has a significant influence in most societies, it does not necessarily have the same impact as it does in the United States. The United States, being one of the wealthiest and most powerful countries in the world, has a significant investment in remaining that way even at the expense of some of its members.

We, as individuals in this society, have become comfortable with our standard of living and with the access we have to resources and power. To ask an American to jeopardize their lifestyle by allowing the federal deficit to keep rising or by raising their taxes is not a decision the average American would be happy to make. Very often, a limited understanding of the federal economy affects most Americans when they make their political choice. Grasping the role of the economy in society and having a good working knowledge of how different budgetary plans can affect the deficit, as well as taxes, will provide child welfare social workers with skills to advocate for favorable decisions for social services through intelligent economic planning. Advocating for and supporting those politicians who embrace innovative ideas for the economy, without sacrificing the well-being of families and children, is a positive step the social worker can take in working with families and children.

Political Agendas

Just as important in understanding the economy is the understanding of the political issues and platforms of political parties. Politicians often use the economy to play on the average American's political decisions. Instead of having a complete grasp of all the issues, most Americans will support those politicians whose ideas appear to aid them individually. It is crucial for you, as a child welfare social worker, to understand not only the political issues, but also the platforms different political parties have for resolving social problems. It is also critical that you play an active role in politics and the election of those individuals who support families and children.

SUBSEQUENT POLICIES

Emerging from the economics, ideologies, and political influences of the society are the creation and implementation of policies that affect in negative and/or positive ways the families and children living within the society. The purpose of these subsequent policies is to improve certain conditions for a group of people; however, often a policy that improves one situation can negatively affect other situations. For example, the implementation of "work fair programs" to put welfare recipients to work leads to an increased need for safe, approved day care spaces for children of these recipients. With day care spaces for low-income children barely serving 20 percent of those in need now, how a childcare program can be set up quickly to handle thousands more children is hard to envision. Thus, one policy designed to handle what is considered a social problem will often create another social problem.

As significant as this situation is, the fact remains that very few policies or services are based on actual practice research. Policymakers then create policies without knowing about the ways in which they need to be implemented. Globally, as conservative influences move across countries influencing economic and political issues, the creation and implementation of policies in the area of social services are reflective of these influences. Although welfare reform in the United States affects all aspects of social services, its impact on child welfare is yet to be completely understood. As the continued implementation of welfare reform occurs, there will be greater restrictions and inconsistencies in services across the United States. Examples of this can be seen in the block grant plans that will allow states to decide their own funding and types of services in social welfare programs. It will be the social worker's responsibility in working with families and children to seek consistent and supportive policies and programs to meet child welfare needs. This will require the professionally trained child welfare social worker to work toward equity of resources politically to bring about changes in the field.

Highlight 1.2 is an example of the kind of dilemma many trained social workers face in agencies where policies without a practice research foundation affect child welfare.

The following example is a common one for social workers working in the field of child welfare services. You will become aware from your training of the needs of your clients and the services that are most appropriate, yet may be unable to access these resources because of conflicting policies in the programs. Your understanding of ideologies, economics, and politics will prepare you to create the changes needed.

❖ HIGHLIGHT 1.2　Child Welfare Dilemma

Susan Rutgers, a social worker in a state Children and Family Service Organization, was assigned to work with the Mitchell family following an accident in which Tommy, age 3, had suffered a severe burn on his right arm. Children and Family Services had become involved upon notification by the emergency room doctor and hospital social worker that Tommy had been left at home in the care of his 8-year-old sister while their mother worked a late night shift. An initial investigation had been handled by the child investigation worker and Susan was now providing social services to the family. The investigative report had indicated that Ellen, the mother, was recently divorced and had taken on extra shifts at work to supplement their financial needs. Ellen had initially argued that her 8-year-old daughter was very mature and she had not felt it was wrong to leave Tommy in her care for 4 hours. However, Ellen did not want to run the risk of losing custody of her children and stated she would not continue in taking extra shifts and would not leave the children alone again.

The difficulty for Susan, however, was that she knew without the financial support needed for the family, Ellen might be forced into even more difficult situations. Susan recognized her role was not to simply enforce a plan by which Ellen stayed home, but to aid in creating a stable environment for the family. The resources available to Ellen and her family were limited within the program that Susan worked. Susan believed her responsibility to the children required further action, but short of placing the children in a foster home, she believed there was very little she could do. The consequences of an out-of-home placement in this type of situation were as risky as not providing additional services in Susan's mind.

Susan had the resources to oversee the safety of the children even to the extent of placing the children in foster homes. However, she had little resource for providing the family with more financial aid or for providing childcare to the mother to enable her to take extra shifts, due to these added resources being identified as not necessary according to agency resources. Even though Susan recognized the emotional as well as economic savings from the use of childcare and financial aid over foster care placements, the system in which she worked had cut back in this area and Ellen's family did not qualify for these additional intensive services.

Personal Responsibility and Work Opportunity Act (PRA)

Following is a discussion of the welfare reform policies and their effect thus far on child welfare services. Social welfare reforms approved in 1996 as the Personal Responsibility and Work Opportunity Reconciliation Act had many of the same qualities of the Elizabethan Poor Laws. One such quality was the difference made between the "deserving" and "undeserving" poor. Twelve features of the bill were originally designed as shown in Highlight 1.3.

❖ HIGHLIGHT 1.3   Initial Content of the PRA Act

1. Creates Bock Grant/Entitlements. Replaces AFDC, emergency assistance, and the JOBS program with Temporary assistance for Needy Families (TANF). States have full discretion in how these funds will be given.
2. Requires states to operate a welfare program but do not have to be uniform across the states.
3. Institutes a five year lifetime limit on cash assistance and recipients must work 2 years. Most States will require parents receiving assistance to participate in community service after 2 months on assistance.
4. Benefits for legal immigrants reduced by $22 million.
5. Most programs have already been eliminated in terms of services to illegal immigrants.
6. There will be family caps on benefits so that in some states those families already on assistance will receive no more even with the addition of another child.
7. Prohibits individuals who have been arrested and convicted of a felony drug charge to not receive benefits under the TANF program.
8. Cut $2.9 billion from nutritional programs for children.
9. Reduces the access of children for assistance with certain disabilities including maladaptive behavior.
10. Cuts funding by $28 billion including food stamps. This will affect close to seven million families with children.
11. Reduces support for families needing child care if they are receiving cash assistance. Also may prohibit families unable to access child care to return to work with a possible time limit in assistance. (Summary; NASW, 1996)

While this was the preliminary stance of the Personal Responsibility Act, the negative response as well as the initial consequences have led to several changes.

As noted, the consequences of this new legislation are currently being determined, but a study by the Urban Institute, a liberal-leaning think tank, predicted that the legislation would thrust an additional 1 million children below the poverty line (NASW, 1996). Changes in the formula that affects social services for families have had a significant impact on the type and nature of the intervention given in child welfare situations. From what we know of how economic conditions effect social service programs, it is easy to understand why there are an increasing number of difficult child welfare situations as the poverty level rises and the services provided diminish (U.S. Department of Health and Human Resources (1997). This makes an even greater difference in the kind of intervention models that can be provided to the family and child. We know from history that increased child welfare cases generally lead to more out-of-home care. It would be a devastating blow for families and children to lose intensive family-based care programs. Yet, the new practice models will need to continue to be intense and managed within a short-term process in order to make changes that can improve the child's life. They will also need to address issues related to the community and the prevention of further child welfare difficulties through the use of macro strategies and skills. If child welfare practice models do not do this, it is very possible there will be a movement back to the focus on placement of the child outside the home and on the further increase of children living in poverty. In order to prevent substitute care from becoming the primary solution to most child welfare situations, child welfare social workers need to address the relevant issues and policies that will affect these areas from a preventive focus.

Welfare reforms have further increased the exchange between the field of child welfare and the social work educator. Several conferences and meetings have been held as a result of these changes and the effects of these reforms on families and children. Social workers who understand the issues that need to be addressed regarding the changes in resources for families will be the ones who can best serve their clients and account for their interventions.

Ozawa and Lum (1996) stated that their research surrounding the effect of lowering income transfers to low-income families with children found not only an increase in the number of children living in poverty but also an affect on the future outcome of our society due to this poverty. In a world of changing technology with advanced methods of providing different services, it would seem imperative that some of these energies be spent on ways to aid American families and children living in poverty conditions. The future of our society appears dependent upon this being a part of our focus in child welfare. The issues raised in the last section can be more completely examined from the perspective of professional social work development. The paradigms in social work practice have never completely reconciled the importance of their roles in both changing poverty policy and applying good interventions for broad and preventive practice. Developing the profession of social work through a joining of these approaches in a manner that is both helpful to clients and reality based for social workers in the field is imperative.

BRIDGING THE GAP BETWEEN THE PROFESSION AND POVERTY

The role of the social worker in bridging the gap between the profession and children and families in poverty clearly lies in the ability of the child welfare social worker to not only work within both paradigms but also cross the boundaries between residual types of intervention and universal prevention.

Residual and Universal Care

It is sometimes difficult, because of the conflicting paradigms and often specialized training in schools of social work, to see how front line workers in child welfare can impact in both residual and universal ways. It is also important, however, to recognize that this will be the only manner in which change really occurs. Theorists and researchers such as Lindsey (1994) and Costin, Kargar, and Stoze (1996) rally behind the idea that the residual approach to child welfare is adding to the lack of change in the overall welfare of families and children in the United States. They point out that by focusing so much on individual cases and protection of the child rather than welfare of all children, social workers are not able to make the holistic changes necessary for real results. While the authors agree with this theory, we take another approach to the controversy of residual versus universal treatment. We believe that while child welfare social workers are in the midst of residual situations, they also have a responsibility and opportunity to move toward universal changes and treatments. Although their time will be limited by their individual cases, Lindsey (1994) points out that beginning to think about social work in child welfare differently is the first step. Therefore, as you move through the chapters of this book and review the examples, you will see protocols and actions related to changing policies, strengthening and training families for advocacy, and imparting effects on the political and economic machines within this society, while dealing with case interventions.

Vosler (1996) suggests that in order for social workers to effectively work with families in poverty, they need "(a) accurate descriptions of current societal *reality*, (b) an understanding of poverty and inequality *trends* over the past several decades, and (c) an understanding of populations that are particularly *at risk* for poverty and resulting difficulties" (p. 167). The understanding of *reality* of the poverty situation in the United States allows the social worker to see beyond a narrow focus and understand that poverty is not an individual issue but an environmental one. Reviewing *trends* enables the social worker to recognize that economic change can be affected as it has been in the past for particular groups of people. Recognizing those *at-risk* populations in our society aids the social worker in identifying quickly those families that are more likely to be affected by poverty. Strategies to counter the effects of economic hardships abound within the macro literature related to economic policy changes. Less common are strategies that address working with children and families who are experiencing economic hardships from a preventive as well as residual type of social work intervention. Vosler (1996), as well as others, supports the idea of intervention from a multisystemic perspective in working with families. Yet the specific strategies for implementing a multisystemic approach on both a micro and macro level for child welfare have not been detailed out into a specific model of practice.

The next section of chapter 1 introduces some of the ideas associated with a bridging model of practice for child welfare. This model, SWPIP, is representative of a bridging of the profession's paradigms into an approach that is both preventive and treatment oriented.

OUT OF THE BOX
METHODS IN CHILD WELFARE

Working together with the families we serve toward more positive aspects in our ideologies, family-oriented economic and political decisions, and family-friendly policies will move not only families forward but also our society. As you read through the next section of this chapter on the definition of out of the box approaches, critically analyze how already established services and programs might be enhanced to create prevention of child welfare situations. Out of the box thinking is not a new term; it has been utilized in many arenas to describe ways in which to be innovative and constructive. McPhee (1997) utilized this term to describe methods for understanding and changing child welfare in a complex analysis of systems within the societal context.

In the box thinking is the approach most social workers now take within the context of this work within the child welfare setting. In the box thinking implies that most social workers practice their profession from within the contextual and structural parameters of the child welfare organization in which they work. From this perspective, they are clearly following the roles and policies of the agency and carrying out the responsibilities of their position; however, this does not necessarily mean they are best able to practice within the framework of the social work profession. The Code of Ethics clearly states the social worker's responsibility to the organizations in which he or she works:

IV. The Social Worker's Ethical Responsibility to Employers and Employing Organizations
　　L. Commitments to Employing Organization—The social worker should adhere to commitments made to the employing organization.
　　　　1. The social worker should work to improve the employing agency's policies and procedures and the efficiency and effectiveness of its services.
　　　　2. The social worker should not accept employment or arrange student field placements in an organization which is currently under public sanction by the National Association of Social Workers (NASW) for violating personnel standards, or imposing limitations on or penalties for professional actions on behalf of clients.
　　　　3. The social worker should act to prevent and eliminate discrimination in the employing organization's work assignments and in its employment policies and practices.
　　　　4. The social worker should use with scrupulous regard, and only for the purpose for which they are intended, the resources of the employing agency.

It also clearly delineates the social worker's responsibility to clients:

II. The Social Worker's Ethical Responsibility to Clients
　　F. Primacy of Clients' Interests—The social worker's primary responsibility is to clients.
　　G. Right and Prerogatives of Clients—The social worker should make every effort to foster maximum self-determination on the part of clients.
　　　　1. The social worker should serve clients with devotion, loyalty, determination, and the maximum application of professional competence.
　　　　2. Social workers' greatest responsibility is their relationships to clients.

3. Social workers should not be involved in any conflict of interest when serving a client (Summaries: Kirst-Ashman & Hull, 1996).

When you examine these sections of the Code, the question becomes how do you ameliorate these two areas if they are in conflict, as they often are, in child welfare? If the agency is limited by its constructs and systems and the clients need a different approach, what is your responsibility and how might you go about lending the leadership that is needed? These questions can be more adequately answered from the perspective of out of the box thinking (McPhee, 1997) and an understanding that as a front line social worker you have the ability to create change without foregoing your responsibilities to the agency.

Out of the box thinking is not simply about major changes, it is about making systems work for people and society through small steps and tasks. Just as we would not ask a client to make major changes, we cannot expect the child welfare system to undergo as dramatic a change as from a completely residual approach to a completely universal or preventive approach, even if this is the best idea. It will take time and effort for child welfare agencies to begin to respond to a more macro way of thinking to change the inequities in society and thus prevent a child welfare crisis. However, a model of practice that supports the integration of both micro and macro practice, as well as the use of innovative and out of the box methods, may begin the process of taking steps toward resolving some of the inequities in society.

In response to these concerns, this text presents a model that can be utilized in all areas of child welfare. The SWPIP model applies an empowering approach that can help clients create change for themselves in their environment. The model is based on the knowledge, purposes, values, skills, and processes of the social work profession. The underlying frame of the practice model is made up of best practice protocols, which allow for a collaborative strengthening approach between the social worker and the family and/or child. Yet, at the same time, the model takes into account the policy issues that affect child welfare agencies and seeks to inform and modify these policies with accountable practices through innovative services and programs. Frequently, child welfare social workers, who *are* part of the public child welfare field, are blocked from implementing their professional training because of the limitations of the policies and programs available. These limitations have often emerged as a result of specific ideologies in society rather than based on practice research. This is key to understanding that the role of a child welfare social worker is not only to apply the appropriate practice models, but also to work for policies that are reflective of the best types of practice. Social workers in all areas of child welfare programs can provide the best welfare services to children based on professional training when that training practice helps inform policy.

Although many policies flowing from conservative ideologies do not reflect a social work perspective, the SWPIP model works with these policy constraints to bring about change. This type of model is important in the field of child welfare so that despite ideologies, the practice of social work with families and children remains beneficial rather than harmful.

SOCIAL WORK PHILOSOPHY

The idea that the context of child welfare practice needs to be understood under the rubric of a consistent social work theory and model is inherent in good professional practice. The fact that the social work profession itself needs to take a leadership approach in constructing these practices regardless of economic or political constraints is a goal the profession is struggling to achieve. This is where the future social workers in the child welfare field can provide leadership. The strength of the social work profession lies in its ability to integrate its knowledge and skills into models of practice in different fields of public and private child welfare services. It also lies in the individual social worker as the possessor of this knowledge and these skills.

In order for the social work profession to offset the negative and reinforce the positive effects of societal issues as they relate to children and families, it is important for social workers and the families and children they serve to gain greater knowledge of societal issues and to develop skills in advocacy, negotiation, organization, and policy implementation. The profession itself can also begin to respond to the impacts of these issues as they affect children and families by building and implementing models of practice in child welfare utilizing advocacy, negotiation, organization, and policy implementation. To accomplish this, we must turn to the roots of the social work profession and empower the families and children we serve through strengthening services. The practice models we develop must encourage and increase the social work profession in the field of child welfare armed with knowledge and effective approaches to counter negative aspects of these policies and to reinforce the positive aspects.

The turn of the twenty-first century is proving to be an especially significant time in the changing global perception of social issues and policies. Now, more than in the last 100 years, the social worker in the child welfare field needs to step forward in creating an environment in which services for families and children are at the forefront of all societies. As you think about the preceding three strongly influencing factors of ideologies, economics, and politics, it is important to examine them as they affect what is happening today at the turn of the century. Are these factors that need to be countered or advanced by the strategies of the past or do they require new initiatives? In what manner can we as a profession move to not only impact the negative ramifications of these factors but to turn their positive aspects in a direction which is productive for the families and children with whom we work? As you read through the chapter on the programs and services that have been put in place to help counter the effects of poverty and neglect on children, (chapter 5) we hope you critically analyze how these programs might have been enhanced to prevent child welfare situations. This is where you begin to think outside the box and provide the necessary leadership to make child welfare work for families and children.

SUMMARY

This chapter has provided you with an overview of the relationship between child welfare, the social work profession, and poverty. An historical account of how the profession, as well as societal issues, have affected the well-being of our children has been presented within the context of understanding the residual approach to child welfare services. We have suggested that concern over these residual-only services and the ways in which inequity in our society affects families and children can best be addressed through an out of the box model (SWPIP) of child welfare practice. This model focuses the issue of implementing the two paradigms of social work practice (preventive through social reform and residual through individual case treatment) by combining the two perspectives through one practice model utilized within the present system of child welfare. This model demonstrates the leadership that the profession of social work can provide to the child welfare field.

QUESTIONS FOR DISCUSSION

1. Discuss the historical role of social work in the development of child welfare.

2. In what ways does poverty affect families' and children's involvement in child welfare?

3. Describe the three societal issues that impact welfare poverty and services.

4. Give examples of how welfare reform has affected families and children within our society from articles you have read.

5. Describe what "out of the box" refers to in terms of making changes in the child welfare system.

6. Discuss why it is important that the two paradigms in social work be joined together.

A Model for
the Profession
in Child Welfare

INTRODUCTION

The purpose of this chapter is to address the major components of the Social Work Protocols in Practice (SWPIP) model. After discussing the model, a brief overview of the social work profession is examined. The purpose of this review is to aid the social work student in understanding how professional social work practice fits within the context of the child welfare arena and to clarify the foundational base of the professional SWPIP model.

A CHILD WELFARE PRACTICE MODEL

Social Work Protocols in Practice (SWPIP)

As noted, the research and writings on child welfare to date have focused basically on residual policies, services, and programs available for children and their families. Because the child welfare field is governed by these policies and services, very little material concerning the application of a universal model of practice has been implemented. The actual practice in the child welfare field has been dictated by the political and economic policies currently applied to families and children. Presently, a solution-focused or brief treatment model has become a mainstay of residual treatment. The reasons for this type of practice approach centers on the need for an intensive intervention that produces change and does not focus on problems but on strengths and solutions. Although this approach is positive, it does not necessarily move the child welfare field into a holistic social work model which intervenes in the policy area as well.

An additional reason for the lack of a professional social work practice model that defines child welfare issues stems from the fragmentation of policies and services that are available to children in this country and the changing economic and political structure of services. Where particular states provide services and programs through one major organization, other states provide their services through several different organizations. There are also generally several different social workers involved in each case from each organization who attempt to intervene in the family. Many of the individuals working with the family may have the title of social worker but have very little training in the field. Thus, their intervention into the family may be based on the context of their organization rather than underpinned by the values and beliefs of the social work profession.

A major principle in the model proposed is that the approach taken must have a consistent and underlying base of values and ethics that interconnect between the child, family, social worker, environment, and society.

Strengthening Practice Continuum

As you proceed through the material regarding the SWPIP model, you will find that the structure of this child welfare practice model is not based on a "field of services continuum" (see chapter 4), but rather on a strengthening practice process continuum. The authors refer to this as a strengthening practice continuum in that the practice being provided is the empowerment of the individuals to take action for themselves and to move up a continuum that leads to independent family situations. Strengthening practice involves the social worker empowering the client and educating him or her in community actions that they can employ to bring about change for themselves and/or other families and children.

Most child welfare cases can be guided by the continuum of the strengthening practice process applied in all child welfare situations and systems. This continuum of practice is based on an intervention that recognizes the

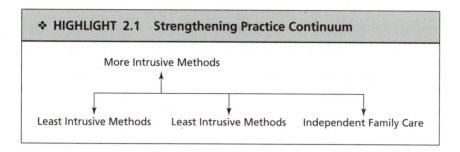

least intrusive method at initial intervention and yet continues to work for an even more empowered situation with a goal toward independent family-based care. Highlight 2.1 shows the strengthening practice continuum.

It is possible along this line of the continuum, once contact has been made and the family situation assessed, for the practice method to become more intrusive as a result of protecting the child. The continuum would then move back to a less intrusive method as it leads to independent family care regardless of whether the child is with their biological family or an adoptive family.

The strengthening practice process continues despite a shift in the level of intrusive methods. It may seem like a contradiction that a child welfare social worker can be more intrusive in a family (for example, place a child at risk in foster care) and still be working toward a strengthening process with the family and child; however, as long as the goal is independent family care and all services are offered, families can move in that direction.

Protocols and Tenets

The term tenets stands for those canons that serve as the foundation of a particular belief system. Examples of tenets will be seen in later sections of this text which utilize the components (tenets) of professional social work practice.

Protocols develop as a result of thought, experience, and fact. In other words, protocols in the SWPIP model are produced as a result of the experience of the authors and other child welfare workers, as well as the research to date on the practice area being examined. These protocols and the subsequent steps to be followed in the practice model of SWPIP serve as the foundation.

While many models define a particular theoretical underpinning, the SWPIP model applies a more eclectic approach to practice. This does not mean that the practice approach is not based on substantive theory. As you read more about the SWPIP model you will begin to recognize the theories and approaches which provide a foundation. These include but are not limited to systems, crisis, psychodynamic, empowering, political, organizing, and cognitive theories and approaches. The SWPIP model, however, is based on more than a number of theories. Foremost among its belief system is the value base of social work practice supplemented by a frame of reference for practice focused on the person in environment, a systemic strength's perspective that is sensitive to diversity, and a commitment to equality and equal access for the best development of each member of our society.

PROTOCOLS IN SWPIP

The protocols in the SWPIP model are guidelines for appropriate behaviors and skills used in the different fields of practice. Generally, a protocol is a description of a step to be taken by a worker to ensure that a situation is resolved. These situations call for actions that do not risk damaging consequences. The medical field has long had sets of protocols for different procedures and their initial use by social workers occurred in medical social work. The child welfare field moved toward the inclusion of protocols in most fields of services in an attempt to provide a more consistent and reliable form of social work intervention. Although each child welfare situation is different, establishing a set of standards from which to make decisions and form approaches provides the child welfare worker with a means of stabilizing families through established practices.

Difficulties arise when the protocols established do not reflect research of practice but rather policies reflective of ideologies, economics, or politics in a society. The SWPIP model is based on a series of protocols that have been established as the most effective steps or process to follow in intervening in a child welfare situation. They reflect practice experience and research done on practice. These protocols differ from others you might become aware of in child welfare as they do not reflect the policies of the child welfare agency but good practice. Protocols for child welfare practice are listed in Highlight 2.2.

❖ HIGHLIGHT 2.2   Protocols for Child Welfare Practice

PREPARATION PROTOCOLS

1. Establish yourself early as an active member of your community who advocates for families and children.
2. Develop good relationships with the different constituencies in the community.
3. Initiate and foster good personal connections with individuals throughout governmental and social service agencies, as well as natural helping networks.
4. Practice being a good educator and presenter on family and child welfare issues in the community by establishing relationships with the media.
5. Review the list of resources available in your community and make note of those you believe are additionally needed.
6. Become an active member of your local National Association of Social Workers and be involved in the political issues in your community, state, and nation.

RELATIONSHIP BUILDING PROTOCOLS

7. Advocate for programs that separate the investigative function of child welfare from the interventive function as involuntary clients build relationships with the social worker more easily and quickly if the primary social worker is not the one who does the initial investigation.
8. Your development of a positive relationship with the child and/or

family are key elements for the success of the intervention.

9. Skills in genuineness, empathy, human dignity, and warmth are critical for building a relationship with a child and/or family.

10. Building positive relationships with formal and informal community services are critical for the child and/or family with whom you are working.

11. Aid and strengthen the child and/or family to build natural helping networks as a key to their success and maintenance.

ASSESSMENT PROTOCOLS

12. Assessment of the risk to the child is the most important child welfare assessment to be done in cases of neglect, emotional maltreatment, physical abuse, and sexual abuse.

13. When working with the family and child, engage a strength's perspective in the assessment.

14. The risk assessment instrument utilized needs to be a reliable and valid instrument, however, your experience and decision-making abilities need to be valued as well.

15. Nondeficit assessment is an essential part of a diversity strength's perspective in child welfare.

PLANNING PROTOCOLS

16. Planning with the family and child is more successful when their involvement is valued and mutual interaction occurs in the process.

17. Case management is a significant part of planning and involves both formal and informal interactions within the community.

18. Planning and contracting for service needs to reflect the family's cultural background and needs.

19. The child welfare social worker serves as the case manager for their families and facilitates their interactions with the community.

IMPLEMENTATION PROTOCOLS

20. Carry out your agreed part of the plan and do not agree to actions that you cannot do.

21. Respect the family's needs to make changes and adjust the plan if there are necessary reasons that do not adversely affect the welfare of the child.

22. Utilize both micro and macro interventions in child welfare situations. Until major changes are made regarding the economic inequality of families, the child welfare situation will continue to worsen.

23. Educate the family to advocate and take action for themselves with others in their community.

24. Being able to think outside the box and use innovative techniques and services to aid a child, family, and community allows the family and social worker to make the greatest use of services.

EVALUATION AND ENDING PROTOCOLS

25. View evaluation from both a process and outcome perspective.

26. Families are an important part of the evaluation process and their ability to provide that evaluation is an important step in their independent family process.

27. Evaluation provides information for not only the individual case but for future cases and the programs, policies, and services utilized.

28. Compiling case evaluations can provide data to make changes in policies that affect families.

29. Ending intervention is the overarching goal of your work with the family and as such provides the family with a positive launching point.

30. Dealing early with the reactions family members may have to ending allows the family to move forward easier.

Continued

❖ **HIGHLIGHT 2.2** *Continued*

---

31. Focusing on the accomplishments the family and child have made and encouraging their continued use of social support resources is an important part of ending.

FOLLOW-UP PROTOCOLS

32. Follow up allows families and children to review their successes and know that the child welfare social worker is concerned about their welfare.

33. Follow up also permits the social worker to follow through on the larger macro actions related to policy and program changes.

These protocols are not only the foundation of the SWPIP model but also "necessary but not sufficient" conditions for practice in the child welfare field. Each of these protocols is based on a value of the social work profession. The protocols also play a major role in the practice continuum process by providing practice methods for moving toward your goals. Additionally, these protocols allow the social worker to move between fields of service as needed and to implement all available resources at any given point on the continuum rather than being limited to one field of service. As you read through each chapter, it is important to remember that your responsibilities are tied not only to these protocols but also to the profession and the agency in which you are employed.

PHASES OF THE SWPIP MODEL

The outline in Highlight 2.3 shows the specific phases of the intervention model. These phases are very ingrained in the traditional social work process, however, their underpinning of protocols and emphasis as a strengthening continuant that begins and ends with the child welfare process set the model apart in many ways from other social work related child welfare interventions.

❖ **HIGHLIGHT 2.3   SWPIP Phases and Processes**

PREPARATION PHASE

Prepare yourself to work effectively in your environment and its systems through networking and the establishment of power.

RELATIONSHIP BUILDING PHASE

1. Establish an immediate relationship with the child and family based on warmth, genuineness, empathy, positive regard, and empowerment.
   a. Warmth
   b. Genuineness
   c. Empathy
   d. Positive Regard
   e. Empowerment
   (Evaluate Process and Outcome)

ASSESSMENT PHASE

2. Assess the situation briefly and thoroughly based on the following systems:
   a. Child
   b. Nuclear Family
   c. Extended Family Systems
   d. Social Systems
   e. Resource Systems
   f. Programs and Services
(Evaluate Process and Outcome)

PLANNING PHASE

3. Plan and contract for intervention with all systems.
   a. Case review and coordination
   b. Involve family in planning process
   c. Contract with family and support services for their roles in implementing plan.

IMPLEMENTATION PHASE

4. Implementation of plan.
   a. Continued implementation of interviewing skills and practice techniques
   b. Continuing coordination of services
   c. Support and empowerment of child and family
   d. Identification of barriers and resolution
   e. Monitoring of services and plan
(Evaluate Process and Outcome)

EVALUATION AND ENDING PHASE

5. .Evaluate outcomes and terminate services.
   a. Evaluate outcomes
   b. Terminate services
(Evaluate Process and Outcome)

FOLLOW-UP PHASE

6. Follow up from a multisystemic perspective.
   a. Family
   b. Community
   c. Program and services
   d. Policy
(Evaluate Process and Outcome)

The different phases of the SWPIP model are familiar to most social workers as they follow the social work problem solving process. It is important to look at the phases through a holistic view rather than as separate pieces of the process. From the beginning, the social worker must be preparing for the rest of the intervention in order to move the treatment along. This does not mean that the social worker is determining what happens in each phase, but is preparing the way for the clients to define how each phase will work for them.

Phase I   The Preparation Phase or Phase I of the SWPIP model is an area that is often overlooked in other models of practice. It is important to recognize that when a social worker practices from a multisystemic approach he or she must first have established the relationships necessary in their community to make this practice effective. If you as a child welfare social worker enter a community without this preparation there will certainly be a time lag in terms of the aid you can provide. Understanding and forming appropriate relationships with all facets of the community in which you work provides you the opportunity to start immediately from a person in environment perspective.

Phase II   Phase II of the SWPIP model is the key entry point into the family. It must be done with care and concern. As the primary social worker becomes involved with the family, it is important for the social worker to establish a relationship of trust, honesty, and partnership with the family and child. Dependent upon the child welfare situation, as will be noted in the following chapters, the difficulty of this process will be dependent upon the reason the social worker must enjoin with the process.

Phase III   Phase III of the SWPIP model is critical to both the process and the outcome of the intervention. Having a complete and thorough understanding of the situation is key to planning and coordinating the intervention needed to improve the child and family situation. This assessment involves understanding not only the internal functioning of the family but the external functioning of the family. How are they proceeding in the environment? What are the social and/or community supports they have? What programs and/or services are available for the family? How can the family be aided and empowered to bring about change in their lives through their strengths and talents?

Phase IV   Phase IV of the SWPIP model may appear similar to the contracting and goal-setting phase of many problem-solving approaches. Where this phase differs in the SWPIP model is the emphasis on involving those systems and individuals who will be involved with the family from this point on. The emphasis at this point in the process is on the involvement of all the systems in working toward the goals the clients have set. If the social worker does not now coordinate the rest of the systems toward these goals time and support can be lost to the family and child.

Phase V   Phase V of the SWPIP model is the heart of the model in that this is where the contract and plan are implemented. It is critical to recognize that implementation of the plan will not occur if this plan has not involved all participants in the decision-making process. Following through on implementation will require intensive, consistent application of goals and tasks through a treatment approach based on brief treatment and solution-focused interviewing and practice skills.

Phase VI   Phase VI of the SWPIP model is the ending phase of the intervention in that it is the termination of services to the child and family. It is the point at which the outcome of the plan is evaluated. The outcome of the plan can have a significant impact on the termination in that the outcome may determine if intervention continues. One of the reasons the SWPIP model emphasizes evaluation as a continuous process is to avoid the difficulty of not reaching the appropriate outcome. By evaluating the process, changes can be made as the intervention is happening rather than at the end. Also involved in this phase is the reinforcement of the skills the family and child have learned to resolve their difficulties. Review of how the family has resolved their difficulties and how they plan to keep positive development going is important to reinforcing their progress and ability to create and maintain change.

Phase VII   Phase VII of the SWPIP model is the follow-up phase that occurs at several levels. It is the point at which the child welfare social worker examines the follow-up situation at a point agreed to by all members of the systems involved. Additionally, follow up includes not only concern over family members involved, but the community and the policies that set parameters on the case situation. Although it is hoped that the child welfare social worker will be working on the multisystemic perspective from the beginning, it is critical that a follow-up assessment be made of any changes that occurred as a result of this case. A basic diagram of the SWPIP model utilizing the strength's continuum, protocols, and phases is outlined in Highlight 2.4.

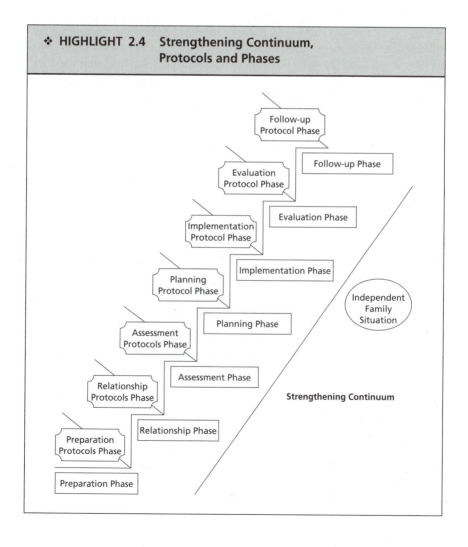

❖ **HIGHLIGHT 2.4   Strengthening Continuum, Protocols and Phases**

These different parts of the SWPIP model form an approach to child welfare which is both new and yet at the same time consistent with other reliable social work approaches. Let's now review those core components of the social work profession that enable and facilitate a multi-systemic approach to child welfare.

PROFESSIONAL CONTEXT

Early in the profession's history, social workers were in the forefront of the development of social programs for dealing with social difficulties as they related to families and children. Individuals such as Jane Addams, Ellen Gates Starr, Charles Crittenton, Lillian Wald, Florence Kelly, Edith Abbott, Grace Abbott, and Julia Lathrop worked through settlement houses, charity organization societies, and maternity homes for unwed mothers, providing aid to children and families. Many early forerunners of the social work profession focused on aid to children and families through the provision of kindergarten services, health care, socialization, empowerment of families, and the networking of communities. This early response to families can be identified as practice from a multisystemic perspective of intervention. The use of this unique intervention perspective is part of social work's identity. Whether a professionally trained social worker specializes in one-on-one services; group or family treatment; community development; and/or policy, planning, and administration, their overall training includes an understanding of the importance of all approaches to helping a system or systems within this society. The value of this multisystemic focus is clearly unique to the social work profession and enables child welfare social workers to deal with issues for children and families in a variety of ways. This context has provided the direction for the development of many different aspects in social work that will be reviewed in the first section of this chapter.

Social Work Processes

The processes involved in social work intervention rely heavily on the understanding of the theories that undergird the social work profession. Although some would argue that the practice of social work is based on borrowed theories, it is the application of these interacting theories that establishes social work's authority over their use in practice. Theories related to systems, families, child development, communities, empowerment, group work, crisis, psychodynamics, cognitive and behavioral attributes are only a few of the areas with which social workers need to be familiar. Child welfare social workers also need to be familiar with theories related to economics, politics, and research, as these are the tools by which social workers can advocate for families and children and play an active role in changing the environment.

Person in Environment

The "person-in-environment" focus of social work practice serves as an identifying strength of the social work profession. Understanding the individual, the family, and the environment within a practice context has served as an underlying base of social work practice for over 100 years. Many theorists have proposed excellent models of practice to fit with this frame of reference, such as Germaine and Gitterman's ecological model (1980) and Reid and Epstein's Task Centered Practice (1977). Emphasizing the importance of an approach that implements a person-in-environment intervention through working not only with the child and family, but also with the extended family, the institutions in the community, and local and national policies, is an unique contribution of the social work profession to the field of child welfare.

The difficulties with this intervention lie in the reality that seldom, if ever, are child welfare social workers able to deal with all the external and internal influences affecting children and families. Often, we only have enough time to work with the individual needs of the children and families we serve and none to deal with the problems of the policies and institutions that are affecting them. One area that appears to be missing in this scenario is an understanding of how this frame of reference for social work practice can be most effectively integrated into the field of child welfare. Models of child welfare practice that interconnect all the systems from a strength's perspective will meet the needs of children and families and have the most success. We will now examine the strength's perspective from a person-in-environment frame of reference.

Strength's Perspective

It is important to recognize that a trained child welfare social worker who comes into an intervention with a child and family from a strength's perspective will most likely be involved with the case from both an internal and external focus. A strength's perspective is not a new phenomena in the social work profession but is one that is being integrated into current practices more than in the past. A strength's perspective, according to Saleebey (1992), serves the purpose of providing the client with an empowering frame of reference by dealing with the situation from relying first upon the strengths of the client. Through a strength's perspective, the child welfare social worker strives to view the family/parents/child from a focus on the attributes, talents, and resources these members have to make changes in their own lives. This approach brings more people into the case situation who are working toward the same goals and, thus, the external environment is more likely to be affected and utilized.

Multiculturalism

As social workers, we often think that it goes without saying that a multicultural perspective is one that is part of our inherent understanding in the child welfare field. In reality, however, there are very few of us that have as complete a perspective as we would like on multiculturalism. A multicultural perspective in the child welfare field requires not only an understanding of differing ethnic and cultural characteristics, but also a recognition of our own preset beliefs about families and children from other cultures and how these beliefs affect our practice.

To more fully understand another's culture, traditions, and beliefs, it is important to not only read about them but to give ourselves an opportunity to experience them first hand. Social workers who have the opportunity to interact with individuals, families, or groups who differ from their own cultural backgrounds can more comfortably recognize differences as positives rather than as negatives. Additionally, social workers who can recognize not only differences but strengths in diverse multicultural situations of child welfare are more successful in their endeavors. To be able to recognize these strengths, we must first be open to seeing them. This often calls for our stepping away from our own cultural background and allowing ourselves to embrace differences. Our ability and desire to do this stems from the profession's value base.

VALUES

At the core of the social work profession are the underlying values that guide the principles of the models of practice in all fields. These values are exemplified in Highlight 2.5, as noted by the National Association of Social Workers (NASW) (1982).

❖ HIGHLIGHT 2.5   Social Work Values

1. Commitment to the primary importance of the individual in society
2. Respect for the confidentiality of relationships with clients
3. Commitment to social change to meet socially recognized needs
4. Willingness to keep personal feelings and needs separate from professional relationships
5. Willingness to transmit knowledge and skills to others
6. Respect and appreciation for individual and group differences

7. Commitment to develop client's ability to help themselves
8. Willingness to persist in efforts on behalf of clients despite frustration
9. Commitment to social justice and the economic, physical, and mental well-being of all members of society
10. Commitment to a high standard of personal and professional conduct.

SOURCE: NASW Standards for the classification of social work practice, Silverspring, MD, 1982.

Value 1: Primary Importance Is the Individual in Society   Through an understanding of how the individual's rights are foremost in ensuring equality within a society, the social worker can make decisions based on human beings rather than on statistics and policies. When the importance of one human being is diminished over another, then society cannot work toward the equality or the betterment of all. When children are diminished within our society, the future of all is placed in jeopardy. This value adds to the belief in multisystemic interventions that influence policies for all families, not just treatment for one.

Value 2: Confidentiality   Confidentiality is of key importance in a child welfare situation. Although this value can often cause conflicting situations with protection cases, the protection of the child remains of highest priority. It is important that the social worker attempt to maintain confidential records and interviews to the fullest of his or her ability in order to build trust with the child and family. There are, of course, those times in child welfare (when a child or teenager becomes endangered) that it is inappropriate to maintain confidentiality. The safety of an individual overrides the value of confidentiality. For example, you are seeing a family in family counseling when you discover that the 10-year-old son gets locked in his room for often a day or more by the stepfather. Despite your desire to maintain trust and rapport with the family, this type of situation must be immediately acted upon and reported to the child abuse authorities. The manner in which this is handled is what sets social workers apart from other professionals. Your rapport with the family can be the path through which they contact child welfare themselves.

Value 3: Social Change   A commitment to social change requires the social worker in the child welfare field to be constantly working toward the development of policies that protect and promote the child and family. This means that the social worker not only works in a one-on-one situation with a child and/or family, but is involved and empowers families and children to be involved at the community, state, and national levels in bringing about social change to improve the lives of all families and children. Examples of this include an adoption worker who works on a task force in his or her community to promote the establishment of an emergency care shelter for children, or a group of families in a community who promote change within their local school district for more sufficient funding with the social worker's aid.

Value 4: Separate Individual Emotions and Needs from Professional Relationships   This value requires that the social worker be able to set aside his or her own personal emotions and needs in child welfare cases and respond to the needs and welfare of the child and his or her family. Although many of us would like to believe that this is not a difficult thing to do, it often is an issue that can arise before you know it is occurring. For instance, a social worker becomes involved in a family situation which has similarities to his or her own early childhood family and begins to react to the situation in a personal rather than professional manner. The social worker in this situation may become more attached to the child, show anger toward the mother, and consequently make judgments about the situation that are inappropriate. Being aware at all times of your reactions to particular cases in dealing with transference and counter-transference is imperative.

Value 5: Transmit Skills and Knowledge   Social workers must take part in educating others about the knowledge and skills needed. This may include running community parenting classes, giving at-risk pregnant mothers skills in handling a baby, helping a teenager learn to problem solve, or helping a group of parents learn how to promote a safe sex environment in their community. In the field of child welfare it is just as important for the social worker to transmit knowledge and skills to the community. Through this endeavor, policies and issues for the betterment of all families can be influenced.

Value 6: Respect and Appreciation of Differences   It is often easy in a child welfare situation to view a family system from what middle-class white America suggests is a healthy environment. This is not to say that the ideas from this viewpoint are wrong, but they are not the only way of understanding things. For example, a mother who works, has a cluttered home, and raises her voice when disciplining a child may be an excellent mother as compared to someone who remains at home but participates little in their child's development. In many cultural settings, a raised voice is a natural part of the family milieu and not a dysfunctional behavior. Social workers must understand and be comfortable with differences between family situations and know when their own personal values may be affecting their vision of the family with whom they are working.

Value 7: Enable Clients to Help Themselves   The role of the child welfare social worker in aiding a child and family is to enable the family to resolve their own issues through the strengths and skills the child and family bring, as well as those you will aid them in building. Although there will be particular circumstances that require the child welfare social worker to take more directive actions and make more concrete decisions (child abuse and neglect), every effort should be made in even the most difficult situations to allow the clients to make their own choices. This encourages the decision-making process of the client as well as the development of their abilities to problem solve.

Value 8: Continue Efforts Despite Frustrations   In many of the child welfare situations encountered, social workers become frustrated because of the lack of services and resources the agency can provide. They may also become frustrated because of the lack of ability of family members to respond to the needs of their children. Despite these frustrations, it is important for the social worker to continue to work toward resolving the issues in the most innovative and empowering ways possible. It may mean the social worker needs to take a step back and reconsider their approach or listen more carefully to the children and families they are serving. Whatever the reason, it is important for the social worker not to allow their frustration and/or burn-out to overcome them. Recognizing differing situations and levels of skills in families enables social workers to better understand and accept their own frustrations. The importance of working together with your families to make change can also reduce your frustration as families themselves undertake change and your responsibility becomes less.

Value 9: Social Justice, Economic, Physical, and Mental Well-being of All This value requires the social worker to advocate and become not only socially conscious but politically active. We need to support those policies and political figures who support equality for all in social and economic justice, as well as physical and mental well-being for all members of our society. In child welfare, you may be the only voice the child has to receive the services he or she needs, and your proactive actions politically will affect the families and children you serve.

Value 10: High Standards of Personal and Professional Conduct This value reminds the child welfare social worker that regardless of any situation that is encountered, the worker must maintain high standards in his or her conduct. This may mean not becoming defensive when verbally attacked by a client, maintaining appropriate interactions with a client who is difficult to deal with, not becoming romantically involved with a client, modeling appropriate behavior in your personal life, and so forth. As a child welfare social worker your role in modeling good parenting and respect for families in the community is critical to families understanding what is appropriate in their own family.

ETHICS

Closely related to the values of the profession are the ethics or guidelines by which decisions are made and particular situations are handled. Ethics are different from values as they serve as guidelines for values to produce correct professional behavior. Although as social work students you may be familiar with the NASW Code of Ethics, it is important to review these guidelines in every class. For this reason, the Code is contained in Appendix I of this book and is important for you to review at this time. It is also significant to recognize that child welfare situations are ones in which social workers may experience the most difficulty in deciding the appropriate course of action from a professional view. The NASW Code of Ethics can aid the professional social worker in understanding what the professional issues are and direct the decision.

SOCIAL WORK KNOWLEDGE BASE

Political and Economic Issues

At play in the child welfare field are the changing political and economic systems that underlie the financial support of child welfare programs. With each changing governmental administration, the supporting base of child welfare practice, services, and policies change. The current situation is a good example of this phenomena. With a strong conservative movement in power, policy-makers have designed welfare reform through block grants and changing funding strategies related to child welfare by leaving decisions in this field up to individual states. In making these decisions states could seriously compound the issues related to the differences in services given to children. As states are given the responsibility of making their own decisions regarding child welfare funding, the mandated federal policies and matching funds become diminished, and the risks of differences between states in kinds and types of services becomes even greater. Without an understanding of these issues, social workers and their families and children will be unable to make changes that are needed.

Educational Knowledge Base

Within the social work education system, the Council of Social Work Education provides an overview of guidelines for the development of a competent social worker at both the BSW and MSW levels. Part of the role of the Council is to provide guidelines for the knowledge base needed within the profession. As part of the new standard guidelines, the following areas are mandatory for student understanding and skill development. In terms of the field of child welfare practice, it is important for certain aspects of these areas to be specifically understood.

Human Behavior and Social Environment

An understanding of human behavior and the social environment is critical to intervention in the child welfare field. A comfortable working knowledge of child development, family development, age appropriate skills, and the effects of the environment (families, institutions, organizations, communities, and society) on a child and their family are a necessary part of assessing, intervening, and empowering in a child/family situation. Additionally, it is important that development of family be understood from a nondeficit perspective. This requires the child welfare social worker to be sensitive to the cultural differences of the families with which they work. Although understanding family development may give you some guidelines by which to assess a situation, they should never be mistaken for the "right" or "wrong" way a family may develop. Different cultures and families develop in different ways and it is important to be sensitive to these differences from a nondeficit perspective.

Social Work Practice Theories and Skills

Theories, skills, and treatment approaches related to social work practice abound within the profession. However, it is critical in child welfare practice that the social worker have a working knowledge of crisis, family, child development, systems, cognitive, behavioral, psychodynamic, and case management theories. Additionally, the worker needs to be able to implement interviewing skills and practice methods in the areas of psychodynamic practice, family therapy, behavioral and cognitive therapy, brief treatment, solution-focused treatment, case-management, community development, policy development, and grass roots organizing.

Brief treatment and solution-focused methods serve as a foundation for the interactional skills used in certain applications of the SWPIP model. Solution-focused treatment (Berg, 1994) emphasizes focusing on solutions in family/child welfare situations rather than on the problems. The techniques developed in this model fit well with the SWPIP focus on strengths, empowerment, and client change. The SWPIP model blends the components of these approaches with a multisystemic perspective of the situation. The use of approaches can easily be extended to the communities, agencies, neighborhoods, and groups you are working with.

Social Work Policy

Understanding how policy develops, is defined, and then is implemented is critical to working in child welfare. Although, as child welfare workers, we are often constrained by the policies set, as social workers it is important that we understand how they can be best implemented or changed for the betterment of families and children. Policies set such important guidelines within the framework of child welfare that to not understand these policies and how they develop will put a social worker at a disadvantage. Along with this understanding is the need for the development of skills that aid in changing inappropriate policies or affecting new ones. These actions in our profession are what set the profession of social work apart from other professions. We do not just work with individuals, families, groups, or communities, but also the society and environment affecting families and children.

Policies do not just affect clients. Policies affect the child welfare social worker in terms of pay, vacation, and benefits. One of the most important areas a social worker in the child welfare field must be aware of is the high amount of burn-out and the turn-over rate of child welfare workers. Addressing policies within your own work environment that are not effective for you and promoting those policies that are critical to not only your well-being but your ability to help clients and systems is imperative.

Social Work Research and Evaluation

The implementation of social work research and evaluation is often seen as an afterthought to much of social work practice; however, with the changing state of economic policies and funding sources, it is necessary that social workers are able to evaluate not only their practice, but also the programs that are implemented in the field of child welfare. To be able to help families and children, we must be able to prove to funding sources and constituents that the skills and practices used are effective. In the SWPIP model presented, you will find that the evaluation of the practice is not done only at the end of the implementation, but also during an analysis of process at the end of each phase. Without knowing if the phase has been accomplished, it becomes more difficult to accomplish the next step in the model. It is also important for the family and child to recognize their ability to accomplish tasks and move forward through a review at the end of each phase. Being able to review their growth and strengths helps move families further ahead. Different evaluation tools will be introduced in each section of the book to enable the reader to become familiar and comfortable with the use of these tools. This analysis at the end of each phase of the SWPIP can be done as a verbal discussion with the family in summarizing the point to which you and the family have come.

Social and Economic Justice

Fundamental to an understanding of social work and its goals is a belief in social and economic justice for all people. Regardless of race, gender, age, religion, or sexual orientation, all individuals are entitled to equal opportunities and an equal economic standard of living. Despite these beliefs, as noted, social workers in the child welfare field have had little time to do more than residual types of practices in working with each case. It is important to recognize that as long as the profession of social work promotes economic and social justice in all fields of practice, we will succeed in making major changes. Without a focus on macro and external issues at some point in practice, we are not doing real social work. How do you then as a child welfare social worker find the time to work toward these goals? Through the families and children you are serving, you can strengthen them to bring change into their own environment and create social justice for larger groups of families through advocacy and action. Your activities and the specific ways you can accomplish this will be discussed through the SWPIP model.

Diversity

As has been noted in the discussion of multiculturalism, an understanding of differences between people and a respect for these differences is an important part of a nonjudgmental attitude in child welfare. Although there are certain standards that are necessary for the quality of life for children, not all these standards will be met the same way. One family culture may demonstrate support and love of their child by outward affection while another might utilize a method that is not as apparent. While we as social workers will have expertise in what provides a family and child with a healthy and happy environment, we cannot be so rigid in our thinking and normative training that we cannot see other ways as beneficial. In fact, the role of diversity in society can be seen as a means for all of us to understand and accept differences in each other. One of the important areas in child welfare in which diversity is critical is in our acceptance of all people for who they are and their lifestyles. Whether it is a gay or lesbian youth, a single-parent home, a communal family situation, or an interracial couple, we as professional social workers need to see the strengths and individuality of each person or family—not their label.

Populations at Risk

Populations at risk overlap with diversity and multiculturalism, but they are not mutually inclusive. There are many different oppressed groups such as children, the elderly, the physically and mentally challenged, gays and lesbians, and women who are affected by discrimination within society, as well as individuals from cultural, racial, and religious minorities. Populations at risk include many diverse groupings of individuals. In child welfare settings, the child is generally not only at risk but very often the family in which they are raised as well as the community in which they live. For example, in a poverty neighborhood, a 4-year-old child raised in a poor single-parent home in a drug-impacted neighborhood is within a multiple at-risk situation for the child, family, and community.

SOCIAL WORK ROLES

You are probably already familiar with the importance of understanding and being able to implement the roles that make up the social work profession. In the SWPIP model being presented, every role of the social worker is of equal importance. These roles include: enabler, educator, advocate, activist, mediator, initiator, broker, and empowerer. Roles are not simply to be called upon as play actors might call upon a role. These roles will emerge as a personal pervasive part of your personality as a social worker and need to occur automatically as you practice child welfare.

Enabler   An enabler performs the role of aiding the client in accomplishing their goals. Enabling involves skills in communication, support, encouragement, and empowering which helps the family successfully complete tasks or find solutions related to obtaining their goals.

Educator   A social worker educates and helps build knowledge in their families as well as in the systems in which they interact. Through greater knowledge and education, a social worker can employ methods of empowerment that encourage the families to make their own decisions and accomplish their own goals from the steps they take.

Advocate   An advocate is a role a child welfare worker is always playing. We begin by advocating for the child and the family through establishing more productive programs and services for them and then training these families and children to advocate for themselves and others.

Activist   An activist is a role that was identified with more in the 1960s than in 1990s, yet in child welfare practice being an activist is a task that is required regardless of the decade. An activist does not wait for change to occur, but takes action to produce the change and lends leadership for the best interests of families and children in their society.

Mediator   The role of a mediator is to listen to all sides and to bring about a compromise in a situation. In being a mediator, you will be expected to understand both points of view and be able to bring about a consensus by aiding each member of the family in examining their feelings and position in light of the other side.

Initiator   This role is one in which the child welfare social worker identifies a need and calls attention to it by making others aware of the issue and motivating others to work toward resolution of the issue.

Broker   The role of broker is in the linking of the family system with the services and programs that are available in the community. Being a broker is not just about referring families and children to services, but is also about understanding the quality of those services and establishing networks that help them connect to those services.

Empowerer   Being an empowerer is about strengthening the talents and resources families and children already have within them and helping them utilize these strengths to make changes in their external environment.

SOCIAL WORK SKILLS

Relationship Skills

There are many interviewing skills that social workers develop in the course of being trained in the profession. Five of these skills are basic to the profession and play a significant role in the field of child welfare: empathy, genuineness, warmth, positive regard, and empowerment. Although you may have received skill training in these areas, their implementation in child welfare has some specific aspects that you need to be familiar with.

Empathy   This skill denotes the ability of the social worker to respond to the child and/or family in a manner that conveys the worker understands how they are feeling. This does not mean you have the same feeling or that you agree or condone the feeling. It simply means that you understand the feeling that is being conveyed and have an acceptance of that feeling. For example, a child welfare situation might involve the mother explaining to you, as the child welfare social worker, how she becomes depressed and frustrated and feels like slapping the children at times. As the worker, you have empathy for her situation because of her lack of financial and emotional support. You can understand that frustration and depression often leads individuals to strike out at others. This does not mean you condone or accept this behavior, but that you understand the feelings of frustration and the consequences of these feelings.

Genuineness   Genuineness is a skill that involves being comfortable with who you are as a person and allowing the naturalness of your personality to come through as the social worker. When you are able to do this, then you are able to be accepted by the child and family and to be trusted much more easily. Genuineness is about being honest with the child and family in terms of who you are and how you respond in a situation. For example, a young teenager is afraid to tell her parents she is pregnant and considers running away as an option. You feel frightened for her, knowing how hard it is out in the real world, and also afraid that she will get hurt in the process. Being genuine means that you share your feelings of fear for her in an honest manner.

Warmth   This is a skill that involves the social worker's ability to convey a sense of caring about the person they are working with. In child welfare situations, this can be a very difficult skill to possess toward particular family members. There are often situations in child welfare in which we feel anger and resentment toward adult family members. To be genuine and warm at the same time requires a great degree of understanding about what causes child maltreatment situations and a belief in their ability to change. In other words, in order to be genuine and warm to others, we must have the ability to be empathetic despite the situation. Warmth may be demonstrated in both verbal and nonverbal ways. For example, your tone of voice and choice of words can express warmth, as well as your facial expression and posture.

Positive Regard   Positive regard is different from empathy in that it requires more than just a basic understanding of a situation—it requires the individual who is a social worker to have a strong positive value of all human beings and their ability and drive toward goodness. Only through a value belief such as this can individuals who have committed acts such as sexual abuse on a child be seen with positive regard. Regardless of what the person has done, the social worker in the child welfare situation needs to view the individual as a human being deserving of respect and compassion. Again, positive regard is separate from condoning or approving behaviors that harm a child.

Empowerment   Empowerment is a term that has been around in the social work field for some 20 years. Its early history is tied with the ecological perspective. The role of empowerment is to aid individuals in achieving a stronger sense of self-esteem and to deal with an unrealistic sense of personal inadequacy. Through this process the individual, family, and/or group/community becomes empowered to create change in their environment.

Case Management Skills

In addition to these skills there are several other areas in which the social worker working in child welfare must have a significant grasp. The skills in case management are mandatory for the child welfare social worker. These skills include the abilities to organize, coordinate, mediate, sustain, evaluate, and integrate services.

Organize A social worker in the child welfare field must be able to be organized and have the leadership abilities to help others organize around a plan. This does not mean you must be obsessive-compulsive in your behaviors, but that considering the fact that many situations in the child welfare field will involve high case loads and numerous responsibilities, it is important for the child welfare social worker to be able to organize systems involved in the treatment plan in a collaborative manner. Organization is more than a simple process of controlling papers, however, it requires the interpersonal skills necessary to aid in organizing groups around a consensus and bringing about a plan.

Coordinate The skills required in coordination of plans and people often revolve around the social worker's personality. Are you a person who other people trust? Can you lend your leadership skills in a manner that is not controlling? The talents to mediate and allow others to make choices are the kinds of abilities that will allow the child welfare social worker to coordinate with the family and other systems.

Mediate The ability to mediate requires understanding strategies in conflict resolution. How might a task be accomplished when the family and other systems do not agree on the method of accomplishing that task? How can you intervene in a manner that produces a plan acceptable to all involved? And if this is impossible, how can you accomplish the plan with the involvement and consensus of all others?

Sustain Sustainment requires the social worker to maintain the hopes, challenge, and empowerment of all involved in a child welfare situation. This may mean that the social workers will have to sustain themselves through difficult times and situations. As noted, overload in child welfare practice is not unusual. Child welfare social workers must have a means of relieving stress and maintaining a positive attitude for themselves in order to support the families and other systems with which they work.

Evaluate Child welfare social workers must have the skills and abilities to evaluate their own practice and make known to others the positive and negative outcomes of their practice. Only by establishing what works in child welfare practice can we hope to eliminate the need for child welfare agencies and the role of government in the protection of the child. Without the skills of evaluating programs, policies, and your own practice abilities, you will not be able to justify your work or the need for specific programs or services for families and children. Social work students often question the need for evaluation skills but once in the field come to recognize their significance.

Integrate Services The skills called for in the integration of services require the social worker to not only be aware of the services available but to be able to pull together those services in a manner that is constructive for the client and the systems working with the client. For example, in the case of a teenager involved in a drug/alcohol situation, the child welfare social worker must have the skills to bring about the best services for the teenager by integrating the services needed with the systems involved. If the family court, school, and/or other community agencies are involved, the child welfare social worker must know how to differentiate between agencies to obtain the appropriate services for the teenager.

As has been emphasized throughout this second chapter, the skills involved in aiding families and children are extensions of the natural skills in which social workers are trained. By utilizing both the foundation of the social work profession as well as this multi-systemic approach to child welfare, child welfare social workers will be able to aid not only the child and family but provide a stepping stone for families to create their own change within this society.

SUMMARY

This chapter has provided an overview of the social work profession as it relates to the values, skills, knowledge, and theories needed to work within the child welfare field. The belief system of the social work profession serves for the implementation of the SWPIP model. The strengthening practice continuum has also been presented as a foundational piece of the SWPIP model. It serves in direct contrast to the current service continuum that focuses on residual practice. This continuum provides a direction for child welfare workers that is both preventive and interventive in nature. The protocols in the SWPIP model are defined as best practices to be implemented within the differing fields of social work practice and are briefly defined as they relate to child welfare and the phases of the model. Finally, you have had an opportunity to review the phases of the SWPIP model as they will be presented within the context of specific child welfare situations throughout the text.

QUESTIONS FOR DISCUSSION

1. The "person in environment" perspective has a unique meaning for the profession of social work. Discuss how this occurred from a historical perspective.

2. Discuss three values of social work that may create conflicts for you in the role of a child welfare social worker.

3. Describe how knowledge of human behavior and the social environment integrates theory and practice in the child welfare field.

4. Utilize "out of the box" thinking and describe a role social workers could play in child welfare.

5. Briefly review the major components of the SWPIP model and the ways in which they fit together.

6. The strengthening practice continuum implies that all families have strengths. Give an example in a child abuse situation of a possible amily strength that may be present within a family.

3

■

Protocols and Practices

INTRODUCTION

This chapter will present each protocol in relation to the phases of the SWPIP model and describe how the protocol can be applied. It is important to recognize that the protocols include guidelines regarding interventions from both a residual and universal focus. Many of the practice protocols detailed here have been validated as best practices through research and clinical experience.

PREPARATION PROTOCOLS

Protocol 1: Establish Yourself Early as an Active Member of Your Community Who Advocates for Families and Children   What makes early involvement and advocacy in the community so important for the child

---

CASE 3.1   Application of Preparation Protocols

Morgan Eberle graduated from Cretin University in May with a BSW. She sent her resume to several agencies but was really interested in working with the Children and Family Service Agency in the new city where she and her partner were moving. She had wanted to work in adoptions but was open to other areas, although she was a little nervous about protective services. Morgan had completed her internship with the local Children and Family Services in the adoption unit and had really enjoyed it.

About 3 weeks after moving to the new city, Morgan received a letter from the Children and Family Service Agency asking if she would like to interview for a Protective Service Worker I position. Morgan made the appointment immediately and over the course of the next few weeks interviewed in the agency with several different people. Although she still was somewhat nervous about the protective service position, she accepted it when it was offered. Morgan really liked the supervisor in the unit and the supervisor believed she would learn the job quickly.

As Morgan prepared to start her full-time job, she remembered several things her professors had told her about preparing to work as a social worker in a new community and she wondered if she should be preparing for the position in other ways than simply reading the procedure and rule book. Morgan called her good friend at the Children and Family Service Agency where she had interned to share the good news. After her friend started asking her questions about other social workers in the area, such as: who in the community was supportive of family and children, what other agencies were resources for them, and countless other questions, Morgan began to realize that she needed to do a lot more preparation other than just reviewing the agency book.

---

welfare social worker? At times children and families go unnoticed and unrecognized as a major building block of our society. The child welfare social worker plays a major role in fostering the recognition and importance of children and families in their community. The child welfare social worker's role is to keep the issues and concerns of their young clients and their families visible. The ability of the worker to be a part of the community is often overshadowed by the case load that the worker must deal with. Additionally, the case loads may contain difficult situations that involve numerous meetings and interventions. During the preparation phase you may have an advantage in establishing yourself as a part of the community, as your case load may be at its lowest while you familiarize yourself with the agency. This is not always the case in all child welfare agencies, as you may be asked to take a heavy case load immediately; however, it is critical to become as familiar as possible with the community and its members. When you are able to establish yourself quickly, you are also able to influence resources for your children and families. Byington and McCammon (1988) in their study of a volunteer group, found that through networking individuals could enhance their influence and access to resources of unmet needs by becoming more known as advocates in their community. The authors suggest that networking may be the main method of achieving resources for many individuals. The role you play as the child welfare social worker to not only network, but to model the steps for learning how to network will be very important for empowering families and children.

There are many things you can do during the preparation phase to familiarize yourself with the community and let members know that you are a part of the community and an active advocate for families and children. Spend some time at the schools, religious institutions, and other public arenas in town to introduce yourself and talk with members of the community about what they see as their concerns about families and children. Take part in town halls, community meetings, and open forums about different community issues to make your presence familiar to others and make them more open to speak with you. Remember, the most important thing you can do to become part of the community is to listen. Others hear what you say more readily, as you know, when they believe you have listened and heard them. Once you have become familiar to the community, take part in the discussions and emphasize the importance of children and family in any decisions the community is making.

Protocol 2: Develop Good Relationships with the Different Constituencies in the Community and Learn as Much as Possible About the Cultures of the Families with Whom You Will Work   The second protocol under the preparation phase refers to the importance of good relationships with agencies and individuals in the community. Moreover, personal contacts within these agencies is viewed as a way to create smoother paths for families and children in obtaining services. These contacts mean very little, however, if you do not understand the cultures and backgrounds of the children and families with whom you are working. Whether you are working in a large city or in a rural community, there will often be different cultures living among one another. Understanding the cultures in terms of their behaviors, language, familial relationships, and interactions will enable you to work more effectively with the families and will allow the families to recognize your efforts and respect for their cultures.

There are many steps you can take in familiarizing yourself with a culture other than your own. Becoming part of the community through attending different community activities and discussing issues particularly relevant to that community will help tie you to members. If the language is different from your own, it is important for you to begin to speak some of this language. It will be next to impossible to empower your families and children if you cannot speak with them or communicate to others what their needs are. Cohen (1992) notes that "recognition needs to be given to the unique cultural characteristics and the interdependence of people and their resource systems" (p. 245) in order for child welfare workers to effectively aid families of color. The issue goes further than simply understanding the different cultural issues, social identities and the language. It means that it is important for you to work within these differences and their meanings to bring about effective change.

Protocol 3: Initiate and Foster Good Personal Connections with Individuals Throughout Governmental and Social Service Agencies and in the Natural Helping Community   The third protocol in this phase recognizes the importance of the initiation and ongoing relationships with all the different constituents in an area. Whether the city council or local governing board agrees with social work's values and positions on families and children should not matter when it comes to providing services to your client. Many political individuals will welcome the counsel of local social workers and be happy to assist with problems in the community if you can produce the facts and information they need to understand the problems. Probably one of the best methods to meet influential individuals is to attend local religious gatherings, have breakfast at a café or diner that is known to cater to the city hall crowd, attend city council meetings, and take part in the social service and philanthropic networks that are available in your community. As you have introduced yourself into the community as suggested in protocol 1, you can now intervene more by knowing who the "players" are in the community and being able to work with them on issues related to families and children.

As important as knowing who has the power in a community and being able to work with them to bring about positive change, is knowing your counterparts in other social service agencies. By being able to contact someone you know on a more personal level, you will be able to facilitate resources for children and families that might otherwise be more difficult to obtain. Generally, there are numerous opportunities to meet other social service workers in a community. Being part of the professional organization and attending meetings, contacting other agencies and introducing yourself and your services, joining task forces around community issues, and becoming part of the general community are beginning ways to make and maintain ongoing relationships in other agencies. This type of networking enables the child welfare social worker to also have an ongoing knowledge of the changes in different agencies and to be familiar with the services that are available. Kirst-Ashman and Hull (1996) define agencies that have ongoing relationships with one another as complementary. They work together to not only provide services but to refer clients to one another for those services they can provide. These are the types of relationships that are the most beneficial between two social service agencies. Those relationships that do not connect or are competitive often place the needs of the agency before the family and child.

Protocol 4: Practice Being a Good Educator and Presenter on Family and Child Welfare Issues in the Community and Utilize Media Resources When Necessary   Providing the community with information regarding issues affecting families and children requires the child welfare social worker to be comfortable with presenting information and knowledgeable about the information being given. Of key importance in this endeavor is your own training, understanding, and presentation of the issues that surround children and families. Making sure of your data through research that is valid, keeping pace with new initiatives, and being able to present the material in a manner that is understandable and interesting can significantly raise the profile of the issues of families and children at risk in your area. Many child welfare agencies have set up volunteer speaking bureaus and have trained staff and volunteers to present material to different organizations in the community. When you are personally advocating for families and children, you need to be able to use your own strengths and limitations to work toward methods in which to create change.

Protocol 5: Review the List of Resources Available in Your Community and Make Note of Those You Believe Are Additionally Needed

In any beginning social work situation it is critical to make yourself familiar with the agencies and services that are available to the families and children in your community. There are, of course, several ways to do this and most communities have booklets available that describe the agencies, services, and requirements for individuals to acquire those services. These are often called the Community Service Handbook or some other similar name. These handbooks can be invaluable in establishing what services are available, what overlaps, what is needed, and who can be contacted in each agency to explain the services in more detail. If a community resource handbook does not exist in your community, this is one of the initial tasks you could initiate and undertake with other agencies in the area.

Understanding what services are missing can be gathered to some degree from a handbook; however, it will not be until you start working with families and individuals that you will begin to see those things that are really needed. For instance, the closest hospital may be 30 miles away from the community in which you work and they may have only one ambulance. This may not seem important at the time, but let a house fire occur with several people in the house and the services will be desperately missed. It is important to not just examine those agencies that serve social service functions, but to also look into the services that are available through other institutions. Talk to the professionals in these areas about their concerns over what services are missing in the community. For instance, does the local school have a way of testing for learning disabilities and serving children who have them? If not, what is being done about needs such as these?

The significance of protocol 5 is to aid the social worker's entrance into a new community and the utilization of services. Along with this is the importance of recognizing early on the strengths and limitations of the community's resources. While understanding more clearly where services are needed or are redundant may involve your experience with cases, you will also become aware of the types of needs children and families have during different periods of their development. It is a review of these resources that may be important to investigate. For example, along with educational services, are there specialized services for children with specific behavior problems within the community?

The utilization of formal services in the preparation phase of the SWPIP model involves gaining an understanding of (1) what services are available, (2) the quality of those services, and (3) how to build relationships with individuals who can sponsor and provide these services.

Protocol 6: Become an Active Member of Your Local Association of Social Workers and Become Involved in the Political Issues in Your Community, State, and Nation Taking the time to be an active member of your professional organization is very beneficial to working with issues for families and children within your community. By being a part of the professional organization, you are able to (1) stay in touch with other social workers in the community, (2) know the latest information about local, state, and federal political situations that may affect the families and children with whom you work, (3) have opportunities to take part in political issues and make a difference in the policies that are decided, (4) find support and collective thinking about issues related to families and children, and (5) stay up to date on the opportunities for innovative interventions with families and children. As mentioned, the use of the professional organization can be invaluable in many ways, not just for yourself but for your clients. As in any organization, there may be issues or decisions that you do not agree with, but if you are a member of the organization you will have more of an opportunity to question these decisions and influence the actions that are taken. Your role to model strengthening and empowerment behavior must begin with you—and be modeled for clients.

RELATIONSHIP BUILDING PROTOCOLS

CASE 3.2 Application of Relationship Building Protocols

The Kemlay family had lived in the neighborhood for 2 years in a house located on a large lot on one of the more quiet streets. The neighbor who had called the Child Abuse Hotline stated she had never seen Mrs. Kemlay or her daughter out of Mr. Kemlay's sight. She mentioned that soon after their move to the street, she had taken some cookies over to introduce herself but had found Mrs. Kemlay reluctant to ask her in.

What had caught the neighbor's recent attention and caused her to make the call to the hotline had involved a scene she had witnessed the night before when she was watering her garden. She stated she heard the Kemlay's door swing open loudly and turned to see the daughter run out of the house toward the street. Mr. Kemlay was running after her with what looked like a belt in his hand. He grabbed the girl by the arm and dragged her back in the house. The girl had been yelling and crying but she could not hear what was being said. The neighbor stated that she did not want to get involved in other's business but couldn't sleep all night and had noticed the girl didn't get on the school bus this morning. She wanted someone to check to see if the girl was all right.

The caseworker on duty at the child abuse hotline contacted the local authorities at Children's AID Society. The child protection team leader immediately assigned the case to Samantha Tierney who was a case investigator. Samantha looked up the number of the Kemlay family in the phone book and found it was unlisted. After having run the Kemlay name through the child abuse records and found no open or closed case, she decided to go out to the home and talk with the family. Knowing she would be walking into a family situation unannounced, Samantha prepared herself to approach the family with caution but also with openness to the situation. She knew that information on the abuse hot line could sometimes be unreliable. As Samantha approached the door she heard

yelling coming from inside. After knocking, the door was opened by a young woman in her teens. An older woman came to the door behind her. The older woman appeared to have been crying.

Samantha: "I'm Samantha Tierney and I have come from the Children's Aid Society. We have been informed that there may be a problem we could help you with and I wanted to speak with your family to see if any help was needed."

Older Woman: "My husband is not home and he does not allow anyone in the house when he is gone."

Samantha: "I don't want to cause any problems for you, but I am going to need to speak with you, your husband, and your daughter. Perhaps we could contact him at work and let him know I am here and would like to speak with him?"

Protocol 7: Advocate for Programs That Separate the Investigative Function of Child Welfare from the Interventive Function as Involuntary Clients Build Relationships with the Social Worker More Easily and Quickly If the Primary Social Worker Is Not the One Who Does the Initial Investigation   Protocol 7 is not only a key factor in this phase of the model but to all forms of interventions in child welfare protection. The process involved in forming a positive relationship requires skills in interviewing and a solid base of understanding of social work values. One of the major conflicts you will have as a child welfare social worker is to balance the roles of investigation and therapeutic intervention. While many theorists and researchers call for the separation of these tasks (including the authors), we also believe the tasks need to be carried out by professionally trained child welfare social workers. Advocates for the investigative process being handled by the law enforcement services (Holder & Corey, 1986; Pelton, 1991; Lindsey, 1994; Costin, Kargar, & Stoeze, 1996) recognize the importance of the initial impact involving the agency that will continue to work with the child. However, there is also the concern of the involvement of the law enforcement personnel if they have not been trained or taken part in workshops with child welfare social workers to coordinate their efforts. A critical component to success in child welfare protection is the joint training of many individuals in a community to recognize and respond to children in need. If these types of services are not being initiated, it would be important for you to help develop these skills with other professional individuals.

Regardless of the training, if you are responsible for both the investigative as well as interventive function in child protective work, it is critical that you assume the role of providing services to the family through a good relationship.

Protocol 8: Your Development of a Positive Relationship with the Child and/or Family Are Key Elements for the Success of the Intervention The importance of the relationship in the child welfare field can often be taken for granted. It is in child welfare situations that many of us will struggle the most with being able to maintain relationship skills. Working within child welfare situations, especially in protective cases, will test your own compassion and strength to be able to understand a person's actions and at the same time not condone them. Anderson (1992) examined the interactions of social workers in child welfare situations and found four different types of interactions primarily used: (1) mediating help and support with rare and positive contact, (2) controlling and exercising authority with negative contact and superficial contact only when necessary, (3) treatment-oriented work with regular contact and a close relationship, and (4) purely investigatory work with neutral contacts. The findings of the study support the supposition that the type of contact is determined by the type of problem with which the social worker was dealing. Although this would seem to be a likely outcome, it is not a finding that indicates that different interactions with different types of cases is necessarily good. An additional study by Anderson (1992) indicated that the treatment-oriented focus was the most positive and effective in building a trusting relationship. Many researchers have identified in their studies of child welfare situations that the outcome of the interaction between a child welfare social worker and their family was to a large degree determined by the relationship of the social worker with the parent—not by the type of problem (Winefield & Barlow, 1995; Drake, 1994).

The question then becomes—how do you go about establishing a positive relationship in even involuntary child welfare cases? Protocol 6 describes the importance of separating the investigative and intervention functions of the child welfare social worker but there are other means. Often, the relationship situation can benefit from the social worker visiting with the family in their home. Balgopal, Patchner and Henderson (1988) note that in a study of 34 involuntary child protective service cases, the findings indicate families more engaged in the intervention program with their worker were less likely to drop out of parenting skills training. Additionally, Colapinto (1995) has found that involuntary families in the child welfare system are more likely to lose their own power of making change through their family processes as the family's function begins to be consumed by the child welfare agency. The role of a positive relationship of the child welfare social worker with the family allows the family to balance and utilize its own processes to create positive change. In many ways, you as a child welfare social worker can serve in establishing a positive transitional process that can be integrated into the family. The verbal and nonverbal messages initially given a family can have a significant impact on the perception of the relationship by the parent and can aid this positive transitional process to take place.

Protocol 9: Skills in Genuineness, Empathy, Human Dignity, and Warmth Are Critical for Building a Relationship with a Child and/or Family　　Research in the area of counseling and therapy has long concluded that the most positive outcomes are more often a result of the social worker expressing empathy, genuineness, human dignity, and warmth (Nugent, 1992). The skills involved in allowing these traits to be at the forefront will be challenged to a large degree by the attitude of families who are involuntarily receiving your services. Drake (1994) found that parents and families in the assessment phase, as well as other phases in child welfare intervention, were more successful if the worker and parent/s had initially developed a positive working relationship. It is important to remember that a defensive or confronting attitude can immediately turn the family against you. Recognizing that each situation has its own uniqueness and that individuals are capable of making changes is probably one of the reasons you went into social work. Having a perspective that most families love their children and want what is best for them will also help you. Although we must recognize that there are certain individuals to whom this does not apply because of a mental deficit or unique situation, the majority of parents do want to keep their children from harm. If your initial reaction to the family is to listen and understand, you will receive more information, be able to make more informed decisions about the situation and gain the confidence of the family to make changes.

It is important that not only positive attitudes are integrated into your relationship with the child and family but that also genuineness and honesty form a major part of the trust that you will build with the client. Be honest and genuine with the family and child. Do not keep issues from the family and they will not keep issues from you. How we treat a family will reflect back the family's treatment of us and the amount of progress they can make.

Protocol 10: Building Positive Relationships with Formal and Informal Community Services Is Critical for the Child and/or Family with Whom You Are Working　　Establishing positive relationships with informal and formal community services early is very important, but if you do not maintain these relationships and constantly establish new ones when there are changes within the agency, neighborhood, or community, you will lose your ability to influence services and resources. There are many changes you will experience within the community in which you work. Some agencies have significant turnovers as well as changes in policy and administration. Particular neighborhoods and communities can experience transient populations but still generate stable networks within these communities that individuals may turn to for support and resources. Part of your role as a child welfare worker will be to identify these informal support networks in a neighborhood or community and help strengthen them as a resource for families and a means for you to be integrated into the community.

To give you a better understanding of how this might work, let's assume that you have several families you are working with who live within a five block area. While visiting these families you begin to hear one or two names more frequently associated with the neighborhood. It could be an older neighbor who lives down the street and sits outside frequently exchanging conversations with others, the superintendent of an apartment building who is always offering aid to others in the area, or a pastor at a local church who is very interested in outreach and advocacy for his or her neighborhood. Whoever it might be, it may represent an individual or group of individuals who care about others and would be happy to aid or work with you in establishing a supportive network in the neighborhood. Contacting this person or pulling several of these people together from the same community to discuss what issues they are concerned about and in what ways they might be willing to help out can provide a base of a natural helping network in the community where families and children could turn for resources when it is impossible for you as the child welfare worker to be there. It is also an empowering method for those in the community.

Protocol 11: Aid and Strengthen the Child and/or Family to Build Natural Helping Networks as a Key to Their Success and Maintenance   Research clearly indicates that those families who have more emotional and social support do better in parenting, having healthy children, and preventing child maltreatment (Garbarino, 1980). Many of the families you will work with in child welfare will not have these kinds of resources. They will often be single parents without extended family in close proximity or with families who are not interested in supporting them. Another type of family may be a closed family in which the parents do not allow outside intrusions although the supports are available and there. It is critical to aid all families in reaching out for not only formal supports but for informal supports. There are natural helping networks located in all communities and neighborhoods. It will become an important task to help pull these natural helping networks together and give them support for the aid they provide those families who do not have these supports or who do not know how to reach out to become integrated as part of these natural helping networks.

Many times, as child welfare social workers, you will believe that your case loads and responsibilities prohibit you from reaching out in a macro manner such as this, but in reality by reaching out into communities and neighborhoods to set up natural helping networks, you will be aiding yourself through having other individuals involved in helping families and children in their communities.

Natural helping networks exist not only in communities, but also through institutions. There may be teachers in a school who are interested in helping or medical personnel who are willing to volunteer their time to create differences in the lives of families and children with whom they work. Families will need to be encouraged to reach out, connect, and build these social networks for themselves. Often, working as a network of social workers within your agency can enable a team approach to operate within a neighborhood and/or community.

ASSESSMENT PROTOCOLS

CASE 3.3   Application of Assessment Protocols

Patrick Kerns had worked with Children and Family Services for 3 months when he was asked to make an assessment of several family home situations in the same apartment development. A few days prior to this assignment there had been an article in the local newspaper condemning this same neighborhood apartment area. The article was on the poor conditions of the apartments and of the fact that the families were afraid to allow their children outside because of the drug dealers and violence in the surrounding area. Several phone calls to local politicians following the article had promoted the city mayor and state governor to order the building inspected, the police to place double teams in the area, and for the Family Service Agency to check out the well-being of the children living in the dwelling.

Patrick knew there had not been any specific complaints of child abuse or neglect and that his visit to these homes was in response to political pressure following the newspaper article. Patrick had three families he was assigned to visit in this apartment building while other caseworkers were assigned the rest. These families all received state and family income support. The fact that he was intruding into family situations due to a

newspaper article did not cause Patrick to feel good about the situation. When he had called the families in the building, most were annoyed with being intruded upon and he believed very much that this was like "blaming the victim." He determined that he would assess the situations in the building in as nondeficit a manner as possible.

The next day Patrick contacted the three families again and agreed upon a time that they felt was most convenient to meet. The first family he visited was the Doloro's. Marissa Doloro was a single mother, age 23, who lived alone with her three children, Arron, age 5, Lynn, age 6, and Steve, age 8. Ms. Doloro had never married and the father of the children had not lived with her for over 2 years. When Patrick arrived at the home, the children had just returned from their grandmother's where they had been staying for the week. Ms. Doloro explained that she had sent the children to her parents so they could have a "vacation." She stated that they did not go out much before or after school because of the concern she had over the problems in the neighborhood. She stated she knew the children got very bored but that she did not want to risk something happening to them.

Protocol 12: Assessment of the Risk to the Child Is the Most Important Child Welfare Assessment to Be Done in Cases of Neglect, Emotional Maltreatment, Physical Abuse, and Sexual Abuse The questions behind the use of out-of-home care in the 1960s and 1970s led to an emphasis in family-based services and family preservation; however, other questions are now being raised as to whether we as child welfare social workers are concentrating too much on the preservation of the family and not enough on the protection of the child. As you will learn in chapter 6, there are several issues that must be examined in protective services cases when attempting to make decisions about whether or not a child can remain in a home while the family receives aid. The lack of foster care homes has also led child welfare social workers to question what the worse case scenario may be for the child—leaving them in a home that needs immediate intensive services or placing the child in a large institution, such as a detention center, because there are no foster homes available. Regardless of the philosophy of the agency in which you work or the resources available, a child should never be placed or left in an at-risk situation. Making this decision is difficult and there are many differing types of risk assessment tools you can utilize to help in this process; however, the child's safety must be the foremost issue in your mind in working with the family.

Protocol 13: When Working with the Family and Child, Engage a Strength's Perspective in the Assessment If you are familiar with most assessment forms and techniques, you realize that many of them focus on the problems and issues related to family. In doing an assessment of the family and child after the "risk assessment" that you or an investigative worker has already done, your focus needs to be on the strengths and resources the family already has. Compton and Galaway (1994) indicate the focus of an assessment from an empowerment perspective is a mutual endeavor. The expertise of the client, as well as their experience, is a very important aspect of a strength building assessment. Gutierrez, Parsons, and Cox (1997) reiterate the importance of both the micro and macro systems being assessed. Many of the families with whom you work will be from an economically disempowered group and their understanding and assessment of both the external as well as internal forces will create a picture of hope for them as they come to recognize how external influences beyond their control may be affecting their lives. Highlight 3.1 is a figure by Cox and Longres (1981) in Gutierrez, Parsons, and Cox (1997) that identifies the assessment components from a strength's perspective (p. 12).

This figure clearly illustrates how the family's assessment of themselves takes on a very systemic and strength's-focused approach. On many levels this process of assessment is like a cognitive intervention into the family's life. By participating in assessing the situation and understanding how other factors play into their lives, the family can begin to think differently about how to handle many of the situations they face.

Protocol 14: The Risk Assessment Instrument Utilized Needs to Be a Reliable and Valid Instrument in Which You Are Trained and Experienced in Using   The use of a risk assessment instrument will be talked about in more detail in chapter 6; however, it is critical to recognize that whatever instrument for risk evaluation you utilize in working with families and children needs to be a reliable and valid one. Issues of reliability and validity are concepts that can be misunderstood when you are practicing—however, part of your social work education is to develop the ability to not only understand but to utilize research methods in an accountable way with your clients. Reliability ensures that the instrument you are using accurately tests what you are seeking, while an instrument that is reliable can be utilized over and over again to test the same type of situation. For instance, if you were seeking to test the risk to a child remaining in their biological family you would use specially designed and tested instruments such as the New York Risk Assessment Instrument (1992) or the Child at Risk Field (Holder & Corey, 1986), not a family stress measurement. The instrument you choose would have been tested for validity, and you would know that the instrument can be used in any child protection situation and will measure the same from situation to situation.

Many issues emerge when you utilize a risk assessment instrument to determine whether a child needs to be removed from a home. The removal of a child from their biological family has serious consequences for both the child and the family. While they may have suffered maltreatment or neglect within their family, it may also be the only sense of security and nurturing they have experienced. Removing a child from their home is a traumatic experience for them. The placement of a child into a foster family or group care situation requires the utmost care and consideration. Risk assessment instruments, even those that have been tested and proven effective, are not without their flaws. Part of your training in social work is to not only utilize good instruments but to also utilize your own "use of self" to make decisions that are in the best interest of the child first, as well as the family.

Protocol 15: Nondeficit Assessment Is an Essential Part of a Diversity Strength's Perspective in Child Welfare   We know that the assessment of the family and child needs to be completed from a strength's perspective for the purpose of building and empowering the family from the beginning. While it is important to understand the limitations of the families you work with, it is even more important in child welfare to assess the family from a diversity perspective and look for out of the box ideas for making use of that diversity. As we have noted, in the assessment phase we need to be focused on both internal and external factors that are affecting the family's or individual's strengths to cope with their problems. However, a clear assessment cannot occur within the context of a single lens—either your's or the family's. The situation must be examined through many lenses, those of the family, culture, and society.

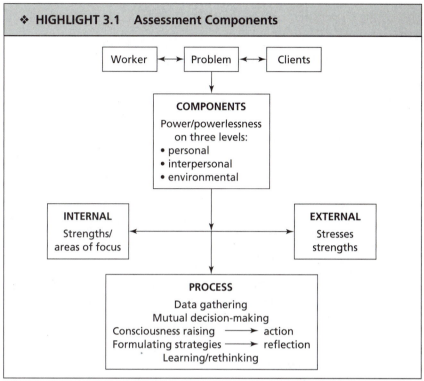

❖ HIGHLIGHT 3.1   Assessment Components

Worker ←→ Problem ←→ Clients

COMPONENTS

Power/powerlessness
on three levels:
• personal
• interpersonal
• environmental

INTERNAL

Strengths/
areas of focus

EXTERNAL

Stresses
strengths

PROCESS

Data gathering
Mutual decision-making
Consciousness raising ⟶ action
Formulating strategies ⟶ reflection
Learning/rethinking

SOURCE: From *Empowerment in Social Work Practice,* by Gutierrez, Parsons, and Cox. © 1997. Reprinted with permission of Wadsworth Publishing, a division of Thompson Learning.

Nondeficit assessment is essential for dealing with diversity in a multicultural society. Nondeficit assessment requires you as the child welfare social worker to focus on the strengths of the family through their cultural perspective, not yours. Although there are situations that must be maintained as consistent for the well-being of all children, there are many situations in which the environmental conditions of the family, although different from general societal ideals, can still be very strong and positive. For example, a large portion of minority families who love and care for their children do not have the same resources as those in majority families. The United States Census Bureau indicates that an average of 68 percent of African-American single-parent families are living below the poverty line, as compared to 48 percent of Caucasian single-parent families. The conditions and resources of families living below the poverty line do not necessarily produce the same kinds of environmental conditions as those with more funds. There may be many generations of a family living under one roof or the children may live for the largest part of a time period with an extended family member. Children may share a room with several siblings or may only have access to a few changes of clothing. These are situations that may exist in many loving families and do not need to be changed or seen as a deficit.

PLANNING PROTOCOLS

CASE 3.4   Application of Planning Protocols

Sean had been working with the Leing family for approximately 3 weeks. Ms. Leing had recently had a child who was born with a series of medical problems that required the child to remain in the hospital for several weeks. Once the infant returned home there would be additional needs and resources required. The Leing family had just experienced the loss of Ms. Leing's mother and sister in an automobile accident. Ms. Leing had been experiencing a deep depression for the last several weeks following this accident and had not been in a positive emotional state upon admittance to the hospital. There were three other children in the Leing family and Mr. Leing had recently accepted a job with a trucking company that kept him on the road at least three days a week. There were no extended family members living near the Leing's, nor did they seem to have other support to help with the needs of the family after the child returned home. The hospital social worker on the pediatric floor contacted a child welfare worker (Sean) who focused on working with families with special needs.

Sean, Beth (the hospital social worker), and Mr. and Ms. Leing met together on the day Ms. Leing was discharged from the hospital. At the meeting, Ms. Leing's depression was quite noticeable as was Mr. Leing's concern over their children. Ms. Leing was anxious about being able to visit their new daughter in the hospital when she would not have transportation or care for her other children during the day. It quickly became apparent to Sean from what was being described that there were several concrete issues that must be dealt with in order for the Leing family to maintain itself: Ms. Leing's depression, care for the other children while the parents visited the hospital, transportation to the hospital for Ms. Leing when Mr. Leing was away, possible homemaker services for Ms. Leing for a temporary amount of time after her discharge, and possibly other services once the new baby returned home depending upon Ms. Leing's depression and the needs of the child.

While Sean recognized these issues, he focused for several minutes on the positives and strengths in the family, the new job position for the father, the raising of three children, the well-being of their new daughter and her coming home, and the strength of Ms. Leing recognizing all she had been through this past year. He then began to turn the conversation to what the Leings thought would help them—not listing off the services he had raised in his own mind. The Leings were very responsive to his questions and appeared most interested in Ms. Leing being able to see her daughter as frequently as possible in the hospital. Sean suggested several ways they might manage additional childcare and transportation. These included homemaker services that he could set up on a temporary basis, and possible individuals the Leings might know in the neighborhood or within their community they had not thought of using as a resource. Sean also mentioned that there was a means of transportation for individuals in the area without cars to and from the hospital. Generally, this service was for the elderly, but he believed that there might be a

Continued

CASE 3.4 *Continued*

---

way to arrange the service with the volunteer organization that ran it.

Sean set up a meeting at the Leing's house the following day to try to pull some of these resources together. The volunteer director of the transportation services agreed to meet with him at the Leings the next day. When Sean and the director arrived, they found that a Ms. Maris, the teacher of one of the Leing children, was also there. She had been very supportive of each boy when they had taken her class. Ms. Leing had contacted her upon her return home to seek information about childcare. Ms. Maris had offered to meet with everyone as she knew several resources for after school care on a temporary basis that would not cost money. All Ms. Leing would need to do was to give back the days in the form of childcare when she was well enough.

Sean encouraged Mr. and Ms. Leing to lead the meeting in discussing what their needs were and what options were available. Once the transportation and childcare issue had been resolved, Sean asked the parents about how he might further aid them as he recognized that there would be some additional stresses in the family. Ms. Leing mentioned several additional areas that were concerning her: being alone at night when she felt so down, her anxiety over when her daughter would return home, and her concern for her other children that they would feel abandoned if she placed them in childcare.

As Sean continued to talk with the mother, Mr. Leing spoke up and mentioned how important he thought it would be if his wife could see a doctor about her depression and maybe she could do that when she went to visit her daughter at the hospital. As they talked, Sean began to more clearly understand what issues were affecting each member of the family and he began to make mental notes of the supports each of them could obtain in the community. A plan began to emerge through this discussion and would involve other members of the community, however, Sean was certain that the Leings felt good about the meeting and felt they were listened to and served.

Protocol 16: Planning with the Family and Child Is More Successful When Their Involvement Is Valued and Mutual Interaction Occurs in the Process Social workers are very familiar with the importance of mutual work with the client and this becomes even more critical when you are dealing with a child welfare case. Your involvement in the family, whether voluntary or involuntary, is a threat to the security and equilibrium of the family. Whether the issue is about child protection or about day care, families are often suspicious of governmental intervention even when it is given as aid. Your ability to give the family and child choices when you are dealing with them enables you to form a relationship more quickly and is more likely to create a situation in which the family and the child want to work toward goals that bring about their independence from your involvement.

Enabling the family to be part of the process involves being able to let go and allow the family to make decisions that may not be in sync with your initial thoughts. For example, there may be a situation in which an infant is in need of immediate care due to a lack of parental skills and the parents' inability to provide the nurturing so needed in early development. The infant may not need to be completely removed from the family, but there may be ways in which the child and parent could receive the appropriate care immediately, with the parent receiving the training at the same time.

Protocol 17: Case Management Is a Significant Part of Planning and Involves Both Formal and Informal Interactions Within the Community   Case management has a significant role in child welfare. As noted by Maluccio, Fein, and Olmstead (1986), the role of case management includes: "evaluating goal attainment, collaborating with foster parents, negotiating and coordinating the roles of various service providers, referring parents to appropriate community resources, planning and managing parent-child visitation, helping parents develop and use resources in their social networks, and monitoring the delivery of services on behalf of the family" (pp. 69–70). Although these skills may appear basic to most social workers, it requires a great deal of coordination to bring these different services and the families together. Your ability to have formed a positive relationship with the family, as well as with individuals in community agencies, will aid in your case management efforts. Without case management, the likelihood of the family and child becoming lost in the social service system with little involvement in the decision making process, becomes greater.

When you serve as a case manager it is important to recognize the roles and skills of the others involved in the case. In doing this, you can facilitate the skills of the team in those areas in which they are most experienced and develop a plan that does not allow for the overlapping of roles or services by members of the team. While facilitating this process, it is important to recognize that the family is part of the team. Their input and ability to be involved in the decisions to accomplish the mutual plan is important to the success of the intervention. Although their involvement may be viewed by some on the case team as unnecessary (you may be working with disciplines that differ from those of social work) it is important to establish this social work value as quickly as possible so that the family is involved from the beginning of the process. Macaskill and Ashworth (1995) found that social work professionals supported the involvement of parents in conferences at a much higher rate than other disciplines. In supporting this involvement, results of these types of conferences are seen as more effective.

Protocol 18: Planning and Contracting for Service Needs to Reflect the Family's Cultural Background and Needs   When you are planning services and programs with families, as in assessment, it is important to be aware of their specific cultural and or/individualized needs. Difficulties frequently arise from not acknowledging or recognizing these specific needs. Religious issues are an area that child welfare social workers often overlook. Setting up a plan and the utilization of services needs a focus that takes into account the issues of culture, race, religion, and other personalized characteristics of the family. In order to accomplish this task, you as the child welfare social worker advocate for an awareness that there are individual characteristics in the family that must be recognized and receive attention. Your ability to become aware of these characteristics involves the family sharing with you what these are through their comfort and openness to letting you be a part of their reality. Establishing this comfort level, according to Devore and Schlesinger (1987), requires a process of "(1) stage setting, (2) tuning in (Middleman & Goldberg, 1974), (3) attending (Egan, 1975), and (4) preparatory empathy (Shulman, 1984)" (p. 184). This process speaks to the worker preparing a physical space that is comfortable for the family (this may be the family's home) and preparing for the opportunity to become more in tune with the family's reality as it differs from the social worker's. Through this preparation, the worker is able to be empathetic with the feelings and ideas the family or child expresses that may differ from the worker's. This is an important process of listening and displaying skills that pay respect and give importance to what is happening within the home.

Protocol 19: The Child Welfare Social Worker Is Most Effective When Serving as the Case Manager for Their Families and Facilitating Their Interaction with the Community   Many agencies offer case management services to their clients; however, when you are working from a child welfare perspective, it is important that the services be coordinated through the services being provided to the family in the child welfare agency. As the child is of utmost importance in terms of safety, your ability to serve as the case manager enables you to make the priority the safety and needs of the child. As a social worker in child welfare you may also be asked to work with other disciplines in the planning and management of a case. It is important to recognize the roles of these individuals and allow their expertise to be a part of the plan; however, the values and skills that you as a social worker have in case management and in working with family and child welfare situations places you in the unique position of having expertise and authority in an interdisciplinary situation. Aaronson (1989) argues that the dual role of the case manager and social worker offers an opportunity for the social worker to assess the situation more closely and have a hands on interaction that allows for providing immediate services.

IMPLEMENTATION PROTOCOLS

Protocol 20: Carry Out Your Agreed Part of the Plan and Do Not Agree to Actions That You Cannot Do   As a social worker you may want to provide all the alternatives you can to help the family and child, and yet this may not be possible because of the parameters of your agency. In an effort to support the family be very specific about what you can do, explain

---

CASE 3.5   Application of Implementation Protocols

The recent arrest of her 16-year-old son had affected Ms. Lyons enormously. Jamal was the youngest of her three sons and had always been very studious and hard working at school. He had not been in trouble before. Her second oldest son, Michael, had some difficulties when he was younger, hanging out with a gang of kids who always seemed to be getting into trouble, but he had outgrown that and was now married and holding down a good job. The arrest was even more upsetting to Ms. Lyons as it involved drugs. The family had gathered quickly to support one another and by the time the youth worker from the local family service agency met with them at the detention center, they had already formulated a plan to help Jamal.

Meilani had been a child welfare youth social worker for about 3 years, yet she did not think she had seen many other families as anxious as this one to try to resolve the situation. The only concern was that the family did not believe that Jamal had been involved with the drugs. They felt he had been set up by gang members in the neighborhood. While Meilani did not know every detail of the case, she was aware that Jamal had been picked up by the police during a raid at a "crack house" and that he had been high at the time. Meilani assured the family that she would check on Jamal's well-being and would attempt to gather as much information as she could. She met with Jamal in the interview room and was surprised by his ability to focus and talk about his situation since the legal authorities had stated he had been high at the time of his arrest 2 hours earlier. Because of the seriousness of the charge, Jamal had to remain in the detention center until the next day when a hearing was set. At the hearing, Meilani worked with the public defender who had been assigned to Jamal's case to ensure that Jamal was released to the custody of his family. Meilani's responsibility over the next few weeks before the formal hearing would be to work with Jamal and the family to assess the situation, make plans for monitored supervision, and provide a recommendation to the court regarding the arrest. Over the course of the next few days, Meilani had come to believe that the officers must have been mistaken at the time of the arrest. A blood and urine analysis indicated that Jamal had not had drugs in his system at the time of the arrest.

---

the limitations of your role, and help the family look for ways they can obtain the services they need that you cannot provide. Carry out your part of the intervention plan as you agreed in the contract. Do not change or make adjustments to what you will do without first consulting with the family. Do not agree to provide the family with services you cannot. Make very clear your role and their role in the work to be done.

To accomplish this building of trust and the establishment of the family and the social worker's responsibilities, it is important to work through a strengthening perspective. Simon (1994) suggests that "asking as much dedication to problem solving from the clients as from yourself" will aid in establishing not only the expectations of both responsibilities, but also in strengthening the family to know that they have the power to make a difference and that it is not just the responsibility of the social worker.

Protocol 21: Respect the Family's Needs to Make Changes and Adjust the Plan If There Are Necessary Reasons That Do Not Adversely Affect the Welfare of the Child   A family that has been working toward identified goals may at some point want to change these goals as other issues arise that affect their ability to carry out the initial plan. Regardless of what the issues are, it is important for you as the child welfare social worker to be open and acknowledging of circumstances that may occur to make a difference in their situation. If you are working from an empowerment perspective, then the family and/or child must be given the opportunity to make decisions that differ from the initial contract. While these changes may not be such that they jeopardize the contract that has been established, especially in relation to protective service cases, they must be recognized as part of what is an ongoing process between the family and the child welfare agency. When families recognize that they have the ability to make changes even if they are under the auspice of a governmental agency or institution, they can integrate an empowerment that may move them from hopelessness to action.

Protocol 22: Utilize Both Micro and Macro Interventions in Child Welfare Situations. Until Major Changes Are Made Regarding the Economic Inequality of Families, the Child Welfare Situation Will Continue to Worsen   Regardless of the type of case you are working with, it is important for you as a child welfare social worker to examine the situation from an environmental and possible inequitable perspective. These perspectives need examination from how they have affected not only the family situation but also how they are affecting other family situations. The inequality may take the form of a lack of economic resources, such as after school care, a drug-infested neighborhood, and/or a lack of adequate housing. Your use of measures to bring about change from a macro focus requires the use of different roles than those dealing with residual cases. As an advocate and change agent, you will be required to assume a leadership role in the changes that must be made for children and their families. This role will diminish as families take on these actions. As welfare reform assimilates into the contextual environment of social services, it is important for child welfare social workers to take an active part in seeking macro changes in policies and programs that will benefit and prevent the need for child welfare services. The role of the families and children with whom we work is even more important to creating change within the environment. Cowger (1994) notes:

> Clients, not social workers, own the power that brings significant change in clinical practice. A clinical social worker is merely a resource person with professional training on the use of resources who is committed to people empowerment and willing to share his or her knowledge in a manner that helps people realize their own power, take control of their lives, and solve their own problems (p. 294).

As we empower the families with whom we work, together we will move forward in creating change and bringing about an environment in society that is more equitable.

Protocol 23: Educate the Family to Advocate and Take Action for Themselves With Others in Their Community It is impossible to be everything to everyone, but it is not impossible to help others become those things they most want to be and strengthen them to obtain the services and resources they want for their community. As noted in protocol 22, your role goes beyond residual services as a child welfare social worker and embraces the macro goals of empowerment for societal change. The families with whom you are working in a neighborhood or community are the most powerful weapon available. Their ability to be heard and have their issues addressed must come from them. Pulling together to make things happen for a community is what will continue to bring about real change. Simon (1994) states that making leadership development a constant priority of practice and policy through personal, group, and community involvement is an important empowerment technique for social workers. This development of leadership among families creates an environment of not only natural helping networks, but also an environment in which societal change becomes very real and possible. Lum (1996) describes this macro level intervention as a "natural response to program cutbacks, reduced services, and restrictive eligibility-requirement tests" (p. 272). Lum, whose emphasis is on empowerment of people of color, clearly delineates the ways in which this may be accomplished.

As laid out in this text, Lum emphasizes the empowerment of families to create the changes needed. Methods of accomplishing these changes can be through political impact intervention and legal advocacy intervention. Political impact intervention impacts on society through the coalition of groups affected by negative policies, to pull together in the election of politicians who will bring about change. Legal advocacy intervention is about bringing change through the courts in relation to large classes of people who experience discrimination because of a particular characteristic. For example, a class action suit might be considered by single-parent mothers who receive less income than their male counterparts based on their gender.

Protocol 24: Being Able to Think Outside the Box and Use Innovative Techniques and Services to Aid a Child, Family, and Community Allows the Family and Social Worker to Make the Greatest Use of Services The use of out of the box ideas and techniques is part of a constructivist approach to dealing with social problems and issues. Although child welfare agencies attempt on many levels to provide innovative and best practice techniques and programs, they are often limited by the context of the governmental auspices under which they provide services. The recommendation to think outside the box is not about a radical focus on not working within the parameters of the child welfare agency. Although there may be a time when you are forced to acknowledge that the best practices for a child and/or family may not be within the context of your agency and you will need to advocate for changes, utilizing out of the box techniques does not necessarily require a rearranging of the social service agency parameters. Small out of the box methods that do not go against agency policy, but rather refine it or create situations in which several policies may be integrated, can serve your clients from a multi-systemic perspective. One example that you will read about in chapter 4 recognizes the importance of children and parents remaining together yet protecting the best interests of the child by placing both the parent and the child in a family foster home. This is different, yet within the context of the agency, and very viable in terms of an intervention process that utilizes the macro approach of foster care placements that include many members of the community.

EVALUATION AND ENDING PROTOCOLS

CASE 3.6 Application of Evaluation and Ending Protocols

The first year of the Mentoring Co-Op Program at Lincoln High School would be winding down in about two weeks. The program, sponsored by the State Department of Children and Youth, was designed to run for only nine months a year. Jacob Lagar had worked with the program since its initiation a year ago. He had been a juvenile case manager with the Department of Children and Youth and had been working in one of the group homes for boys when the governmental grant he had applied for had been awarded. The Department immediately gave him the opportunity to direct the new pilot program in the inner city high school. The program had been designed as a way to help juvenile boys/girls at risk of dropping out of school to connect with an adult in the community who had success in graduating from high school and developing a business in the area. Each identified teenager had been matched with a man or woman in the area who had volunteered to take the youth into their business to work 10

hours a week. The volunteers had also been selected on the basis that they would volunteer at least 2 hours a week in working with the youth on school or personal issues. Jacob had served as an advisor for both the youth and mentors during the program.

Of the 25 teens who had entered the program in September, 22 of them had remained in school throughout the year and 20 of them had passed all their classes. Jacob knew this was a good indication that the program was working but he also realized that his view was not worth as much as statistics that could back up the results. Through initially reviewing the records and talking with teachers, Jacob had identified close to 70 teens who were in need of the program, but with services available for only 25, he had randomly selected those from the 70. He had set up a chart to monitor the progress of the other 45 and planned to review those figures as soon as possible.

Protocol 25: View Evaluation from Both a Process and Outcome Perspective   The importance of evaluation cannot be underestimated. It not only serves the agency in accounting for these services with funding agencies, but also helps you to more fully understand the quality of your own work with children and families. Evaluation that also involves the family and child can provide them with feedback about their success and/or areas on which they need to continue working. Evaluation as an outcome measure examines what has changed in the family over the length of the intervention and reviews the goals that have been achieved and those yet to be achieved or modified. Process evaluation, however, involves an ongoing examination of not only the outcomes from the intervention, but also the interaction and changes that are occurring while the work is going on. Process evaluation can often serve as a guide to the intervention and aid in directing the methods that will be used.

In the phases of the SWPIP model, both types of evaluation are part of each phase. The outcome and process evaluations at the end of each phase are gathered through examining short-term goals for each phase that are evaluated on a regular basis with the family and child. For example, a short-term goal may be to have established a contract and plan with which the family, child, and you are satisfied. At the end of the planning phase, you and the family/child can review whether the process involved in establishing the plan was satisfactory and in what ways this process was important. A method by which to do process evaluation not only at the end of a phase but as part of each session would be to discuss how the interview went, how the services are working, and what the family and child believe they have accomplished each week. This supplies feedback not only to you but also to the family and child and gives them an opportunity to see their growth as autonomous and as part of a process that they control.

Protocol 26: Families Are an Important Part of the Evaluation Process and Their Ability to Provide That Evaluation Is an Important Step in Their Independent Family Process   As noted in the previous protocol, families need to be a part of the evaluation process as much as they need to be a part of any factor in the intervention. When you begin where a family is, you need to also recognize where they believe they have gone or are going in terms of the intervention. Hepworth and Larsen (1993) note that when clients give feedback in the evaluation process, it can be invaluable for the social worker as well as the client in knowing what worked and what did not work. The social worker adds this knowledge to his or her understanding of interventive processes and can utilize or modify these interventions for future families. The involvement of the family in the evaluation also aids them in understanding their successes and strengths in bringing about change in their own lives. The ability of the family to recognize their role also helps promote their involvement in sharing with other families how to go about creating change in their lives. The success of those families can serve not only as models, but also as part of a natural helping network within a community.

The participation and involvement of families who have been successful in working with child welfare programs in training other families in the skills of becoming a strong independent family can be a critical bridge between micro and macro practice.

Protocol 27: Evaluation Provides Information for Not Only the Individual Case But for Future Cases and the Programs, Policies, and Services Utilized Evaluation provides information for not only micro case situations but also for macro issues. It is important when working in a community with many different systems to evaluate those institutions and services that have been utilized by the family and child. Kirst-Ashman and Hull (1993) note that quality assurance reviews are one form of evaluation of service outcome. This type of evaluation can be accomplished by a review of records and from information gathered with the families and children who have received the services. It is also important to aid the family and child in being recognized as the consumer of the service and the ones who can verify the effectiveness of the intervention and the ways in which it could be modified to be more effective.

This type of evaluation, however, is not just about an evaluation of the organizations that are utilized. Consistent and ongoing evaluation of individual cases can create a substantial file of similar case situations that can be evaluated based on the effectiveness of the interventions, programs, and policies that affected families. A method to gathering this type of ongoing data is to record consistently the process of the case situation and the outcomes of each interaction.

A thorough review of these processes and outcomes allows the child welfare social worker to recognize specific issues and themes that can be identified and evaluated for their worth. For example, the use of a particular method of interaction, the specific processes involved in the family or child making use of a resource, or the identification of specific resources that may become broader natural helping networks are all examples of the themes and characteristics of cases that might be gathered for use in working with families and/or making changes in policies and practices. This process of evaluation is just as important to your work in child welfare as anything else you do. If this analysis of cases is handled professionally and with knowledge of the practice research, you can make significant changes in bridging the gap of micro and macro practice.

Protocol 28: Compiling Case Evaluations Can Provide Data to Make Changes in Policies That Affect Families As you gather information from your evaluations about each of your case situations, you can bring together these findings to examine similarities and patterns in the families' environment that affect their ability to function and bring about change in their lives. As noted in protocol 27, this compiling of data is a form of practice research that can bridge the gap between micro and macro practice. Bridging between residual and preventive practices is what the SWPIP model emphasizes in its application. This kind of analysis is done often in child welfare agencies, but without the goal of bridging practice with policy. Many child welfare agencies, for example, will review workers' charts evaluating for appropriate procedures and actions taken with a client. The purpose of this examination is generally to assess a worker's performance, however, this same process could be used for a more positive objective of identifying the practices that work and the environmental factors that play into whether a case situation has been strengthened or weakened. This accumulated data can be utilized as information for policymakers and politicians to create change within an environmental context for families. This is another form of bridging the gap between residual and preventive types of services and programs. It brings into play the connection between practice and policy and how this connection might be utilized for the betterment of all families.

Protocol 29: Ending Intervention Is the Over-Arching Goal of Your Work with the Family and as Such Provides the Family with a Positive Launching Point The goal of the strengthening continuum, as noted, is to end services with a strong and nurturing independent family environment for the child. Part of your role will be to make real for the child and/or family this ending goal from the start of your work. Even if the initial action you must take in a protective service case is to place a child in foster care, there needs to be a clear understanding with the family and child that the purpose of the intervention is to establish an independent family environment that can provide nurturing and strength for the child. In many of the case situations you will deal with in child welfare this will not be a difficult task. When working with a family with special needs, a delinquent teenager, or an expectant young mother, you will find that instilling this perspective of a strong family is not difficult. Your responsibilities focus on facilitating the strengths in these types of situations and helping individuals see that they can utilize their own characteristics and strengths to not only produce this type of environment for their family, but to be able to maintain and continue sustaining their growth. Your purpose from the start of interaction is to exit the family as quickly as possible with the knowledge that they have the ability and tools to handle their family situation.

In protective service situations, however, the family will feel a lack of control immediately upon your unwanted presence. Often, because child welfare social workers have been identified in the media as individuals who do not aid a family but tear it apart, your intrusion will be seen as a means to disrupting the family system. Your ability to clarify your role and the purpose of strengthening a family environment for a child (beginning with the biological family) will enable you to bring about change in a much more positive way. As noted, it aids you in child protective situations to not be the investigator who makes the decision about the neglect or maltreatment and to enter the family with the goal of ending the intervention in a positive manner.

Clarifying early on the goal of ending also aids the family in letting go of your support. Despite difficult protective service family situations, the majority of families will establish a very positive interaction with you if your approach and interactions have been appropriately utilized. This positive interaction for many families will become something they depend on. The fact that many of these families will be single mothers with little support or resources can make you a very important person in their lives. Your ability to help them form other social networks and resources, as well as to make clear from the beginning the goal of ending your interaction so they become a strong independent family unit, prepares the family for your leaving early on and helps them move toward developing their own strengths and supports for when you are not involved.

Protocol 30: Dealing Early with the Reactions Family Members May Have to Ending Allows the Family to Move Forward Easier Despite your efforts to prepare the family and/or child early about your departure from their lives, there are often difficult reactions that emerge from ending. Even if you are working with involuntary family situations, you may find that your relationship with the family and child are difficult to end even if you have been able to build the relationships the appropriate way. Hepworth, Rooney, and Larsen (1997) note that the general negative reactions to the ending process for clients include: (1) clinging to therapy and the practitioner, (2) reporting recurrence of old problems, (3) introducing new problems, and (4) finding substitutes for the practitioner. Your awareness of these types of reactions and dealing early with the family and/or child in ways to handle these feelings will make ending much easier for both you, the family, and child.

In different ways, these negative reactions can become positive if the family and child understand what they might experience and can utilize those emotions in a positive way. For example, they might reach out for other types of social supports or become a social support for a group of families in their community. Preparing families to not only end with you but to begin their independent family life with strong social supports and resources is part of the practice you are implementing.

Protocol 31: Focusing on the Accomplishments the Family and Child Have Made and Encouraging Their Continued Use of Social Support Resources Is an Important Part of Ending Focusing on the accomplishments of the family and/or child during the ending of the intervention is a way of sustaining their continued efforts and resources for their own problem solving. By maintaining focus on the strengths and accomplishments of the family and child, you are sending a message about their ability to be independent and become a strong family unit. It is equally important to tie these strengths to their ability to sustain their strong family unit through recognizing that the social supports and resources they have formed will continue to enable them to function well. Rzepnicki, Sherman, and Littell (1991) have found that the failure of clients to maintain themselves include, among other issues, the lack of opportunities in the environment for social and leisure activities, the absence of positive support systems, and the lack of reinforcement for functional behaviors. When we examine these causes of maintaining positive outcomes, it is easy to recognize the importance of social supports and resources. These must be established and maintained if the family and child are going to succeed. These supports and resources must include many more informal or natural helping network supports as the more formal supports will end with the intervention. Your ability to help a family and child understand the importance of these informal networks, and to either create these for themselves or be involved on a continuing basis with those that already exist, will help maintain their growth.

FOLLOW-UP PROTOCOLS

CASE 3.7 Application of Follow-Up Protocols

Tiffany Esposito had been a social worker in the child welfare agency in a rural community for almost 5 years. She liked her job and liked working with the families in the community. It was not an easy position, but the administration in the agency was very progressive and open to the workers utilizing the best skills they had learned. One of Tiffany's cases that had ended very successfully was on her list of follow-up calls. The family had been a part of the intensive preservation program in which Tiffany worked. The mother was young, age 17, and lived with the father of their child, a son, age 2. The family had initially been referred by the hospital social worker as an at-risk case. The initial intervention with the family had provided parenting classes, homemaker services during the first three weeks following the baby's birth, and some brief social services provided by a caseworker. The family came under the family preservation program and on Tiffany's case load. During this intervention, Tiffany developed a very positive rapport with the family. The mother, Emily, was anxious to provide a good environment for her child, yet felt overwhelmed at the prospect of becoming a mother. The father, Ron,

also age 17, had a job at a grocery store stocking shelves at night so he could finish his high school classes during the day. They received very little support from their extended family as Emily's family had not wanted her to have the baby or marry Ron and Ron's family had little ability to help them as there were five other siblings in the family. It became apparent to Tiffany early on that the family needed strong supports to continue to function, as well as the parenting and skills classes.

Initially, Tiffany provided this positive reinforcement and support but quickly moved the family to finding others who could provide this. Emily's older sister, Janis, was the first real support the young family developed. With encouragement, Emily had contacted her older sister and the sister had responded in a positive manner to aiding Emily in babysitting and moral support. As Janis began to interact with Emily and the baby, Emily's mother and father began to mellow toward the couple. Soon the extended family was a part of Emily's and Ron's life. Boundary issues and establishing their independence with their extended family as they provided

Continued

CASE 3.7 *Continued*

---

support was a major part of the work Tiffany did with the family. Emily also returned to classes and finished her GED at the same time Ron graduated. The baby, Ron Jr., was developing in a very positive manner as the extended family and friends of Emily and Ron interacted in their lives. The intervention by Tiffany ended on a very positive note and Tiffany had strong hopes for the future.

Approximately two months following the ending of the intervention, Tiffany contacted Emily and Ron to see how things were going. Although they reported some issues with the extended family about boundaries, in general they felt positive about their family and how they were handling these issues.

Protocol 32: Follow Up Allows Families and Children to Review Their Successes and Know That the Child Welfare Social Worker Is Concerned About Their Welfare It is important that you as the child welfare social worker follow up on the families and children with whom you have worked, even though in ending you have given them the message that they have become a healthy independent functioning unit. By involving yourself in the family, you need to ensure that contacting them is not a questioning of their ability to be independent. However, a follow-up call will also give the family an opportunity to review with the social worker their successes and talk about those issues they are dealing with. The social worker in responding in a strengthening mode reminds the families of their strengths and the tools they have learned to resolve their own issues. It is also a time to encourage the family to become as involved as possible in areas in their community that enable them to strengthen themselves as well as aid others. For example, in the case of Emily and Ron, the child welfare social worker encouraged their involvement in the parenting classes given to other young families. Suggesting that Emily and Ron might serve as trainers not only reinforces their success but also aids them to think about a way in which to help others. They become a part of the natural helping network that they depended on so strongly and that will provide support to others who are in similar situations.

Protocol 33: Follow Up Also Permits the Social Worker to Follow Through on the Larger Macro Actions Related to Policy and Program Changes One of the most ethical responses you as a child welfare social worker can have after dealing with a residual case is to integrate the information and findings from your work with the case(s) into the macro arena. The majority of the child and family cases with whom you work will have similar issues, and, as noted, high among these is economic inequality within society. Additional issues that may be similar in many of your cases include chronic mental illnesses, special needs children, substance abuse, racism,

ageism, and sexual orientation. These issues reflect the underlying broader in-
equalities within our society and as long as they continue so will the numbers
of families and children on welfare case loads. You have already started this
practice by being involved in the community and by taking part in policy and
political issues through case review. By bringing these issues to the forefront
as you carry out your macro roles, you can influence and make significant
changes in other lives. Part of bringing these issues forward include not only
your involvement, but the involvement of successful clients in bringing about
change for others. Your practice in a residual case needs to bring a broader focus to your family after they have achieved their own successes. By involving
the families you work with to advocate for resources and needs once they
have become strong, or while they are building strength, builds on the ability
of the community to make a difference and end inequitable situations. Individuals in a society, by coming together as a group with a focus and purpose,
are what change situations. Seeing your families and children as not only individual cases to be aided, but also as strong families to create broader change,
is what will make a difference in child welfare.

SUMMARY

Chapter 3 has provided you with a detailed description of each protocol as it
relates to the phases of practice in the SWPIP model utilized in child welfare.
Examples of these protocols in action were presented to introduce each phase
of the model. The value of these protocols is in understanding their relevance
not only to each phase, but also the importance of their implementation
throughout the model of practice. Protocols have served as guidelines for
many professions and the ones listed in this chapter are reflective of the values
discussed in chapter 2. This list can easily be added to as your experience in
the child welfare field and the profession increases.

QUESTIONS FOR DISCUSSION

1. Preparation protocols reflect your
   establishment as a child welfare
   worker in the community. List
   several you would initially do in
   the community where you are a
   student.

2. Describe how relationship protocols establish the relationship with
   the client in the context of trust.

3. Implementation protocols
   involve the participation of both
   the family and social worker. How
   can the family be part of a macro
   intervention?

4. Describe nondeficit assessment.

5. When does termination begin
   and why?

6. Use a specific example to
   explain follow-up protocol 32.

4

■

Child Welfare Services: Formal, Informal, and Out of the Box

INTRODUCTION

A critical part of understanding the types of interventions you can provide is your ability to utilize both the formal and informal services available in the child welfare field. In working from the strengths continuum, you can provide more services out of the box and focus on preventive and innovative interventions for families and children within a multi-systemic approach. This chapter will examine the different services currently available in child welfare and present several ways to integrate more innovative and preventive methods and programs.

CURRENT SERVICE CONTINUUM

The structure of child welfare training and child welfare agencies has focused on approaching problematic family situations from a residual service program continuum and perspective. The emphasis on more formal service programs rather than a flexible practice model is due in large part to public policies defining the services in programs. In an effort to provide aid to children and families in need, programs and services that serve specialized functions in support of or in lieu of the family have become the mainstay of public child welfare.

These programs and services, as noted in chapter 2, have been commonly categorized as supportive, supplementary, and substitute. They have been explained by many child welfare experts (Kadushin & Martin, 1988) as being on a continuum of least restrictive to most restrictive. The reason for this description has been the shifting in public child welfare to a protective focus (Lindsey, 1994). This focus in turn has been influenced over the years by the perception of what is the best course of action for the child. The question becomes whether to leave the child in his or her home while receiving services or to remove the child to temporary care until it is determined whether or not to reunite the child with the biological family. This debate has had far reaching effects on child welfare services and will be discussed in greater detail later in the text; however, as you read through this chapter, you will come to understand how this debate has had much to do with the concepts of permanency planning, family-based care, family rights, and the best interests of the child.

Despite the effort of the profession to discern the best approach, the fact still remains that most child welfare services have developed from a perspective of what is available and fits within the context of the public child welfare organization. This is not to suggest that the services and programs in the formal child welfare system are not valuable; however, they can be limiting and are often implemented through a process that is not concerned with strength building. To better understand the strengths and limitations of the more formal residual system we will thoroughly examine the continuum upon which these services have been based.

CHILD WELFARE SERVICE CONTINUUM

Highlight 4.1 shows the child welfare service continuum as it encompasses supportive, supplementary, and substitute services.

Supportive services are seen primarily as those services provided for children within their home. They include, but are not limited to: (1) homemaker services; (2) Temporary Assistance for Needy Families (TANF), and other types of financial and in-kind aid; (3) social services provided in child and family disruptive situations; (4) parenting skills classes; and (5) self-help

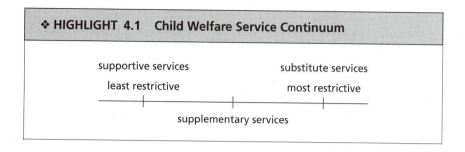

❖ **HIGHLIGHT 4.1   Child Welfare Service Continuum**

supportive services   substitute services

least restrictive   most restrictive

supplementary services

groups. These services are family based in nature and represent the least restrictive environment. This term is based on a belief that the best environment for the development of children is within their own families if the family can be supported to provide a safe and loving home.

Supplementary services are primarily programs provided to the child and family in order to assist the family in the raising of the child. Supplemental services can include, but are not necessarily limited to: (1) respite care; (2) day care; (3) homemaker services; (4) parenting skills classes; (5) TANF and other financial and in-kind aid; (6) supportive agencies, such as Big Brothers/Big Sisters; and (7) social services provided in disruptive family situations. As you can note from this list, many of the supportive and supplementary services overlap.

Substitute services (the most restrictive service) encompass: (1) emergency care, (2) foster care, (3) adoption, (4) community care, and (5) institutional care. These services are at the opposite end of the continuum from least restrictive care. These services involve the child being placed out of the home of the biological family and into the care of others. Generally, the intention of substitute care was for a temporary amount of time in an out of home placement while issues within the child's family were worked through or another environment was established for them. Substitute care was the predominate method of handling most child welfare cases before the 1970s and 1980s.

Ivanoff, Blythe, and Tripodi (1994) note that the differences between these types of services are reflective of the aforementioned continuum of least restrictive to most restrictive care on the part of a child welfare agency. They further note that both supportive and supplementary services are offered to support the family remaining intact and tend to be family focused, although the welfare of the child is not neglected. Substitute forms of care, however, are more protective in nature and have more focus on the child. As a child welfare social worker, you will need to assess the family in deciding which types of services are most appropriate in each case. There will often be times in protective child welfare work where you will be the only one making this decision. This can be one of the most significant decisions a social worker makes. Your understanding of which of these services is the most appropriate to be implemented will determine the child and family's course of intervention. Although risk assessment tools are part of this process, the child welfare social worker still utilizes their own decision-making skills in making these assessments.

The established service fields as related to the child welfare service continuum in public child welfare are familiar to most social work students. These include, but are not limited to: day care, foster care, adoption, child protection, homemaking services, aid to pregnant adolescents, and community and independent living. However, it is important to recognize these service areas do not necessarily describe how the practice process is to be implemented. Alone on a continuum they are limiting because they do not explain how or in what manner the varying resources and supports available from the community can be utilized in making these services not only effective but also preventive. Although most of you will be familiar with these fields of service described in terms of policy and history, the actual practice in these service areas in conjunction with preventive approaches, created though the community, have not been emphasized in social work education. Specialized training programs that do respond to the practice and training needs of the social worker in the child welfare field are often implemented by the agency in the community. The practice process related specifically to child welfare is unique in many ways to other forms of social work practice. It frequently begins by nonvoluntary design, with the social worker being viewed as an interloper into the family. This process is then further hampered by the residual focus of the intervention in working with the family.

Another factor related to the manner in which this service model is operationalized is that the service fields, although conceptualized on a continuum of least restrictive to most restrictive, are not organized on an infrastructure in the child welfare agency based on a continuum of practice. Most child welfare agencies compartmentalize services and divide the social worker's role according to the service provided rather than the case's needs. Often, a family and child who come into the child welfare system may receive a disjointed, unorganized approach to practice. They may become entrapped in a process that worsens because not all of the care available at the least restrictive point of the continuum has been recognized or implemented. This design is very different from the strengthening practice continuum which focuses on the strengths of the family and child and moves toward the least restrictive environment through the goal of achieving an independent, healthy family situation. In this model, each individual case is assessed after investigation and the same social worker continues to work with that family in their service needs.

As we have noted, many of these formal services overlap in their classification. For example, homemaker services can be seen as both supportive and supplementary, while foster care can be interpreted as both a form of substitute care as well as a supplemental service. What distinguishes these services is their primary purpose as it relates to each individual case situation and how they are utilized to achieve an independent family living situation for each child.

INFORMAL SERVICES

Understanding what services are available and how they are provided within the child welfare system is an important part of your training, but services are not just about what the formal public child welfare system can provide, services can also come from informal systems that may include extended families, friends, neighbors, communities, or nonsocial service organizations, such as schools, hospitals, or even work settings. The use of informal services has not been a focus of public child welfare because these services have generally not been easy to integrate and have not been part of the more formal system; however, because the SWPIP model is built around a multisystemic approach to the welfare of children and families, informal services become as important as formal services. SWPIP is based on utilizing services that are inclusive of preventive types of care as well as residual care. Preventive services can be part of formal systems; however, because child welfare policies tend toward residual care there are limitations to the financial resources used for preventive services within public child welfare agencies.

FORMAL AND INFORMAL SERVICES WORKING TOGETHER

To better understand how both formal and informal services can be integrated, this chapter will review both types of services in more detail and suggest ways they may both exist within social service organizations.

SUPPORTIVE SERVICES

Homemaker Services

Homemaker services in child welfare situations are not used as frequently as they have been in the past (Yoshikami, 1983). They are generally offered under the auspice of an agency and are part of an overall treatment plan. Homemaker services are utilized to supplement the needs of a family with children when the primary parent is unable to provide the homemaking needs in the family or when a child has special needs and the parents are not able to provide all the services the child requires. Homemaker services have also been utilized in emergency situations where the primary parent may be unable to care for the child due to hospitalization, imprisonment, or other situations where the parent will be gone for a limited amount of time. The use of homemaker services during this period is for the protection of children not being removed from their home (Brown, Whitehead, & Braswell, 1981). The reasons behind the need for homemaker services may include: (1) a parent who is ill, (2) a deceased parent, (3) respite care for a parent with a special needs child, and (4) parents who do not have parenting skills and need extra help through training.

Homemaker services have been replaced to a large degree by volunteers who work with at-risk parents to teach them how to handle basic household skills and raise children. Volunteers may also work with families who have parents who are critically ill or are experiencing mental health difficulties. Although homemaker services still exist in some agencies, the focus on supporting the whole family and not just focusing on the mothering role, as well as utilizing volunteers for cost efficiency, has led to a lessening in the use of these services. Homemaker services are often seen by those who have protective services involved in their family as the positive side of intervention, while the child welfare social worker plays the negative role (Pecora, Whittaker, Maluccio, Barth, & Plotnick, 1992).

As noted, more informal types of homemaker services utilize volunteer programs that focus on helping at-risk parents. These tend to be preventive in nature as parents are not necessarily identified after an incident, but because of certain factors about them that may make an incident of child neglect or abuse more likely. For example, teenage parents, parents with drug and alcohol addictions, parents with mental illnesses, and so forth. Examples of these types of volunteer programs can be seen throughout the United States. Your goal as a child welfare worker is to ensure that opportunities for such programs are developed in your community. Whether the child welfare agency you are working in has these types of preventive programs will often depend on your willingness to work with individuals and institutions in the community to establish them. The use of these volunteer programs also needs to extend beyond the limits of professional auspices and become networked in a community of neighbors.

TANF and Financial/In-Kind Services

Temporary Assistance for Needy Families (TANF) has replaced Aid for Families with Dependent Children (AFDC), Emergency Assistance, and the Job Opportunities and Basic Skills (JOBS) program through the Personal Responsibility and Work Opportunity Act (PRA). TANF provides temporary financial assistance to needy families. This assistance is allocated to states through block grants/entitlements. The change from AFDC in the PRA was to promote families to not stay on public welfare but to move forward in supporting themselves through work programs and opportunities; however, as discussed in chapter 1, the opportunities have not yet been put in place for individuals and families to procure jobs and a financial income capable of supporting families. The changes to financial aid for the poor through TANF has provided no guarantee that needy families will receive the assistance they need. States have so much discretion in deciding the eligibility of families to receive any services, whether they are financial or in-kind, there is no consistency of what aid can be provided. Additionally, the limitations placed on certain families, like new immigrants, who tend to be among our poorest, has begun to concentrate more poverty in these areas. Services such as food stamps, housing, health care, and education have now all been limited to such a degree that the prospect of greater poverty in this country for more children and families is inevitable.

While there are many informal services that exist to provide aid to children and their families, they cannot be expected to offset the increasing numbers of families who do not have support. The major informal provider of financial aid and in-kind services to families and children has always been from spiritual and religious denominations. Popple and Leighninger (1996) note that according to a 1986 survey by Netting, 14,000 social service agencies were affiliated with national religious groups. Netting notes from this study that this is probably an underestimation, as these numbers represent agencies and not all the programs that may be offered by religious groups through other means. The types of services these organizations offer are as varied as those that are offered in public welfare agencies. In many cases they are residual in nature and seek to supplement the family with food, clothing, and money. In other situations there are preventive programs that focus on financial and in-kind aid. An example of this might be seen in a church or temple sponsoring immigrant families into their community. The importance of being involved in your community through informal networks has been discussed in chapter 3; however, it will be opportunities in working with spiritual or religious organizations that may provide access to the types of preventive services needed.

Social Services

Social services in formal child welfare are generally defined as, but not limited to, counseling services for families with child protection, juvenile delinquency, special needs, and adolescent pregnancy cases. These services are offered differently according to which state is providing them. As with many other federally funded social service programs, states are given discretion in how they utilize the monies from federal block grants. In some states, the emphasis in child welfare may be on investigation and protective services while the counseling services are contracted out to another state or not-for-profit agency. In another state, the work of investigation, protective services, counseling, foster care, and adoption might not only be handled within one agency but might also be handled by one child welfare social worker. In other states, the investigation work is handled by the legal authorities, such as police, and the child welfare social workers only provide social services or counseling to the members of the family. In some situations, for example, specialized programs that work with the spouse of a sexual perpetrator, as well as with the sexually abused child and the perpetrator, have existed for several years in child welfare agencies as part of their ongoing services.

Social services in the form of counseling have always been a primary function of social workers since their work in charity organization societies; however, because public welfare agencies began with the Depression and out of a need for more concrete services, the primary function of social workers in these agencies has been to supply concrete needs. Yet the concrete resources that each state provides is seldom enough to help pull a family up to a point where they might be able to concentrate on more of the emotional issues within the family. In cases where the emotional interactions in the family must be dealt with, many child welfare social workers are limited in the amounts of time they can spend in these areas. Contracted services in these situations have come to play an important role. Family Service of America, Child Guidance Clinics, Community Mental Health Centers, and HMOs, to name a few, often work under contract with public child welfare agencies.

Informal services provided by religious organizations and programs within other types of institutions, such as schools and hospitals, have been utilized to a large degree to provide counseling or pre-counseling services to individuals and families. Parent training, pre-marriage classes, and retirement courses are a few of the types of classes that are often offered free-of-charge in a community through hospitals, schools, and religious organizations.

Natural helping networks within neighborhoods and communities are once again being looked to for supportive services as budgetary cutbacks influence what can be obtained through more formal services. Natural helping networks as discussed in this text are those networks available within a community or neighborhood that have always been there but have not been utilized in a more structured manner. The use of natural helping networks is not new. Historically, natural helping networks in neighborhoods and communities were the only ways in which to obtain extra support during difficult times. A neighbor who watches children while parents are at work, a community of farm families who help to rebuild a home destroyed by fire, a church group that organizes a food and clothing pantry for those in need, and a group of concerned neighbors who organize a crime prevention watch are a few definitions of natural helping networks. As budgetary cuts occur, more development and use of natural helping networks are needed to counter those social forces affecting families and children and to provide social services as well as in-kind services.

Parenting Skills

Training in parenting skills is another form of supportive services in child welfare practice. As mentioned, parenting skills classes and programs are provided through child welfare services, hospitals, schools, and maternity homes to educate young and at-risk parents. These supportive services can also take on a preventive vision and are offered through more informal means. Parenting skills are also often part of a protective service contract in which the worker and the family have determined that extra training is needed. These skills are sometimes delivered within the family's home or through programs in the community. The difficulties with having programs in the community that a welfare family needs to attend include transportation, childcare, and time scheduling. Whenever you are working with a family on a contract, you will find that these issues need to be addressed in order for families and children to be able to take advantage of the services provided.

More informal types of parenting skills classes can be identified in mutual aid or self-help groups. These community groups are often initially organized by a professional, however, the work is done through the individuals or families themselves without the help of a professional person. Examples of this are Parents Anonymous, Families with Mentally Ill Members, Families with Children in Foster Care, Alcoholics Anonymous, and Foster Care Families. The value of these informal groups is the lack of stigma attached to membership and the ability to take part or not.

SUPPLEMENTARY SERVICES

Many of the same services available in supportive services also serve supplementary services. These services will not be discussed again; however, there are a few that provide for special situations and can be viewed as possibilities for broadening their use in other child welfare cases.

Respite Care

Respite care serves as a way to relieve parents of their responsibilities for limited periods when their stress is overwhelming in dealing with children with special needs or chaotic family issues. Very often respite care is provided by volunteers who are arranged through agencies to help a parent or family with the special needs child for several hours a week, over a weekend, or through a vacation. In other situations, children can be dropped off at centers for limited periods while parents have time to be stress-free for a few hours. Use of these services has been through both formal arrangements with child welfare agencies setting up the programs and through informal arrangements with religious organizations, volunteer agencies, and special social service agency programs.

Day Care

Day care is a vital supplementary service that increases in demand constantly. In 1990, a National Academy of Sciences report, by Hayes, Palmer, and Zaslow, estimated that close to 16 million children under the age of 6 and another 18 million between the ages of 6 and 13 had a parent or parents in the labor force. It further projected that by the turn of the century, close to 80 percent of school age children and 70 percent of preschool children will have a parent or parents in the labor force. Of these children, less then 10 percent of these placements are being provided by regulated day care in the form of centers and family day care. This leaves approximately 20 to 30 million children in some form of unregulated day care.

Day care has become such an important component of family life in the United States that families who can afford to will spend enormous amounts of monies to provide the best care. The American family can spend anywhere from $100–$1000 a week for two children in childcare. Obviously, from these figures it is easy to understand why families below the poverty line or receiving welfare funding must have greater access to reasonable childcare if they are to attempt to become a part of the workforce. The increased numbers of single-parent families with children, as well as the number of dual working parents, has made day care a necessary and critical component of family life in the United States.

The Personal Responsibility Act has added to the issues that childcare is now facing. An NASW governmental release (1996) notes that this Act in October of 1996 established that childcare would be funded with matching block grant/entitlement to the states. NASW estimated that this funding will create a shortfall of approximately $1.8 billion less than what is needed. Increased numbers of parents are being required to find childcare space for children under age 6 so that they may take part in following the state's work requirements under this law. Because the number of spaces needed increased and the amount of funding for these spaces has decreased, there is little hope for quality care for the majority of children receiving any type of welfare subsidy. The care of our children has never been highly valued in this society, as is seen in the changing economic programs and the lack of financial support to parent children under the age of 6 at home.

The day care services provided have generally been directed through three main streams: working parents, young child education, and for the remediation of family deficits (Child Welfare League of America, 1988). The last two streams have been the major focus of formal services within the child welfare agencies; however, with the new Personal Responsibility Act, child welfare social workers have become even more involved in attempting to find regulated care for new working parents. Regulated childcare centers and day care homes are authorized through most state offices of child welfare. It once again depends upon the state in which you work as to who will oversee these agencies.

There are several different programs and services provided through formal governmental sanctions. These include: Dependent Care Tax Credit, which allows a credit against the federal income tax; a guarantee for child day care under certain conditions in the Personal Responsibility Act while parents are completing their training and obtaining a job; childcare subsidies to low-income families where the tax credit would not be as helpful; and Head Start, an early childhood education program for disadvantaged preschoolers. Additionally, there are other formal services that might be available within the state child welfare agency, including subsidies for families at risk for childcare services and childcare food programs for needy children (Child Welfare League of America, 1990). How these services will be provided is subject to the discretion of the state in which the client lives.

Working with families and agencies to establish more regulated services will be a major activity of the child welfare social worker in the future. With the Personal Responsibility Act stipulating that families on welfare be trained

and assume jobs or not receive funds, many families will be in need of afford-
able day care services. Because the jobs many of these individuals will take
will provide incomes that make their children inaccessible to quality day care,
it will be critical for quality care supplemented by the government to be
available. Many research studies have suggested that it is the early childhood
environment that can create in children the qualities of hope and motivation
(Baily & Baily, 1986; Garbarino, Gutterman, & Seeley, 1986). Studies such as
these suggest that without quality regulated care for everyone's children, our
society will not be led in a positive direction.

Informal services are often available in the childcare field and include
family care, in-home day care, unregulated family day care, cooperative programs, and neighborhood outreach care services. While these types of informal services exist where there are no formal regulated care spaces available, it
is important to recognize that not all care is good care. While comparison
studies of regulated and unregulated care have shown little difference (Fosberg, 1981) there are those situations that are not safe for children. Helping
groups of families in neighborhoods develop their own resources for day care
is a positive approach, but this must be matched by careful planning in setting
up the arrangements and in how the services will be monitored. In most
states, self-help groups establishing day care will need to meet the standards of
the state in operating a childcare center. The costs and requirements can be
high to bring an informal care center into regulation; however, this is part of
your role as a child welfare social worker to aid in the development of the
resources to accomplish these goals. In some cases, a co-operative center may
be necessary because not all parents need child care from 8:00 in the morning
until 5:00 at night. In fact, the need for late evening and overnight care has
greatly increased as parents take employment that requires their presence away
from the home in the evening and at night. When this happens, not only is
care often needed when the parent is at work, but care can also be needed
when the parent is at home during the day trying to sleep. There are many
instances where some form of childcare is needed 18 hours a day in some
families.

SUBSTITUTE SERVICES

Substitute forms of service incorporate the majority of time and financial
resources spent in public child welfare. Although family-based care has played
a major role in the changing public child welfare system, the residual focus of
care still leads to many out-of-home placements.

Foster Care

Foster care has been a major intervention since the beginning of philanthropic endeavors to help children. Often these early endeavors involved
the farming out of children from the city. Children abandoned or without

parents were often placed on trains from cities and sent to farming areas to become laborers or adopted children of families in rural areas. Foster care took on a more formal aspect with the initiation of public child welfare services. Although out-of-home placement was of a more institutionalized nature during the mid 1900s, the issues surrounding the need for children to have a single home environment began to emerge during the 1960s as the concept of childhood began to be discovered. The emergence of childhood as an important aspect of our society and its future led professionals to emphasize the use of more foster care situations. The growth of foster care as a method of out of home care became very popular and has been used extensively since. Although there have more recently been attempts to lower the number of children placed in foster care, there are still an estimated 500,000 children placed in this type of foster care each year (Terpsta, 1992). These high numbers and the increasing focus on leaving a child in the foster care system led to many of the family-based services now being utilized.

Permanency Planning   Issues surrounding the lack of service given to the child, the biological family, and the foster family once the placement had been made led to an emphasis on permanency planning. Permanency planning began in 1959 as the result of a study by Mass and Engle (Popple & Leighninger, 1996). Their estimates of approximately 170,000 children remaining in foster care throughout their childhood, as well as the fact that very little was being done to work with biological families and children to reunite them, reinforced permanency planning. The seven principles to be used in permanency planning, according to Meezan (1983, p. 13) were:

1. There must be early identification of cases in which family dysfunction can lead to the placement of the child.

2. There must, whenever possible, be work with parents and children in their own homes to prevent entry into the placement system.

3. Removal of a child from home must be based on specific guidelines and should occur only after it has been determined that the parents, with agency supports, cannot mediate the situation with the child in the home.

4. Before or shortly after the removal of the child from a home, there must be an examination of the various placement alternatives, and the child must be placed in the least detrimental alternative available.

5. There must be established for children and their families a time-limited casework plan designed to achieve, as soon as possible, an appropriate permanent placement. Appropriate services must be provided to establish and carry out this plan.

6. There must be established a consistent set of guidelines regarding the termination of parental rights, which can be implemented if children cannot return to their homes.

7. There must be sufficient resources available for the child who cannot return home to ensure that a permanent substitute home can be arranged.

Permanency planning is regarded as an important endeavor today as well as in the 1970s. Permanency planning initially created significant change within the foster care arena by promoting the adoption of children within specific amounts of time and by forcing biological parents, child welfare agencies, and courts to recognize the importance of not allowing a child to float through the foster care system indefinitely. By 1984, the number of children in foster care was reduced to 275,000; however, this number had significantly risen back to 553,000 in 1995 (U.S. Department of Health and Human Services, 1996) due to budgetary cutbacks, homelessness, drug epidemics, and other economic stressors (Downs, Costin, & McFadden, 1996).

Training in Foster Care   In order to accomplish the goal of permanency planning, the training of foster care parents has taken on a new perspective. Although foster care initially focused on the care of the child in a stable home for a fee paid, foster care is now being reexamined as a more structured process by which foster families are carefully selected and trained in their responsibilities. Issues regarding foster care families in the past have strongly brought into question how a strengthening continuum toward independent family care can be achieved. Whether or not the child is able to be returned to their biological family, the foster family plays a major role in decreasing the harm done to a child by their removal and in the child being returned to their biological family or by establishing a nurturing independent family life in another way. Because of these issues, foster families are being selected more carefully in most states and receiving training to enable them to aid the child placed with them. Additionally, training has focused on developing a cooperative relationship between the foster parent and the biological parent. The purpose of this cooperative relationship is to aid the child and biological family in maintaining contact and fostering success.

Removal into Foster Care   Aiding a child and the family through the foster care situation requires many skills on the part of the social worker and the foster care parent from a micro systems perspective. The actual removal of the child can be a traumatic experience for everyone. The decision to remove the child, as discussed in chapter 3, and in greater detail in chapter 6, is a difficult one and needs serious thought before the step is taken. Because family-based care now is intensified within the child welfare system, this is a very difficult process. Being aware of the factors affecting your decision, as well as the utilization of a good risk assessment instrument, will help you through. Research related to this process clearly indicates that child welfare social workers can be affected in this decision by certain variables. Zuravin and De-Panfilis (1997) found that issues of substance abuse and maternal characteristics significantly influenced the placement of a child. These types of variables also play significant roles in the risk assessment scales and the likelihood of potential harm.

Once the difficult decision has been made to place a child in a foster care situation, there will be numerous concerns to deal with as a child welfare social worker. The emotional trauma for both the family and child (whether this is a voluntary or involuntary placement) is a significant part of your work. Parents will feel anger, depression, grief, and a sense of failure when this occurs (Jenkins & Norman, 1972). Parents may also experience a sense of relief from fear for their children and/or the responsibilities of raising the child. Dealing with these feelings immediately and appropriately is critical in aiding the family through this difficult process and understanding the reasons for the placement. Normalizing these feelings and identifying them as strengths as part of their parenting concerns for their child will also help. There will also be feelings and thoughts of hopelessness and fear of never being with their children again. These feelings often add to a parent not following through on a contract with the child welfare agency. They will react in such a demoralized manner when they believe nothing they can do will help them regain the custody of their children. It is your role as a child welfare social worker to counter these reactions. You can accomplish this through focusing immediately with the parent on the plans and the visitation guidelines that can be set up with the child. Focusing on the strengths of the family and their ability to accomplish their goal of raising their own children will aid in the separation process.

Children, like their parents, experience very mixed feelings in placement. The initial reaction to being removed from their home and placed in a strange environment is generally one of fear and confusion. Additionally, anger and guilt become a major part of their internal processes as they often come to believe that they have done something wrong that has led to their placement (Trasler, 1960). Abandonment and relief are also feelings children may experience. The ability of the worker and the foster family to quickly build trust with the child will aid in relieving the emotional trauma that can occur. Explaining clearly to children what is happening and allowing them whatever choices they can make in this process will help them in feeling empowered in this difficult situation (Fahlberg, 1991).

Some factors that have been overlooked in the past regarding foster care placement, but which we now know must be considered, include the placement of sibling groups together, the use of extended family foster care, and the quick resolution of the issues so the child can be returned if the environment is safe. The issues surrounding the placement of siblings in the same foster or adoptive home have become significant, as shown in studies by Staff and Fein (1992) and Grigsby (1994). These studies have consistently shown more aversive effects on children from separating sibling groups.

The use of extended family foster care or kinship care is an important aspect to be considered before children are placed in nonfamily homes. Berrick, Barth, and Needel (1993) found that kinship care of children in contrast to nonfamily foster care was less harmful to the child in dealing with a transition from their home. Mills and Usher (1996) also found that kinship care case management can help maintain family continuity through kinship placement stability. Kinship care is especially important in those family cultures where extended family plays such a significant role.

Reunification   The process involved in the reunification of the child with their biological family following foster care is a careful process that begins at the same moment the child is removed from the family. If the family is aware from the beginning that the first goal is the return of the child to the home through work with the child welfare social worker, foster family, and the child themselves, then families are much more likely to become involved in the intervention and take an active role in bringing this situation about. According to Pecora et al. (1992) there are several guiding principles to understand, including seeing the reentry into the family of origin as being based on a continuum. This entails the family beginning with writing and phoning the child, moving to visitation, and then partial reentry into the home before returning completely to the home. Secondly, from an ecological perspective, there needs to be involvement of all family members in the reunification process and an emphasis on the empowerment of all family members. Third, and finally, there needs to be an interaction and a planning toward this reunification by all those involved in the situation. Carlo (1991) in his study of out-of-home care found that parental involvement led to a greater degree of family reunification. Bicknell-Hentges (1995) identified several stages in the reunification process that deal with emotions, including: (1) defining the family, (2) fear and distrust, (3) idealism, (4) reality, (5) second phase of fear, and (6) return. The social worker, foster parents, family, child, and other systems that are affected by this process need to understand these stages and recognize the normality of them.

Independent Living   Independent living is a term utilized for situations in which adolescents who have been living in foster care now are at an age and a stage where they can live on their own. Independent living has not only been used for foster children, but also for many adolescents who for whatever reason are no longer able to live with their families and are given the opportunity to live on their own. Independent living services began as a reaction to the results of foster children leaving their homes and going out on their own. Foster children tended to be more developmentally delayed than other adolescents their age and many did not have the ability to manage on their own. Wood, Herring, and Hunt (1989) found that adolescents discharged from foster care were more likely to have behavioral and emotional problems and difficulty in assimilating into the culture. Many of these adolescents ended up on public welfare or homeless as they did not have the skills to support themselves (Maluccio, 1990).

In 1989, the Independent Living Initiative was added to the Social Security Act. This Act provided special services to those adolescents who had begun to live on their own. The Act specifically provided aid toward socialization, education, and counseling. Although the Act began to insert funds into the programs for emancipated adolescents, many needs continue to be unaddressed. Needs for housing, medical care, and ongoing support remain limited. Despite the many Independent Living Programs, their financial base has now been called into question by welfare reform. Research has shown very positive outcomes for independent living situations with the use of limits, transitional programming from foster care to independent living, and the use of mentors (Malton, 1998).

Adoption

Adoption is another form of substitute care and is utilized in situations where children have lost their parents, been given up for adoption, or have become wards of the state because parental rights have been severed. There are anywhere from 50,000 to 100,000 children available for adoption in the United States each year through adoptions by public and not-for-profit agencies, private resources, and foreign programs (Cohen, 1992; Pecora et al., 1992; Child Welfare League of America, 1988). Despite these numbers, the numbers of couples wanting to adopt far outweighs the children available for adoption. Healthy nonminority infants are in great demand but very few are available. The majority of children available for adoption consist of older, ethno-racial, and special needs children. These children arrive in the child welfare system and due to their special needs, age, or ethno-racial background do not receive the same opportunities for adoption as white, healthy infants.

Many children who arrive in substitute care in the child welfare system are also not able to be adopted due to the fact that their parents' rights have not terminated. The Adoption Assistance and Child Welfare Act of 1980 was a significant piece of legislation designed to promote the prevention of placement of children out of home and the adoption of those children who had to be removed and whose families did not follow through on plans to regain their custody. The purpose of permanency planning was to provide for children in foster care the opportunity to have a plan for a permanent family placement within a certain period of time. As noted, permanency planning did initially have a positive effect, but because of rising numbers of children in need of care, this policy has not kept up with these increasing numbers. Therefore, there are many older, ethno-racial, and special needs children who are available for adoption but are not adopted because of these issues.

The process involved in the adoption of a child is a sensitive one and one that needs to be handled with care. The role of the social worker in the adoption process is to provide the best family possible to meet the needs of the child. In order to do this, assessments are undertaken to evaluate the adopting family and their strengths as well as the child's needs. Although many children will respond to an adoptive family in a positive way if care is taken in arranging the adoptive process, it is important to recognize that some children will not fare as well despite the strengths of an adoptive family due to their earlier histories of care and trauma. Social workers doing complete assessments of the child need to recognize the importance of sharing this data with the prospective parents. Ensuring that the family has as much information as possible and is prepared for issues that may arise will offset the possibility of an unsuccessful adoption that does enormous harm to both the child and the family.

There are many interventions that can be used in aiding a child to transition into an adoptive family. Among these, the use of life books stands out as an innovative method of aiding the child. Life books help adoptive children understand the process their life has undertaken. These books include information about the biological family, adoptive family, and foster families, if applicable. They frame the child's life through pictures, legal documents, letters, and other personal material.

Because there are many more children who are not first choice for adoption, many social service agencies have modified their view of what make a perfect adoptive couple. For most of the history of adoption, adoptive couples were seen as needing to be young, financially secure, and within what was considered the traditional family situation; however, child welfare social workers have come to realize more and more the importance of a loving family environment rather than a traditional one. Many more single-parent families, older parent families, lower-income families, and parental family units reflective of more nontraditional lifestyles are being considered as adoptive family situations today.

Interracial Adoption   An issue that has created increasing conflict is the issue of interracial adoption. In the child welfare system, there are proportionately more ethno-racial children available for adoption than Caucasian children. In fact, African-American children make up close to 39 percent of all children available for adoptions (National Committee for Adoption, 1986). While the Child Welfare League of America supported the placement of a child without prejudice to race of the parents, it also acknowledged the importance of cultural and racial support for children. The League emphasized, however, that the placement of a child should be for the best interest of the child and not for the adoptive parent. While some studies have indicated that children adopted interracially are well-adjusted (Feigelman & Silverman, 1983; Simon & Alstein, 1987) there is still strong belief by many researchers and practitioners on the importance of same race adoption. The Indian Child Welfare Act of 1978 is one of the most significant pieces of legislation to address the issue of interracial adoption. This Act was enacted to offset the numbers of placements of Native-American children with other ethnic racial families. Findings during the period preceding this Act indicated that Native-American children were being placed at alarming numbers in Caucasian homes and being removed from their Native-American communities. The Act provided a procedure that must be taken for the placement of any Native-American child. The procedure includes preference being given first to the extended family, second to other families in the child's tribe, and third to families of other Native-American tribes.

Those professionals who protest interracial adoption have also begun to promote the placement of children within their own ethno-racial group by reaching more into specific ethno-racial communities to seek out placement for more children. An example of one such program is the Illinois Program entitled One Church/One Child. This program, begun by Father Clements in

1979 in Chicago, promoted the adoption of one African-American child in each African-American church in the Chicago area. This outreach program resulted in the adoption of 37 African-American children within a few years. This program has now been adopted throughout the United States (Veronico, 1983).

Special Needs Adoption Children with special needs who are in need of adoptive services make up large numbers of older children without families. The issues surrounding these factors were addressed in the 1980 Adoption Assistance and Child Welfare Act. This act enabled the offering of subsidies to families to encourage the adoption of special needs children. These subsidies were to serve as a means for a family to obtain resources for the child with special needs. Although there was a fear that families would be adopting as a means of obtaining a subsidy, this has not appeared to be the case (Cole, 1987).

Black Market Adoption Black market adoption is a term used to refer to the "selling" of children for profit. In these situations, a third party is generally involved in finding infants and young children for adoption and setting up deals with their parents (generally a young single mother) in exchange for financial gain. Although many independent adoptions occur, the financial support is generally limited to the medical care and minor support of the parent during the pregnancy.

Adoption Process The process involved in adoption requires the child welfare social worker to be open and sensitive in his or her understanding and assessment of potential parents. Once a referral is made to a child welfare agency of the availability of a child for adoption through legal termination of parental rights, voluntary termination of parental rights, or abandonment, the social worker will examine those families who have filed for adoption and attempt to match the families with those children who are available. The difficulty in this process is that many children who are in need of adoption will be older or of an ethno-racial background for whom there are fewer family opportunities (McKenzie, 1993).

McKenzie (1993) has also observed the system barriers in the adoption process including the reunification phase, preparation for adoption planning (including termination of parental rights), and adoption planning (pp. 67–68). These planning stages before adoption often cause delays in the process. These delays are difficult on both the child and adoptive family. Although they are an important and required piece of the process, special attention to the needs of the parent and child during these periods is critical.

The process of adoption also requires an extensive home study of the potential adoptive parents. These home studies are utilized to provide the social worker with an understanding of the situation in which a child is to be placed and an opportunity to aid the family in preparation for the child. While a home study needs to identify issues that may be harmful to a child (such as a criminal abuse record, a history of child maltreatment, etc.) most of these home visits should focus on aiding the potential parents in their prospective parenting role. In the past, home visits were utilized more as a moral analysis of the parents.

Although an infant may be placed immediately in a home, an older child might visit the home for limited periods before an adoption takes place. This is due in part to the fact that the majority of adoptions that disrupt are with older children (Rosenthal, 1993). Very often, adoptions occur with the foster parents who have been caring for a child. Although controversial studies exist, foster care adoptions are less likely to disrupt according to several child welfare experts (Downs, Costin, & McFadden, 1996; Gil & Amadio, 1983). This fact has led more and more agencies to seek out foster parent situations in which an adoption is a high priority.

Residential, Community, and Group Care

There are many different types of residential and community care that have been designed for children and adolescents. Historically, community-based care in group settings tended more toward the use of institutional care during the early part of the twentieth century. From the beginning of children being placed within work houses and orphanages, institutional settings have generally been perceived as very negative environmental placements for children. The use of orphanages has not been generally supported since the mid 1900s, however, during the late 1980s there was a movement to reinstitute these facilities. The reasoning given focused on the numbers of drug-related births in terms of "crack" babies and the increasing need for out-of-home placement (Pecora et al., 1992). The end result, however, was not a movement back in this direction because of the negative outcome results of institutional care for children.

The definition of residential or substitute group care has varied throughout the history of child welfare. Initially, out-of-home care placements in group settings consisted only of institutionalized settings and were more likely to be for the care of homeless or parentless children. Substitute and residential group care, however, has narrowed in its definition of the type of situation by which a child comes to be placed. Most homeless and parentless children are now placed in foster care homes, adoptive homes, or shelters for limited periods. However, children who have been identified by the state and/or their parents as having behavioral problems often related to delinquency, substance abuse, or mental health are the ones more likely to be placed within an institutional or group home setting today. During 1990, Gershenson estimated that 750,000 children would be admitted to juvenile facilities, 200,000 to child welfare facilities, and 50,000 to psychiatric hospitals or treatment centers.

Outcome studies related to the placement of children in residential group settings appear strongly related to the continued involvement of the family during the placement and the community-based support following the placement (Fanshal, 1982; Curry, 1991; Whittaker, 1988). Residential placement for rehabilitation is best seen as a continuum according to Pecora et al. (1992) as it pertains to positive outcomes. This continuum focuses on the continuation of the child's relationship with the family and community during and following the placement. The following listing describes different types of residential care.

Group Home Settings   In order to more clearly differentiate between institutional and group home settings, an overview will be presented here. Unlike institutional placements, group home settings are more limited in numbers of children in residence, generally have a behavioral and/or cognitive approach to therapeutic change, and rely heavily on peer group influence. The use of smaller group homes or cottage-like settings for adolescents came about as a result of the deinstitutionalization of institutions in the 1960s. This focus made clear how many individuals were often forgotten in state facilities by family and even the agencies that placed them there. The movement in the 1960s back to community or small group care led to the establishment of therapeutic situations where the medical model of treatment was not the primary focus. In particular, children and adolescents were encouraged to work through their peers as well as in family therapy to bring about change in their lives. These smaller programs continue today and focus mainly upon psychiatric issues, substance abuse, and/or delinquency as the major criteria for placement. Generally, placements in even these smaller group settings take place as a last resort when outpatient intervention has not worked.

Therapeutic Settings   Most residential and group home settings incorporate a therapeutic approach to intervention with children and youth. Although most remaining training schools for delinquency claim to be rehabilitative, very few are. The therapeutic approach, as mentioned, includes the use of groups, one-on-one counseling, family work, and work within the community to support the child in school and in socialization.

Shelters   Shelters are generally utilized in emergency situations related to short-term care. These shelters can be for the care of children removed from a neglected or abusive home when a foster care placement has not been established, for runaway youth who do not have homes, and for pregnant adolescents waiting for the birth of their child.

State Facilities for Delinquents   The use of institutional care has become more limited to those situations of delinquency and crime. Although there is generally a hierarchal process involved in the types of facilities in which children are placed outside their family because of delinquency, many states have kept prison-like facilities for youths. The hierarchal process involved for most delinquent adolescents today involves first a family-based approach in which the youth is left in the home and the family and youth are provided intensive services. The next approach is through community-based group homes where youths are given an opportunity to resolve their issues without being removed from their peers, and finally in state run facilities and institutions when no other resources have been able to affect change. The decision to utilize large state-run facilities for children and adolescents is a very serious one. Because their development at this point is still in process, the placement of young people within this type of setting tends to have a more negative effect than positive. A decision of this kind can be made by the court without input from family members or professionals working with the child.

Wraparound Services   Wraparound services is a new term being used in the area of child welfare but an old form of community care. This approach to child welfare service is defined as a means of providing the child and family continuous service through one primary social worker who coordinates and contracts all services through the community. Although this term of service intervention is new, the method and process are not. The theory behind the wraparound process is a newer version of how child welfare practice was done in the 1950s and 1960s. During these periods, the family and child were handled completely by one social worker who saw the case through to its termination. As you recall from chapter 2, several of the protocols established for the SWPIP model of child welfare practice fit well within a continuum context and focus on a strengthening process beginning within the least restrictive types of services obtained, not only through the agency, but also throughout the community.

OUT OF THE BOX
SERVICES AND PROGRAMS

Out of the box services and programs within the context of child welfare involve more than techniques and methods, they are about a philosophy that envisions beyond where these services are and creates what is possible for what is needed. The use of more macro services and programs that are preventive in nature and that create change in policies to bring equity into the lives of families and children are in themselves out of the box simply because this has not been done consistently in child welfare. The ability to not only envision these types of services but to also implement them is a skill in which social workers are trained and yet cannot be done within the parameters of residual child welfare agencies. As in working with clients and asking them to create change through small steps instead of giant leaps, a front line child welfare social worker can begin to create these types of changes through small out of the box steps in their work with families. This does not preclude major changes being made in policies to affect all families, but it does give front line child welfare social workers an opportunity to make a difference where there are very few opportunities for a difference to be made.

We will now begin to look at some of these out of the box services and programs that you as a child welfare worker may be able to create for your families and children. It is important in examining these different ideas to understand that they do not need to fall only under the labels of supportive, supplementary, and substitute services. These services and programs can be referred to as "strengthening," since this term describes the strengthening continuum which is a major base of the SWPIP model.

Strengthening Services and Programs

Strengthening services and programs are based on the premise that families and children are inherently strong in their abilities and desires to keep their family together, therefore the services and programs described here will be ones that are based on that premise. They will be described related to specific needs of families and children rather than to the services that are provided. Some of the examples may seem like major endeavors, however, use your creative thinking to envision smaller steps taken to these goals.

Holistic Family Foster Care   Holistic family foster care is a term used to describe a foster care situation in which the entire family might receive care. An example of this would be a program in which foster families were trained in taking in not only the children but also the single mother who is having difficulty providing for and caring for her child or children. In many cases these types of programs are focused more on young single mothers with little knowledge or support in caring for their child. Foster families would provide space for the mother and children in term of providing the family with a shelter and training skills to get started on their own. The foster parents would provide information on parenting skills, aid the mother in learning to care for her children, and provide support and positive reinforcement to the mother in her learning and caring for her family.

Another form of family-like foster care comes in the form of what is called Foster Care Communities (Canadian Broadcasting Company, 1998). These communities are neighborhoods or streets where the homes have been purchased by the child welfare agency and are co-owned by the foster parents. This community would be linked by a community center that was specifically focused on the needs of these families and children. The unit operates as a neighborhood network and serves as mutual aid support for the families.

School-Based Agencies   For the most part, schools have not seen themselves as providers of social services, however, as Loughborough (1997) points out: "Parenting is no longer the main role of a single social unit; we are all responsible for the safety and growth of all children" (p. 26). Schools are the mainstay of the interaction between society, the family, and the child. Programs such as day care have finally begun to be accepted as part of the public school service to the community. Moving beyond this is a need to recognize the ability of schools to be providers of a variety of programs. The term providers in this sense does not refer to utilizing funding or resources of human capital from the schools, but in terms of allowing the location of different agencies, programs, and services on the grounds in order to facilitate the needs of families and children. This type of shift to a multifaceted community school provides all families and children with the opportunity to not only obtain services they need but to also work together to bring about focus on families in our society.

Wolf (1991) has indicated that the prevention of emotional and physical abuse of children would be best served through the implementation of general awareness of family roles and responsibilities at an early age. He advocates for educating children at both the elementary and secondary level about their needs and the role and responsibility society and the family have to provide for these needs. The social worker's part in this goal might be the presentation of these issues and the organizing of parents within a school district around issues in their community.

Mediation Programs   While most individuals continue to think of mediation as part of business or legal negotiations, more and more social workers are finding that the skills in mediation can help them immensely in the child welfare field. Kassebaum and Chandler (1992) have noted that negotiation skills in child welfare situations appeared to be the best practical solution in child abuse cases. Both social workers and family members found that a negotiation approach to dealing with different factors in protective cases that brought together the concerned parties had a positive effect for outcome in the cases.

A proposed use of mediation in the child welfare system appears especially appropriate to adolescents according to Godman (1998). Considering the issues adolescents face when they attempt to remain independent within the child welfare system, the use of mediation seems to give back some of that sense of independence and at the same time provide a safety net for the adolescent. Additionally, because mediation includes learning skills such as listening, communicating, problem solving, and conflict resolution, these skills can be invaluable in the development of the adolescent (Godman, 1998). There are examples of programs that have implemented this mediation process for adolescents, among which Teen Mediation Program in Vancouver is one of the more well-known for its work in resolving issues of teens and their families (Godman, 1998).

Outdoor Camp Programs   Outdoor camp programs have provided services to children and their families for many years. Camps for children began during the mid-1900s as a means for children and their families to receive recreational activity either together or separately. Since the 1960s, there has been an increasing development of camps that focus more on the therapeutic needs of the child. The philosophy behind most therapeutic camps in the 1990s is on the development of the strengths and self-esteem of the child, as well as requiring the child to learn to work with others in dealing with life on a day-to-day basis. Outward Bound is an example of such a program. Designed to aid adolescents who have behavioral difficulties, this program develops their strengths and skills to create a positive environment where they survive and work with others in a wilderness setting. Most programs such as this are time limited and carefully planned for the individual needs of each child.

Mutual Aid Groups, Self-Help Training, and Advocacy Groups   The utilization of self-help groups has long served as a means for empowering individuals to care for themselves and make their own decisions. Groups such as AA, Parents Anonymous, and Single Parent Organizations have had a significant impact on many families served by the child welfare agencies. Additionally, advocacy groups that focus on the development of consumer leadership have had an enormous impact on changing policies in society as they affect particular groups. Examples of this include the gay and lesbian coalitions, the gray panthers, and welfare rights groups. An example of a group that has benefited children is the Community Action Project for Children (CAPC) (Cooke, 1998). This organization of individuals, who had received child welfare services, came together to produce a community-based coalition of parents and professionals concerned with the well-being of children. Many of the activities of this group have focused on creating a center where young children can receive an early, successful start through socialization activities, education, recreation, a toy lending library, childcare, support groups, parent education groups, and outreach activities. The center developed in partial response to the stigma attached to child welfare agency centers and the need of the community to provide their own neutral facility where families can be seen from a strength's perspective rather than from a problematic perspective (Carruthers, 1998). This group is what is known as a mutual aid support group. They are able to support one another and at the same time take actions to better their families and communities.

Family-Centered Programs   Although we will discuss at some length the family-centered and family preservation programs now being instituted in the United States, it seems important to identify here examples of expansions of these programs on a wider-based scale. Wells and Tracy (1996) suggest that an expansion of services from a family-based perspective in child welfare would provide a type of tertiary prevention for children and families. This expansion would not be limited to short-term care, but would involve a long-term plan that would provide an elaborate assessment of the needs of families and children and then the procedures needed to carry out these services. This would require the involvement of many professionals, such as physicians, psychologists, addiction counselors, and educators, as well as social workers. This type of family-centered care would refocus the policies in our society back onto the needs of families and children and provide a recognition of the preventive types of services that are needed (Nelson, 1995).

Child Advocacy Programs   Advocacy for children's rights in this country has existed since the early 1900s, however, the real emphasis began in the 1960s. Advocacy in child welfare systems is a major part of bridging the gap between preventive and residual intervention. Litzelfelner and Petr (1997) note that the special program in Seattle began in 1977 called Court Appointed Special Advocates (CASAs) has served as a model for development throughout the United States. Between 1990 and 1994, the program grew by

78 percent. This program provides trained volunteers sponsored by the court system to advocate for the best interests of the child in child welfare situations. The training of these volunteer child advocates has not included social workers to any great degree. Litzelfelner and Petr argue for more involvement on the part of social work in providing technical assistance and training for these volunteers in order to help them understand the profession's strength's base form of practice.

Homeless Family Shelters   A type of care that has developed in many cities is related to homeless families and the development of shelters that serve the needs of all family members. These shelters prevent the separation of parents and children and at the same time aid the family in developing resources for themselves. Philips, Dechillo, Kronenfeld, and Middleton-Jeter (1998) found that the use of shelters for homeless families served many positive changes in the short term. An extension of this idea has been the development of homeless family apartments that serve the needs of a family for longer periods, with employment counseling and child welfare services.

SUMMARY

This chapter has given an overview of the present service continuum in the child welfare field in terms of residual services. A brief review of these formal and informal services has been examined in light of the current issues and trends which child welfare social workers must deal. The final section of this chapter presented some examples of out of the box services and programs in which you, as a child welfare social worker, can create innovative ways to bridge prevention with intervention. These services can be developed and applied within the present child welfare system based on a strength's perspective.

QUESTIONS FOR DISCUSSION

1. The Child Welfare Continuum is currently based on services. Discuss the three areas of services and give examples.

2. How can mutual aid groups be utilized in the formal child welfare field?

3. Discuss your view of interracial adoption.

4. Describe why training for foster parents is important for biological parents.

5. Using an adolescent runaway case example, describe how wrap-a-round services might be applied to assist this adolescent.

6. Choose an out of the box service program described in the chapter and discuss the steps needed for this program to be operationalized in your local community.

5

◼

Neglect

Samuel, an African-American, age 5, had been seen in the emergency room approximately six times in the last year. The emergency room social worker, R. J. Hull, had begun a list of those children and their families most frequently seen, in order to better identify cases that may be the result of abuse and/or neglect. Samuel's case did not appear to be one of direct physical abuse. The injuries and illnesses that Samuel had been seen for had been very likely in terms of the circumstances explained by his mother, aunt, and sometimes grandmother who had all brought him in on different occasions. What was beginning to concern R. J. was the num-

ber of situations and the circumstances surrounding the accidents or illnesses. None of the doctors had reported the case for referral to social services. As so often happened in the emergency room, many different doctors had seen Samuel and although there were some questions as to how the accidents and illnesses might have been prevented, none believed that Samuel was purposely being abused. This was more likely a case of "neglect," as well as the "activity level" of Samuel himself.

R. J. recognized that not all children were alike, that some were likely to be more active and take more risks while others were not. Samuel was definitely a risk taker. At the age of two and a half, he had attempted to climb to the top of the monkey bars in the park where he was playing with his cousins and siblings. The result of that adventure was 12 stitches. Two months later, Samuel had almost drowned at the public pool while being supervised by his 10-year-old sister. Samuel had developed bronchitis some 3 months before and had not been seen at the emergency room until he had a high fever and fluid in his lungs and the doctors had to admit him for pneumonia.

The physicians in the emergency room were reluctant to call in social services under conditions like this as it appeared that his family cared about him and that the illnesses and injuries were not purposeful. They believed calling in social services would provide more problems for his family and themselves. The medical personnel did not want to see Samuel taken away from his family and also believed child welfare services would or could do nothing to change the situation. R. J. had urged the doctors and nurses to let him know about cases like this, but in a busy emergency room, no one seemed to have the time. He had held a workshop on the services that could be provided in a case like this; however, until the doctors and nurses could see the results of how social services could be helpful in a neglect case, it was doubtful that they would call upon them.

INTRODUCTION

The issues surrounding the neglect of children in the United States are numerous. A NCCAN (National Center for Child Abuse and Neglect) study in 1993 estimated that close to 1.5 million children in the United States were neglected in some way each year. Neglect as defined in this study did not include one time situations but was a study of chronic pervasive neglect. Neglect of children has been closely tied to the economic situation of the family and the environment in which the child lives.

While child welfare has generally considered neglectful situations of less immediate concern than an incident of physical or sexual abuse, recent research (Ontario CAS Study, 1996) indicates that it is in neglectful family situations where the child is more likely to suffer severe injury while under the supervision of child welfare authorities as compared to the abusive case situation. There are many reasons why findings such as these may have begun to emerge related to neglect. In most states the investigation report in a case of neglect is approximately 21 days, as compared to an abusive situation that generally must be investigated within 24 hours. Additionally, most child welfare agencies have not seen neglect as an issue as serious as physical or sexual abuse and therefore children are more often left in their homes without intensive support services (Minty & Pattinson, 1994). Because neglect is often seen as an act of omission rather than commission, child welfare social workers and their agencies have generally not placed intensive support services in these homes. As the case loads of many child welfare social workers are so high, it is difficult for workers to handle all cases with the same intensity. Neglect cases have usually come second to physical or sexual abuse situations;

however, new findings are raising serious questions about the interventions and efforts that need to be placed on neglectful family situations. For these reasons, the authors have decided to discuss the issues of abuse and neglect separately as they are different situations and ones that must be dealt with in both different and similar manners.

DEFINING NEGLECT

Part of the difficulty in understanding how dangerous a situation might be rests on the complex and diverse definitions of neglect. As we have mentioned, neglect generally is seen as an act of omission rather than commission and, therefore, recognizing whether or not neglect is occurring is often dependent upon a child coming into contact with a child welfare agency through other institutions, such as hospitals or schools. To better understand the definition of neglect, the following terms (modified in part from the Child Welfare League of America, 1991) are offered as a base of description from understanding:

1. Physical Neglect: Physical neglect involves the neglect of the child to the point that there is physical risk to the child. This neglect may be affected by things such as hygiene or housing conditions, lack of health care or the lack of treating illnesses.

2. Environmental Neglect: Environmental neglect includes factors related not only to hygiene within the home situation, but also the safety of the areas in which the child plays or receives care.

3. Emotional Neglect: Emotional neglect may be the lack of love and nurturing given to the child. One type of neglect in infants and young children is sometimes described as "failure to thrive." Failure to thrive involves emotional, physical, and developmental signs of neglect or abuse. Generally, factors related to failure to thrive include a child not being fed appropriately, held, or stimulated by the parent or caretaker. This lack of nurturing is sometimes brought on by factors affecting the parent or caretaker and/or factors that create an interactional problem between the child and parent (English, 1978).

4. Educational Neglect: Educational neglect includes truancy of the child from school, not enrolling a child in an educational program, or failure to provide for a child who has special needs.

5. Neglect of Supervision: Neglect of supervision refers to the parent not supervising the child appropriately. This may include the child being left unsupervised, locked out of the home, or allowed to be gone out of the home for lengths of time without attention being paid to their whereabouts.

6. Neglect of Childcare: Neglect of childcare includes leaving a child underage alone or in the care of someone who is not qualified to care for them or who abandons their child.

These definitions of neglect can often be difficult to discern unless they are blatant acts, such as a child being abandoned or noticed by a professional who has a child under their care. There are also many factors that play into the relativity of a child being seen as neglected. In the United States, there are numerous deteriorating neighborhoods in which many children in poverty situations live. Their families have little hope of moving beyond this situation as what is offered to families is often "residual" in nature.

When we define neglect, it is critical to be aware of the role society plays in allowing these situations to continue. The view of financial efficiency in the United States affects the funding of social services for families through viewing issues from a very narrow and immediate perspective. What might save us $50 in taxes this year can often become more important than the fact that $50 could pay for a program that might save society $2000 in the future. For example, a young child receives a special program for dealing with a learning disability that will enable the child to do better in school and obtain a productive profession. Compare this to cutting the program now and the young child becoming an unemployed adult because of not learning to build upon his or her strengths.

Causes of Neglect

There are many factors that are related to the neglect of children. Among these, as we have noted, poverty is highly correlated with neglect (Lindsey, 1994). This is not simply because of a lack of material goods or resources. Lindsey states if we consider the fact that some 5 million children are living below the poverty line then in fact "de facto" they are being neglected. By whom are they being neglected—society, the family, or both?

Many of the outcomes of poverty in a family can relate to neglected children. This does not mean, however, that all children living below the poverty line are being neglected by their family; however, in many families the lack of resources creates an environment of stress, a sense of demoralization, and often depression and a lack of hope. When these conditions occur, the child's opportunities for a positive living environment decrease. The term often used in talking about poverty is called the "feminization of poverty." By this researchers are referring to the fact that the largest proportion of families living below the poverty line are headed by a single mother. It is also the single mother family that receives the most notice from welfare agencies through these families using their services.

Additional factors of child neglect include psychological factors that may not be related to the family's economic situation. Depression in parents, a lack of intelligence or understanding of what a child needs, a history of a neglected childhood for the parent, as well as substance and drug abuse, are but a few of the factors associated with neglect (Polansky, Chalmers, Buttenwieser, & Williams, 1981).

POLICIES

Policies related to neglect and abuse are very similar. Chapter 6, which deals with physical abuse and emotional maltreatment, will give a detailed accounting of the history of these policies; however, this chapter focuses on those major policies that have the most effect on neglectful family situations.

From an historical perspective, it was during the 1960s and 1970s that the visibility of child abuse and neglect was heightened through its documentation in the United States. The realization by society of the high incidences of abuse and neglect within U.S. families caused all 50 states to create laws requiring the reporting of all suspected cases of abuse and neglect (Zuckerman, 1983). Additional legislation was enacted during the 1970s to further offset the spread of child abuse and neglect. In 1974, the Child Abuse Prevention and Treatment Act served as an impetus for the improvement of reporting and intervention into families where children were at risk. These programs were integrated and coordinated with other family services, such as income maintenance. Although the level of service in the 1970s did not exceed the level received by families in the 1960s (Blitsch, Mears, & Sharna, 1995), the services became more specialized as more attention was placed on families with abused and neglected children. This recognition for specialized services for children was identified in the 1980 Adoption Assistance and Child Welfare Act. This Act provided more attention to the specialized needs of children in at-risk families, as well as requiring specialized children services to be combined with other social services related to families. The Act helped identify neglected, abused, dependent, handicapped, and delinquent children as targets of concern.

The 1980s and 1990s have been turbulent times for child welfare as the tide of economic and political ideology has affected the administration of services. As neglect is strongly tied to the economic conditions of the society, there have been numerous shifts in emphasis and resources given to child welfare related to this issue. The Family Preservation and Support Act of 1993, which focused on intensive family services to children at risk and their families, was an attempt by advocates for child welfare reform to cut back on the number of children being placed out of their home. This Act, which enabled many state and not-for-profit agencies to obtain funds for intensive programs to families and children in family preservation/family support, provided a means of financing child welfare services and programs to families in neglectful and abusive situations.

However, the Personal Responsibility and Work Opportunity Act of 1996 increased the likelihood of neglectful situations for children as more families receive less financial support or are forced to work outside the home without funds or spaces for adequate childcare resources (Vann & Rofuth, 1993). Because many of the federal funds that have served neglected children are now being given in block grant allocations to states, it is feasible to assume that many states will reduce their funds for intensive child welfare programs.

The 1990s also saw the increase of the popularity in the conservative right and the belief that families on welfare do not deserve added financial support for programs and services that can benefit them. This philosophical and political ideology comes on the heels of a period of history in which the United States has seen dramatic fluxes in the economy and equally dramatic changes in public views of social programs for families and children. As the financial ramifications of welfare reform expand across the budgets of the states and communities, the outcomes appear to be a move toward cut backs in social service programs for the poor. Subsequently, the hardest impact will most likely fall on children who are neglected due to economic factors (Meyers, 1995).

PROCESSES AND PROCEDURES

The processes and procedures involved in a child being identified by a child welfare agency as neglected or at risk of being neglected is, as mentioned, generally the result of the family's involvement in another institutional system, such as a school, hospital, or welfare system. Because the family may be receiving services related to a lack of financial resources, it is not surprising that many of the cases related to neglect or child maltreatment may be low-income families. As discussed in chapter 1, the significance of poverty related to a family being involved with the child welfare system is reflective of these issues. A family in poverty is already within the system for financial reasons and is more visible for situations of neglect and abuse.

As you will also discover in chapter 6, the process involved in a case of neglect involves the referral, investigation, finding, and dissolution of the case. Although neglect cases have not received the same intensive evaluation as maltreatment cases, the decision factors involved in a neglect case are very similar to those involved in an abuse situation. The safety of the child, whether neglect or abuse, is the most important factor being assessed.

SERVICES AND PROGRAMS

Services and programs for neglected children and their families are also similar to those for maltreated children. They can include on a formal basis: homemaker services, health care, day care, and protective service actions that are residual in nature. However, preventive types of services and programs can be more easily provided for neglected children than for maltreated children. An example of one such program is Head Start. Head Start is an early childhood educational program provided for low-income families as a way of starting children early onto a path of a positive education. Begun in 1966 as part of the "War on Poverty," the emphasis of the program was to also empower the families of the children involved by having them active in the phases of developing the program. In 1990, Head Start was expanded through the Head Start Expansion and Improvement Act. This Act not only expanded services, but also included an increase in funding for the programs. Studies by researchers such as Zigler and Styfco (1994) have found positive results for children placed in this program. The findings suggest that Head Start can have a positive impact on the abilities of young children in early educational situations.

Residual types of programs, such as homemaker services, parenting skills classes, group support endeavors, and therapeutic services, have aided in helping families in neglect situations to move beyond a current crisis. However, while all of these services can be of benefit to neglectful families, Pecora, Fraser, and Haapala (1991) point out that the majority of services most useful for neglectful families are concrete services such as financial assistance, housing, food, childcare, and employment opportunities.

Many programs and services are being developed in communities based on multidisciplinary teams providing intensive services. This model for organizing child welfare services follows a family-based approach to aiding families in their homes. Professionals in the community form teams to provide services to families in need of an outreach endeavor. Some of these programs are in child welfare agencies and others may develop from institutions in the community such as hospitals, schools, and/or mental health agencies.

Different forms of aid for families and children can be created through mutual aid groups. Cameron (1990) argues that a variety of informal helpers are underused in child welfare where their involvement might be the one thing that is needed. Examples of mutual aid type programs include "lay home visiting" and volunteer family support (Cameron et al., 1997; Pallone & Malkemes, 1984).

CULTURAL DIVERSITY

Because this is the first chapter that contains specific cultural content, it is important to note that the comments made in each of these sections refers to research that has been carried out through many studies related to that particular cultural group. As in any situation, the characteristics and behaviors mentioned are based on a significant proportion of any research sample and exceptions for many reasons occur in all groups. For example, the economic, class, religious, geographic, age, and acculturation factors of any individual or family in a society affects their behavior regardless of their cultural background.

African-American Families

African-Americans make up 13 percent of the current population in the United States with over 80 percent living in urban areas (U.S. Census, 1997). Hill (1972) attributed the strength of black families to strong kinship ties, flexibility in family roles, and the value placed on religion, education, and work. These kinship ties have remained strong and perhaps grown in strength because of the tremendous stress and pressures placed on African-Americans. Kinship bonds for African-American families do not necessarily follow only bloodlines. It is very common for individuals to be included in a family who are neither related by blood nor marriage. Children will often talk of aunts and uncles unrelated to them. These strong bonds and networks serve as supports for families and communities. Children may often be raised by grandparents or other family members while the elderly are also cared for on a collective basis. Informal adoption of an African-American child is not uncommon as parents often recognize that an extended family member can provide more supervision or guidance than they are able to at the time. This placement is not seen in the African-American community as negative as it demonstrates the parents' love of the child and their desire for the child to have his or her needs provided for. As is the case of Samuel, all the adults in the family are a significant part of his care and need to be included in any plan.

The roles of males and females in the African-American family tend to be more flexible than in white families. African-American females have historically worked outside the home as they were the ones who were more likely to receive employment. Because of this reason, there is more of a sense of egalitarianism in the parental roles. Although males are still seen as the heads of the households by women and children, the family's definition of this is not necessarily based on who works (McGoldrick, 1996).

Sensitivity to these issues is important in your intervention with African-American families. It is also as critical to be self-aware of your reactions and role in terms of your own cultural and racial background. Recognizing in Samuel's family the importance of the close relationships and the environmental circumstances that may be affecting his care is part of the awareness critical to the child welfare social worker.

SWPIP PRACTICE MODEL

Phase I: Establish an Immediate Relationship with the Child and Family Based on Warmth, Genuineness, Empathy, Positive Regard, and Empowerment   In child welfare situations involving poverty and neglect, it is often initially difficult for the new social worker to understand or relate to the living conditions of the family. Social work graduates often do not have any personal experience with poverty or living in a family situation where the conditions are dangerous to the children involved. Many social workers, at both the BSW and MSW levels, come from middle-class families whose desire to aid children and families often comes from very little experience in dealing with diverse or poverty situations.

A nondeficit approach to both the initial phase and the assessment phase in a poverty and/or neglect situation is a requisite to the SWPIP model. A nondeficit approach requires the social worker to view the family not only from a strength's perspective but also from a diverse frame of reference. Diverse in the sense that families living in poverty conditions may be different from the social worker in terms of income level. The ability to recognize that income level may affect a family, but not necessarily reduce the family's desire and ability to provide a loving environment for their children is an important recognition for both the family and the social worker. Highlight 5.1 looks at the environmental situation of Samuel's family so that we can assess where the strengths lie.

❖ HIGHLIGHT 5.1   Samuel's Environmental Situation

Sarah Sheridan met with Samuel's mother, Ann Williams, and grandmother, Molly Williams, at their apartment following their initial meeting at the hospital. Ms. Sheridan noted that the apartment consisted of three bedrooms, a living room, and kitchen. The apartment was clean and tidy but sparsely furnished. The mother shared that Samuel and his brothers slept in one bedroom on bunk beds, her daughters and nieces in another, while she and her sister slept in the third bedroom. The grandmother used the couch in the living room as her bed. During the visit, the younger children who did not attend school (Samuel, his brother Mat, age 4, and his cousin Tohesia, age 4, played in the kitchen with pots and pans and helped the grandmother make a cake. Ann, although initially nervous by Ms. Sheridan's visit, began to relax as Ms. Sheridan shared a cup of coffee and talked about the children. Ann shared that she worked from 6:00 p.m. until midnight each day while her sister worked from 8:00 a.m. until 5:00 p.m. In this way, one of them was home with the grandmother all the time and there was always one of them present when the children were

home. In Ann and the grandmother's opinion, the difficulty with Samuel was that he was overexcitable and was always into things. The family had tried several different ways of ensuring he was safe but just when one adult would think the other adult was watching him, he seemed to disappear.

Ann also stated that sometimes the family was just so overwhelmed with eight children in the apartment and three adults they never felt like they had time for anything other than work. Samuel's father and son to Molly had been killed only 6 months earlier in a fishing accident. That was when she had moved in with her mother-in-law and sister-in-law. They had decided that the only way to help her manage was by sharing the responsibilities together. She stated that although the apartment was sometimes crowded, they did generally manage to get along. She stated it was difficult to plan anything with all the people in the house and her time for Samuel was limited because of her work. His 10-year-old sister, Kerry, did watch out for him a lot and was very responsible as the oldest child.

In reading through this example, what do you see as the strengths and resources that are positive in Samuel's family situation? How might they be used to work with the family regarding Samuel's frequent accidents? The major strengths that you have probably already picked up on are the strong family bonds, the responsibility the adults in the family carry, and the caring environment surrounding Samuel. Whether or not Samuel displays "overexcitability" or is "hyperactive" is yet to be determined.

As you gather more information about the family, you will want to ask questions about Samuel's relationship to his father and his behavior before moving into the apartment with other members of his family. What is important in this phase of the intervention is to listen, identify strengths, and reinforce those positive aspects of the family through statements which empower. For example, you may want to express to Ann Williams and her mother-in-law your respect for their strength and the manner in which they are attempting to raise eight children. An example might be: "I am really impressed by the care and concern you have for your children and grandchildren. You have an enormous amount of strength and love to provide the kind of home environment you are trying to do." You will also want to show your empathy and concern over the loss of Ann's husband and son of Molly. Letting them talk about this loss may be one of the appropriate focuses of this initial meeting once you have satisfied yourself that Samuel's safety is not in jeopardy from ongoing treatment or neglect in the family. Although Samuel's safety remains your first concern, your decision in how to intervene in this family would initially be from a family-based intervention. Therefore, the first step is to establish your relationship with his mother and grandmother and let them share those issues that may be impacting on Samuel's neglect. Is Samuel experiencing neglect because his mother and grandmother are still grieving their loss? If so, why are the other children not experiencing similar difficulties? What are the issues surrounding Samuel that cause him to have more accidents than the other children? Highlight 5.2 is an example of how focusing on the loss of the husband and son may lead into issues regarding the care of Samuel, as well as establishing a positive relationship with the family.

❖ HIGHLIGHT 5.2   Relationship Building with Samuel's Family

Social Worker: The loss of your husband must have had a great impact on you and your family, Ms. Williams. (*concerned facial expression*)

Ms. Williams: (*tears appear in her eyes*) Yes, we had our problems like everyone else but we were really devoted to each other. He was especially fond of Samuel. You know that was his father's name and grandfather's name. It was really hard for all of us when he died. I couldn't believe it and I didn't know how we were going to manage. If it hadn't been for my daughter, and my mother and sister-in-law, I don't know what I would have done.

Social Worker: You seem to have a very supportive family in your mother and sister-in-law.

Ms. Williams: I do, but sometimes I'm not sure who is in charge. We all have our good days and bad—and whoever feels the best watches Samuel.

Social Worker: Do you have rules for Samuel and the other children?

Ms. Williams: Yes, but his father was really the only one who could make Samuel mind. Samuel doesn't necessarily follow the rules. And my mother-in-law sometimes lets Samuel do more than the other kids because he reminds her of his Dad.

Social Worker: Might that be confusing for Samuel?

Ms. Williams: I know it is.

Phase II: Assess the Situation Briefly and Thoroughly Based on the Following Systems   *A. Child* Assessment of the child in a neglect case is as critical as assessment of a child in an abuse situation. The safety of the child is the primary focus of this assessment. One particular form of neglect that must be assessed immediately in cases of infant neglect is "failure to thrive." This condition was first diagnosed in the 1970s and is characterized by poor physical growth, retarded motor and social development, and malnutrition (Pecora et al., 1992). Many of the studies into this area emphasize the importance of the interactions between the mother and child (English, 1978). Further, Evans, Reinhart, and Succop (1983) describe the issues of neglect as having an important affect in this condition occurring. Samuel will need to be spoken with individually to give the fullest safety assessment of the situation. This individual interview with the child is part of any safety assessment in an abuse or neglect situation. The manner in which this is handled is very important to establishing your trust with the child.

B. Nuclear Family As you can gather from the last set interactions (Highlight 5.2), you are moving more into the assessment of the family. Assessment of the nuclear family in a poverty and/or neglect situation, as noted, also requires a nondeficit perspective of intervention. A nondeficit perspective requires the social worker to assess the strengths of the family situation from both an economic as well as cultural dimension. Thus, the child welfare social worker needs to recognize that a family, such as the Williams, has many positive attributes. For example, the Williams' extended family system provides additional support for Samuel while his mother is working. The availability of Samuel's grandmother and aunt are resources the child welfare social worker can call upon to help in Samuel's family situation. Another strength is the family's demonstrated concern over Samuel's upbringing and appearing to be taking steps to ensure his safety.

Significant information to gather in this phase is not only about the family dynamics and developmental processes, but also to assess the view of the child within their family. Has the child experienced these types of accidents for a long period or are they of more recent origin? Has the child ever been tested for hyperactivity by a professional? What has Samuel's growth pattern been? Has he been on target with his developmental milestones? Does the family compare Samuel to the other children? How would the family members describe Samuel's relationships to others in the family?

Spend time with the child in their own environment. How does he handle himself with other children and the adults in his family? Is he fidgety or can he play by himself for at least 10 minutes at a time? This is where the knowledge of child and family development becomes critical. Knowing how a child of 5 typically behaves allows you to assess the situation free of any personal biases of child development. It is also critical in this assessment to understand that in different cultures or backgrounds typical behaviors are occurring that may not be what you from your own background might expect. For example, Samuel might demonstrate his ability to read by looking at cereal boxes rather than books because the cost of books may be beyond the family's means.

C. Extended Family Systems The extended family system in a poverty and/or neglect situation can be a significant resource for the child welfare social worker. African-American families, as noted, have extended families who play a significant role in child rearing and care resources. This kind of support may not be as available in all families and the lack of human resources affects the family. Understanding the differences in cultural setting and the importance of the role the extended family plays is critical for the child welfare social worker. Knowing what resources are available to help the family stay out of the child welfare system and to achieve their own goals is accomplished through recognizing the family's strengths.

The reasons for families becoming involved in the child welfare system are often related to the fact that they have no extended family or friend support system and must utilize the services provided by their community. There are at times difficulties that can accompany a strong extended family who take part in a child's life resulting in a blurring of roles as to who is responsible and sets the limits in the child's life. As in Samuel's situation, there are many adults taking charge of the family but with different rules and ideas. The result is that sometimes the whereabouts of Samuel is unknown because each adult believes the other has their eye on him. Additionally, Samuel does not yet understand his boundaries because they change according to who is watching him at that point in time. With so many people coming and going in the apartment for work, church, school, and so on, it is difficult to keep up with a 5-year-old like Samuel, as Samuel's family will attest.

D. Social Systems Many of the families we find in low income situations do not have access to social systems for support. Social systems such as churches, social groups, family organizations, and friends, are often luxuries low-income families cannot afford because of transportation issues as well as time limitations. Depending upon the individual family situation and often the cultural background of the family, some of the families will have "closed systems." Closed systems reflect the fact that the family has very little to do with others outside of their nuclear family. Although a closed family is frequently seen in cases of physical or sexual abuse, families living in poverty and/or whose children are suffering from neglect seldom have social resources on which to call. Because many poor families do not have these outside resources, they are often overburdened and unable to express their frustrations to anyone other than someone within the family.

In the Williams family, the system is closed in the sense that the two female adult mothers have little time to seek outside support or activities because of their work and child raising responsibilities. The grandmother, however, does keep involved with her church and friends from the church. Although the children attend church, their mothers do not. In some ways this family system is open to outside social supports in that the family allows the children in the family to take part in outside activities as much as can be allowed with their time limitations. This is a positive sign in the family that they are willing to be open to their children sharing in outside activities, but are so time limited they are not able to seek this support out as much as might be helpful.

E. Resource Systems The resource systems available to low income and/or neglectful families are often limited to income transfers and protective service resources. Depending upon the state and its policies toward giving resources to families with children, the systems can provide a range from financial supplements to childcare benefits and work/training programs. Which programs are provided and how they are provided can make a significant impact on the intervention utilized with the family. The major resources needed in a child poverty or neglect situation tend to be those that are the most concrete. Increased childcare subsidies, food stamps, low-cost housing situations, school meal programs, Medicaid, and SSI are all programs that may fit with the needs of the Williams family. Additional resources to aid Samuel because of hyperactivity or grief reactions can be provided as complements to concrete services.

F. Programs and Services The programs and services to be assessed include those that have previously been used by the family, as well as those that the family have not had contact with. Although many low-income families find themselves in the public system of aid, they often do not receive the same information. One family may be informed of the WIC Program while another may not. Being very clear on all the resources and services that can be provided for the family and children you are working with is one of the major responsibilities of the child welfare social worker. Being able to inform the family on not only the availability of the services but also the means of accessing them is critical to the family taking advantage of all that is provided. For example, a service that requires the parent to go to a particular building and apply for the services means the social worker needs to be able to aid the parent in obtaining transportation to the office and in how to fill out the forms without taking away their view of themselves as competent. Very often the families we serve through the child welfare system are so demoralized by the circumstances and regulations they must overcome that they give up on the process before they begin. Additionally, the cultural background of each family is going to affect how reluctant they may be to access services. Sensitivity to these differing backgrounds and the issues about accessing services are a requisite to being able to help your client obtain their needs.

As in the case of Samuel, the social worker and mother decided that some of Samuel's need related to his opportunity to be more stimulated outside the home. Neither Ms. Williams nor her sister had ever utilized the Head Start program in the community but now believed that this might be a positive outlet for their younger children still at home. This would additionally enable them and the grandmother to catch up on other responsibilities while the children were in the program in the morning. Samuel's mother decided to go back to computer school 2 hours a day while the children attended Head Start. This was funded through a special training program that Ms. Sheridan had found in the community for single mothers like Ann.

Phase III: Plan and Contract for Intervention with All Systems

A. Case Review and Coordination Meeting A case review and coordination meeting for a family living below the poverty line or in need of services to help prevent neglectful situations due to financial issues, will require the child welfare social worker to spend more time on building those networks with agencies and people who can work together to provide well-developed and non-overlapping services. Although this expenditure of time may seem extensive in the beginning, once these relationships are established they can be utilized again and again for cases in shorter and more planned amounts of time. For example, if you establish relationships with significant individuals in different agencies in the community and organize regular meetings between these workers on a regular basis, you will find that many cases can be handled in one session. By providing these regular meetings, different agencies and workers come to know one another and can more readily know what changes in programs are occurring within their community. Although you as a child welfare social worker are coordinating the meetings to provide the best services for your clients, you will find that this kind of cooperation enables the other members of the social service community to meet together to work on other issues. In part, you are providing a strengthening process to other social workers in the community by giving them access to more information and a means of employing their joint strengths together. Partners in the case plan for Samuel might include the director and teacher of the Head Start program.

B. Involve Family in Planning Process The family's involvement in the process of coordination of services is critical to their own feelings of self-esteem and empowerment. Their ability to help identify their needs and what services could most benefit them is an important step in providing the family with skills to bring about change in their environment. As the members of the Williams family became involved in the planning process for the safety of Samuel, they were able to recognize and identify those areas of their lives where they could create change. A unique technique associated with solution-focused treatment (Berg, 1994) is what is called the "Miracle Question." Highlight 5.3 shows how the "Miracle Question" would be used in the planning process phase with the Williams' family.

❖ HIGHLIGHT 5.3   Application of the Miracle Question

Social Worker: Ann, if you could wake up tomorrow morning and all your problems were solved, what would be different?

Ann Williams: Well, my husband would still be alive. And I guess I want to have a better paying job so I could give my children more of what they need. I would also want to get a bigger place to live. I don't really want to leave my sister and mother-in-law, but we do need more space and a yard for the kids to play in.

Social Worker: If these things happened, what do you think would be the first thing you would notice about yourself?

Ann Williams: Well, I would be less tired and I would not feel so lonely or helpless.

It is at this point that the social worker can focus on the change in the family member and how this change might be brought about through the intervention process. In many ways, the change in the client is a way of focusing on the goals and tasks the family member can accomplish.

Think about how Samuel's mother being less tired and less lonely might help prevent neglect to Samuel and his siblings. Although the protection of the child is a priority, it is critical that you as the child welfare social worker recognize that there are a lot of underlying issues that play on these types of child welfare situations. It is imperative for you to understand these and to help family members recognize their own issues and how changing them can affect the entire family.

C. Contract with Family and Support Services for Their Roles in Implementing Plan The actual contract with the family and the support services that will be given are significant in that this may be one of the few times the family has an opportunity to set some objectives and be empowered to accomplish them. Although an example of a contract will be presented in other chapters in this text, it is important to recognize that when you are working with a family who has little power because of their financial status, the contract should, for all intents and purposes, be theirs to plan. To the family, this contract can represent little more than a guide to gain control of their lives. It can help represent how they are not necessarily the cause of the problem in their situations. It can help identify that there are environmental factors in the society that have affected their ability to move forward. This recognition for a family in poverty conditions is crucial to the members beginning to believe in themselves and their ability to bring about change in their lives. As shown in Highlight 5.4, in the case of Samuel and his family, the contract clearly identifies the strengths of the family members and the uncontrollable areas that affect them.

❖ HIGHLIGHT 5.4 A Verbal Contract with Samuel's Family

Social Worker: I know you want what is best for Samuel and you and I have discussed the areas that need to be addressed to ensure Samuel does not have so many accidents. Let's just go over those areas we have talked about and then see if we can come up with a way to ensure Samuel's safety.

Ann Williams: Well, I know we've talked about Samuel needing more stimulation than he gets being in this house all day. He needs to get out and be around different children and learn how to control some of his impulsive behaviors. I also know that we have talked about how sometimes it's confusing in the house because when all the children are around, sometimes we don't let each other know who has an eye on whom.

Social Worker: That's right. It's hard to keep an eye on eight children and even harder when three adults are trying to do it at the same time without knowing who has said what.

Ann Williams: Well, my mother and sister-in-law have agreed that we will tack on the refrigerator a schedule of who will be watching who when. We will also make sure that Samuel isn't going to all of us to do something and that only one will be responsible for him at that time. I've also let my daughter know that I want her to help me, but that I have to make the major decisions for all of us since I am the Mom. I think she was a little hurt by that, but I told her I couldn't have done all I had after her Dad died without her help. I hope she isn't feeling too left out now.

Phase IV: Implementation of Plan *A. Continued Implementation of Interviewing Skills and Practice Techniques* Critical to any implementation of the SWPIP model is the continued use of interviewing skills and practice techniques that fit with this model of intervention and that provide the client and social worker with an opportunity to change situations and resolve difficulties. In a case of neglect based on conditions initiated by poverty, the skills of empathy and positive regard for the family are crucial to making any difference. By giving the family positive regard, looking for and identifying strengths the family members have, and assisting them in applying these strengths to their situation, the child welfare worker can bring about positive change quickly. For example, in Samuel's family situation, it was very clear to Sarah Sheridan, the social worker from the Department of Children's Services, that the Williams' family members loved and cared about Samuel. There was never any question that Samuel was ignored. On the contrary, the difficulty appeared to be that so many adults were involved in the care and raising of Samuel that no one was quite sure of what the other was doing.

Once Sarah and the family had identified the issues and set goals and tasks to be carried out around those issues, it was Sarah's responsibility to continue to encourage and support the Williams family in the changing of their environment. Although you try to examine all the issues that will affect the family's plan as the goals are being set, it is impossible to know what will happen as the plan progresses. With a relationship built on warmth, empathy, positive regard, genuineness, and empowerment, the social worker can call on different practice techniques to aid family members in reaching their goals.

It may come as a surprise to many social work students that many individuals, especially those who are low income or lack educational training, do not know how to problem solve. One of the most important techniques a child welfare social worker can give to a family living in poverty is the ability to understand and be able to problem solve. The process of problem solving appears simple to most of us, yet we have been constantly trained to critically assess and problem solve. Highlight 5.5 is an example of the steps involved in the problem solving process that can be learned by your families.

❖ HIGHLIGHT 5.5 Steps in Learning the Problem Solving Process

1. Acknowledge the problem.
2. Analyze the problem and identify the needs of participants.
3. Employ brainstorming to generate possible solutions.
4. Evaluate each option, considering the needs of participants.
5. Implement the option selected.
6. Evaluate the outcome of problem-solving efforts (Hepworth & Larsen, 1986, p. 416).

❖ HIGHLIGHT 5.6   Problem Solving Childcare in Samuel's Home

Social Worker: Let's talk about how Samuel last fell down and had to be taken to the hospital.

Mother: Well, I was at work and my sister said she left him playing in the bedroom with his toys. My mother-in-law said that she asked him if he wanted to go to the store with her when he was in the bedroom and he shook his head. So my mother-in-law left for the store and my sister thought he was in the bedroom, but instead he decided to follow grandma to the store so he went out behind her and fell down the stairs.

Social Worker: So, it sounds like some of the issue is who is watching Samuel?

Mother: Yeah, sometimes we get very confused with who has whom.

Social Worker: What kinds of things do you think you could try at your house to make this less confusing?

Mother: I'm not sure what you mean.

Social Worker: Well, the problem seems to be that Samuel has several people watching him and each one thinks the other knows what he is doing. But that isn't the case.

Mother: Well, maybe we could have a schedule with who would watch him when and they could always be responsible.

Social Worker: That's a great idea! Can you think of anything else?

Highlight 5.6 shows how each of these can be modeled and learned in Samuel's family's case.

From this example we can see that the social worker is helping the client identify the steps in problem solving by modeling each step. Thus far, they have acknowledged the problem and are now brainstorming about possible solutions, as in steps 1–3 of problem solving. As the mother comes to practice this with the social worker more often, it will become part of her way of making decisions.

B. Continuing Coordination of Services Continuing coordination of services in any model is critical for the success of the intervention. It is the child welfare worker's responsibility as well as the client's to be alert when any member of the contract plan is not fulfilling their responsibilities or carrying out their assignments. Often, clients tell us of how they attempted to fulfill some part of their contract only to find that other individuals involved in this process did not complete their part so the client could accomplish the goal.

The process of dealing with a situation like this in an appropriate manner can help the client learn how to problem solve their own situations and improve their sense of self-confidence. For example, suppose a childcare worker in an afterschool program has been part of Samuel's contract to ensure that he does not take any impulsive risks on the playground. One afternoon the worker does not come to work and does not inform anyone else at the child-care program to watch for Samuel. Although the childcare program is aware of the responsibilities they have toward Samuel, they do not reassign another worker to give Samuel guidance. When Samuel's aunt arrives at the program to pick up Samuel, she is concerned to learn that the worker did not come to work that day. Although Samuel has not harmed himself, the fact that the childcare center did not follow through is important. Highlight 5.7 shows how supporting the family member to confront this situation rather than to be afraid of the consequences is a step toward independence for the family and safety for Samuel.

This type of empowering through support and the use of role playing can make a significant difference in a person's life (Saleebey, 1992). If you can

---

❖ HIGHLIGHT 5.7 Empowering Samuel's Family

Ann Williams: *(telephone call to Ms. Sheridan)* I wanted to call and tell you about something that really upset me today. My sister-in-law went to pick up Samuel at the afterschool program and found that his special childcare worker, Marie, had not come to work today. The school didn't bother to assign anyone else to watch him.

Social Worker: I am glad you are sharing this with me. You must be feeling very angry about this as well as frightened that they did not carry through on their agreement with you.

Ann Williams: I am angry, but I don't know what to do. I don't want to have to worry about Samuel and whether they are really watching him and helping him make good decisions.

Social Worker: What would make you feel better about their care and their doing what they say?

Ann Williams: Well, I had thought I ought to change where he stays, but that's hard because they go and get him from Head Start and they are the only ones who provide transportation. I was wondering if you could talk to them?

Social Worker: I would be happy to talk with them for you, but I really think you can explain to them better what you want them to do and to follow through on their agreement with you. You are a very strong person and I know you can make them listen.

Ann Williams: I just don't think they will pay any attention to me.

Social Worker: Well, I could go with you but wait in the other room while you talk with the director of the program just to give you support.

Ann Williams: I would really appreciate that.

Social Worker: Then let's agree to when we will meet there, but first let's practice what you are going to say when you meet with the director. Why don't you try it out on me right now? Let me help you with it. It's always good to be prepared.

help your families learn to stand up for themselves in a positive appropriate way and succeed at small steps, this can often have a domino effect that leads into other parts of their lives. For example, as Ann Williams is able to appropriately confront the director of the childcare agency and get the results she wants, she may also be able to confront her mother-in-law or boss in an appropriate manner and bring about change in her environment that is more productive for her.

C. Support and Empowerment of Child and Family Continued support and empowerment of the child and family involves not only verbalizing their strengths and supporting their steps of accomplishment, but also entails the child welfare social worker encouraging the involvement of the family in community and agency issues. The child welfare social worker might identify those individuals in their case loads who express desire to bring about change in services and provide for them access to environmental supports, such as evening childcare, transportation, and group support for the purposes of helping accomplish this broader goal through attendance at a welfare rights meeting or a neighborhood support group.

If the environmental supports a family needs are not available or if they need modification, it is the professional responsibility of the social worker to affect this situation. Yet as professional social workers in child welfare we know we do not have enough time for all the issues that need to be dealt with and that clients need to learn to help themselves through community action and negotiation. Your role then becomes one of helping clients mobilize and affect change in their communities. For example, if there are no after-school day care programs in your community, the clients you serve could be organized and trained in ways to develop needed resources. It is essential that you use the SWPIP in child poverty and neglect situations where families can be supported and empowered. Families in poverty often learn to give up and not initiate change in their lives because they feel helpless. Much of this is due to their focus on simply surviving. By training families in community development and aiding them in accomplishing small initial steps, you can facilitate dramatic change in a community as well as in members of families.

D. Identification of Barriers and Resolution The role of the child welfare social worker is not to just provide support and a plan, the child welfare social worker aids in the plan and contract being accomplished by helping the family members identify the barriers to accomplishing their goals. In poverty situations there can be many barriers and most of these turn out to be representative of concrete services that are needed. Unlike some other child welfare situations, concrete issues such as childcare, transportation, and education are basic barriers to clients accomplishing their goals.

In light of this, many of the obstacles you will need to aid families in overcoming will be related to basic needs. Being able to help them provide transportation to an appointment or provide childcare so the parent can attend a class or meeting is critical to children and families achieving their goals.

Helping family members identify barriers to their goals early and develop solutions to resolving these barriers will increase the likelihood of success in a case situation. Building on networks and neighborhood bonds can bring about these macro changes.

E. Monitoring of Services and Plan The importance of continuously monitoring services and the plan of intervention is essential to success. This monitoring includes not only the tasks set out by the families and yourself, but also includes the regular monitoring of external services and programs by having case meetings with other members of the intervention team to ensure that all aspects are moving smoothly.

If you ask a social worker in an agency about team meetings and coordination, you may hear some moans about the amount of time this kind of meeting can take and the issue of less time for the social worker to work with the child and family; however, as a social worker you will find that it is just this kind of case coordination that also involves family members in the intervention that creates success. There are numerous ways to coordinate these meetings around several families and to make the best use of time; however, these meetings will be of little value if the child and family are not included in the monitoring of the service. It is only they that can shed light on the ways in which the plan is or is not working for them.

Phase V: Evaluate Outcomes and Terminate Services Evaluating services in a neglectful situation can be both fulfilling and disappointing. It can be fulfilling if the family has been successful in accomplishing its goals, not just for the protection of the child but also for the growth and empowerment of the family. It can be disappointing because often we bond with families and ending our relationships can be quite difficult. You will find that there are many children and families who you will want to continue working with despite their need. It is important for you as the child welfare social worker to recognize when your needs are feeding into the process of termination. It is equally important for you to recognize that the family may not want to terminate services and although they are doing well may, as in other social work interventions, relapse or find ways to keep you involved. That is why it is important from the beginning of the intervention to make known that there will be a completion of the services and you will no longer be involved in the family at a particular point. Although the family may first resent your involvement, they may come to see it as a support they would like to keep. Helping them network with others and work as change agents in their community can also alleviate some of the termination issues.

A. Evaluate Outcomes Evaluating outcomes is a critical part of the SWPIP process. You will be able to evaluate outcomes easily if the goals and contract are set up appropriately during the contract phase. The goals will serve as your measures of the outcome in the situation. The use of assessment tools to measure the success of a goal can be a very empowering technique when working with families in poverty who believe they have no successes. The use of a self-scoring sheet related to a goal or the use of a standardized questionnaire, such as the one noted in chapter 3, gives the family a way of visually measuring their success and empowering their continuation of change.

It is equally important at this point in the discussion of the evaluation that we once again mention the ongoing evaluation of the process in each phase of the SWPIP model. This ongoing evaluation should be done with the children and families in order to reinforce their accomplishments and to give them incentive to continue through the intervention plan. Evaluation of obstacles such as policies and laws are also important. It's at this point and even before that clients can be encouraged and empowered in political change strategies.

B. Terminate Services Termination of services in any child welfare situation will involve many of the same aspects of any social work treatment situation. There may be a number of different responses that families and children have to the termination of services. If an intervention has successfully kept the family together and improved the conditions of poverty and neglect, then termination is a much easier process than if the child has to be removed from the family and the family's parental rights are terminated. Your ongoing relationship with the child in this type of situation will be critical to their adaptation to a new environment and family. With the emphasis in adoption becoming a major issue, many children will find that if their families are unable or refuse to make the efforts to provide safe and healthy environments, they will be placed in new family homes. This type of outcome will not be the termination of services for the child, but may only be the beginning of intervention for adaptation into a new family.

Phase VI: Follow Up from a Multisystemic Perspective   *A. Family* The family will need to be contacted following termination to determine if the services they received were satisfactory. Have any changes occurred in the community or agencies with whom they have been working that have hampered their continued growth? Has the family maintained their level of functioning the same as at termination? Has the level of functioning increased or decreased? What are the factors that have affected their level of functioning? How might they be helped to regain their level of functioning if this has not been maintained?

It is hoped that the skills the families learn will enable them to provide healthy, safe environments for their children, yet we all know that without intensive supports or with the loss of particular resources it is easy to fall back in our forward progress. It is the responsibility of the child welfare social worker to follow up on all cases within a certain amount of time (6 weeks) to ensure the continued safety of the child and development of the family.

B. Community The role of the child welfare social worker in working toward policies and programs that will reduce poverty and neglectful situations needs to be a major piece of the worker's advocacy role. The reason this is so important is not just because of concern for the families who currently need the services, but with the reality that the future of society is dependent upon the young. A lack of good development resources for a major portion of our population will lead to nothing but deterioration of our society.

Follow up in the community is not just based on the families we have served, it must be based on preventive types of endeavors to protect other children and families from falling into the system. Therefore, our work with the community needs to be forward thinking and involve all members of the community. Facilitating families to bring about programs and changes that will prevent poverty and fight neglect in all family situations is a key component of the SWPIP model. The skills for doing this include those that focus on organizing, mediating, and empowering families. Aiding families in a neighborhood or school system to recognize the power they have and uniting them in common causes for the betterment of their children and families is part of the multisystemic approach. As you move through the text, the skills for this phase will be discussed in more detail.

C. Programs and Services Following up on which services and programs have been the most helpful enables the child welfare social worker to provide feedback to particular programs and reinforce their continuation of services or their modification of them. It is also important for you to recognize which programs and services are not available to the families in your community and need to be provided. For example, the lack of childcare services in a community can significantly endanger the lives of the children in your community. The step to take in a situation like this is to help organize cooperative and regulated programs of childcare for families to prevent neglectful situations.

D. Policy It is the responsibility of the child welfare social worker to examine the policies and how they are affecting their families and children as they move through their intervention process; however, it is often not until the end of the intervention that the social worker can take the time to examine which policies have been helpful and which have proven to be barriers to the family. This is also the opportunity to evaluate from their case loads, policies that have created difficulties for several families and to take steps to make changes in these policies. Changing policies is not an easy endeavor due to the fact that many policies are decided upon at upper bureaucratic levels that involve the social worker expending time at political and change levels beyond the parameters of their agency position.

Often when we talk of community development and change, social work students miss the importance of the preventive nature of this process. In child welfare social work you may be so busy with your case load that you will not believe you have enough time to attend neighborhood or task force meetings in the community. Yet it will be through your participation and interventions on a macro level that prevention will become a priority.

SUMMARY

This chapter has provided you with an overview of the role of poverty in creating child welfare situations, especially as it affects neglect situations. The role of poverty expands beyond neglect and affects most issues in child welfare practice. The Personal Responsibility & Job Opportunity Act has had a significant impact on how child welfare services are being provided. This chapter focused on an overview of how child welfare social workers can utilize their skills to make changes in families suffering from poverty and empower them to provide the best care possible for their children.

QUESTIONS FOR DISCUSSION

1. Discuss the causes of neglect.

2. Describe how the adults in Samuel's family were inconsistent with the children.

3. Explain how the cultural backgrounds of Samuel and his family create strengths in terms of his care.

4. Describe how poverty can affect a neglectful situation or a view of one.

5. Give your view on whether neglect can be more serious than abuse.

6. Discuss barriers in resolving neglect cases and ways in which barriers may be diminished.

7. Explain how a family like Samuel's might be empowered to create change in their community and in what types of programs.

6

■

Abuse and Emotional Maltreatment

Shelly, a 13 year-old eighth grader from an Hispanic family background, pulled her sock further over her knee. She hoped Ms. Shanks didn't see the bruise on her leg. Her Mom didn't mean to hit her, but when she drank she just got mad and didn't know what she was doing. It was home room period and Ms. Shanks asked Shelly to speak to her in the hallway for a few minutes. Ms. Shanks asked Shelly how she had gotten the bruises on her legs and if they hurt. Shelly didn't want to tell what had really happened so she said she fell down the stairs. Ms. Shanks asked how she had fallen and Shelly replied that she had tripped. When Ms. Shanks put her arm around Shelly's shoulder, Shelly began to cry. If you tell me what really happened maybe I can help, Ms. Shanks said.

INTRODUCTION

The overwhelming statistics regarding child abuse can be discouraging to the social work student as well as the child welfare social worker; yet, remember it will be your work in the child welfare field that will make a difference. It is estimated that every second of every hour of every day there is a child being abused. Estimates of severe physical abuse of children in the United States are approximately 10 percent, while hitting and spanking are estimated at close to 100 percent (Knudsen & Miller, 1991). The Child Welfare League of America estimated that in 1986, 2.2 million children suffered some form of abuse and neglect. In fact, the American Humane Association noted in 1987 that reports of suspected abuse had increased by 233 percent since 1972. Some of the latest statistics regarding child abuse estimates 2,877,461 reported cases of child abuse and neglect in the United States in 1993. Of these reported cases, 1,004,080 were substantiated. This amounts to 35 percent of all reported cases being substantiated by child welfare agencies (Child Welfare League of America, 1995).

DEFINING ABUSE AND
EMOTIONAL MALTREATMENT

Substantiation of abuse is dependent upon the definition given to abuse. As an individual raised in a family context, you have probably formed your own ideas of what defines abuse or emotional maltreatment. These definitions have been a source of contention for many years and the debate continues today. Many individuals do not consider hitting or spanking to be abuse. They would argue that only situations that leave visible signs of abuse need be noted. Others argue that any type of physical or emotional punishment administered by an adult to a child is abuse and should not be allowed. Definitions also differ between cultures and societies. The authors take the approach that abuse in any form (physical, neglectful, or psychological) can affect not only the present well-being of children, but their development and future as functioning adults. As a child welfare social worker, you will be asked to establish in your mind clearly the definitions of abuse and emotional maltreatment. Highlight 6.1 gives definitions of abuse and emotional maltreatment.

❖ HIGHLIGHT 6.1   Defining Abuse and Emotional Maltreatment

1. Physical Abuse: Physical acts by parents or caretakers that caused physical injury to the child or might have created this scenario.
2. Emotional Maltreatment: Acts such as berating, ignoring, abandoning or isolating a child which creates a situation of impairment for the child. (Modified in part from Child Welfare League of America definitions, 1990)

Abuse, neglect, and emotional maltreatment, as mentioned, are difficult to define, yet these definitions clearly impact upon the services, programs, and practices that can be provided for the child. Abuse and emotional maltreatment may also be a one time incident (although rarely), an episodic occurrence, or an ongoing daily event in a child's life. Abuse, neglect, and emotional maltreatment, however, do not occur only in families, but may also be the result of treatment from another child or adult outside the family or in the context of an institution or community setting. For example, a child who has misbehaved in a classroom is struck hard across the face by a teacher causing a nose bleed, a teenager in a group home is abused by several other teenagers after lights are turned out, or a child who is being cared for by a day care agency is left in a crib all day with no diaper changes or feedings.

The society in which the child is raised has a responsibility to protect all of its members. Children, who are among the most vulnerable, are in need of definitions that clearly articulate when the protective branch of the society needs to step in. The state or government has come to serve as a parent (*parens patriae*) to all children in situations of physical abuse, sexual abuse, psychological abuse, and/or neglect. This term implies that the government has a responsibility to take on the role of parent to all children in need of protection. Through this conceptualization, a third party becomes involved in the child and parent relationship in order to protect the child (Kadushin, 1987). You, as a child welfare social worker, will often play this role. How the government becomes involved and, in particular, how you as a social worker intervene, is crucial to the future of any society's welfare.

It is important to once again acknowledge that despite a society's definition of abuse/emotional maltreatment, sensitivity must be given to the role of ethnic, cultural, and religious diversity. Within the society, differing subcultures and perspectives must be recognized in implementing any child welfare policy. The government, for example, can set guidelines for the definitions of abuse and emotional maltreatment and then find that they conflict or contradict a cultural norm or religious belief. For example, the concept "spare the rod, spoil the child" is not one taken lightly by several religious groups. Understanding these differences is not the same as condoning them. We do not as child welfare social workers agree with these definitions but we must take our definition of why they are occurring into account. Many child welfare social workers find themselves battling religious beliefs as well as parental rights when attempting to uphold the policies of the child protection system.

POLICIES

Although programs regarding the protection of children grew rapidly during the first part of the 1990s, the focus on child abuse and emotional maltreatment died down and did not receive the same attention until the latter part of the 1960s. This reinvestment in the protection of children grew out of several different arenas. The 1960s were a time of upheaval in the United States.

Issues surrounding civil rights, women's rights, and the Vietnam War were prevalent in the minds of most Americans. It was during this period of raised social concern that information and research began to emerge noting again the high number of child abuse situations, the differences between states in providing protection and service, and the lack of care in many areas due to nonregulation and inconsistency of legislation.

In 1965 a conference was held by the United States Children's Bureau on the battered child and the "battered child syndrome" (Kempe, Silverman, Steel, Droegen, Mueller, & Silver, 1962). Research and information at this conference gave rise to serious concerns about the current plight of America's children. It was found that voluntary agencies were no longer providing the kind of protection that had been instituted in the early 1900s. Instead, public programs had been expected to take on this responsibility without the resources to do so. There was clearly no consistency in the type of services being provided to children and families across the states or local communities (Kadushin & Martin, 1988). Additionally, as institutions were receiving considerable scrutiny during this period, the situation of abuse and emotional maltreatment toward children who were institutionalized was becoming more visible. A study in 1962 (Kempe, et al.) of institutional settings noted 302 cases of child abuse so serious that the child needed to be hospitalized.

Title XX, a title added to the Social Security Act in 1968, made child protective services mandatory in all 50 states. During the 1960s and 1970s the educational and medical system's concern over child maltreatment caused it to be re-embraced as significant within society. Pediatricians became strong advocates for children and set about creating an environment in which the protection of children became a high priority for the government. The U.S. Senate Subcommittee on Children and Youth began in 1971 and focused on child maltreatment as an issue, led by Senator Walter Mondale. This issue found strong support from the American Medical Association and the National Association of Social Workers. There was no opposition to child maltreatment as a national issue in 1972, as very few politicians could deny the crisis nor wanted to look as if they were unconcerned with American families and children during this period.

The Child Abuse Prevention and Treatment Act of 1974 was a federal act that provided direct financial assistance to states in their provision of programs related to child abuse, neglect, and emotional maltreatment. The Act required that all states receiving federal assistance must have "statutes that protect all children under age 18, cover mental injury, physical injury, and sexual abuse; include neglect reports and abuse reports; guarantee confidentiality of records; guarantee legal immunity for reporters; and provide for a guardian *ad litem* for children whose cases come to court" (Kadushin, 1984, p. 223).

Public Law 96-272, Adoption Assistance and Child Welfare Act of 1980, was designed as a means of assuring the child permanency planning within 18 months of intervention by the child welfare system. Permanency planning became the focus of the child welfare systems as more and more children were being lost within the care arena—"lost" in the sense of being forgotten by the system. Although the emphasis was on providing the child with a functional family, it did not necessarily state that this family had to be a biological one. Some parts of this law redefined child welfare services, as shown in Highlight 6.2.

❖ HIGHLIGHT 6.2   Defining Child Welfare Services

". . . public social services directed toward the accomplishment of the following purposes: (A) protecting and promoting the welfare of all children, including handicapped, homeless, dependent, or neglected children; (B) preventing or remedying, or assisting in the solution of problems which may result in, the neglect, abuse, exploitation, or delinquency of children; (C) preventing the unnecessary separation of children from their families by identifying family problems, assisting families in resolving their problems, and preventing the breakup of families; (D) restoring to their families children who have been removed, by the provision of services to the child and the families; (E) placing children in suitable adoptive homes, in cases where restoration to the biological family is not possible or appropriate; and (F) assuring adequate care of children away from their homes, in cases where the child cannot be returned home or placed for adoption." (Section 425.a)

Samantrai (1992) notes that this new legislation gave definition to welfare services for children and families and did much to expand the role of government in family life. Up until this point, separating the child from the family in order to protect the best interest of the child was the predominant measure taken in the field of child welfare. This law, according to Samantrai, swung the pendulum of the paradigms in child welfare from legalistic separation to the implementation of social services for families.

The Act, however, was never implemented in the ways it was intended, as the Reagan Administration suspended its implementation for several years. In 1983, the Act was reinstituted with less involvement from outside consultants and more power given to the states in terms of how each would respond to the legislation. Samantrai's study of the impact of this law during 1985 and 1986 gives indications that although many states varied in their efforts to provide preventive services and family strengthening approaches, the majority of the states attempted by means of the law to implement services that would be used to support a family in crisis. It is important to note that Samantrai's findings indicate that clearly those states that had a governor and key legislatures in favor of implementing the law more often led to the appointment of a child welfare director who tried to implement family support intervention and permanency planning services. Samantrai states that it was also during this period that the social work profession began to play an important role in political action by working for the election of leaders sensitive to the needs of families and children.

The Family Preservation and Support Act of 1993 is one of the most recent additions of legislation dealing specifically with children in abusive, neglectful, and emotional maltreatment families. This Act attempted to enhance support for family preservation programs through expanded financial and in-kind services to agencies that implement and support these types of programs. The results of this Act are yet to be fully assessed as these programs continue to be implemented and developed. Early results of outcome studies are mixed, yet many government-supported agencies are implementing family-based programs as a positive response to the bleak outcomes of the past. Both public and private child welfare agencies are seeking funding through the Act to start and/or continue forms of family preservation in child abuse, neglect, and emotional maltreatment situations.

Difficulties in these programs have arisen as a result of differing ideologies in terms of the planners and the ability of the creators to empirically account for the outcomes. Generally, most outcomes appear to have clinical significance (in that those working directly with the families and the families themselves attest to the positive support that is available). But as yet, there are very few empirical and/or long-term studies that show not only clinical change but fundamental change in long-term consequences for the families.

Policies surrounding child abuse, as in all other aspects of the field of child welfare, are affected by the ideologies, politics, and economics of the time. Although policies generally are reflective of the acts that have been instituted, there are many instances where states have integrated federal legislation in order to obtain federal funding for programs only to have the programs instituted more reflective of the ideologies, politics, and economics of the state rather than of the federal legislation.

For example, federal legislation, such as the Adoption Assistance and Child Welfare Act of 1980, was reinstituted in 1983 with more power given to the states, but was implemented very differently among states. Although this law was initially designed as a means of providing permanency planning for children, it very quickly began to take a new form of interpretation in the area of family-based care. Family-based care took the Act one step further in that many states did not necessarily stop with the idea of a functional family, but considered the biological family to be the best functional family. Many programs began to reconstruct their emphasis around the biological families. As these special programs were implemented and tested, many differences emerged between traditional child welfare services and these new family-based services. For instance, in some states, the primary investigator of a child abuse report became the provider of services to the family, while in other states the functions of investigator and service provider were separated out as part of the family-based programs. These changes then began to affect traditional programs as many child welfare agencies began to adopt certain aspects of these family-based services, but not all.

It has been inconsistencies such as these among states that makes the implementation of a model of child welfare practice so difficult to employ consistently. The intent of this Act, as noted, was to "ensure that child welfare agencies made reasonable efforts to enable children to remain safely at home before it was found necessary to place them in out-of-home care" (Child Welfare League of America, 1990, p. 6). More often than not, however, agencies have been unable to make reasonable efforts because they lacked the resources (such as trained personnel, financial support, and a well-established practice model) needed to ensure the safety of children in their homes.

The Child Welfare League of America Standards of Services for Abused and Neglected Children (1990) makes clear, however, that there are basic values and assumptions that you as child welfare social workers must believe and use consistently. These standards were designed as an underlying base of practice to provide services to strengthen and preserve families with children. As you read through Highlight 6.3 notice how closely the standards reflect that of the social work profession that were reviewed in the first chapter of this book. Also notice how the standards are closely tied to the protocols of the SWPIP model.

❖ HIGHLIGHT 6.3   Child Welfare League Standards

1. All families need support at some time, although the type and degree of support needed may vary.
2. A child's development and ability to cope with life situations are enhanced by a healthy parent-child relationship and the positive functioning of the entire family unit.
3. Most parents want to be successful and effective parents, and help their children to grow into healthy, fully functioning adults.
4. Families are influenced by their cultural and ethnic values, as well as the societal pressures in their community.
5. Parents are likely to become better parents if they feel good about themselves and thereby can feel competent in other important areas of their lives, such as their jobs, schools, their own families, and social relationships. (Child Welfare League of America, 1990, p. 10)

PROCESSES AND PROCEDURES

Before describing the types of services and programs available in child abuse and emotional maltreatment situations it is important to understand the general system of processes and procedures that have been put in place to handle abusive and/or emotional maltreatment situations. These processes and procedures are clearly reflective of residual approaches to intervention. They are residual in that they occur only after a difficulty has developed. Family-based care programs were designed for both residual and universal situations in that they are for reported cases of child abuse and families that might be at risk.

Systems Procedures

The sequence of events that occur in an alleged child abuse and emotional maltreatment situation are: (1) the report, (2) the investigation, (3) the decision, and (4) the intervention. The report is the initial awareness that the child protection agency has with an incident of alleged child abuse, neglect, and/or emotional maltreatment. Certain professions are required by law to report suspected child maltreatment or face fines and punishment. Among these professions are social workers, teachers, doctors, nurses, therapists, psychologists, and counselors.

In most states there is a 24-hour hotline available for individuals to call to report suspected abuse and emotional maltreatment. The reporting of a case may be anonymous. This has raised issues among the public when the agency is used by a parent in a divorce or custody case to cause problems for the other parent; however, with the increased public awareness of child abuse, reports have increased by 68 percent since 1987 (Child Welfare League of America, 1995). As previously noted, there are over 2,000,000 reports made with some 35 percent of the cases being classified as substantiated (Child Welfare League of America, 1995). Reporting of cases varies by ethnicity. Lindholm (1983) found that proportionally for their cultural numbers, Hispanic children were most often reported, at 32.5 percent, while African-American and Caucasian children were reported at approximately the same rate (26 percent). Rates involved in substantiated cases differ even more. Lindholm (1983) further suggests that African-American children are more likely to be physically abused than Caucasian and Hispanic children and yet less likely to be sexually abused. Differing findings in this reporting pattern may be related to cultural differences in child rearing and/or prejudice toward a particular culture that leads to overreporting in particular regions of the country.

The investigation into a suspected case must be handled within 24 hours of the report by law in most states. This requires the child protective worker or investigator to meet with the family within 24 hours of a report. This is a difficult time limitation in that it may be too long due to the possible danger to the child and may also be too short depending upon the number of cases the worker is assigned. It can also become more difficult due to accessibility to the family (if they are at home, if they answer their door, if they respond to the agency trying to contact them). It is also critical at this point of entrance into the family that social workers recognize diverse family situations. This does not mean that an investigation outcome will be affected because a family has a different set of cultural rules; however, it does mean that if you, as the social worker, are required to do the investigation, you can recognize and respect differences related to culture, ethnicity, and religion. These factors allow the social worker to enter the child abuse, neglect, and emotional maltreatment situation from a different perspective.

Most decisions in child abuse/emotional maltreatment cases are made as (1) substantiated, (2) unsubstantiated, and/or (3) indicated. Thirty-seven states use only substantiated and unsubstantiated, while thirteen others include the decision of indicated. Indicated implies that while the case cannot be substantiated there is a high risk of abuse or neglect present (Child Welfare League of America, 1995). The consequences of this decision weigh heavily with you as the child welfare social worker or investigative officer doing the investigation. This is a decision that requires you to have extensive interviewing skills and an ability to get at facts from the perspective of many different people.

Many factors must be taken into account when making this decision. Foremost in these cases is an understanding of diversity as it relates to child rearing and homemaking practices and your own attitude as a social worker toward these areas. While there are many cultures for whom "sparing the rod spoils the child" is a belief, there are additional circumstances under which the society must protect the safety of the child. Teram (1988) suggests that it is at this point in child protection when child welfare social workers must make a decision about a family situation and a plan for remedying it that the worker begins to experience the most difficulty. Your training and understanding of a model of child welfare practice that considers this diversity is necessary for your success. The decision at this point in the process will also be dependent on a valid and reliable risk assessment instrument in which you have been trained.

Once a decision has been made as to the findings of the report, the child welfare social worker or investigative officer must decide what is the best course of intervention for the child in this case. As noted, there is more of a growing tendency in many states to leave the child within the biological family and provide intensive supports. Sensitivity to the cultural diversity of the family is also important in the decision related to the intervention. Does the family allow others to enter into the family or can an extended family system help provide support during this crisis period? What cultural and/or religious factors play into the situation and may affect or be used to aid the intervention? How might the strengths of these factors be part of the healing process?

In many cases intensive supports and/or extended family systems are not available and the risk to the child in the home becomes too great. It is at this point where the removal of the child from the home begins to involve substitute types of services. Working with a family after having removed a child places the child welfare social worker at much more of a disadvantage in attempting to provide a treatment environment that will empower and reunite the family. It becomes difficult for the family to be empowered and utilize their strengths when they believe all their control and power has been taken away by the loss of their child. However, the safety of the child is primary and without the resources to ensure this, no other decision can be made.

It is also important for you as the worker to be aware that it is at this point where feelings of failure and burnout can greatly increase. Especially as more and more agencies embrace family-based care and the goal of working with the maltreated child within the family, child welfare social workers will begin to see their efforts as failures when children are removed from the home (Teram, 1988). Your ability to understand that not all situations are conducive to family-based care, but that the appropriate model of intervention may be to bring the child into a loving outside family context, will guide you through these dilemmas.

SERVICES AND PROGRAMS

In child abuse, neglect, and emotional maltreatment cases, all states are required to serve an investigative function and then provide services for the child and family. The services in these cases, as noted, have primarily been defined as supportive, supplementary, and/or substitute forms of care (Magazino, 1983). The history of which services are most often used in child maltreatment situations has changed throughout the years. As mentioned earlier, there was a period in child protection when substitute care was the core response. Very little thought was given to changing the environment in which the child lived. Instead, there was heavy use of foster care, orphanages, and institutional placement. Programs were developed around the placement of children in these substitute situations.

Initially, as more and more concern grew over the numbers of children in foster care and permanency planning (the planning of long-term care for a child in the foster care system) became so important, special training for foster parents was developed. Early emphasis in child maltreatment situations still focused on removing children from their homes and reconstituting families through work with the foster family and/or an adoptive family. Although biological families were part of the consideration in the permanency planning for the child, they generally did not receive enough services to change their environmental situations during the period in which their children were removed. Normally, they were given an opportunity to complete a contract of behavioral change over a period of time in which their children might be returned to them. Often families gave up hope of getting their children back because the lack of resources within the child welfare system were not enough to empower them to complete their contracts. Even when children were placed back in their biological homes after being removed, very few families had received enough counseling or supports to help in decreasing the possibility of an abusive situation.

As noted in the policy section, this approach has changed during the last two decades. Now the predominant belief is that the biological family is the least restrictive environment and the best place for a child to develop if safety and nurturing can be assured. This belief is reflective of changes that have occurred not only within our society, but also within the service delivery systems. In the 1970s, a growing understanding about the healthy development of children, as well as a recognition that longer term foster and institutional care of children could be just as damaging as the biological home, led to these changes. At the turn of the century there is a new emphasis to secure safe, healthy homes for all children. Governmental pressure is currently pushing toward the reunification of a family within 12 months or the adoption of the child into a new family.

Although the original concept of permanency planning did not focus on the biological family, it eventually supported the concept of focusing on the rehabilitation of the biological family as a priority in intervention (Maluccio, Fein, & Olmstead, 1986). The recognition that the biological families were not affected solely by their individual personalities, but also by the ecological environment and factors surrounding them, have caused most child welfare programs to begin reaching back out to the biological family in a more focused, systemic manner. It was out of this that the reemphasis on strengthening the biological family reemerged and the interventions in family-based care took a priority in the child welfare field.

Intensive Family-Based Care Programs

As noted, intensive family-based care programs and services have become more of a mainstay within this society. The beginning of intensive family-based care appeared simultaneously throughout the country. The focus of these types of programs was based primarily on the policies emerging from the Adoption Assistance and Child Welfare Act of 1980; however, the Family Preservation and Support Provisions of the Omnibus Budget Reconciliation Act of 1993 (pp. 103–166) provided significant financial incentives in child welfare funding to lead many states into the area of intensive family-based care.

Interestingly, these services have not been used just in abuse, neglect, and emotional maltreatment cases, but have been implemented in other areas of welfare, including poverty, substance abuse, the elderly, and disabilities. Features of these programs include: (1) intensive work over a shorter period of time, (2) coordinated services and full involvement of the family in the process, and (3) a multisystemic approach to intervention.

In intensive family-based care, the model of practice is focused on preserving the family for the sake of the child through the provision of intensive services that deal with the ecological and environmental factors affecting the family, as well as with the issues of individual family members. The early models of intensive family-based care generally included a caseload of two to four families, a primary worker who nurtured and maintained a supportive relationship with the family, case-managed intervention with a wide range of services involving a number of different workers, and the availability of assistance for the family on a 24-hour basis. Treatment and intervention were based in the home with the family at the center of the intervention process. In this brief intervention model (2 to 4 months) the family was empowered to make changes and supported in their decision making (Pecora, Fraser, Haapala, & Bartholomew, 1987).

A large majority of these programs were supported by additional funds through Title IV-A and Title IV-E of the Social Security Act. Significant in these programs were the strength's perspective and the respect of cultural diversity from a multisystemic perspective. Currently, many forms of these programs are funded through the new Family Preservation and Support Act of 1993.

The difficulty, as noted, is that the research consensus about what is most effective in intensive family-based care programs has yet to be developed. Planners and researchers are working on validating much of their own work, but have not necessarily joined together with others to make a consistent difference in the child welfare field. Steps toward this goal have begun with national workshops on intensive family-based care, as well as a new journal (*Journal of Family Preservation,* edited by Alvia Sallee) dealing specifically with articles utilizing this approach. Taken further, the real value of the family preservation movement will be in its development as a prevention rather than a residual program for many different areas of social problems. Studies have noted the successful diversion rates of open child protection case loads when intensive family-based care programs are initiated in preventive forms (Hooper-Briar, 1996).

Yet prevention has not been established as a priority in many of the programs. Many states do little to collaborate or replicate other programs in these areas because of resource allocations. Each state is once again directed from its political, economic, and societal ideologies on just how intensive family-based care should be done, and these directions are often reflective of the lack of funding for child and family programs.

Despite these differences, these programs have helped define the most recent standards set by the Child Welfare League of America (CWLA). In the CWLA standards of child welfare practice, included are descriptions and goals of both FRSE (family resource, support, and education) and FC (family-centered services). These two areas have much in common in that one (FRSE) represents a service that is community based and assists adults in their roles as parents, and the other (FC) represents a belief that families staying together is a critical priority for the betterment of society. It also states that services provided toward the goal of this belief will be for the betterment of the child, family, and community. Both these service areas are used extensively in providing intensive family-based services to families dealing with child abuse, neglect, and emotional maltreatment. CWLA has gone further than many of its counterparts in correlating and reporting the best possible standards and protocols to be set in child maltreatment situations.

Although the child welfare practice model presented in this text is based on many facets of intensive family-based care, the authors are not without concerns regarding these programs as they intervene into situations of child abuse, neglect, and emotional maltreatment. Arguments abound as to whether keeping abused or neglected children in a home under an intense intervention situation is a risk worth taking. A few researchers argue that the risks to the child are too great. They speak of case examples from these programs where children have suffered further abuse or died. Highlight 6.4 gives an example of family preservation failure.

❖ **HIGHLIGHT 6.4 Family Preservation Failure**

Sarah, age 4, was found to be abused by her stepfather after being seen by a doctor who found burns on her hands and arms caused by cigarettes. In an effort to keep Sarah with her mother and brother, an intensive family-preservation program was put into place to create change in the environment. The stepfather, who was arrested following the report by the doctor, showed no indication that he wanted to be a part of the family and moved into another home. Intensive work began involving the mother and children receiving support and resources to prevent an abuse situation from occurring again. However, after three weeks in the program, the social worker arrived on a Monday to find that the stepfather had moved back in with the mother's permission and Sarah had several bruises on her back and legs. Without the aid of the mother to keep the stepfather away from the home or for the stepfather to want to change and get help for his actions, there was no recourse but to remove the child.

The opponents of intensive family-based care would state that the second abusive situation could have been avoided if Sarah had been removed immediately. Richard Gelles, director of the University of Rhode Island Family Violence Research Program, believes that there are some families who will be unable to change their behavior. Gelles' book, *The Book of David: How Preserving Families Can Cost Children's Lives* (1996), illustrates his growing concern over residual types of family preservation programs that risk the child over the family.

The responses to these criticisms reflect that most families selected for intensive family-based care programs have been screened for risks to children and that in the research done in these programs, some 5 percent to 50 percent of cases do end in the child eventually being placed in out-of-home care (Nelson, 1995). Once again, you as the child welfare social worker will face the difficulty in maintaining a balance between protection of the child and keeping the family together; however, the right decision is to always err on the side of protection of the child in dangerous family situations.

The positive clinical processes and perceptions of these family-based programs appear to support the continued implementation of the Child Welfare Act of 1980 and the Family Preservation and Support Act of 1993 through more preventive types of programs. Studies that thoroughly evaluate family-based programs might explain many of the difficulties that have recently been seen. Specific training models that highlight the important facets of these programs of practice, whether dealing with a child abuse situation or a delinquency situation, would go far in the prevention and provision of child welfare services. A model that can be implemented in child welfare situations that will protect the child while still maintaining the overall integrity of providing a functional family unit (either biological or surrogate) is key to the well-being of children and our society.

Another argument that has emerged against family-based care programs is the high cost compared to what has been considered the normal cost in child protection. Yet when the cost of foster care is taken into account, as well as the effects the placement of a child may have on the child, the differences in costs can dramatically shift. The cost of a child placed in foster care for approximately 6 months may seem nominal as compared to a family being in family-based care for 2 to 6 months with intensive interventions and the involvement of numerous resources; however, when the long-term results and costs are calculated in terms of the family treatment and the overall outcome for the child, the picture is quite different. Children who have been maintained in their biological family environment with intensive change taking place eventually leading to a long-term stable home can be less costly than children placed in and out of foster care and not provided with a stable environment to help them develop as a healthy, functioning adult.

Tied to intensive family-based care are the interviewing and practice techniques related to brief treatment, family therapy, and solution-focused therapy. These three therapeutic interventions are used frequently with family-based care in that they provide an intensive approach to positive change. While the techniques in these approaches are appropriate for all families, it is important to recognize that not all child welfare situations (for example, sexual abuse) can be handled so quickly.

Just as changes are occurring in the child welfare field that might produce better programs and services for our children, political ideologies have begun to shift once again. One well-known term in the 1990s, as noted in chapter 1, is what is known as welfare reform. Although new welfare reform legislation has just been integrated into the public welfare system, social workers in the field of child welfare with abused, neglected, and emotionally maltreated children are just beginning to experience the consequences of this reform. Even though child protective services in the field have been spared, there is a significant impact on family-based care services as changes have occurred to financial aid programs such as AFDC, childcare services, health, and education. States may consider supporting programs that cut expenses at the front end rather than at the back end (for example, cutting funding in intensive family-based care programs to save monies and then using these funds to supplement the use of foster care).

As social welfare reform continues to be implemented, it is most likely that social workers will increase their case loads, thus not having the time to spend in intensive intervention in a family. The amount of time spent with a family will become limited due to the number of cases. One case worker overseeing all of these cases without the benefit of supplemental support and services will most likely be forced to turn to foster care unless a different means of empowering and changing families and children can be found. Use of intensive family-based care can continue, however, if we as a profession can validate its success and support politically those individuals who can see from a long range and broader view. As part of your use of protocols in the SWPIP model, you as a child welfare social worker, will need to empower the families and children in your communities to advocate for support and change. Highlight 6.5 is an example of a case situation in which you may find yourself as a result of heavy case loads.

❖ HIGHLIGHT 6.5   Making a Critical Decision

Amy Lyons has just arrived at the Child Welfare Agency as a child welfare social worker. She has been in the position for approximately two weeks. She assumed the 62-family case load of her predecessor and has opened three new cases herself. Although many of the cases involve neglect, several have been "founded for abuse." Amy must make regular visits to all the homes on her case load in order to help the families fulfill the contracts both she and her predecessor developed regarding issues around the abuse, neglect, and emotional maltreatment. She has a BSW degree and has had training in her internship in child welfare, but this did not prepare her for the heavy case load and the concerns she often carries with her regarding particular family situations.

Most recently, Amy was called to the school regarding a teacher's report of suspected child abuse. The young girl, Shelly, had received several bruises on her legs and had shared with Amy, after initial denials, that her Mom had accidentally hit her with a broom. Amy recognized that she needed to meet with Shelly's mother that day in order to make a decision regarding the risks to Shelly and the steps that needed to be taken. Yet she also knew that with 62 open cases many of the families also needed to see her this day. She made the decision to see this new case immediately. In only two weeks she was performing what she called "triage," which involved seeing the cases most at risk first.

Prevention Programs

One of the most growing concerns in child welfare today is the establishment of prevention programs. As mentioned, due to economic, political, and societal ideologies, preventive types of programs are generally the last service on which funds are spent rather than the first. Reasoning behind this philosophy clearly relates to the limited amount of funds often made available in child welfare situations and the need to reach out to those families already in critical need. The focus of residual care has always taken precedence over prevention because of the danger involved in already abusive family situations. You will often find yourself running from family to family in a crisis mode until a model of child welfare practice in your agency truly begins to incorporate preventive techniques. In the SWPIP model, these techniques involve the strengthening of the families and children with whom you work to bring about change in their environment through collective means.

Etiology of Abuse and Emotional Maltreatment

Understanding why families abuse is perhaps one of the most difficult processes for social workers. There is no clear cut research that identifies reasons for violence against children; however, it is also difficult to present a practice model unless the social worker understands the underlying causes of abuse. Gil (1971) has stated that the profile of an abusive family is more likely to include one or more of the following: (1) a history of childhood abuse, (2) an environment of poverty, (3) no social support, (4) alcoholism or drug use, and (5) a child with a special need. It is not surprising that these characteristics imply more about the environmental situation than about the abuser or victim. Therefore, it is necessary that the model of child welfare practice you employ have methods for dealing with these issues.

As noted, there are situations in which the characteristics of the child may increase the likelihood of abuse (Gil, 1971). This study found that children with disabilities (physical, mental, learning, etc.) tend to be the children who are more likely to be abused. Statistics suggest that over 25 percent of children reportedly abused suffer some type of disability (Child Welfare League of America, 1995). Family situations in which this is part of the issue can be more easily identified before abuse occurs and families can be helped from a preventive perspective. There are also other issues in a family's life that can indicate a potential at-risk situation, including poverty, mental illness, age of the parent, substance abuse, history of family violence, and cultural and/or religious beliefs about the use of physical discipline in rearing children. Whether or not the family you are dealing with has one or more of these characteristics, it is important to understand that there will be enormous differences between how these families will respond to intervention from outside sources. Equally important is how you as a child welfare social worker may be able to respond to these family situations from a preventive focus for not only a particular family but for many families in a community. Although protecting children in child welfare still takes precedence over any other issues, recent movement by social workers has been to reach out to all families, stabilize their environment, and strengthen them to create change for themselves and others through networking and empowerment.

CULTURAL DIVERSITY

It is important in working with families from an Hispanic cultural background to recognize that different geographic locations of families affect their culture and behavior. According to Delgado (1992), Hispanic families in the United States consist of four basic groups: Mexican-American, Puerto Rican, Cuban, and other Spanish-speaking people. Most Hispanic families are structured on a hierarchical basis with loyalty being the significant value of the family. Mothers are respected and children are loved, but fathers are the ones who generally receive the highest respect (Falicov, 1983). There is a high degree of cohesion in the family and, as in African-American families, extended families are a major part of the life of the nuclear family. Despite these factors and the Catholic background, Hispanic families have a large rate of divorce (14 percent) and 18.2 percent of Hispanic children live in single-parent families (Delgado, 1992). In Hispanic families, the extended family takes on a special role. Research has shown that while Caucasian families are more likely to turn for help to a friend or neighbors, Hispanic families turn to the extended family first for support (Keefe, Padilla, & Carlos, 1978). For the child welfare social worker, these factors affect how you approach the Hispanic family and the courtesy you pay to the hierarchical system. It is also important to understand that with this strong extended family cohesion, your choices of support may best be gathered from more informal sources, such as the family, if this is at all possible. Sadly, the records indicate that these informal supports are not considered first and Hispanic families have experienced an overuse of substitute care through child welfare services (Delgado, 1992).

Language can also be a major barrier and it is appropriate for the child welfare social worker to be conversant in the Spanish language as this is denoted as a sign of respect for the culture. As noted, your behavior with an Hispanic family should be more formal and respectful. It is not until you become more acquainted with the family that informal interactions can occur. Initial focus should be on the individuals in the family rather than on procedures and processes in the agency if this is at all possible. Once a relationship has been established, the contract agreement may need to be developed from a more informal process, as the Hispanic focus is generally on people. The process of working through issues should always be culturally sensitive to the different backgrounds and cultural beliefs of the family with whom you are dealing. As with other diverse cultures, acculturation is of key importance in the treatment relationship. How acculturated a Hispanic family is adds to the diversity of Hispanic families. Acculturation plays a major role in determining just where the family is in relation to societal issues and parenting roles. One of your first responsibilities in all families will be to assess their acculturation into the society as this can often indicate what interventions are most appropriate.

THE ALCOHOLIC FAMILY

In Shelly's family, the visible difference appears to be in the economic level of the family. As a single parent, Shelly's mother's opportunities are likely limited by her educational background and economic status. While we do not know the specific cultural background of the family, it is very possible that the family's cultural traditions affect the parenting within the family.

Of particular significance in this case is the role the alcoholism may play now or in the future for the children. The role of economic factors affecting the use of alcohol by children is noted by Lindsey (1994). He noted that opportunities are limited for many children in oppressed groups, and as a result of this situation there is an "increased need for residual services for such problems as drug and alcohol abuse, delinquency, and teenage pregnancy" (pp. 193–194). Although studies differ as to the percentage of substance abuse in children, Windle, Windle, and Scheidt (1995) note in their study of 802 alcohol treatment patients, the significantly high levels of childhood physical and sexual abuse.

Dore, Doris, and Wright (1995) in examining their research statistics related to substance abuse and child welfare note the crucial need for child welfare workers to be prepared to utilize skills and knowledge to intervene appropriately in substance abuse cases. Mitchell and Savage (1991) note that there are as many as 675,000 children seriously mistreated by a substance abusive adult. Your intervention into the family will be affected by the circumstances surrounding the income level, the substance abuse, and the parental history in the family.

The best training for social workers includes knowledge about programs such as AA (Alcoholics Anonymous), Hazelton (Intensive Interventions) and even programs that do not focus on abstinence and treatment but on harm reduction. Harm reduction programs are very controversial in that individuals are encouraged to cut back drinking rather than stop. While the authors believe that AA and other abstinence/treatment programs are best, in child welfare the consideration of harm reduction initially with intensive supervision may be the best alternative until the parent begins an abstinence program.

SWPIP PRACTICE MODEL

The SWPIP model in child maltreatment is based in part on family-based care and the protocols necessary to intervene in a difficult family situation with intensity and immediate impact. Implicit in utilizing this approach within a child maltreatment situation is the protocol of the use of one worker to focus on the family in a supportive and protective manner. It has been clearly established through research that the most successful approach (especially when dealing with a child abuse or emotional maltreatment case) is that the social worker who investigates the case not be the worker who follows through on the intervention into the family.

Many state agencies have begun to utilize this approach to intervention in child maltreatment cases by providing a separate intake or investigative worker to assess the abusive situation. The child welfare social worker who then intervenes with the family to monitor protection of the child and provide services to the family serves as a support for the family. You, as the child welfare social worker, will have fewer obstacles to face from the family if you have not been the social worker who made the decisions regarding whether or not maltreatment occurred and how disposition of the case is to be handled.

Utilizing the SWPIP model within a child maltreatment situation requires very well-developed skills. The protocols of the model are difficult to introduce into a physical abuse, neglect, or emotional maltreatment situation unless you have a full understanding of the issues in each family situation and the practice skills necessary to utilize this model. Regardless of the debate between the importance of child protection versus family-based care, most trained child welfare social workers recognize the difficulty in intervention from either perspective. The following model integrates not only the protocols and processes that define the SWPIP process, but also provides a solid social work practice basis for working with child maltreatment cases. Specific techniques and tools have been selected from brief and solution-focused treatment to allow the social worker to best provide for the family and child. Examples of different techniques in each chapter of this text will provide you with an extensive range of methods in dealing with differing child welfare situations. [Protocols are cited in the following case.]

Phase I: Establish an Immediate Relationship with the Child and Family Based on Warmth, Genuineness, Empathy, Positive Regard, and Empowerment　In a child maltreatment situation, it is not difficult to understand how being the investigator of a case intrudes with this initial phase. You are entering as an outsider into the family with the power to remove a child from that family. The role of authority in the protection of the child clearly is not a comfortable role for the family. You may be viewed initially as an enemy out to destroy their family. While there are cases where families do not care about the removal of their child, the vast majority of families love their children and desire, for all the reasons any of us would desire, to keep their family together. So it is with fear and often anger that they encounter you, the social worker from child welfare, who is there to investigate issues of child abuse or emotional maltreatment. It is for just such a reason that it has been recommended that the person who investigates not be the same person who intervenes with the family (Protocol 7); however, this may not always be the case in all child welfare agencies. Part of your advocate role as a social worker will be to work toward implementing a program that allows for the separation of investigation from treatment.

Regardless of your initial contact with the family, you must be prepared to present yourself in a manner that is conducive to the well-being of the child and family. In part, your skills in a child abuse situation will generally be in dealing with what is termed an "involuntary client." Although this may initially be the case, it is important to remember that if you can provide the type of services needed in a manner that is strengthening and empowering to the family members (Protocol 13), they may quickly become a voluntary case. Highlight 6.6 gives several methods to remember when approaching a family regarding a child maltreatment situation.

As you may surmise from this list, these methods assume the child welfare social worker is both the investigator as well as the service provider. As has

---

❖ HIGHLIGHT 6.6   Practice Methods

1. Use your authority in a warm, personal, supportive manner and show an understanding of the parents' feelings about the problem.
2. A family may feel less fearful of your authority if you demonstrate a nonthreatening and noncoercive attitude.
3. Help your client to see that you represent a reasonable authority so that he or she can learn that other authority figures can also be reasonable.
4. Demonstrate your authority in a manner that indicates that you have no hidden agenda; that is, be honest.
5. Clarify your protective service role and function. Do not retreat from your responsibility; make the family aware of the expectations for change and the consequences of no change in their behavior. Make them aware that you will develop a plan for your work together and that there are consequences should the changes in their behavior not occur and their child be considered at risk.
6. Make the family aware of your knowledge that Child Protective Service intervention can be traumatic and you will do your best to minimize that trauma. Remember, the experience may be traumatic for both children and parents.
7. Avoid insensitivity to parental feelings since insensitivity may create anger, hostility, and resistance and will make it difficult for you to establish a helping relationship.
8. Do not allow your behavior to convey to the parents that they are the enemy and that you are working against them.
9. Avoid excessive reliance on your legal authority (Filip, McDaniel, & Schene, 1992, p. 45).

---

been noted, playing both these roles can lead to difficulties in providing service. Whether or not you are within a system that requires this dual role, Highlight 6.7 gives additional methods to use when engaging the family in the SWPIP intervention.

Foremost in the application of these skills are the social worker's ability to implement professional "use of self." Use of self is a key technique in any practice a social worker undertakes with individuals, families, groups, and/or communities. Use of self implies a conscious use and understanding of your personal reactions to a situation, but from an empathetic and supporting framework (Protocols 8 & 9). It also implies an understanding and working through of your own personal reactions and feelings about difficult family situations. It does not mean that you tell stories about yourself, but that you can give an indication to the family of how you understand components of the situation. Through an application of this skill, the social worker in the child maltreatment situation has a greater opportunity to affect positive change in the lives of the family and child. Highlight 6.8 is an example of an initial contact situation, followed by a sample phone conversation in Highlight 6.9, and a sample home interview in Highlight 6.10.

❖ HIGHLIGHT 6.7   Additional Practice Methods

1. Listen carefully to the family members' feelings, trying to understand how the situation may have reached this point. This is not condoning the behavior, but rather accepting that there are factors that play into all abusive situations that can be improved.
2. Know yourself, what your personal reactions are to the situation, and what your professional responsibilities are. It is your responsibility to ensure the safety of the child, but this can be accomplished by non-judgmental communication and reaching out to the family.
3. Allow the family to make decisions about the intervention within the context of your protective function. Remember, the family will be more likely to follow through on a plan and/or contract if they have had some part in making it. Empower the child and family as much as possible to deal with environmental issues and make changes themselves.
4. Be very clear about professional issues of confidentiality and the limits of your decision making. Helping the client to understand the limits of your role allows the client to assume some of the responsibility.

Think now about how this social worker responded to the mother. She was warm, supportive (from a strength's perspective), and yet firm in her interaction (Protocols 12 & 13). Now consider the same situation if the social worker had come in following an investigative report, as shown in Highlight 6.11.

❖ HIGHLIGHT 6,8   Initial Contact

Initial Interaction (in dual role)

Amy met Shelly at the school with her teacher in the counseling office. Amy had found Shelly very frightened and shy when she was initially introduced.

Amy: Hello, Shelly. My name is Amy and I am here from Children's Services. I would like to talk with you about your bruises.

Teacher: Shelly, Amy can help you if you can tell her how you got those bruises.

Shelly: It was an accident.

Amy: How did the accident happen, Shelly?

Shelly: Mom was cleaning up some things last night and I broke a glass off the table, she went to sweep it up and the broom hit me.

Amy: Have you had these kinds of accidents before, Shelly?

Shelly: Sometimes Mom has a bad day and I get in the way. She loves me and is always sorry after it happens, and it usually only happens after she has a bad day and has to lay down with a headache.

Amy: Well, maybe I can help you and your Mom with her bad days, Shelly. I need to call her and talk with her about these accidents.

❖ **HIGHLIGHT 6.9   Phone Conversation**

Mother: Hello?

Amy: Ms. Lopez, this is Amy Lyons calling from Family and Children's Services. I'm calling in regards to your daughter Shelly.

Mother: Is she all right?

Amy: Yes, Ms. Lopez, I am at the school with her now and she is fine. I would like to come over to your home this afternoon if I could to speak with you about Shelly.

Mother: What do you want to talk about?

Amy: I think it would be best if I could speak with you in person. I know Shelly will be home about 3:30 and I would like to talk with you and then with both of you if I could. I can come now, it's 2:00, and then see Shelly when she arrives home.

Mother: I don't know, I am supposed to go out this afternoon. I guess you can come over now but I don't know what you want and

I am not sure I want you in my house.

Amy: I understand you're being anxious over the visit. Let me explain that I am a social worker for Family and Children's Services and in that capacity I need to meet with you. However, my role will be to help you with your family situation. I would like to talk with you now so we can get started on that.

Mother: I don't need any help.

Amy: I recognize that as a single mother supporting yourself and your child, it may not seem like someone outside the family should be involved in any way; however, sometimes we all need help and in this case I am required to speak with you before we can make that decision together.

Mother: All right, come over.

Notice how much easier it is now for you as the social worker in a child abuse situation to connect with the parent. You are not entering to make a judgment of the situation. That has already been done and you are there to provide support and guidance to help the family create a new situation for themselves as well as protect the child. Do not think this role is easy. The family will still be suspicious of you and you will have to engage them in an ongoing working relationship in order to gain their trust and enlist their willingness to change. Research supports this approach as the most productive in the sense that as parents begin to trust you, changes are more likely to occur (McCallum, 1995).

Phase II: Assess the Situation Briefly and Thoroughly Based on the Following Systems   *A. Child* Your first priority in the assessment of any child maltreatment case will be a risk assessment related to the child (Protocol 12). If you serve as the investigator, this will be your main initial assessment, but if you serve as the supportive social worker, you will review the initial risk assessment done by the investigator and do an ongoing risk assessment process

---

❖ HIGHLIGHT 6.10　Home Interview

Amy: Ms. Lopez, the situation I am here about concerns the bruises on Shelly's legs. The school is required to notify Family and Children's Services if they believe a child might need some help in their family situation. Can you tell me how Shelly received those bruises?

Mother: That school is always interfering. I didn't know she had any bruises. She's always falling down. What did Shelly tell you?

Amy: She was very reluctant to say, but she shared with me it had been an accident with a broom last night.

Mother: I didn't know she had an accident. She's very accident prone and she doesn't tell me when she does something silly.

Amy: The bruises on her legs would be very hard to get from an accident with a broom. In fact they were quite large and numerous.

Mother: Well, I don't know how she got them. Probably out playing at recess. They never watch the kids at school and then try to blame us parents for all the issues.

Amy: Shelly didn't go out for recess today. She came to school with the bruises and I understand she has had similar bruises before.

Mother: I don't hurt my daughter . . . I love her. I don't need you people interfering. Shelly and I do fine. *(screaming)*

Amy: *(calm voice)* Ms. Lopez, I am not here to create problems. I want to help you solve them.

Mother: I don't need any interference from outsiders, including that school. I don't need any help. We get along fine.

Amy: At this point, Ms. Lopez, I believe there is ground for a substantiated case of abuse with your daughter. I really want to work with you but if you aren't able to tell me what is happening, there is little I can do.

Mother: *(starting to cry)* I don't want to lose my daughter. I am a good mother. I didn't mean to hit her. She broke several glasses when she was washing dishes and I got too angry. I won't do it again. I really love my daughter.

Amy: I know this is a very frightening process having someone from Family and Children's Services come to your door. I am not here to break up your family, Ms. Lopez, but I am here to ensure the safety of Shelly and to work with you so that these situations do not continue. Let's you and I talk together now about what's been going on and in what way I can help. I need to let you know that I will be filing a report with protective services regarding my findings. I want to work together to resolve this situation, however, I must ensure Shelly's safety so we will need to discuss the situation you have at home right now and make some decisions.

Mother: I was just angry at her. I just swatted her with the broom. I never intended to hurt her.

---

through the length of the case. Of initial concern in this assessment process is the evaluation of the risk situation in which the child is placed. There are many tools that can be used for risk assessment in a child abuse situation. Holder and Corey (1986) note that there are four areas of critical decision

---

❖ **HIGHLIGHT 6.11   Initial Interaction (Social Worker as Supportive Intervention)**

Amy: *(meeting at door with Shelly's mother)* Hello Ms. Lopez, I am Amy Lyons from Family and Children's Services. I believe Mr. Meridith shared with you I would be coming today.

Mother: Yes, he did. Come in. Mr. Meridith told me that you would be here to help me with some of the problems I'm having. You're not here to take Shelly away are you?

Amy: *(smiling warmly)* No, Ms. Lopez, although there is concern for Shelly's well-being as you know, we believe that you are an important person for Shelly to be with and may just need some help in pulling things together. I am here to work with you figuring out what things need to be done so you can stay on track. It is important to understand that I must be assured of the safety of Shelly at all costs. I know you are concerned about that also and I think together we can come up with a plan to resolve some of the issues that have emerged for you and Shelly lately.

---

making in risk assessment: (1) if the child is in immediate risk of danger, (2) what services or actions are necessary to protect the child during the investigation, (3) if the child should be removed from the home, and (4) is there a case plan that can be developed to address the child being at risk? (Pecora, Whittaker, Maluccio, Barth, & Plotnick, 1992). These are the questions you as the social worker will have to answer before making any decisions regarding what services can be used.

Pecora, et al. (1992) further suggest that there have been three different types of risk assessments developed: (1) matrix approaches, (2) the empirical-predictors method, (3) family assessment scales, such as the Child Well-Being or Family Risk scales developed by the Child Welfare League of America, and the Child at Risk Field (CARF) developed by Holder and Corey (1986). They further note how difficult a risk assessment becomes as the child protection worker may not know exactly which areas or issues to focus on. The 14 open-ended questions and anchored rating skills developed by Holder and Corey are shown in Highlight 6.12 and can aid you in identifying what risks exist.

Possibly the most difficult area in assessing risk is the fact that despite all the scales and matrixes, none are perfect. Many do not take into account the multicultural, gender, or age issues as they relate to the child and family. Among these, there are several points to be considered in the child welfare social worker's mind as they process each case. These points are shown in Highlight 6.13.

❖ **HIGHLIGHT 6.12   Risk Field (CARF)**

1. How is the child viewed by the parents?
2. How does the child present self, specifically as related to behavior/emotion?
3. What is the child's current status and vulnerability?
4. What are the pervasive behaviors, feelings, or levels of adaptation apparent in the parents?
5. What is the history of the adults (parents) in the family (recent and past)?
6. What are the parenting practices in this family?
7. How do parents relate to others outside the home (nonrelatives)?
8. What are the demographics of the family?
9. How does the family function, interact, and communicate?
10. How does the environment, which includes extended family, support the family?
11. What surrounding circumstances accompany the maltreatment?
12. What form of maltreatment is apparent?
13. How does the family perceive or respond to the intervention?
14. What influences, external to the family, will reduce intervention effectiveness?

Holder and Corey (1986), as found in Pecoria et al., pp. 243–244 (1992).

B. Nuclear Family Assessment of the systems within and surrounding the child and family are essential components to planning any intervention strategy. Having established a relationship with the family will enable you as the worker to intervene in a positive way. Methods of doing assessments abound in the social work child welfare practice field. What makes the assessment different in a child abuse situation is the immediacy of the situation. The importance of accurate and thorough information based on not only the issues related to the child and family situation, but also the strengths and supports that are visible within the situation, will help determine the immediacy of risk to the child (Protocols 13 & 15).

There are two major assessments that are done in child maltreatment cases. The first is the risk assessment of the child, while the second is a more extensive assessment for intervention in the family.

Most assessments in social work are done on the basis of biological, psychological, and sociological components of the child and family situation.

❖ **HIGHLIGHT 6.13   Points to Consider**

1. Know your own limitations.
2. Do not make the decision without the use of a reliable instrument.
3. In making the decision, utilize your own experience in assessing all factors.
4. The safety of the child is the first priority.

Inherent in a good assessment is the ability of the worker to integrate these areas as they relate not only to the child and their development, but also to the family and its development. The family itself follows a developmental cycle that can be short-circuited by environmental factors. Understanding these environmental factors and their effects is important in intervening in a violent family situation.

A written assessment of family members, the situation, and the dynamics taking place in the situation is critical to beginning to coordinate a treatment plan. There are many different forms that have been developed in child welfare agencies to facilitate this assessment. It is important before examining one of these example forms to reiterate the importance of the protocols and methods shown in Highlight 6.14 when doing any assessment, be it for risk or for treatment.

C. Extended Family Systems The preceding assessment does not include all the areas that the social worker may have covered before making a decision about an intervention plan. The social worker may have spoken with family members, neighbors, and other systems (such as the family's church) in making this decision. Additionally, a thorough review of records, as well as an assessment of the environmental situation of the family, is extremely important. Family of origin material is especially relevant in abuse situations as it may be a repetitive pattern; however, the initial written assessment may not be as detailed as an intervention plan may be. An intervention plan will include details that theoretically lead to the decision to be made.

It is important for you to understand that this assessment needs to be done as thoroughly and as quickly as possible in order to protect the well-being of

---

❖ HIGHLIGHT 6.14   Additional Assessment Principles

1. Be sensitive to cultural values, multicultural differences, and to the family strengths as well as limitations (Pecora, et al., 1992).
2. Include the family in understanding the importance of the assessment and how it will aid them in resolving the situation through solution-focused tasks.
3. Although there are many different pieces of information to gather, keep the initial assessment as simple but thorough as possible.
4. Assessments need input from many different sources, so do not just assess a situation based on one system's perspective (such as the school, the family, or the extended family). All perspectives are critical. Also, remember that information can be found in records, not just in talking with someone—the family doctor's records, a hospital's records, as well as previous difficulties at the school.
5. When gathering the assessment, empower the family and child as much as possible, allowing them to talk about what they believe are the issues. Do not, however, lose track of your focus of the assessment which is first for the protection of the child and second for the stabilization of the family.

the child and the family. Gathering such an assessment is very difficult when there is limited time and the situation may be very tense. Remember to gather the information not simply by moving through the questions on the form, but by discussing with the family and child all aspects that they desire to share. It is significant that some of the best assessment information is gained through simple communication rather than through a structured form. Highlight 6.15 illustrates how the social worker can gain information without following a structured interview.

Visual assessment methods are also very helpful in gathering data quickly and in a manner that provides an overview of more than the problematic situation. In visual assessments, you can also pick up more quickly on the strengths within the family. A common visual tool for assessing family dynamics and the developmental cycle of the family is known as the Kinetic Action Drawing and is shown in Highlight 6.16 (Schachte, 1978). In this technique the social worker has different family members draw a picture of something the family does together. Through these drawings, the social worker can assess how communication occurs, what level of interaction the family has, and how individual family members feel right now.

Always remember when assessing any family situation to look for the strengths of the family even in the drawings. Clearly, from Shelly's drawing, the issues of drinking begin to emerge, but there are signs of strength in the family from how the family appears to be together. The person at the end of the table is the father who Shelly continues to hope will come home.

❖ HIGHLIGHT 6.15   A Nonstructured Interview

Amy: I will need to gather some information about you and your family situation before I can provide you with services I believe will help. Let's start by talking about your family now. I know you have Shelly who is 8 and Kevin who is 4. Do you have any other children?

Mother: No, I had a miscarriage once. I was about 4 months pregnant and fell down some stairs. I was only 17 and was not married yet.

Amy: That must have been a difficult time for you. *(leaning slightly forward toward Shelly's mother)*

Mother: It wasn't easy, because I didn't really slip. Shelly's dad pushed me down the stairs after we got into a fight. He was always doing something like that. I stayed with him anyway and we got married but it didn't last long. He left when I was still pregnant with Kevin. I hadn't heard from him until about 9 months ago when he came and said he wanted a divorce so he could marry someone else. Like he'll be any better with anyone else.

Amy: It must have been hard seeing him again.

Mother: It wasn't easy, especially after I had just lost my grandmother. I've been feeling real low—like no one wants to be with me. I know my grandmother loved me, but I still feel real alone now. More than I ever have.

❖ **HIGHLIGHT 6.16   Kinetic Action Drawing**

D. Social Systems The purpose of an assessment is not simply to focus on the family and child, but to also provide an overview of the external systems that impact the family. A common tool for analyzing external systems and their relationship to the family and child is the Ecomap. The Ecomap was devised as a method of obtaining information related to the openness or isolation of a family. It provides information about how the family and its members handle issues both internally and externally. The Ecomap can be used quickly to gather information about linkages the family and individual members have with outside systems. In doing an Ecomap it is important to share with the family the importance of outside resources and linkages and to explain that a visual presentation of these resources can often be helpful not only to the social worker but also to the family (Protocol 11). An example of an Ecomap can be seen in Highlight 6.17.

You can note from this Ecomap the lack of support this family has on the outside; however, it is also important to notice where there are some supports that may be called on in future situations, such as with the Sunday School and church, as well as with the school system and Shelly's teacher. By empowering the family with this information and training them in how to seek out additional supports you are aiding them in reaching more resources through prevention tactics. The more external supports, the less possibility of child maltreatment.

E. Resource Systems The resource systems available to a family are defined as those systems within the community that can help provide services, programs, or resources to aid in the intervention with the family. Most resource systems

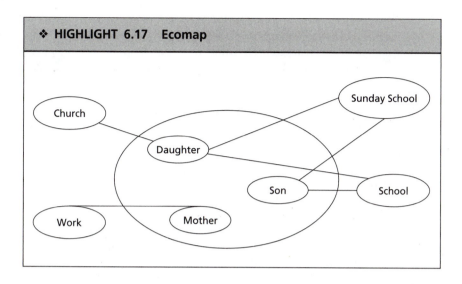

❖ HIGHLIGHT 6.17   Ecomap

overlap with social systems and/or programs and services. Examples of re-source systems in a community might include the school, church, women's shelter, public aid office, juvenile probation office, legal services, family shelter, family court program, to name a few. Assessing what resource systems a family may have available to them means understanding what needs the family has and what resource systems can provide them. This is also the point at which the child welfare social worker and family can begin to make some decisions about who it will be important to include in working on a collaborative treatment program.

F. Programs and Services It is necessary in the assessment of all child welfare sit-uations that programs and services provided by the resource systems in the community also be evaluated related to each case situation. It is important to begin this process long before your work with cases. In part, understanding the resources of the community in which your families live is critical to pro-viding the services needed. The social worker's understanding and connection with these services provides not only a significant resource to the child and family, but also to the community and agency the worker serves (Proto-col 3). Understanding program and service resources involves more than just knowledge—it also involves the worker being able to utilize those programs and services in the most productive manner for their families and children. This involves the child welfare social worker not only knowing all the ser-vices and programs that can be provided, but also the workers involved in these areas, and the eligibility requirements of particular programs and services (Protocol 5). Having collaborative relationships and networking among social services agencies and workers is valuable to the child welfare social worker. It allows you to readily assess which services and programs may be the most

---

❖ **HIGHLIGHT 6.18   Excerpt from a Community Agencies Network Book**

AGENCY	CONTACT	PHONE
American Cancer Society Eligibility Requirements:	Sarah Jenny	884-1536
AIDS Support Group Eligibility Requirements:	John Lyndon	498-7834
Parents Without Partners Eligibility Requirements:	Mary Johnson	886-9874

---

helpful for the child and family. Highlight 6.18 shows a sample excerpt from a Community Agencies Network Book.

Once a complete assessment has been done, a written assessment is necessary to help provide the social worker, the family, and other members of the intervention plan with collaborative guidelines and an understanding of the situation. Highlight 6.19 is an example of a written assessment.

Phase III: Plan and Contract for Intervention with All Systems   In the third phase of the SWPIP model, it is critical that the social worker involve all systems in the planning and contracting of the intervention. The

---

❖ **HIGHLIGHT 6.19   Written Assessment**

PERSONAL INFORMATION: Identifying Information
Name: Shelly Lopez
Address: 214 Wilton Rd. Sugan, California 32317
Phone Number: (532) 675-8923
REFERRAL: Ms. Shanks, Sugan Grade School, Sugan, CA.
PHYSICAL CONDITION: Shelly is a 7-year-old Hispanic girl of medium build and height. She is cleanly dressed and her hair is combed into a ponytail. Shelly's physical appearance appears normal except for three bruises on the back calf of her left leg and two bruises on the back of her right thigh and calf. The size of the bruises range from 2 inches to 6 inches. There does not appear to be

any additional physical injuries on Shelly. The bruises appear new as they are the color purple. The school nurse reports there are no fractures or breaks to the legs.
EDUCATION: Shelly is in the second grade at Sugan Grade School and generally is an A and B student. Ms. Shanks, her teacher, reports that over the last month, Shelly's grades have been dropping and she has seen bruises on Shelly's legs at least three other times. Ms. Shanks notes that this has been a recent change and she had not noted difficulties before. Records indicate that Shelly has been a good student and there have been no concerns over her until this last month.

PRESENTING PROBLEM: The presenting problem is suspected physical child abuse. Shelly reports being "accidentally hit with the broom." Ms. Lopez stated after some initial denial that she had "swatted Shelly with the broom" after the child had broken some dishes.

FAMILY INFORMATION: Shelly lives with her mother, Racine Lopez, age 32, and her brother, Kevin, age 4. Ms. Lopez states she has been divorced for 3 months and works as a toll booth operator three blocks from their house. Ms. Lopez states she has worked for the state for 3 years. Shelly's father's whereabouts are unknown and Shelly has not seen her father for 5 years according to Ms. Lopez. The family receives no government assistance and there is no financial support from the father. Ms. Lopez states that her family lives in Arizona and that the father's family has never been involved with the children. They also live in Arizona. Ms. Lopez does not believe she has much outside support as she has no family in the area and very few friends. Ms. Lopez noted that she has been more depressed in the last few months and that her reactions with the kids are affected by this.

When asked about recent stresses in the family situation, Ms. Lopez reported that her grandmother had recently died and that she had been quite close to her. She also stated that she had felt quite lonely since that loss as she had talked with her grandmother at least once a week for the past 10 years.

Ms. Lopez noted that generally she disciplined the children by making them stay in their rooms, but that lately she seemed to lose control and swatted at them although she knew this was wrong. Ms. Lopez denied any alcohol, drug, or mental health problems in the family, although she stated that her father had a drinking problem at one time.

FAMILY OF ORIGIN: Ms. Lopez notes that she was raised by her maternal grandmother following the death of her mother from cancer. She states she was the youngest of three children. She has two older brothers whom she has not seen or heard from for over 10 years. Her grandmother recently died and she expresses she has experienced depression and stress from this situation. Reasons for lack of contact with her brothers could not be explained by Ms. Lopez. She states that she never knew her father as he left the family before she was born. She describes her upbringing as positive from the love of her grandmother but very lonely.

SOCIAL WORKER'S ASSESSMENT OF SITUATION: It appears that the case of physical abuse can be substantiated by the own admission of Ms. Lopez. The abuse appears to be of recent origin and not an ongoing practice in the family. This change in behavior on Ms. Lopez's part appears to be related to some depression and stress she is experiencing from the loss of her grandmother. Although Ms. Lopez denies a substance problem, it should be noted that there is a family history of substance abuse. Ms. Lopez appears genuinely remorseful about the abusive situation and is willing to work with the agency in any way to correct the abusive situation and stabilize the family.

RECOMMENDATION: Due to a lack of prior history of abuse, the rating on the Child Well-Being Scale, and the motivation of Ms. Lopez, I am recommending an Intensive In-Home Support Program for the family with the child remaining in the home. Ms. Lopez and the family are strongly in need of social support, treatment for emotional issues, and further support for single parenting.

child and family system is not the only system involved in child abuse situations. The resources of the extended family, childcare system, health care system, educational system, and community resource systems are all vital to implementing any plan with a child and family in an abuse and/or emotional maltreatment environment. These systems are all involved in the interaction of the child and family. A coordination of these systems is necessary in order to prevent inconsistent messages and interventions.

A. Case Review and Coordination Meeting Case review and coordination in child maltreatment situations requires the social worker to be skilled in case management as well as in interactional relationships. Case management in all child welfare situations is a core intervention skill that will be used throughout all areas of child welfare (Protocol 17). Highlight 6.20 notes features of the case management process (Vourlekis and Greene, 1992).

Case management services have phases in their process. Most case managers understand that to accomplish their goals they must follow the process shown in Highlight 6.21.

Highlight 6.22 gives an example of the case management process.

B. Involve Family in Planning Process Critical to good intervention in a child abuse situation is the involvement of family members in not only the planning of the intervention but also the coordinating of the services. Once a

---

❖ HIGHLIGHT 6.20   Case Management

Social work case management practice:

- is a process based on a trusting and enabling client-social worker relationship
- utilizes the social work dual focus of understanding the person in the environment in working with populations at risk
- aims to ensure a continuum of care to clients with complex, multiple problems and disabilities
- attempts to intervene clinically to ameliorate the emotional problems accompanying illness or loss of function
- utilizes the social work skills of brokering and advocacy as a boundary spanning approach to service delivery

- targets clients who require a range of community-based or long-term care services, encompassing economic, health/medical, social, and personal care needs
- aims to provide services in the least restrictive environment
- requires the use of assessment of the client's functional capacity and support network in determining the level of care
- affirms the traditional social work values of self-determination and the worth and dignity of the individual and the concept of mutual responsibility in decision making

---

❖ HIGHLIGHT 6.21   Case Management Process

1. Engage all systems and individuals to be involved in a mutual and positive manner
2. Establish quickly the roles of the differing systems within the case management
3. Work together toward a mutual treatment plan
4. Contract for responsibilities in the process and case
5. Meet on a regular basis to review goals and outcomes
6. Termination must be an agreed upon time with all systems involved
7. Always evaluate the case management process as well as the outcome

---

determination is made on how the child maltreatment situation will be handled, the family needs to be involved in every step that follows. Ms. Lopez was encouraged by Amy to initiate and clarify between individuals in the planning meetings their responsibilities, services, and time schedule for providing service. After the meeting, Amy empowered Ms. Lopez by applauding and supporting her participation in the intervention and asking her to plan the agenda for the next meeting (Protocol 16). This was Amy's beginning step in encouraging Ms. Lopez to take control of her own environment and bring about change.

❖ HIGHLIGHT 6.22   Example of a Case Management Process

Amy contacted the school following the investigation with the knowledge of Ms. Lopez and Shelly. In contacting Ms. Shanks she learned that Ms. Shanks had met with Ms. Lopez during the parent-teacher conference and had found her interested in Shelly's progress. Ms. Shanks agreed to stay in contact with Amy over the course of the rest of the school year to report on Shelly's progress. She also offered to help in any way she could. Amy recognized following this conversation that she had found an initial support for the Lopez family in Ms. Shanks. Amy then contacted the support system for respite care for parents recognizing that Ms. Lopez would need some times of relief in order to attend parenting classes and other support groups that might help her with her depression.

As Amy began to bring these differing systems together, she prearranged several planning meetings for all involved, including Ms. Lopez (Protocol 16). The initial purpose of these planning meetings was to clearly lay out the intervention plan and agree on the services and focus of treatment to be provided. Later meetings were designed to review the progress of all involved and to reinforce all positive outcomes.

C. Contract with Family and Support Services for Their Roles in Implementing Plan
It is critical at this point of intervention into the family to set up a written
contract regarding the expectations and understandings that you, as the social
worker, have with the child and family. In the case we have been discussing,
this contract will involve intensive service provisions from the child welfare
agency worker and the family. The contract will include time lines and meeting dates, goals and tasks, and ideas of how solutions to difficulties can be accomplished. A contract, as noted, is important in giving specific information
to the family and child about the expectations of the plan and as a method for
giving the family and child an opportunity to be part of the plan. Highlight
6.23 gives an example of this type of contract.

Phase IV: Implementation of Plan   *A. Continued Implementation of Interviewing Skills and Practice Techniques* Key in the implementation phase is the
continuation of the interviewing skills and practice techniques that focus on
the strengths of the family and child and direct them to solutions for their
problems (Protocols 20 & 21). For example, you suspect from what you know
that Ms. Lopez drinks and you want to deal with this situation immediately.
Start with a comment on her strength in being a single mother. For example,
"I know it must be difficult for you to support and raise your children on
your own. You have to have a lot of strength and energy to do that." Then

---

❖ HIGHLIGHT 6.23   Contract with a Family Referred for Child Maltreatment

The following agreement has been
constructed mutually with Ms. Lyons
of the Children and Family Agency of
California, Ms. Lopez, Shelly, Ms.
Shanks, Mr. Williams (of respite care),
Ms. Carol (of Parents Without Partners), and Mr. Sills (of AA).

A. Strengths
   1. Openness to change
   2. Strong single mother
   3. Cares about children
B. Goals
   1. Learn appropriate parenting
      skills through group training
   2. Stop drinking and attend AA
   3. Deal with depressing issues in
      relationship to grief

   4. Receive respite services
**C. Responsibilities and Tasks for Res-
   olution**
   1. Attend parenting group meet-
      ings
   2. Attend AA
   3. Social worker will assist with
      transportation and childcare
D. Outcomes and Evaluation
   1. Improved parenting skills—
      progress notes
   2. No use of alcohol in conjunc-
      tion with regular attendance at
      AA—Goal Attainment Scale
   3. Less depression and more re-
      laxed—Depression and Anxiety
      Scales

move into a more direct question related to the alcohol. For example, "Some-times when a person has to be as strong as you do all the time, you want to escape from the situation once in a while. And for some people the way to do this is to drink." When you are dealing with a case that may involve substance abuse, it is best to be direct in your questioning. For example, "I'm wondering if this is the way you escape and how often you need to do it each week to relieve the stress?" The reason this issue needs to be raised directly is to avoid denials and the time it takes to begin to deal with the problem. Although the parent may continue to deny the use, you have broken the ice and can set out incongruencies in her statement with your own observations (beer bottles in an open trash bag, Shelly's drawing, etc.).

Part of the work you will do in this phase will be in dealing with the parent's parenting skills and helping them develop different ways of parenting. The parent might be involved in parenting classes or you might help the mother role play a situation in which she would tend to get upset and have her try different ways of handling these issues. Along with parenting skills are techniques you will use to help the parent deal with their anger and frustration. Some of these may be relaxation techniques, cognitive restructuring, or assertiveness training. Along with these techniques, it is important to continue to focus on the parent's strengths, their previous coping mechanisms, and their ability to change their situation and behaviors (Protocols 22 & 23).

B. Continuing Coordination of Services When implementing the plan, the coordination of services (a case management function) can be given priority in the process. If resources and systems are not coordinated around the contract and treatment plan for the family, little will be accomplished. An established time line with set meeting dates and clarity of roles and responsibilities is critical as noted in the Contract and Planning Phase. The issue of drinking must continue to be addressed and the parent will need to take action around the alcohol issue with any number of services available.

C. Support and Empowerment of Child and Family Possibly one of the most difficult skills needed will be that of supporting and strengthening the family through the process. With so many systems involved and possibly numerous judgmental issues at play, keeping the family empowered is often a challenge. This is in part why it is so important that one child welfare social worker have responsibility for case management and treatment. Also, this process clearly establishes the importance of the Community Network Book and the social worker's ties or connections with outside members of the systems being utilized. If the social worker does not know and feel comfortable with the individuals who will be working with the family and child, all empowerment can be lost. Not using a system or agency may be preferable to utilizing a resource that may not support or empower the family.

D. Identification of Barriers and Resolution As in any process, it is best not to be surprised. When you are working with the family and integrative support systems in developing the contract and treatment plan, it is important to cover what difficulties could emerge at this point. However, it is often the case that difficulties will not be encountered until the plan begins to be implemented. For example, transportation may be an area that could prove to be a barrier. The family may believe they will not have a problem and yet their car could break down, not allowing them to attend required meetings such as parenting classes. Ensuring that the family has covered these concerns and has alternatives to these barriers in case they happen can save not only time but the potential of the entire treatment (Protocol 23).

E. Monitoring of Services and Plan Monitoring the plan and services being provided to the family requires organizational skills that are inherent in case management practice; however, as the primary provider of the treatment, as well as the coordinator, this monitoring process is much more easily supplied. Monitoring within the SWPIP model is more than monitoring the family and child. It is equally important that the other systems be monitored and that the family be empowered to monitor their services also. Organizational skills are crucial to this process because the model calls for a multisystemic approach and this can only be accomplished through the ongoing interaction between systems, services, and the child and family.

As the family becomes more comfortable and trustful about their role in implementation, they can be encouraged to reach out into their environment to facilitate others who may need similar resources. What you are doing in this phase is setting up a preventive outreach program within a community of people through the families themselves. The design in Highlight 6.24 demonstrates how the child welfare social worker fits in this role between the family, systems, and environment.

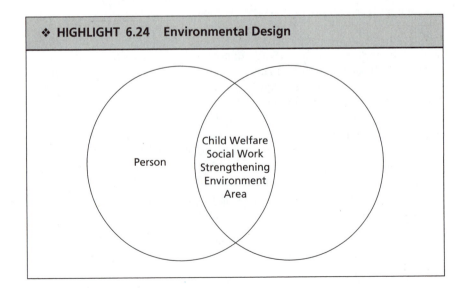

❖ **HIGHLIGHT 6.24   Environmental Design**

Person

Child Welfare
Social Work
Strengthening
Environment
Area

Phase V: Evaluate Outcomes and Terminate Services   *A. Evaluate Outcomes* Evaluation of services is generally an ongoing process that occurs within the context of the intervention (Protocol 25). Although evaluation is a process, it is also an outcome. As an outcome, it has the significance of justifying your practice and services. Knowing how to provide outcome information to your clients, funding sources, and other systems will help secure your intervention and treatment focus. Highlight 6.25 is an example of how an evaluation model for a case may be established and developed.

B. Terminate Services   It may be surprising for students to learn that the termination of services in child welfare should begin as the service starts. Your goal as the child welfare social worker is to provide the child protection and stabilize the family, therefore, the beginning is only one step toward the termination of practice (Protocols 29 & 30).

Phase VI: Follow up from a Multisystemic Perspective   *A. Family* The follow-up phase in a child abuse and/or emotional maltreatment case is an area that has not been dealt with extensively. As Phase V indicates, basic services are terminated at that point; however it is important to remember that the relationship you will have established with this family is a significant one, hopefully not as an intruder in their lives but as a facilitator for the betterment of their family, especially in terms of their parenting skills and the well-being of the child. Highlight 6.26 gives an example of a follow-up situation.

❖ HIGHLIGHT 6.25   Evaluation Model

Goal Attainment Scale for Weekly Score

Goal 1 — Attend AA Meeting

−2	−1	0	1	2
Does not attend or talk to Sponsor	Tries to talk to Sponsor	Talks to Sponsor	Tries to go to meetings	Attends meetings and talks to Sponsor

Goal 2 — Attend Parenting Group

−2		0		2
Does not attend		Talks with Parenting Trainer		Attends

Goal 3 — Deal with Depression Issue

−2		0		2
Does nothing		Work in Depression Workbook		Attends Counselling

---

❖ **HIGHLIGHT 6.26   Follow-up Situation**

Six weeks following the termination of the intensive services offered to Ms. Lopez and Shelly, Amy contacted the family and set up an appointment at the home.

Amy: It good to see you and Shelly again. How are things going?

Mother: Well, we haven't had too many problems, but the state is cutting back on employees and I am worried about what that means in terms of a job for me.

Amy: When will you hear something?

Mother: In about three weeks. I have a lot of seniority but you never know for sure.

Amy: It's important for you to be prepared for what you might do if that happens.

B. Community Follow up in the community includes assessment of the resources within the community, as well as gathering community support for the education and prevention of child abuse, neglect, and/or emotional maltreatment (Protocols 32 & 33). Working through the families to help organize and advocate for resources needed to reduce stress in families is part of the follow-up process. This follow up is based on your work and assessment with many families—more than just the case you have been working with.

C. Programs and Services Like community follow-up, you will be asssessing the programs and services available as well as the quality of what was provided in each case situation. You are quality control for the children and families you serve, therefore it is essential to follow up on the services provided in each child welfare case situation. One way of accomplishing this is to assess from your clients their thoughts on the programs they were involved in and the services they received. By processing data from each family you will be able to identify what needs to be modified and what needs enhancement to the programs and services you recommend.

D. Policy The SWPIP model has demonstrated a few of the techniques and tools that can be used in abuse and emotional maltreatment situations. It is critical for the social worker to understand that it is the risk assessment that allows the model to be utilized in this manner. There may be many occasions when the risk assessment dictates that the child is not safe in the home and must be removed. This does not change the phases or steps that the social worker will move through with the clients, and in particular the family, but it will certainly change the manner and approach that will be taken in dealing with the case. More work will need to be done in working out the trust issues with both the family and child. The removal of children from their home is a serious event and the manner and accommodations being made in this decision will affect the ability of the worker to reunite the family in a stabilized environment.

SUMMARY

This chapter has provided an overview of issues related to abuse and emotional maltreatment. The definitions of these issues and their impact on the policies related to children and families have been examined in light of the impact of the new more family-based services that are being utilized by child protection agencies.

The SWPIP model has been implemented in a manner to provide the student with an understanding of how family-based practice or substitute services can be utilized within not only specialized programs in child welfare but within the established child welfare fields. Preventive work in creating change in economic conditions so families have access to equal resources is a major objective in eliminating child neglect and maltreatment. Understanding how the economic conditions of your community affect these issues will enable you to bring about preventive measures against abuse and maltreatment.

QUESTIONS FOR DISCUSSION

1. Describe the meaning of "parens patriae"

2. Describe the four steps in an intervention of child abuse.

3. Discuss permanency planning and its role in family prevention.

4. Do a kinetic drawing of your own family.

5. Draw your own family's ecomap.

6. What role does case management play in child maltreatment?

7

■

Sexual Abuse

Mandy, a white 15-year-old in the tenth grade, appeared at her friend's house one evening very depressed and preoccupied. After much coaxing, she told her friend what was bothering her. She mentioned that her father was strict and did not allow her to do many of the things her friends were allowed to do, particularly dating. She said her father seemed jealous of the attention she received from boys and wanted her to spend all her time at home where she had assumed many of the household responsibilities. She began to cry uncontrollably upon telling her friend that her father had done "bad" things to her for many years. She confided that he had fondled her on a regular basis from the time she was 10-years-old and started having sexual intercourse with her at age 13. Mandy's friend, although sworn to secrecy, was extremely upset and decided to tell her own mother, who then reported the abuse to the authorities. The Department of Social Services began an investigation of the report, and the findings were substantiated. Mandy was removed from the home and placed in protective custody.

INTRODUCTION

Sexual abuse has emerged as one of the major forms of child abuse, not only in this country but universally as well. Reports of childhood sexual abuse are becoming increasingly common in both the popular and professional press. One national survey reported that 27 percent of women and 16 percent of men had a history of childhood sexual abuse (Finkelhor, Hotaling, Lewis, & Smith, 1990). A similar study of the general population revealed that by 18 years of age 38 percent of women had experienced some form of sexual abuse, while 28 percent had been sexually abused by age 14 (Russell, 1986).

Recent studies of the prevalence of childhood sexual abuse in the general population suggests that sexual abuse continues to be an underreported and undercounted situation by official standards. The issue of disclosure is one that has been given considerable attention by various professional groups and organizations concerned with child sexual abuse. Research on this topic supports the fact that the large majority of sexual abuse survivors, both male and female, never disclosed to anyone that they had been or were being abused. In fact, the research is quite consistent in that not disclosing appears to be the normative response to child sexual abuse. Methodologically sound studies have found that as many as 38 percent of female victims of child sexual abuse (Russell, 1984; Salter, 1992), with estimates of as many as 38 million sexually abused Americans (Crewdson, 1988), do not disclose the abuse as children. This is a relevant fact that you as the child welfare social worker will need to be aware of, as there may be cases you come into contact with where sexual abuse is the "secret" in the families' difficulties.

Aside from the obvious moral problem of sexual abuse, we as social workers cannot ignore the enormous social problems that develop when individuals experience such trauma during childhood or adolescence. Sexual abuse can leave substantial psychological scars on its victims in the form of disturbed self-esteem and an inability to develop trust in intimate relationships. As a result, a large majority of survivors experience difficulty in maintaining long-term relationships, which contributes to the increasing divorce rate. Numerous studies of adults with substantial psychological problems have indicated a plausible connection with a history of child sexual abuse. Studies of various troubled populations such as drug abusers, juvenile offenders, adolescent runaways, prostitutes, and adults with sexual dysfunctions show that high proportions of these individuals were sexually victimized as children (Finkelhor, 1984). The case seems easily made that some fraction of those who are sexually victimized in childhood are affected quite badly by these experiences.

DEFINING SEXUAL ABUSE

Definitions of sexual abuse vary. For the purposes of this text, the authors are employing the definition that is oriented toward mental health issues in child sexual abuse. This is chosen in light of the severe psychological consequences that occur to the victim. The impact of the abuse on the family system will

---

❖ **HIGHLIGHT 7.1   Defining Sexual Abuse**

Sexual abuse is any act occurring between people who are at different developmental stages that is for the sexual gratification of the person at the more advanced developmental stage. This definition assumes a dyadic relationship; however, it is possible to have more than two people involved in a sexually abusive encounter, both victims and perpetrators. Ordinarily the participants in sexual abuse are adults and children, but occasionally both victims and perpetrators are children. The perpetrator may be an adolescent and the victim a latency-aged or younger child. Alternatively, the victim may be the same age as the perpetrator, but at an earlier developmental stage because of mental retardation. (Faller, 1988)

---

also be addressed at another point in the chapter. Highlight 7.1 defines sexual abuse for our purposes.

A more important distinction to understand is the one between incest and stranger sexual abuse.

Incest

Incest is the predominate form of sexual abuse seen by social workers in a variety of settings. It is defined as any form of sexual contact between individuals in which the perpetrator has a familial relationship with the victim (i.e., parent or stepparent, sibling, aunt or uncle, grandparent, etc.). In the more classical case of incest, the interaction between father (or stepfather) and daughter begins as appropriate displays of physical affection then gradually progresses to sexual behavior. The psychological trauma arises in large part from the fact that the child's trust in the father, the primary protector, has been violated. The problem becomes much more advanced if the abuse occurs over an extended period of time and, upon disclosure, the child fails to receive the necessary support from the mother or other significant adults.

Stranger Sexual Abuse

With regard to another form of sexual abuse frequently brought to the attention of social workers, that of stranger rape, there is a significant contrast in the resulting psychological trauma to the child. Generally she or he receives support from parents and the adults involved, thus lessening the depth of long-term emotional consequences. The degree of trauma can also be affected by the use of force on the part of the perpetrator. If significant force is used and results in injury, this may contribute to emotional problems on the part of the victim and will require an appropriate therapeutic intervention.

To sufficiently understand the dynamics of the problems associated with child sexual abuse, it is crucial to develop an awareness of the fact that the interactions in the abuse situation may not necessarily involve physical contact

---

❖ **HIGHLIGHT 7.2   Sexual Abuse with No Physical Touching**

1. *Sexy talk* includes statements the perpetrator makes to the child regarding the child's sexual attributes, what he or she would like to do to the child of a sexual nature, and other sexual comments.
2. *Exposure* includes the perpetrator's showing the victim his or her intimate parts (breasts, penis, vagina, anus) and/or masturbating in front of the victim.
3. *Voyeurism* includes instances when the perpetrator either covertly or overtly observes the victim in a state of undress or in activities that provide the perpetrator with sexual gratification. (Faller, 1988, p. 12)

---

between the perpetrators and the victims. Faller defines the three types of sexual abuse in which there is no physical touching in Highlight 7.2.

Interactions which do involve physical contact between the perpetrator and victim are defined in Highlight 7.3.

POLICIES

The advent of the 1900s brought about a significant number of societal changes, particularly in the areas of sexual mores and the structure of the family system. The changing sexual attitudes and behaviors that have been associated with the beginning of the "sexual revolution" in the 1960s have contributed to the problem of sexual abuse to some degree. According to Finkelhor (1984) one major affect has been the erosion of traditional, externalized controls over sexual behavior:

> Forces such as the religion, parental authority, and tradition no longer have as much legitimacy in controlling behavior and enforcing sexual norms as in the past. One result has been that many people are confused about the state of sexual norms. One group for whom this state of confusion is particularly serious are those whose sexual behavior in the past was regulated primarily by strong external controls. The loss of these controls may have propelled them in an antisocial direction. (p. 112)

In tandem with the decline of external controls has been a progressive change in the portrayal of sexuality in the media. The perceptions arising from these changes have influenced sexual behavior on the part of men and women alike and the roles that they are expected to assume within the sexual relationship. For many, the expectations might be unrealistic, thus inducing them to turn to children for sexual gratification as opposed to risking rejection or feelings of inadequacy in attempts to engage in sexual relationships with other adults.

❖ HIGHLIGHT 7.3   Sexual Abuse with Physical Touching

1. *Sexual contact* includes any touching of the intimate body parts, including the breasts, vagina, penis, buttocks, anus, and perineal area. The perpetrator may fondle the victim, he or she may induce the victim to touch him or her, or the victim and perpetrator may engage in mutual fondling or masturbation. Frottage is sexual contact in which the perpetrator gains sexual gratification from rubbing his intimate parts against the victim's body or clothing.

2. *Oral-genital contact* involves the perpetrator's licking, kissing, sucking, or biting the child's genitals or inducing the child to orally copulate with him. The behavior may be *cunnilingus* (oral contact with the vagina), *fellatio* (oral contact with the penis), or *anilingus* (oral contact with the anus).

3. *Interfemoral intercourse* is intercourse in which the perpetrator's penis is placed between the child victim's thighs, a technique that is generally employed with young victims. The terms "dry" and vulvar intercourse are also used for this act, as there may be rubbing of the penis against the child's vulva, but there is no penetration.

4. *Sexual penetration* is characterized by some intrusion into an orifice. Four types have been noted in sexual abuse:
   a. *Digital penetration* involves placing fingers in the vagina or the anus or both. Usually the victim is penetrated by the perpetrator, but sometimes the perpetrator induces the victim to engage in penetration. Digital penetration is a form of sexual abuse found frequently with young victims and is sometimes a prelude to genital or anal intercourse.
   b. *Penetration with objects* is a less frequent type of sexual abuse in which the perpetrator puts an instrument in one of the victim's orifices—vagina, anus, or occasionally the mouth. The most frequent type is vaginal penetration.
   c. *Genital intercourse* involves the penis entering the vagina, however, occasionally the penetration is partial due to the smallness of the victim. There is usually a male perpetrator and female victim, but occasionally a female perpetrator may be involved in genital intercourse with a male victim. The victim in the latter type of situation is likely to be somewhat older, frequently an adolescent.
   d. *Anal intercourse* occurs when the perpetrator's penis is inserted into the victim's anus. This technique often occurs with male victims but it is also sometimes employed with female victims. (Faller, 1988, pp. 13–14)

The changes that have taken place in the structure of the family system, with the widespread increase in divorce throughout the world, has also affected different behaviors within family relationships. While this issue alone may or may not have had a direct impact on child sexual abuse, it has given rise to alternate family systems, such as stepfamilies and conjugal families. These changes have had an impact on the problem of child sexual abuse, the degree of which remains a subject of much debate. According to research in the area of sexual abuse, children are at higher risk of abuse when they live with a stepfather or mother's boyfriend than with a natural father (Finkelhor, 1979; Russell, 1984). In view of the fact that children today are exposed to more stepfathers and parents' lovers as a result of the increasing numbers of divorces, their vulnerability to sexual abuse has logically increased.

It is important to also note that the women's movement in the mid 1900s directed attention to the issue of child sexual abuse, as did the children's protection movement. Advocates involved in both movements joined forces to deal with the problem of abuse from different theoretical perspectives. The child advocates viewed sexual abuse within the context of other aspects of child abuse (i.e., physical abuse, neglect) where the focus is primarily placed on the parents and other caretakers. The feminists associated sexual abuse with the phenomenon of rape and extended the focus to include nonfamily members and strangers (Finkelhor, 1984). Regardless of the differences in these perspectives and the individual approaches to dealing with the problem, both groups made significant contributions to the task of heightening public awareness and promoting policy concerns in this area. Thus, the status and care of children was elevated in our current society.

Given the historical trends that have taken place with regard to the status of children and the changes associated with these trends, it might be assumed that there has been a progressive decline in both physical and sexual child abuse; however, this is an uncertainty and continues to stimulate much debate. The changing status of children does not necessarily infer such, and, in view of the secretive nature of the problem, it is unlikely that this decline is occurring.

Policies associated with sexual abuse are largely reflective of those already discussed in chapter 6 related to child abuse and emotional maltreatment. Legal issues related to child sexual abuse have many different definitions according to the state in which the family lives. It is important for you as a child welfare social worker to be familiar with not only the policies, but also the legal ramifications of child sexual abuse as it relates to your community. Ensuring that the policies and legal issues protect and support the child and their family is an important facet of your work. Although the legal actions against the perpetrator may be appropriate, they must also reflect a sensitivity to the child within their family context.

PSYCHOSOCIAL DYNAMICS
OF SEXUAL ABUSE

The problem of sexual abuse is surfacing as a major underlying issue in a number of dysfunctional behaviors brought to the attention of mental health professionals today. These can often lead to the inability of marital partners to establish a satisfactory level of intimacy in their relationship. Sexual abuse also can have a profound affect on the entire worldview of an individual throughout a lifetime. Without appropriate intervention, the damage associated with sexual abuse can be devastating.

Social workers are becoming increasingly more involved in cases of sexual abuse through not only child welfare agencies but in a variety of settings. Mental health professionals of all kinds are seeing adults who were victims of sexual abuse as children and are seeking treatment. When social workers encounter sexual abuse, it is usually manifested under the guise of another problem that is brought to the attention of a professional. An adolescent who might be exhibiting antisocial behavior, alcohol or drug abuse, and/or running away could be dealing with an abusive home situation. Children who might be having problems concentrating in school, consistently withdrawing from peers, or regressing to childlike behavior of an earlier developmental stage could be manifesting symptoms of sexual abuse. Additionally, children who are brought to physicians for treatment of enuresis, encopresis, or sleep problems may also be experiencing the trauma of abuse.

Social workers also frequently uncover a history of sexual abuse in a variety of treatment settings where adults seek assistance in dealing with problems such as those described in Highlight 7.4.

Likewise, social workers employed in child welfare settings are challenged by the psychosocial problems manifested by children who have been victims of sexual abuse and must deal with them from a "nontreatment" approach. At times these children exhibit sexual acting-out behavior in foster care and can victimize other children residing in the home. They also experience difficulty in peer relationships or in controling their own aggressive behavior. As a result, they frequently engage in predelinquent and delinquent behavior involving some form of aggressiveness or violence. They often appear on the case loads of social workers employed in school systems, juvenile justice settings, or residential facilities who are assigned the task of coordinating services for them.

In order to structure an appropriate plan for services, it is imperative that social workers have a significant level of knowledge of the deep psychological consequences resulting from child sexual abuse. The closeness or intimacy of the relationship between perpetrator and victim affects the level of intensity

---

❖ HIGHLIGHT 7.4   Issues Associated with History of Sexual Abuse

1. Marital discord or unsatisfying sexual relationship on the part of a couple seeking therapy
2. Substance abuse on the part of a spouse
3. Domestic violence where a woman has entered a shelter for protection
4. Suicidal tendencies or ideation
5. Criminal behavior involving incarceration or other criminal court activity

---

❖ **HIGHLIGHT 7.5 Factors in Determining Relationship Between Child and Perpetrator**

1. Biological relationship between perpetrator and victim
2. Legal relationship that exists
3. Relationship between the perpetrator and the victim's families

4. Frequency of contact between the perpetrator and victim (Faller, 1988)

---

and long-term consequences to the child. The degree of closeness in the relationship is largely determined by the factors listed in Highlight 7.5.

In view of the complexity of circumstances surrounding the issue of child sexual abuse, the so-called remedies to the problem are often fragmented, highly simplistic, or superficial and not actually remedies at all. This, to some extent, is due to the societal taboos concerning human sexuality and sexual behavior. It is also a reflection of a general reluctance to invade family privacy, or to interfere with the sanctity of parental autonomy over children (Laird & Hartman, 1985).

As in cases of physical abuse and neglect, the responsibility of child welfare agencies to protect sexually abused children is generally accepted by society and by the law. For this reason, their intervention in such cases is deemed essential by most experts. However, there is continuing debate about what the scope of agency intervention should be (Chapman & Smith, 1987). As discussed in chapter 3, the implementation of the Adoption and Child Welfare Act of 1980, in an effort to provide more permanency planning for children, instituted a priority of family-based care for abused and neglected children. As the result of the impetus placed on family preservation, and the fact that sexual abuse began to be viewed as a problem symptomatic of dysfunctional family patterns, intervention efforts began to focus on remedying dysfunctional aspects of the family system.

PROCESSES AND PROCEDURES

Effective programs for families who have experienced sexual abuse are given low priority in that society and the law must first protect sexually abused children, while child welfare workers are expected to carry out interventions that focus on preserving the family unit while at the same time protecting the child. The legal authority given to child welfare workers to remove children who are in imminent danger of abuse can create a serious barrier in the intervention process with the family.

In a majority of communities there are linkages among agencies that provide services to abused children. These agencies include schools, hospitals, public and private mental health facilities, criminal justice agencies, child protection teams, in addition to a variety of other social service programs. The effectiveness of these linkages is largely dependent upon coordination and communication among social workers involved to prevent the duplication or breakdown of critical services. To prevent this from occurring, the use of interdisciplinary case review teams is a common practice in many communities. Through the teams, various professionals who might be involved in a specific case involving sexual abuse are able to coordinate services and work toward common goals that support the best interest of the child. This involves the establishment of a case plan in which the role of each professional is clearly defined in terms of the service(s) they are able to provide in meeting a specified goal or service objective.

A range of actions may be undertaken on behalf of the victim by child welfare agencies, either through juvenile court actions or through service agreements between the agency and the family. When juvenile court actions occur, the child may be removed from the home and placed in protective supervision. This could be either a foster home, a temporary emergency shelter home, or with family members or close friends for a limited period of time as stipulated by state law. Under certain circumstances the perpetrator is often mandated by the court to leave the home and not have further contact with the child until the completion of an investigation. The purpose of this action is to provide immediate protection for the child while, at the same time, the child welfare agency and law enforcement authorities conduct separate investigations into the abuse allegations. In most states, child welfare agencies are mandated by state law to conduct these investigations and recommend appropriate dispositions to the court based on the best interests of the child. Concurrently, law enforcement authorities conduct a separate investigation of the case to determine if the perpetrator should be prosecuted for criminal charges.

Following a child's placement in protective custody, an evaluation is often conducted by a social worker representing the child protection team. This team functions in a capacity different from the public child welfare agency responsible for protecting the child or the law enforcement agency involved in the investigation. The role of the child protection team social worker is to interview the child to determine (1) if the sexual abuse actually occurred, and (2) the circumstances surrounding the situation. The results of this evaluation are generally provided to the court for consideration in making a disposition in the case.

During the period of time that the child is under the jurisdiction of the child welfare agency (child protective services) and removed from the home, a contract is frequently developed with the family in which specific objectives are outlined and must be met before reunification can occur. In cases where children remain in the home under formal agreement or court-ordered supervision, a service agreement is established that details the services the agency is able to provide in order for the family to remain intact. In either situation the child welfare agency has legal responsibility for the welfare of the sexually abused child and carries out the necessary interventions.

SERVICES AND PROGRAMS

A great deal of controversy continues to surround the use of family preservation/family-based programs in cases involving sexual abuse. Although these family-based programs might be appropriate in many situations in which physical abuse or neglect has occurred, the dynamics surrounding sexual abuse raise concerns about their appropriateness in these situations. In some cases it is clearly not in the best interest of a child to attempt to preserve a family, particularly if it is extremely dysfunctional and the lives of the children are at risk. Nevertheless, the provision of mental health services to children and families in their homes is a new initiative in the mental health field and is a growing trend across the country (Archacki-Stone, 1995, p. 107). The purpose is generally to strengthen the family unit in an effort to prevent the out-of-home placement of sexually abused children. This is done through the provision of intensive support and therapeutic interventions to families in crisis and is usually only appropriate in cases where the perpetrator is not residing in the home. In most cases, other more traditional services have not been effective and the child is continuing to experience persistent emotional and behavioral difficulties.

A number of exemplary programs that provide services for abused adolescents have been developed in recent years. An example of a program is one whose primary purpose is serving adolescents and their families through many different services. The agency would provide emergency programs, such as 24-hour housing shelter for adolescents, in addition to a 24-hour telephone hotline and counseling service. The program would provide information, referral services and ongoing counseling for youth and their families. Adolescent peer counselors would meet on a daily basis with abused youth to provide support, share feelings, and explain agency and community resources. The agency might also provide short-term foster homes for adolescents who are awaiting placement, who need longer term crisis resolution services, or who are preparing to leave home but have not fully developed skills for independent living. A general philosophy reflected would be one that includes a respect for and incorporation of the ideas and self-help abilities of adolescents (Laird & Hartman, 1985, p. 522).

Other programs that provide services to families who have experienced sexual abuse include Homebuilders, or Family Builders, which provide intensive in-home family crisis counseling and life-skills education. These programs also come from a family-based philosophy. The programs are designed to prevent unnecessary dissolutions of troubled families and reduce placements of children into publicly funded care. Homebuilders is based on the belief that it is usually best for children to grow up in their own homes. It draws upon the ecological perspective and developmental concepts as well as the development of competence. Some of the skills required to implement this orientation are assessing the family's strengths, changing the environment, planning goals, setting the limits, contracting with families, teaching specific life or social skills, intervening during crises, working with families in their homes, and individualizing services to meet the needs of a family (Maluccio, 1990). As noted before, these types of programs are questionable because of the severe dysfunctions in families where the act is a result of sexual abuse.

PRACTICE INTERVENTION CENTER

Child welfare workers tend to respond differently to sexual abuse cases than they do to physical abuse and tend to utilize a variety of interventions. Although certain interventions seem to be more popular than others, an appropriate concern is whether the current child protection models of service delivery really fit sexual abuse. The model on which child protection systems are predicated is one of crisis intervention. The use of this model assumes that the maltreatment of a child is precipitated by a stressful event, and that the provision of short-term intervention will enable the family to return to an appropriate level of functioning.

A study conducted by Kathleen Faller (1991) with the University of Michigan indicates that cases of child sexual abuse do not resolve in a timely fashion. In studying 58 sexually abused children for approximately 3 years after initial identification, she found that more than half of the cases were still open with the Michigan Department of Social Services after these 3 years, and almost half of the children were still out of the home. Her findings support that disclosure of sexual abuse leads to major upheaval in the lives of victims and their families, and the short-term intervention models being used are not usually the most effective interventions of choice in these cases. In particular, if the problem is chronic and in large part the result of offender psychopathology, sustained treatment will be necessary to affect change. The victim who has endured years of sexual abuse is not likely to be "cured by a quick fix," nor is the perpetrator who has enacted the abuse.

According to guidelines for family-based practice, whenever possible children should be served in their own homes and home-based intervention should be employed to prevent placement. Moreover, when children must be removed, they should be placed in the least restrictive setting and should be returned home as soon as possible. This family-based perspective has generally been applied to physical, neglectful, and emotional maltreatment situations. This is not necessarily appropriate for cases of sexual abuse in which the victim has usually disclosed the abuse. Because of the pivotal role victims play in the diagnosis, they are frequently subjected to pressure to retract their accusations and are often blamed by the family for the consequences that occur. In order to protect them from this emotional maltreatment, as well as the risk of further sexual abuse, it may be necessary to remove them from the home. Moreover, relative placement may be inappropriate because the child may be subjected to similar pressures from the extended family. Sexual abuse is often imbedded in the family system and is found both intergenerationally and laterally in the extended family, making a family placement potentially high risk. Because the protection of the child is of first concern, their continued stay in the biological family may be impossible unless the perpetrator has left the home and the adult remaining is supportive and willing to take part in the intervention and protection of the child.

CAUCASIAN FAMILY CHARACTERISTICS

The majority of individuals currently living in the United States are of European descent and make up the majority of cases within the child welfare system. Like Hispanic families, however, not all Caucasian families can be grouped together as being of European descent because their specific cultural backgrounds have blended together. Caucasian families, like other groups, can continue the behaviors and traditions of their cultures from generation to generation.

Awareness of any specific cultural and/or religious factors that play into the family's coping mechanisms are part of understanding how to intervene with the SWPIP model. These factors are important in all families and the common mistake a child welfare worker can make is assuming because a family is Caucasian that there are no diverse issues.

In Mandy's family, the perception of the sexual abuse is very important in understanding how the family will respond to the investigation and involvement of the child welfare social worker. How do different members of the family respond to the "secret" existing no longer? In what ways does the family's cultural and/or religious background affect their dealing with the "secret?" These questions are appropriate for all families and yet it bears repeating that these are important issues in Caucasian families also.

> Identify Protocols in the Following Case Example

SWPIP PRACTICE MODEL

The value of the SWPIP model in cases involving sexual abuse is that it can be adapted to a variety of circumstances in both short-term and long-term situations. The success of the model is contingent upon (1) the use of a primary social worker who is intensely involved with the victim and family and (2) the level of knowledge on the part of the social worker with regard to the dynamics of sexual abuse and how to affect preventive services in the community. As in cases of physical abuse (chapter 3), the protocols of the model are integrated and specific techniques are utilized that are unique to sexual abuse cases. The phases of the model and the specific techniques will be demonstrated through the case example mentioned at the beginning of the chapter.

Phase I: Establish an Immediate Relationship with the Child and Family Based on Warmth, Genuineness, Empathy, Positive Regard, and Empowerment   Phase I can be a difficult and challenging task in sexual abuse cases due to the anger and denial that is typically manifested on the part of the family. The victim is likely to experience the stigma of being identified as a participant in the sexual interactions. They may even be rejected by the perpetrator, who may be a person whom they value. In addition, the victim may also be ostracized if the family chooses to side with the perpetrator, or feel "punished" by being placed in foster care or elsewhere outside the home. The family may be torn apart and the child may see herself as responsible for its demise. On the other hand, perpetrators are not likely to admit they have engaged in sexual abuse and will probably deny it. The overall pervasiveness of anger throughout the family system directed toward the professionals involved in the case can be difficult to penetrate.

As the primary social worker involved in this type of case, your power over the family cannot be disregarded. Your attempts to empower anyone in the family at this stage must be based on honesty and a willingness to work through the situation. Your role as an authority figure is a barrier that must be dealt with at the onset and one that may continue to resurface. Nevertheless, the immediate focus should be on the child and the development of a relationship with them. The first attempt to build trust occurs at the first contact and prior to approaching the issue of sexual abuse. Once trust is established, which can be fairly quickly in children, there is likely to be more spontaneity in the relationship. Thus, it is less frightening for the child to reveal stressful information to someone they know as accepting and warm. In some family situations there may be other adult members of the family who can be supportive of the child. It is important to begin to think in terms of the family's own natural helping network when dealing with these difficult issues if these other family members are given permission.

At the beginning of the initial contact, a strain usually exists for the social worker between the need to identify the purpose of the contact and the need to develop a relationship with the child. How this should be handled will vary depending on the case and the age of the child. In most cases, the person who introduces the child to the social worker will have said something to prepare them. Often a good approach is initially to introduce oneself and assume the child has some idea of why they are there. With a younger child, it is helpful to use a toy or game and involve them in play. Toys or games should be selected based on the child's developmental age level and area of interests typical of that age range. Begin with open-ended questions that allow the child to discuss topics freely and do not restrict them to yes or no answers. Initial questions should relate to general areas, such as school activities, friends, family members, extracurricular areas of interest, and so forth. When there is a feeling that the child is comfortable and is responding in a spontaneous manner, it is appropriate to ask why they think they are here. At this point, the relationship should be more developed before clarifying the purpose of the contact.

Faller (1988) suggests another strategy, which is to make a brief initial statement about the purpose of the contact and then move on to more general topics or play. For example, the social worker might describe herself as "a doctor, but not a shot doctor, who helps kids when they have problems or worries." Or you might say, "I help kids when grown-ups do things they shouldn't." After a brief statement about the reason for the contact the social worker can say, "But first maybe you'd like to play with some of these toys" or "But we don't have to talk about it right away. We can get to know each other a little first." Remember, it is extremely important to not push the child and to follow their direction in pacing the interview.

If at all possible, contacts with younger children should be held in their home, or in the place in which they are temporarily residing, rather than an office setting. This is far less intimidating for the child and gives them the feeling of having more control over what might be happening to them. The issue of "loss of control" is a critical one for a child involved in sexual abuse due to the chaotic changes that typically occur following disclosure of the abuse. Therefore, interviewing them in a "safe," familiar environment helps to facilitate the development of a relationship. It is always important to speak with the child alone, either in a quiet room or outdoors and free from the interference of others.

Highlight 7.6 gives guidelines to consider when working with children (Sheafor, Horejsi, & Horejsi, 1998, p. 366–368).

Throughout this initial phase of the model it is critical for the child to identify you as the primary person who will be working with them for an unspecified period of time, if possible. It is also important for the child to understand the involvement of other professionals and what their roles might be. Be clear with the fact that you will be in communication with everyone involved in the case and will be giving the child opportunities to ask you questions about what might be occurring. Children need to understand as much as possible about what is going to be happening to them. They should also be given the opportunity to discuss their feelings about this with you openly and in a safe, nonthreatening manner. In doing so, it is critical to normalize and validate these feelings as much as possible throughout your contacts with them to help them regain some sense of control in their lives.

With older children, particularly adolescents, it is necessary to be explicit about the purpose of your contacting them at the very beginning of the interview. In the case of "Mandy," the social worker would most likely make initial contact with her at school, perhaps in the office of the school guidance counselor, who should be able to assure privacy. Highlight 7.7 represents a typical initial interview in which the social worker attempts to establish a relationship with Mandy and, in doing so, is able to move right into the stated purpose of the interview.

In this phase of the model the social worker attempts to engage Mandy in a discussion about what occurred while, at the same time, reflecting her feelings and letting her know that she empathizes with her. As you can see, the social worker briefly states her purpose for being there and immediately

❖ **HIGHLIGHT 7.6   Guidelines for Working with Children**

1. When planning the interview with a child, determine the child's age and probable level of development, and anticipate how this will affect the child's capacity to understand and use language—but realize that there will be much variation among children even in the same age group.

2. Be clear about why you are meeting with the child and what you need to accomplish during the meeting. Plan several methods to accomplish your goal. Anticipate what might go wrong (e.g., child will not talk, child cries, child will not leave parent, etc.) and plan how you will handle such situations.

3. Prior to the meeting, assemble the play materials that may be needed. Depending on the child's age, provide "open-ended" art materials (e.g., paints, markers, clay, water toys), as well as materials that can be used to portray themes (e.g., dolls, puppets, blocks or Legos for building, toy cars and trucks, toy animals, doll house, etc.). For older children, consider card or board games, puzzles, or simple electronic games. Because play is normal activity for children, it is also a child's natural method of communication.

4. Plan to hold the interview in a space that is familiar and comfortable for the child, but that affords privacy. As an alternative, consider an accessible community space that allows some privacy (e.g., a spot in a park, walk in the schoolyard, a private section of a playground).

5. When first meeting a child, explain who you are and how you want to be addressed (e.g., "My name is Jane Smith. Please call me Jane."). Place yourself at the child's physical level (e.g., sit or squat so you do not tower over the child). Initiate some friendly interaction by showing an interest in items the child may be wearing or carrying, or ask about school, favorite games, or TV shows. If the child refuses to interact, engage in a parallel activity and gradually initiate conversation about the activity. For example, if the child does not talk, but begins playing with a doll, pick up a doll and engage in similar play.

6. If the child appears frightened, attempt to normalize the situation (e.g., "If I were in your place, I would feel scared talking to a new person. You are acting brave by just being here."). It may be necessary to allay the child's fear that he or she is in trouble and the interview is some kind of punishment.

7. If the child is at least 6 or 7 years of age, ask what he or she knows about the purpose of the interview. This will reveal what the child is expecting. Then, in language he or she understands, explain why you want to speak with the child. Ask if he or she had talked to anyone else about this meeting and what others have said about it, or discuss what instructions the child was given.

8. Do not attempt to disguise a professional interview as recreation; this may confuse the child about who you are and your role. Also be cognizant that only very limited confidentiality can be provided to a child. Do not promise that you can keep secrets, but describe what you can do to keep the child protected and safe, as well as what might happen after the child shares information with you. (Sheafor, Horejsi, & Horejsi, 1998, pp 366–368)

❖ **HIGHLIGHT 7.7**   **Initial Meeting in Sexual Abuse Case**

Ellen: Hello, Mandy, my name is Ellen Bowen and I work with the Department of Children and Family Services. I apologize for having to take you out of class today, but I was wondering if we could talk for a moment. Would you like to sit down?

Mandy: (appearing confused and concerned) Okay. What did you want to talk with me about?

Ellen: Mandy, I am a social worker and my job is to talk with teens who might be experiencing some problems at home. I understand that sometimes it's very difficult to talk about problems with a total stranger, and a little scary as well. Maybe you could begin by telling me a little about yourself. You're a sophomore here at Lake City High, is that right?

Mandy: Yes.

Ellen: What are some of the activities you're involved in here?

Mandy: I sing in the chorus and I belong to a service club.

Ellen: Do you have any sisters or brothers?

Mandy: Yes, I have a 12-year-old sister and an 8-year-old brother.

Ellen: (humorously) I'll bet you do your share of babysitting, right?

Mandy: Yeah. (smiling nervously)

Ellen: Mandy, I'm going to ask you some questions and you might feel a little uncomfortable answering them. I just want you to know that I am here to help. My office has received a report that you've been experiencing some difficulties at home with your father. Is that correct?

Mandy: Yeah, I guess.

Ellen: Could you tell me a little bit about these difficulties?

Mandy: Well, my Dad is real strict and he doesn't like me to go out with my friends, especially Daryl, my boyfriend. All my other friends are allowed to date and go out together, and their parents don't give them a hard time. Just mine.

Ellen: I see. Well, how does your mother feel about this?

Mandy: I can tell that she doesn't agree, but she won't go against Dad.

Ellen: That must be somewhat frustrating for you. What do you suppose your Dad objects to?

Mandy: I don't know. He almost seems jealous of Daryl.

Ellen: Perhaps he is. Has he always reacted this way?

---

begins to establish a safe, trusting environment for Mandy to discuss the problems with her father. The social worker would continue to ask more probing questions about the abuse and, at the same time, reflect the feelings being expressed both verbally and nonverbally by Mandy. Highlight 7.8 is an example of how to terminate the interview, giving the child some idea of what they might expect to happen as the result of having disclosed the abuse.

It is important for the social worker to convey to the client that they will be actively involved in the decision-making process in order to help them regain a sense of control. It is also important to not communicate false or inaccurate information to them in order for the relationship to continue to be

---

❖ **HIGHLIGHT 7.7** *Continued*

Mandy: No, only since I've been seeing Daryl.

Ellen: I see. How would you describe your relationship with your Dad up to this point?

Mandy: It's been okay. *(looking down)*

Ellen: I'm sensing that there are some problems there. Could you tell me a little about them?

Mandy: I don't know. *(becoming tearful)*

Ellen: I'm sure this must be painful for you. Perhaps I can help. The report I've received states that your Dad has been doing some things to you that are harmful. Is that correct?

Mandy: *(nods her head "yes")*

Ellen: Are these things sexual?

Mandy: *(nods her head "yes" and becomes more tearful)*

Ellen: When did your father start doing these things to you?

Mandy: When I was about 8-years-old.

Ellen: Would you tell me how they began?

Mandy: When my Mom wasn't home and Dad was taking care of us, he would come into the bathroom while I was taking a bath to make sure that I was washing with soap. Then he would check me to make sure I was getting myself clean all over. He would even check my vagina.

Ellen: I see. How did you feel about that? Were you confused at first?

Mandy: Yes, then I started feeling bad afterwards.

Ellen: Because it was your father hurting you?

Mandy: Yeah, I guess. But later he started coming into my room at night to tuck me in, so he said. Only he wouldn't leave and he'd start rubbing me all over.

Ellen: On your vagina?

Mandy: Yeah.

Ellen: Please go on. *(maintaining eye contact and appropriate body language)*

Mandy: I didn't know what to do. He kept telling me that he loved me and it was okay because he was my father. But I didn't feel okay about it.

Ellen: I'm sure you didn't. You probably didn't know how you were supposed to feel, only confused.

Mandy: *(nodding her head)*

---

based on trust. Notice also that the social worker does not communicate information about the father, but instead comes across as being nonjudgmental and supportive. This, too, is important in view of the fact that most victims of sexual abuse continue to have loving feelings toward the parent abuser. You have now laid the foundation for the remaining phases of the model, the next being the assessment phase.

Phase II: Assess the Situation Briefly and Thoroughly Based on the Following Systems *A. Child* The assessment of a child or teen in a sexual abuse situation is a difficult one as they will be frightened and often feel guilty about speaking against a parent or family member. An example of a beginning assessment that might be done has been covered in Highlight 7.7.

❖ **HIGHLIGHT 7.8   Termination of Initial Session
with Child in Sexual Abuse Case**

Ellen: Mandy, it's important for you to know that I am required to report what has occurred to the appropriate authorities. It's also equally important that you understand that I am going to be working very closely with you at least until this situation is resolved, and longer if necessary. You will have to talk to a judge, but I want you to know that I will be there with you and help you through that. I also would like for you to talk with a counselor who works with victims of sexual abuse and is able to help you understand a lot of what you will be feeling. I'm going to try to arrange for you to stay with a relative for a short period of time, while the court proceedings are going on, and then we can decide together where to go from there.

I would like you to recognize that what has happened to you is wrong and not your fault. There are many other girls your age who have faced this same type of situation and have been able to enjoy a positive family environment in time.

It is significant that the assessment done with the child focus on the child's immediate needs and safety as well as the conditions that have created the situation.

According to Faller (1988, p. 119), the data listed in Highlight 7.9 needs to be considered during the assessment process to determine if sexual abuse has occurred.

While the preceding information is necessary in determining if sexual abuse has occurred, it is also important to obtain other information that reflects a "whole child" perspective. The whole child approach encompasses physical health, cognitive development, emotional well-being, moral development and social behavior. According to Zill and Coiro (1992), the types of data shown in Highlight 7.10 represent a whole child assessment.

Because young children are likely to express themselves more readily in activities, it is recommended that they be given an opportunity to communicate material in an indirect way, such as in play. A variety of activities can be used, but the more common would be puppet play, picture drawing, and the use of anatomical dolls. As a rule, doll or puppet play is employed with very young children, those from 2 to about 6 or 7; picture drawing requires some fine motor development and is useful with children beginning about 5; and storytelling requires language skills and vocabulary, and therefore is most useful with children of school age. The social worker's task is to track the number of times sexual content appears in the play and how it might relate to other information gathered.

> ❖ **HIGHLIGHT 7.9   Assessment Data for Sexual Abuse**
>
> 1. *Physical evidence*. This includes medical findings and evidence collected by law enforcement personnel.
> 2. *Statements made to significant others*. Statements made by the child to family members, friends, or other professionals. Most often the case comes to the attention of authorities because the child has revealed the abuse to someone close.
> 3. *Sexual behavior on the victim's part*. This would include excessive masturbation; sexual interaction with younger children, peers, or adults; seductive behavior; and sexual promiscuity. Sexual acting out takes different forms at different developmental stages and, as a rule, is more likely to be observed in children too young to completely understand its meaning.
> 4. *Sexual knowledge beyond that expected for the child's developmental stage*. Examples would include explicit knowledge in young children about fellatio and cunnilin-
>
> gus, anilingus, intercourse, that the penis gets big and hard when rubbed, that the penis goes into the vagina during intercourse, and that something white comes out of the penis. Such knowledge could conceivably be gained by observing sexual acts or pornographic movies rather than experiencing intercourse, which also constitutes sexual abuse.
> 5. *Nonsexual behavioral indicators of stress*. The symptomatic behavior of children who have been sexually abused may present with a range of problem behaviors of a nonsexual nature (i.e., sleep disturbances, enuresis or incontinence of feces, victim's fear of sleeping in his or her own bed, eating disturbances, school or learning problems, personality and interpersonal difficulties, etc.). Other forms of regressive behavior include demanding a pacifier or bottle again, resuming baby talk, developing clinging behavior, and so on. (Faller, 1988, p. 119)

Puppet Play

In puppet play, children who have not been sexually abused will focus their play on having the hand puppets engage in normal daily activities (i.e., watching television, cooking, parenting, sleeping, going to school, etc.). However, children who have been sexually abused will spend more time undressing the puppets, making sexual comments about them, or engaging them in various types of sexual activity.

Puppet play can be a valuable tool in assessing sexual abuse as the children are more able to communicate verbally their feelings and circumstances surrounding the abuse without having to take ownership of the information. It feels much safer to communicate through the puppet and the child is able to distance herself somewhat, thus allowing the puppet to take responsibility for what is being said. It is important to select puppets that represent nonthreatening characters to children and are appealing. Interpreting feelings and various behaviors that are commonly associated with sexual abuse can be done effectively through the use of puppets (i.e., anger, aggressiveness, sultry behavior, fear, etc.).

❖ **HIGHLIGHT 7.10   Whole Child Assessment**

1. *Physical health, nutrition, and safety.* Examples of basic health indicators are whether the child's height is within the normal range for his or her age, whether weight is appropriate for height, whether there are any obvious signs of malnutrition, and whether there have been any significant delays in growth or motor development. Significant medical history would include whether the child has any life-threatening or life-shortening diseases, or any chronic illness or impairment that causes discomfort or limits play or learning. Whether the child has a regular source of medical and dental care, when he or she last received a check-up, and whether appropriate immunizations have been given would also be important.

2. *Cognitive development and academic achievement.* This heading would include the child's attainment of the skills, knowledge, concepts, and strategies that are needed to succeed in school and, eventually, to deal with the challenges of being an adult. If the child is school age, it would be important to talk with school personnel to obtain information about the child's progress in school. Also useful would be information about the parents' expectations in this area.

3. *Emotional well-being.* The domain of emotional well-being covers the child's overt behavior and his or her moods and feelings as they can be inferred from parent or teacher reports, through direct observation of the child's facial and vocal expressions and conduct, or through interviews with older children and adolescents. Typical problems children might experience would be poor socialization with peers, aggressiveness, hyperactivity, depression or anxiety, phobias, withdrawal from play activities, lying or stealing behavior, etc.

4. *Moral development and social behavior.* This would include information about whether the child has a strong, secure relationship with at least one parent or parent-substitute. Also important would be information about playmates and siblings, whether he or she is developing age-appropriate competencies, and his or her development of culturally-appropriate values, standards, and attitudes. (Zill & Coiro, 1992)

With puppets children are able to play out content that is preoccupying them at the time and is suggestive of sexual abuse. The information indicates to the social worker that there is cause for concern and that there is a need to explore the situation further.

Picture Drawing

Generally there are four types of pictures that are most helpful for children to draw: (1) a family portrait, (2) a self-portrait, (3) a picture of anything that immediately comes to mind, or (4) a picture in the form of a video game of anything that might be bothering them.

Some sexually abused children will draw pictures that indicate a heightened awareness of sexuality (i.e., putting penises on animals or humans, drawing breasts on themselves, etc.). Occasionally, they will draw persons involved in sexual acts and other times the sexual content will be more subtle. There may be a focus on the genital or abdominal area (a zipper drawn in detail); or when they are asked to tell about the picture, sexual meaning emerges. Children who have been sexually abused may also make drawings that depict their emotional reaction to the abuse (such as in the video game drawing). Finally, pictures sometimes indicate an avoidance of sexuality (i.e., an older child drawing her mother as a stick figure) (Faller, 1988).

Storytelling

Storytelling is an excellent method for eliciting traumatic information from adolescents and children. Relating the information in the context of a story reduces the trauma of telling what happened by enabling the child to initially discuss the situation through the character and circumstances of a story. Material that is often communicated relates to information that is salient to the child, as well as things that are preoccupying the child and may be worked through in storytelling (Faller, 1988).

In beginning the process of getting a child to tell a story, it is helpful to use pictures that might depict material relating to sexual abuse (i.e., a picture of a girl looking sexy or sad, or a picture of a father hugging his daughter, etc.). Anything that might be construed as the least bit sexual by the child, or might in some way relate to her own individual experience, would be appropriate to use. The amount of content communicated by the child that relates to sexual abuse is influenced by the frequency of the sexual contact, the length of time since the last incident, and the trauma involved (Faller, 1988).

In the case of Mandy, the scenario in Highlight 7.11 is used to demonstrate the technique of storytelling, which can be used with children of any age level.

❖ HIGHLIGHT 7.11   Storytelling

In an effort to help Mandy discuss what has been happening within her family, Ellen, the social worker shows her a picture of a young girl, approximately her age, standing apart from a group of teenagers and looking very sad. Ellen then asks her to tell her what she sees.

Mandy: That's a girl and her name is Donna. Her father has been doing things to her for a long time.

Ellen: What type of things?

Mandy: He's been having sex with her.

Ellen: When did he start having sex with her?

Mandy: When she was a young child.

Ellen: What happened when she was a young child?

Mandy: Her father would come into her room at night to kiss her good night and things would go on from there.

Ellen: How did Donna feel about what was happening to her?

Mandy: She felt scared and confused.

Ellen: And how did she feel after she told someone what was going on?

Mandy: She felt different from her friends and she didn't think they wanted to be around her. She felt sad and confused.

This scenario illustrates the fact that, in Mandy's case, she feels rejected by her friends as a result of the abuse. The emotional impact of the abuse is evident here and must be considered when planning for an appropriate intervention.

Anatomical Dolls

The use of anatomically correct dolls is also an effective tool to use in assessing abuse. The child is better able to communicate the details of the abuse by demonstrating what occurred with the anatomical parts on the dolls. This allows the social worker to evaluate what the child is saying about the abuse and what he or she is demonstrating through the dolls. Videotaping the interview is permissible for court testimony in some states as it often minimizes the trauma of having the child testify in open court in front of the perpetrator.

Anatomical dolls can be used in a variety of ways and with children of any age level. They are more beneficial, however, with young children who typically incorporate them into play. Highlight 7.12 illustrates the appropriate use of the dolls while interviewing a young child.

❖ HIGHLIGHT 7.12 Use of Dolls

After a relationship has been established with the child, the social worker (Ellen) would introduce the dolls to the child (Mary) and observe the non-verbal reactions.

Ellen: Mary, I want to show you my dolls. They really are very special. Can you tell me why?

Mary: *(looking a little embarrassed and smiling as she takes the dolls and looks them over)* They are funny looking.

Ellen: Why are they funny looking?

Mary: Because the girl doll has boobies and hair down there. And the boy doll has hair too and a 'thing'.

Ellen: What do you call his 'thing'?

Mary: It's a penis.

Ellen: And what is her 'thing' called?

Mary: It's called a vagina.

(The social worker could then ask the child if she has even seen a penis before and ask her to describe what a real one looks like. To get more relevant information about the abuse she would begin probing by letting one of the dolls represent the victim and the other the perpetrator.)

Ellen: Let's pretend this doll is you. Has anyone ever touched you there? *(pointing to the vaginal area on the doll)*

Ellen: Can you show me how?

(The social worker would then hold the male doll while the child demonstrates the incident with the female doll. The social worker could offer the male doll to the child and ask her to pretend it is the perpetrator, then demonstrate what he did to her.) During this process it would be important to note the emotional responses of the child and consider this information when formulating your intervention.

The social worker would then ask questions relating to when this happened. Who did this? How did it feel? Where did it occur? Did it ever happen again? What was she told to do? What did she want to do? If the child is reluctant to demonstrate exactly what occurred with the dolls, the social worker can touch the dolls in various places and ask her if she was touched in these places. She could then ask the child to demonstrate how she was touched while at the same time asking open-ended questions about what occurred.

B. Nuclear Family A complete and accurate assessment of the child's environmental system is needed, combined with the information surrounding the abuse, before an appropriate intervention can be implemented. During the assessment phase subjective judgments are made about whether certain behaviors or outcomes constitute abuse. They are affected by many factors, including the social class and ethnicity of the children and families, workers' frames of reference and personal values, local levels of awareness and local operational procedures, and so forth. It is critical for the social worker to be aware of these factors and how they might impact the assessment and interventions. Of particular importance is the need to have knowledge of a family's ethnic and cultural differences with regard to how they might relate to what occurred. It is also critical that the social worker completing the assessment be comfortable with his or her own sexuality and in touch with her feelings concerning sexual abuse with regard to how they might affect the assessment process.

A range of questions needs to be answered during the assessment, the first and foremost being, "Has the child been sexually abused?" The sequencing of interviews should place the child interview first so that the social worker has made an assessment of whether or not the sexual abuse took place before investigating its dynamics and treatment prognosis. An integral part of assessment in sexual abuse is the process of assessing the immediate family system before the goals of the intervention phase can be established by the social worker. Family dynamics play a major role in cases involving sexual abuse. The social worker's insight into these dynamics is critical to the development of a systemic approach to dealing with the problem.

Defining the Problem

In any family assessment the initial responsibility would be to define the problem that played a major part in precipitating the abuse. In doing so, it is important for the social worker to know that the problem, as it is defined by the client or family system, might differ from the worker's version of the problem. Because the family system will very likely have to make the major changes that are necessary in cases of sexual abuse, it is important to always remain in touch with their definition of the problem while negotiating possible solutions. This will likely stimulate more of a commitment to change on the part of family members.

Asking yourself the following question helps to organize your approach to the case in the early stages and is vital to understanding the dynamics

---

❖ **HIGHLIGHT 7.13   Strength's Approach**

Let us return to the case of Mandy. Interviews with various individuals concerned about Mandy's welfare indicated that Susan, Mandy's mother, was most invested in making a decision about (1) what to do about helping Mandy, (2) how the other children were reacting to the situation, and (3) what to do about her relationship with her husband. After adding this information to other significant details learned about the case thus far

(i.e., the problem as defined by the social worker, the client, and the family system), you would then progress to the next phase of the assessment process: identifying the *strengths* in the family. When focusing on strengths rather than weaknesses, a social worker is able to achieve far more success in working with families who are thought to lack the most basic problem-solving skills.

---

involved: Who is most concerned about what problem? The person who is most upset about, uncomfortable with, or indignant about the situation is the one most likely to take some steps to solve the problem (Berg, 1994). The parent (1) who expresses some willingness to do something about the situation and appears to be dealing with the problem, and (2) who expresses a sense of hopefulness and is receptive to getting help is the one most likely to take steps to solve the problem. Highlight 7.13 shows a strength's approach in dealing with the family of the sexually abused child.

Nuclear Family

Much significant information about family strengths can be obtained by completing a thorough family history. During the course of completing a history on the family it would be important to identify functional patterns of coping and problem solving rather than focusing only on dysfunctional behaviors. It would also be important to pay attention to the strengths of families from various cultural groups as well. Many of these groups have suffered historic discrimination or, as political refugees, have suffered extreme losses. Examples of strengths in the backgrounds of families from other cultures are shown in Highlight 7.14.

❖ **HIGHLIGHT 7.14   Cultural Strengths**

---

1. Demonstration of an interest in keeping alive the folkways, arts and crafts, language, and values associated with their heritage.
2. Evidence of a commitment to take

care of their extended family members.
3. Communication of a desire to preserve family ties through religious, seasonal, holiday, work, or entertainment rituals.

An excellent tool to use in completing an in-depth family history is the genogram (Hartman & Laird, 1983). The genogram is an attempt to map out family coalitions, alliances, historically significant events, life change events, family myths and rules (particularly in the area of sexual norms and values), and other significant issues that may have an impact on the family and the problems they are experiencing. It would be helpful to have both parents, in cases of sexual abuse, complete the genogram separately to evaluate their individual perceptions of family patterns. A sample genogram is shown in Highlight 7.15.

Another instrument that can be useful in the family assessment process is the Index of Family Relations (IFR), which is part of the Clinical Measurement Package developed by Walter Hudson (1982). It is one of nine separate scales designed to secure a measure of a client's attitude toward self, parents, spouse, family, or peers. The IFR measures the degree of stress and conflict within the family, as perceived by a particular family member. Other Hudson scales that focus on the parent-child relationship is the Child's Attitude toward Mother (CAM) and the Child's Attitude toward Father (CAF), both of which are completed by the child (above age 12) and measure the magnitude of problems in the parent-child relationship. The IPA, or Index of Parental Attitudes, is completed by the parent and measures the magnitude of problems in the parent-child relationship, as perceived by the parent. Not only are these scales beneficial to use during the assessment process, they are also useful in measuring the outcome of intervention.

❖ HIGHLIGHT 7.15   Genogram

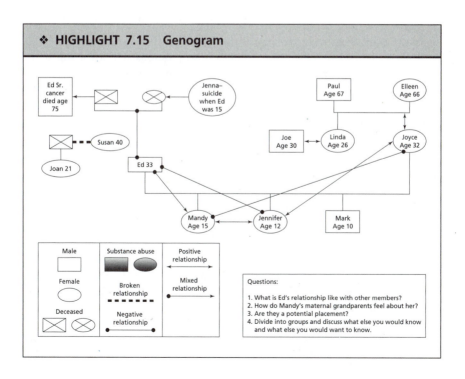

Questions:

1. What is Ed's relationship like with other members?
2. How do Mandy's maternal grandparents feel about her?
3. Are they a potential placement?
4. Divide into groups and discuss what else you would know and what else you would want to know.

❖ **HIGHLIGHT 7.16   Example of Family Assessment Questions**

1. *How does Mandy view her family?*
   If she views her family as a positive system that meets many of her needs for security, emotional support, and assistance when she needs it, then it would be important to emphasize these positive feelings. However, if her view is negative, the social worker can ask how she has managed to acquire her positive traits and give her credit for such. It is preferable to accept the client's perceptions and empower her to use them to her advantage.

2. *To whom in the family does she feel she has the closest relationship, and why?*
   Which family member provides her the greatest amount of support, and has she been able to tell them about the abuse? If not, why?

   How has she been able to maintain that supportive relationship? How might they be able to help each other make the necessary changes that need to occur?

3. *What is her sense of her own autonomy within the family, and does she perceive herself as having some control over the changes that will occur in the family system?*
   Looking at the previous patterns of coping with problems within the family would be important for the social worker to consider here. It would also be significant to consider how much autonomy the client has had in the past with regard to decision making, setting limits, expressing feelings, etc., within the family system.

Again, referring to the case of Mandy, the primary social worker completing the family assessment would ask the questions shown in Highlight 7.16.

Information gathered from the preceding questions will assist the social worker in constructing a broader picture of the problems within the family system, as well as the potential resources to draw on when planning an intervention. The information is also helpful in giving the worker a sense of direction in which to move.

Characteristics of Parents

The characteristics of the child victim's parents is strongly associated with sexual victimization and comprise an important part of any family assessment. The information in Highlight 7.17 should be included on both parents individually, as well as stepparents if they are actively involved and assume a major position in the client system.

C. Extended Family Systems All families have a power structure that defines the amount of influence that each member has upon other members and who will participate in what way in decision making. Children can also play a significant part in the power structure, particularly if they have been delegated appropriate authority over siblings in the absence of parents. As stated earlier in the chapter, this often occurs in cases involving incest in which a child is

---

❖ **HIGHLIGHT 7.17   Parental Characteristics Assessment**

1. Description of current living situation (i.e., who is living in the household; social and economic status of parents; division of responsibilities in home; etc.).
2. Information on family history (i.e., relationship with grandparents; values taught regarding parenting and discipline; communication styles and use of affection in family of origin; etc.).
3. Education level and employment history (i.e., overall functioning in current and previous employments; ability in combining job and parenting responsibilities, etc.).
4. Relationship with children; attitudes toward parenting (i.e., quality of relationship with victim as compared to other children; over-

all situation at time of victim's birth; parental perceptions and feelings about victim; methods of discipline used; etc.).
5. History of substance use and/or abuse; mental illness, and illegal activity (i.e., extent to which these areas related to the abuse; affect of substance abuse or mental illness on child victim; status of recovery; arrest records; etc.).
6. Sexual history (i.e., history of prior victimization of parent(s); sexual practices in the home; sexual patterns of parents; history of promiscuous behavior, etc.).
7. Description of individual roles in sexual abuse; reactions to the abuse; level of mother's commitment to the child's story, and so on.

---

often forced to assume control and decision–making functions beyond her developmental capacity.

Culture also plays a powerful role in defining the allocation of power in families. Many cultures are male oriented and clearly define the female's role as subordinate to that of the male (Hepworth & Larsen, 1993).

Keeping in mind that all families allocate power in some manner, in healthy families the balance of power helps the family system to maintain a state of equilibrium; however, in dysfunctional families the power differential is much more extreme and causes a great deal of stress for family members. In assessing the power structure, it is important to not only determine how power has been distributed in the family, but also whether changing conditions of the family are threatening the power base. You must also assess the extent to which the family's rules allow for flexibility in the power structure and if roles can be adjusted to meet the demands of the family's changing circumstances (Hepworth & Larsen, 1993). In a case of sexual abuse, it would be helpful to know how the child victim views the balance of power within the family system.

Family roles are assigned to each member of a family and are integrated into the power structure of the family system. Often they are delegated to members on the basis of gender and societal expectations. Within the past several decades, family roles have become much more equalized with both men and women sharing many of the responsibilities for parenting. Nevertheless, families continue to experience many difficulties related to role assignments and performance expectations. In assessing role performance on the part of family members it would be important to consider the following: (1) How are roles assigned in the family? (2) How adequately do members perform their designated roles? (3) To what extent are pressures caused by role overload? (4) To what extent are individuals willing to consider adjusting roles?

Communication Styles of Family Members

Problems experienced by some families arise partially because of inadequate communication in which the open expression of feelings is prohibited. In sexual abuse it is particularly important to consider the communication patterns between the parents involved. When eliciting details from the parents with regard to what occurred, one is able to pick up on problematic behaviors in interactions that can become targets of change efforts. Incongruent messages might be communicated in which the verbal information that you hear might be inconsistent with the nonverbal information (i.e., a parent communicates affection for a child but pulls away when the child demonstrates affection). The more distressed a family system is, the more incongruence you may see in the communication of verbal and nonverbal messages.

Extended family systems in child sexual abuse cases can sometimes create more difficulty than aid. The stigma attached to sexual abuse, as well as the fact that abuse may be part of an intergenerational pattern, can create further problems for the child if they are placed in an extended family setting. As noted, often the pressures on the child to deny the problems will come from extended family members and you will need to support and empower the child through this process.

Cultural factors must be considered in assessing communication patterns in families. Problems experienced by some families may arise because of cultural prohibitions against openness. A knowledge of cultural norms is essential before determining that change efforts need to be directed toward promoting more open communication among family members.

D. Social Systems An adequate assessment not only includes an analysis of the problem, the child, and the family, but also the environmental context of the situation. This involves the consideration of the adequacy or inadequacy, and the strengths or weaknesses of systems in the client's environment that might have a bearing on the problem. Social assessment, thus, is aimed at identifying systems that must be strengthened, mobilized, or developed in response to the client's unmet needs (Hepworth & Larsen, 1993). The systems that might be included in cases involving sexual abuse would not only be the family system, but also natural support systems (i.e., extended family members, friends, neighbors, etc.), childcare or school systems, health care, law enforcement, religious systems, and the overall physical environment.

Families in which sexual abuse has occurred tend to be very closed and have little or no involvement with other family members or friendship groups; therefore, in assessing social supports it would be important to note if the child or family have any contact with extended family or friends and what the quality of those relationships might be. Are there feelings of alienation on the part of family members, and should efforts be made to tighten the social network of these relationships for the purpose of offering support for the client system? In cases where a client's environment is completely void of natural support systems, certain environmental changes may be necessary to effectively match needs with external resources.

In assessing environmental systems, socioeconomic and ethno-cultural factors play a major role in the assessment process. Although sexual abuse crosses all socioeconomic lines, reported cases of sexual abuse come predominantly from lower-socioeconomic families, many of whom are socially isolated. The connection between social isolation and both physical and sexual abuse has been frequently noted in the child abuse literature (Finkelhor, 1984). In addition, an awareness of cultural attitudes toward sexual abuse is essential in providing insight into the cultural frame of reference that has helped to shape the client's perceptions of the problem.

E. Resource Systems The resource systems available to families and children who are brought into the child welfare system because of sexual abuse are very similar to those that are involved in the child maltreatment cases as noted in chapter 3. Since the 1970s, many child welfare agencies have begun programs for the children and families involved in sexual abuse cases. The resources available to the family differ to some degree as to whether the child's sexual abuse has been an act of incest or by a stranger.

F. Programs and Services Programs and services available for families with child sexual abuse often depend upon the identification of the abuser. If the abuser is a member of the family, there are specific programs and services in most communities to aid both the child and family through this process. If the abuser is a stranger, there are generally fewer supports available for the child and/or family as this case is seen as more of a criminal process where the focus is centered on the perpetrator rather than on treatment of the child.

Phase III: Plan and Contract for Intervention with All Systems   As in cases involving physical abuse, the planning and contracting phase of the model would include the involvement of all the client systems in setting goals. Therefore, planning and contracting with these systems requires that the social worker be able to set clear priorities and address one problem area at a time. Involving the client in this process is critical to maintaining cooperation and safeguarding the client's right to self-determination. The client can then feel a sense of accomplishment as goals are achieved and new skills are mastered.

A. Case Review and Coordination Meeting Reviewing the case situation and treatment plan with all those involved in the case is a necessary condition for all child welfare cases, but especially in an abusive situation. Ensuring that all those involved understand the intervention approach and are on-board with the process is critical to success. As the primary social worker, you need to be sure that any person involved in the process does not have their own hidden agenda that can affect the outcome of the case.

B. Involve Family in Planning Process It is important to remember that sexual abuse cases, unlike many other cases in child welfare, often involve multi-problem families experiencing serious, long-term issues that have created a high level of dysfunction within the family system. It will be normal for you as the child welfare social worker to feel somewhat overwhelmed by the numerous problem areas that might need to be addressed. Therefore, it is important to begin by involving the client in prioritizing what changes need to be accomplished first and what goal can be attached to it.

After the presenting problem is established, the next step in this phase of the model would be to list the other problems that would need to be addressed in order of priority. Again, it would be important to elicit the cooperation of the client in prioritizing the remaining problems by focusing on each of the environmental systems that should be targeted for change. With each problem a corresponding goal would be negotiated with the client that would reflect the desired outcome of the intervention. For example, if a client is depressed as the result of having been abandoned by a spouse and is lacking social supports, the goal might be to assist the client in establishing a support system to help the client to deal with the feelings of isolation they might have.

In the case of Mandy, the first problem needing attention would likely be the temporary placement of Mandy while the case is being investigated and heard by the court. In most situations involving sexual abuse, the perpetrator might be incarcerated or ordered by the court to leave the home so the child might be able to return with some assurance of safety. In arranging Mandy's return home, the mother and other family members residing in the home would need to concur with this plan. If not, then the first priority might be to locate another possible placement for her until it is decided if reunification is a realistic goal.

Moving Toward the Implementation Phase

In order for an intervention to be effective in achieving desired outcomes, several factors must be taken into consideration. First of all, the intervention approach must match the corresponding problem area and address the appropriate system targeted for change. The client must be able to understand the relationship of the intervention to the goals and be in agreement with the overall plan. This undoubtedly will enhance the level of investment the client might have in the plan and their willingness to follow through with it.

When considering an intervention for a particular client it is also important to be aware of the skills and strengths that the client has, and help match the tasks formulated with the client to utilizing their skills and strengths. For example, if you as a social worker have referred an adolescent client to participate in a management training program and they are not able to read well, you are obviously setting them up to fail in accomplishing the goal of the intervention. Additionally, in formulating tasks for clients it is important to plan with them their involvement and immediately address any concerns they might have in performing the tasks. Other factors to consider when selecting tasks for interventions are: age of the client, developmental level, physical condition, transportation barriers, and other resources the client might need to accomplish the tasks.

With regard to developing an intervention for Mandy, the social worker first addresses a plan that would correspond with the problem of locating a temporary placement for her outside the home. If it is learned in the assessment phase that Mandy has an aunt and uncle who live in the same city and who have maintained reasonable contact with the family over a period of time, then it would be appropriate to evaluate them as a possible placement alternative. The worker would first determine if Mandy is receptive to this idea, then contact would be made with the aunt and uncle to determine if they would be in agreement as well. The next step would be to follow through with the mandates of the agency or court in order to finalize the placement plans.

C. Contract with Family and Support Services for Their Roles in Implementing Plan
In tandem with the process of matching interventions with problem areas, goals would also be set for each of the problem areas needing attention. A goal not only relates to a specific problem area, but it also is the desired outcome of the corresponding intervention. For example, with Mandy the intervention would be designed to accomplish the ultimate goal of reunification. Goals must be meaningful to a client and he or she must view the achievement of the goals as having some beneficial and positive results.

Goals are designed to facilitate the client's sense of success, not failure. Success in reaching a goal is largely determined by the kind of goal agreed upon and the methods used for accomplishment. "Beginning where the client is" is a fundamental rule of social work practice and a critical one to follow in setting goals. A client's motivation can be enhanced by the setting of short-term goals that are meaningful to them and play on their individual strengths. They will then view the goals as having some beneficial results. It is much more prudent for the social worker to agree with what the client wants to change rather than tell them what to change, which is contrary to the value of client self-determination. In child abuse cases, we as child welfare social workers may want to give the parents of a client directions for changing their situation, but unless the client agrees with these changes and has a role in deciding how they will come about, the intervention will not be successful.

❖ **HIGHLIGHT 7.18   Goal Guidelines**

---

1. Goals should be defined in specific terms rather than general terms. The purpose for setting the goals needs to be explained clearly to the client to encourage maximum participation.
2. Goals should specify changes to be accomplished and should be measurable.
3. Goals must be realistic and achievable. They should take into consideration the ability and motivation of the client to accomplish them.
4. Setting short-term positive subgoals directed toward the achievement of a larger goal can be useful in situations where goal attainment is not possible for a lengthy period of time.
5. Goals should be ranked and should correspond with the problems that have been prioritized by the client. Hepworth and Larsen (1993).

Highlight 7.18 provides guidelines that are useful to follow in setting goals.

After goals have been sufficiently established between the worker and client, the next step would be to negotiate a contract with the client, either written or verbal. When establishing verbal contracts the terms should be recorded in the case record for documentation purposes. Just as goals can change over the course of a social worker's involvement with a client, contracts can also change. Whenever a contract is initially developed, and when it is renegotiated at any time during the helping process, it is important for the social worker and client to be mutually involved in this process and agree on the terms stipulated.

Highlight 7.19 is an example of the process of negotiating a contract with Mandy's mother where the goal of reunification has been established.

Phase IV: Implementation of Plan   *A. Continued Implementation of Interviewing Skills and Practice Techniques* The interviewing skills you continue through the implementation process are similar to those utilized in the relationship phase. You must continue to have empathy, warmth, genuineness, positive regard, and be an empowering force for the child and family members. This phase often entails further treatment from an outside agency, as cases involving child sexual abuse are complex and fragmented by the issues.

Because the protection of the child and prevention of further abuse is a priority, the empowering will be focused on the child and the nonabusing parent. As noted earlier, in cases of incest the nonabusing parent is often more passive in nature and needs to be empowered and strengthened to protect the child. The practice techniques can become very complicated if the goal is reunification of the family. There will be legal as well as intense treatment issues to be addressed with the abusing family member. These may be dealt with by

---

❖ **HIGHLIGHT 7.19   Contract Negotiating**

Ellen: We've discussed the fact that Mandy would like to return home, and you would like to have her home as soon as possible.

Mrs. N: Yes, I really feel she needs to be here. We all miss her very much; Mark and Jennifer are always wanting to know when she'll be home.

Ellen: I know this has been very traumatic for them as well. Before Mandy comes home I would like for us to put in writing some of the problems that you have decided you need some help with. How do you feel about that?

Mrs. N: That would be okay.

Ellen: What I am suggesting is that we develop a contract, which we would both sign, that outlines exactly what you want to accomplish in terms of resolving some of the problems you've been experiencing, and how you are going to do this, with my assistance.

Mrs. N: Okay, I'm willing to do that.

Ellen: So, as we've discussed the various problems, what have been your thoughts regarding this most pressing problem that you would like to address first?

Mrs. N: Well, I really need to decide what to do about my marriage. I really believe I want a divorce after what my husband has done to Mandy. Can you help me with that?

Ellen: Yes, I believe so. I'll refer you to someone who does divorce counseling, and I'll also refer you to an attorney who can inform you of the legalities involved.

Mrs. N: Thank you. I really appreciate your help.

Ellen: We'll make this a part of our contract, along with the other things you want to work on, and try to focus on one or two tasks at a time.

Mrs. N: Okay, I really have a lot that I'm dealing with right now.

Ellen: Yes, you do. Would you like to talk about some of the other difficulties you've been having and how they might be resolved?

---

the child welfare social worker or in conjunction with another social worker who has responsibility with the court system. The collaboration between all the systems involved in a sexual abuse case is critical to improving the family situation.

Many of the skills and techniques you will use with the child will be based on building their self-esteem and empowering them to protect themselves. Depending upon the age of the child, it will be important to utilize play therapy or game therapy to help in allowing children to express their anger toward the abuser. Children's anxiety will also be high and there are many different methods for reducing anxiety within children who have been sexually abused. One of these is the use of the technique called "Pink Elephant" (Berg, 1994). Highlight 7.20 is an example of this cognitive thought stopping process.

The purpose of this exercise is to give, as Berg states, "the child a secret weapon" (p. 186). This will help them experience their anxiety with more of a sense of control.

❖ HIGHLIGHT 7.20   Pink Elephant

Ellen: Let's talk about those times when you feel afraid or anxious.

Mandy: Well, sometimes I feel that way when I am walking down the hall at school and a large group of boys are walking toward me. I don't know what I think will happen, but I just want to become invisible.

Ellen: Let's try something the next time this happens. I want you to picture a big pink elephant floating above these boys' heads and it drops down on them. Or imagine that they are all bald and how funny they look. Let's try this and let me know if that has caused you to feel any differently when you see them next time.

Mandy: Okay, I'll give it a try.

B. Continuing Coordination of Services As in child maltreatment, a major part of the implementation of the treatment plan is to continue to coordinate those services that are being provided to the child and family. As was noted earlier, this coordination is critical for the success of the intervention. Because most sexual abuse cases require both short-term and long-term intervention, your ability to work collaboratively with outside service providers over a longer period of time will be essential. We have mentioned that part of your role will be to help decide with the family on whether reunification is the goal. If reunification of all family members does become one of the goals, then you will need to work with the services being provided the abuser as well as the victim.

C. Support and Empowerment of Child and Family Supporting and empowering a family embroiled in sexual abuse may seem incongruent; however, you will find that often times there are nonabusing members of the family who can ensure the protection of the child if they are empowered to take responsibility. This is often the case in the incest relationship between a daughter and father when the mother is willing to do what is necessary to protect her child.

Because the recidivism rate in child sexual abuse cases tends to be very high, it becomes critical that we as child welfare social workers expend an inordinate amount of time in empowering the child and other members of the family in order to not allow the abuse to reoccur. Your focus on empowerment needs to begin from the start with a child sexual abuse case, in particular in order to bring, as mentioned, some control into the lives of this family.

You may also find that you will be the only support a child has initially as other family members beside the abuser may be in denial and angry at the child for telling this secret. It will be your responsibility to decide whether the child can best receive the support they need from within their home or outside their home. Supporting the nonabusing parent to accept the reality of the situation and make tough decisions will also be a critical part of your tasks.

D. Identification of Barriers and Resolution The barriers that can often arise in a child sexual abuse case include the strong emotional reactions that all family members can experience (denial, guilt, anger, blame). These emotions are best handled by normalizing their existence. Assuring family members that these are feelings that are all a part of the process of healing is helpful. The focus is on the healing and strength-building capabilities of the family.

Sometimes the barriers in child sexual abuse situations can be the extended family who refuses to believe the allegations and harasses the child and nonabusing parent to drop the claims. The role of the social worker in these cases is to support the child and nonabusing family members by helping them role play through how they can respond to these pressures.

E. Monitoring of Services and Plan A continued monitoring of services and the plan is critical for the protection of the child and their future. In a child sexual abuse case, very often the child is removed from the home or the perpetrator (in the cases of incest) is removed for the child's protection. A careful monitoring of the services being provided and the intervention plan is needed in order to continue to ensure the protection of the child and their placement in a stable home environment through reunification or adoption. Not following through intensively in child sexual abuse cases like in other child maltreatment cases can lead to the perpetrator returning to the home too soon or the child being left in out-of-home placement indefinitely.

Phase V: Evaluate Outcomes and Terminate Services *A. Evaluate Outcomes* The evaluation of outcomes in a child sexual abuse case involves more than only evaluating the safety of the child. It involves evaluating the impact the intervention has had on all family members (especially in cases of incest) and what interventions need to continue. As mentioned earlier, child sexual abuse cases are not necessarily ones that can improve with brief treatment, but require more extensive types of intervention both for the child, the family, and in many cases the perpetrator. Understanding that you as the child welfare social worker may not be able to provide all these services and will need to ensure that these services continue in some manner with your coordination will be part of the skill you bring to providing successful outcomes.

B. Terminate Services Termination of services in these types of child welfare cases is a difficult process for both the child, family, and social worker. Depending upon the outcome of the case and the circumstances in which the sexual abuse occurred, the child may have formed an attachment to the child welfare social worker based on acceptance and support through the stressful process of discovery and healing. It will be important for you to recognize this attachment and find ways to empower the nonabusing parent in giving the same types of support and acceptance. In cases where the child may not return to the home, it will be equally difficult for you to let go of your involvement with the child as you may be their only tie with their former family. Careful and planned placement of sexually abused children is important for their success in adapting to a new family. Although you may not continue to intervene with the child after a certain length of time, it will be important for you to maintain follow-up contact to ensure they are receiving the services and planned care needed. The termination of your work as the protective service worker only signals the beginning of the work to be done in the adoption process.

Phase VI: Follow Up from a Multisystemic Perspective *A. Family* As has been noted in previous chapters, follow up is a process by which the social worker can assess the present situation of the family as well as how they are continuing to be successful from their work with the child welfare system. In cases of child sexual abuse, it is critical that families be assessed on a regular follow-up basis to ensure that there are no further issues for the child if the child is living in the home. In these cases, it is not simply a matter of seeing if an intervention has continued to work, but it is for the ongoing protection of the child.

In cases where the child may have been removed and not returned to the family, continuous follow up on how the child is progressing and what permanent family plans are being considered is a crucial part of your work. If out-of-home placements are now going to be maximally set at 12 months, with states mandated to utilize adoption procedures after this point, then it is critical that the primary social worker has an ongoing relationship with the child, as well as the family, as this time period nears. If the changes needed to reunite the family have not been successful, the child welfare social worker will need to begin the process of termination of parental rights and preparation of the child for a new home and family.

B. Community Follow up in the community is about ensuring the provision and access to services needed in the community that aid children and families with these difficulties. Are there groups for the sexually abused child and their family? Are there provisions for treatment of perpetrators regardless of the legal consequences so that their abuse will not occur again? Do children have a safe outlet for sharing these types of problems that they know are readily available?

Education is another key element in the community prevention of child sexual abuse. Teaching children to inform responsible adults when something "bad" happens, as well as ensuring that they understand the meaning of "bad," is part of the responsibility of the child welfare worker. Training in schools, churches, and other social institutions on signs of sexual abuse in children is also a step you can take to help prevent its occurrence.

C. Programs and Services As in follow up related to the community, feedback to the services and programs utilized in these case situations is critical to providing the best care possible for the child and family. Ensuring that these services exist is another task you will undertake in your responsibilities. This is often accomplished through meeting as a network of social service representatives and planning the services needed within your community.

D. Policy You as the child welfare social worker will be continually asking yourself as you deal with these types of cases if the policies in place are helpful for the child and family or harmful. It is your responsibility as a professional social worker to bring into action effective policies that address the issues of child sexual abuse. Always be sensitive to those political parties and politicians who are sensitive to these child welfare areas. Campaign for preventive education programs in your schools and other institutions in the community. Work with the police and court systems to ensure that the policies in place for these situations aid one another and do not conflict.

SUMMARY

Chapter 7 has provided an overview of cases involving child sexual abuse. This type of maltreatment situation differs in many aspects from physical child abuse or neglect. The chapter has pointed out how brief treatment and/or family-based care is often the only intervention chosen for these situations and the least likely to be effective. Factors related to the relationship of the child to the abuser and the family dynamics that exist are critical aspects of utilizing the SWPIP intervention model. These dynamics, regardless of cultural background, often have similarities in child sexual abuse families. Being aware of these similarities, as well as the differences, enables you to assess the situation from a more objective viewpoint. Working with children and adolescents who have been sexually abused requires skills that aid the child in discussing the abuse and being able to express their feelings. Whether through verbal expression, play therapy, or creative arts, treatment with the child needs to focus on their emotional expression of hurt and their power to overcome this pain.

QUESTIONS FOR DISCUSSION

1. Discuss the ways in which sexual abuse is different emotionally from physical abuse.

2. Describe your personal response to child sexual abuse and how these responses can affect your intervention.

3. How does assessment in the SWPIP model of practice with sexually abusive families deal with the assessment of the perpetrator?

4. Describe how a community project might be developed that could prevent child abuse.

5. When are children at a higher risk of sexual abuse and why?

6. What role does empowerment play in preventing sexual abuse on children? Give an example of an empowerment program for children.

8

■

Adolescent Sexuality and Pregnancy

Maria is a 16-year-old high school junior whose Hispanic-American family has lived in Arizona for many generations. Over the past year she has been experiencing a number of problems typically associated with adolescence. More recently, Maria has been rejecting the control that her parents have maintained over her and is constantly struggling to be more independent. She is constantly arguing with her mother, and her father has assumed a more passive role when conflicts have arisen. She has been spending a great deal of time with her boyfriend of 6 months, who is also of Hispanic-American heritage. Raphael began pressuring Maria to have sex with him approximately 3 months after they started dating. When she ultimately agreed, the two began to engage in sexual behavior on a regular basis until Maria became pregnant. She then told her parents and they immediately demanded that Maria and Raphael marry, totally rejecting the idea of abortion due to the fact that they are Catholic. Adoption was not a

(Continued)

preferred alternative because they did not have the financial resources to pay for medical care or maternity home placement until the child's birth. Therefore, Maria was referred to a social worker with Children's Home Society by her school counselor, after having made the decision to keep the baby and care for it independently if necessary.

INTRODUCTION

Adolescent sexuality and pregnancy are critical issues in the United States. Although the numbers of teenage births have diminished as a result of abortions and miscarriages, the numbers of pregnancies have not. Recent statistics indicate that there are approximately 518,000 births for women under the age of 19 and around 1 million pregnancies a year (Sugland, Manlove, & Romano, 1997). There are many complex issues that surround teenage pregnancy, beginning with the reasons some teenagers are more likely to become pregnant than others; however, the real purpose of child welfare services related to teenage sexuality is the prevention of pregnancy (Sugland, Manlove, & Romano, 1997). This is not an easy course of intervention, as only half of the teenagers in the United States engaged in sexual activity utilize a form of birth control (Kadushin & Martin, 1987). Additionally, the type of birth control a teenage couple might utilize is generally less reliable than what might be available. The reasons for this are the lack of supports to obtain reliable birth control and the adolescent belief that nothing will happen to her or him (Strauss & Clarke, 1992).

DEFINING CONCERNS
IN TEENAGE PREGNANCY

Teenage pregnancy is defined as a pregnancy of a woman between the ages of 13 and 19, although child welfare is generally only concerned about those children under the age of 18. This age group is not the only group for which pregnancy occurs. Numerous children under the age of 13 become pregnant each year in the United States and the age at which pregnancy can occur has been dropping (Sugland, Manlove, & Romano, 1997). The focus of concern in all these cases involves not only the young mother and father who become expectant parents, but also the child to be born. The role of the child welfare social worker in pregnancy situations for adolescents and children under the age of 18 is often affected by the age of the adolescent, family income, and ethno-racial background. The younger the age of the child, the more likely a child welfare worker will become involved. This is because younger births (ages 14 and under) are more likely to involve physical risk and/or issues surrounding the biological father of the child, such as incest.

The major issues to deal with when working with a pregnant adolescent is aiding her in the decision-making process concerning whether or not to carry the pregnancy to term, the role of the expectant father, counseling with this decision, and if carrying to term, determining whether or not to parent the child or to adopt. Specific issues to be dealt with in each case where the pregnancy is carried to term include the ability of the adolescent to care for the child, the financial resources available, the continued education of the adolescent, counseling issues related to adoption if the child is adopted, and follow up in helping the adolescent with issues of parenting, relationships, and birth control.

Causes of Adolescent Pregnancy

One of the most well-received studies on adolescent pregnancy done by Furstenberg, Brooks-Gunn, and Chase-Lansdale (1989) concluded that the pregnancy of an adolescent was not purposeful but rather due to their lack of attention to the consequences. Additional researchers have found that the vision adolescents may have of their future, based on a negative present situation, can lead to earlier pregnancies (Cervera, 1993). Statistics have also shown that lower-income adolescents tend to have higher rates of births than upper-income adolescents. Race and ethnicity also play into the factors that predict births to unwed mothers. Statistics indicate that per 1,000 females are 15–19, 51 Caucasians, 84.4 Native-Americans, and 112.4 African-Americans gave birth during the years of the studies (Children's Defense Fund, 1994). The differences in these statistics are as likely to be related to income, education, and living conditions as they are to racial characteristics.

What has also changed in the area of adolescent pregnancies are the number of adolescents choosing to keep their children. At this time only 5 percent of adolescents who give birth to their children give them up for adoption. These statistics reflect a change in philosophical and ideological views of single parents and their children. There is more acceptance now of this type of family situation, and in certain cultures keeping the child is seen as the only appropriate way of handling an unmarried mother and her child.

There are many factors involved in the large numbers of teenage pregnancy. The Child Welfare League of America (1996) notes the following: "changes in society's reactions to adolescent sexual activity; limited opportunities for young people; shifts in societal mores and standards of behavior; influence of media exploitation of sexual behavior; alteration in family structures; and the results of poverty" (p. 3) have all had enormous effects on teens becoming more sexually active. The results of this increased sexual activity and subsequent births are increasing risks for sexual diseases and the development of children living in poverty or in homes without the resources needed to achieve their fullest potential.

Adolescents face many different developmental issues during these teen years. They are expected to behave as an adult but are not permitted to do adult activities, such as engaging in sexual behavior or drinking alcohol. Additionally, as our society has changed and family structures have changed, many teenagers come to view pregnancy as a way out of their home and into a more independent and glamorous life. Many preventive programs go beyond the basic sex education courses and look for ways to provide teenagers with hope and a means of obtaining a better life than they had previously experienced in order to encourage them to wait on pregnancy.

POLICIES

There have never been many specific policies designed for adolescent pregnancy. One reason for the lack of policies stems from the societal ideology that adolescents should not become pregnant, therefore policies and programs for them may promote their sexual activity. Perhaps the most common policies have been those that have affected the child's and family's legal rights. In 1968 the Supreme Court ruled that out-of-wedlock children had the same legal rights as those born within a marital situation. This decision led to progress in support, inheritance, welfare laws, custody, visitation, and adoption (Downs, Costin, & McFadden, 1996). The focus of these areas was to provide equity to all involved in an out-of-wedlock pregnancy.

Federal funding has been developed toward adolescent pregnancies and births in the areas of block grants to states for direct services. Medicaid, the Education for all Handicapped Children Act, vocational education funds, the Independent Living Initiative, and the Maternal and Child Health Block Grant, have now been incorporated into larger state block grants as part of these services. Despite these efforts, support for adolescent pregnancy services is very inadequate and is being affected even more by welfare reform (Child Welfare League of America, 1996).

PROCESSES AND PROCEDURES

Processes and procedures in working with adolescents involve preventive types of intervention as well as residual. While focus in the last 20 years has been primarily on the development of sex education to prevent pregnancy; however, this approach has not brought about the kind of change sought (Chilman, 1991). Programs that have begun to work with young children on self-esteem and positive goals for their futures appear to have more significant outcomes (Ooms & Herendeen, 1990). Programs focused on these issues are often initiated as part of a school curriculum.

The process of intervention with pregnant adolescents begins with the identification of the pregnancy. In the past, an adolescent would have little recourse in identifying herself as pregnant without consulting medical personnel; however, it is now easy to pick up home pregnancy tests that will give the results within a few minutes. How this type of medical progress has affected adolescent pregnancy has not been examined, but it may be an important factor in adolescents not having the support they need to either make good decisions about their pregnancies or to receive the support and medical care so needed in the stages of early pregnancy. There are many cases where adolescent pregnancies go unidentified for many months either because the adolescent is attempting to conceal the fact or because they themselves are in denial about the pregnancy. This lack of identification of pregnancy can affect the health of the infant and/or adolescent.

The other issue strongly affected by this lack of early identification or acknowledgment are the number of options the adolescent may have in making a decision. While some abortions are performed in later term, many states have policies that make this illegal. The result is the adolescent either makes a decision based on a lack of action or utilizes abortion procedures that are illegal and often very dangerous.

Once a determination of the pregnancy has been made the adolescent needs to make a decision as to the next step to take. At this point the support of the family members is a critical factor that needs emphasis by the child welfare social worker. The importance of support through this process regardless of what decision is made will have far-reaching effects on the adolescent's sense of self and subsequent life. The decision must be made by the adolescent and she should not be pressured or coerced into a decision (Child Welfare League of America, 1996).

There are basically three decisions the adolescent can make: (1) an abortion, (2) carrying the pregnancy to term and parenting, and (3) carrying the pregnancy to term and allowing for adoption. The father in the adolescent pregnancy situation needs to be given every opportunity to take part in this decision, if possible, and his legal rights need to be clearly laid out for him.

Once this decision has been made, there are numerous counseling areas to be covered depending upon the decision. These may include dealing with feelings about abortion, adoption, or parenting as a young person. Specific details of how the decision will be carried out also need to be worked through with the adolescent, as well as with the support systems she will have in place. Adequate medical care and other pregnancy services need to be arranged immediately to ensure the well-being of both the mother and baby.

SERVICES AND PROGRAMS

There are many services and different types of programs that can be utilized by the pregnant adolescent. Among these services are family planning, parenting classes, schools with special programs that provide for the continued education of the adolescent and day care for the infant, homes for pregnant teenagers, nutrition programs, independent living programs, employment programs, and financial assistance. However, if we consider that the main goal of a child welfare social worker is to prevent adolescent pregnancy, it is important to think about preventive types of services and programs that can be implemented in conjunction with other social service agencies and, if necessary, out of the box.

Preventive programs can take the form of sex education, but need to also include programs that aid adolescents in setting goals for themselves, establishing a sense of respect for themselves, and finding ways to achieve their goals. Independent living programs are one form of service that can be utilized by child welfare social workers to place adolescents out of a difficult home situation and give them new opportunities. These types of programs would not be effective without support. One idea is the use of independent living communities much like family foster care communities where adolescents in independent living situations are placed near one another in communities where they can receive support from one another and from agencies.

Other programs involve the utilization of the school system to provide access to social workers and resources to aid adolescents in receiving services easier and with less stigma. These in-house programs might concentrate on individual counseling, group or family intervention, career planning, and early training in parenting and life management skills.

SWPIP PRACTICE MODEL

Using the case of Maria at the beginning of the chapter, the protocols of the SWPIP model will be addressed in the subsequent section. The focus will be on providing a context within which a primary social worker may establish a practice continuum or process with the teenage parent, child, and parents of the teenager composing the client system.

A Theoretical Approach to Practice with Adolescents

Although a "treatment" approach to practice with pregnant teenagers will not be a focus in the majority of child welfare arenas, some knowledge of a cognitive-social learning theory perspective when working with adolescents can be beneficial in both the assessment and intervention phases of practice. In cognitive-behavioral approaches, certain problem behaviors on the part of the adolescent are targeted and specific cognitions related to the problematic behavior are identified since they function as stimuli in controlling the dysfunctional overt behaviors (Sundel & Sundel, 1993). The child welfare social worker would select appropriate techniques and use their creativity in devising ways of teaching the adolescent more adaptive behaviors to be used in daily life.

Social learning theory draws on concepts from a variety of psychological sources, and theoretical concepts are tested empirically. Essential theoretical constructs include: that behavior is controlled by its consequences and antecedent discriminative stimuli, that complex behavior patterns are learned through imitation of observed models, and that learning and performance of behaviors are commonly mediated by cognitive processes (Zarb, 1992). Particular emphasis is placed on the influence of reinforcement contingencies that occur and shape different aspects of an adolescent's personality through social conditioning. Social conditioning is influenced by the parents' childrearing practices, cultural and social expectations of family and peers, and the adolescent's exposure to influential models (i.e., parental models initially, then later on peer models) (Sundel & Sundel, 1993).

The role of families is central in social work with the pregnant teenager and is consistent with a social-learning perspective. Parenting practices and parent role models shape the personality development of the adolescent. Additionally, the family provides the conditions that contribute to effective socialization and is the primary system to which the adolescent refers for a variety of dependency needs. Therefore, a primary focus of the practice process should be on building family support while, at the same time, empowering the teenager to attain specific goals and objectives that have been mutually negotiated between the worker and the adolescent.

Phase I: Establish an Immediate Relationship with the Child and Family Based on Warmth, Genuineness, Empathy, Positive Regard, and Empowerment A collaborative and positive working relationship is established between the child welfare worker, the adolescent, and the family through a high level of trust and mutual respect. Throughout the relationship the adolescent is encouraged to try out newly learned behaviors in her day-to-day life with the anticipation that they will have more rewarding consequences. The significance of the development of new behaviors will be discussed later as a factor in helping the adolescent to refrain from reexperiencing the trauma of an unplanned pregnancy later.

In working with teenage parents, or teenage pregnancy is general, it is first imperative for the child welfare social worker to have a significant level of knowledge about the various factors that are involved in the issues of teenage pregnancy (i.e., economic, psychological, educational, etc.). Knowledge of the precipitating reasons for an adolescent becoming pregnant is not necessarily critical to the establishment of a meaningful worker-client relationship, nor is it crucial to the success of the practice process. Most studies show that the majority of teenagers become parents unwittingly, and the reasons they formulate for wanting to have the child do not necessarily explain why the pregnancy initially occurred (Sugland, Manlove, & Romano, 1997). The fact is that teenagers become pregnant for many different reasons, not least of which is their lack of use of contraceptives.

A nonjudgmental attitude relating to the adolescent's sexual behavior or reasons for not pursuing a particular course of action in relation to the pregnancy is an integral component of the professional relationship. The establishment of trust between the social worker and adolescent can be jeopardized if the adolescent perceives the social worker as being negative or judgmental toward her situation. In the beginning it is advisable to encourage the adolescent to discuss her feelings concerning being pregnant and becoming a mother. As she begins to open up, the communication of empathy and positive regard for her and the feelings she might be expressing would be critical to this process. An adolescent is likely to experience a need to discuss these feelings as she struggles to resolve them in a way that will enhance her ability to make a number of pressing decisions. Most pressing is the need to make plans about the pregnancy. Understanding the adolescent's possible feelings including guilt, embarrassment, or shame will affect how you aid her in decision making.

During this phase of the model it is not only important for the adolescent to discuss her feelings about the pregnancy, but it is important that the social worker encourage her to talk about her feelings concerning the father of the child. The communication of acceptance of these feelings through the use of open-ended questions and good attending behaviors (i.e., regular eye contact, appropriate body language, frequent empathic responses) is an integral part of this process, in order to facilitate openness and spontaneity.

The theoretical statement about the associations between adolescent pregnancy and child abuse and neglect is referred to widely in the literature on this subject. Family instability characterized by physical abuse, emotional deprivation, rejection, and a lack of parental control are all common elements of family systems in which teen pregnancy often occurs (Sugland, Manlove, & Romano, 1997). Therefore, it is important to explore the adolescent's feelings about her family, particularly in relation to their attitudes and feelings surrounding the pregnancy. In many cases the teenager experiences rejection by the parents immediately after the pregnancy is disclosed, and frequently she is left to resolve the issues surrounding the pregnancy without family support. This can further exacerbate feelings of guilt, inadequacy, and depression regarding her situation.

Utilizing the preceding case scenario, Highlight 8.1 shows the interaction between the child welfare worker and Maria and demonstrates the first phase of the model in which attempts are made to establish a relationship with the adolescent.

During this initial contact the focus is on the relationship and the establishment of trust between social worker and adolescent. It is particularly important not to push the teenager into the position of making some sort of preliminary decision about the pregnancy and to simply normalize what she might be experiencing emotionally. It would be appropriate to encourage her to postpone any decision making until the social worker has made an effort to assist in the development of a plan in collaboration with the family and the teenager.

Before any further contact is made with the adolescent, the social worker needs to contact the family and schedule a face-to-face visit with the

❖ HIGHLIGHT 8.1 Establishing a Relationship with the Adolescent

Ellen: Hello, Maria. My name is Ellen Bowman and I am a social worker with Children's Home Society. I've been asked by your guidance counselor, Ms. Cook, to come talk with you and see if I might be of some assistance to you. We provide a variety of services to young women who are experiencing an unplanned pregnancy.

Maria: Yes, she told me you would be coming.

Ellen: You aren't required to talk with me if you don't want to. Today I thought I would just stop by to introduce myself and tell you a little about our program. I know you've been dealing with a lot lately; Ms. Cook told me you were struggling with a lot of decisions right now. You must be feeling quite confused.

Maria: Yeah, I guess so. Everyone keeps giving me advice and telling me what I "should" do. I just know that I don't want to have an abortion; I really want to keep the baby. I just don't think I can handle getting married.

Ellen: I can understand how you must feel about that. It must seem unfair at times that you have to be faced with so many major decisions at such an early stage of your life.

Maria: Yeah, my parents expect me to know the right thing to do and do it without question.

Ellen: We are able to provide counseling services not only for the expectant mother, but for the entire family as well to help them be a little more supportive. Perhaps this is something that would benefit your parents. Would you like to tell me a little about them and how they're reacting to the pregnancy?

Maria: Yes, well, they're not at all happy about it. They really think Raphael and I need to get married as soon as possible so the baby won't be born illegitimate. But he can't drop out of school right now, and his family isn't able to help us financially. Besides, he really doesn't want to get married anyway, and I'm not sure that I do either.

Ellen: Marriage can be a scary thing to someone your age. Tell me, how do you feel about the idea of being a mother?

Maria: I feel kind of scared. I'm not sure I know how to take care of a small baby. (encourage adolescent to expand on this more).

Ellen: Do you think it might be helpful if I came back in a few days to talk about this a little more? Perhaps I could help you sort through some of the confusion you're having and make a decision that will include the support of your family. Would you mind if I talk with your parents to hear their side of this situation?

Maria: Fine, if you think it'll do any good.

Ellen: We'll see. You seem like such a sensitive, mature young lady. Why don't you call me in a couple of days so that we can schedule another time to meet. Would that be agreeable with you? In the interim I'll speak to your parents to see how they might need some assistance in helping you.

Maria: Okay, that sounds fine. I'll call you next week.

parent(s) with the adolescent's knowledge and permission. Although certain negative attitudes might exist in relation to the pregnancy, it is important to remember that the family remains a central resource for meeting both material and emotional needs. Many adolescents are living with their families when they become pregnant. Like their nonpregnant counterparts, they often turn to them for support and approval. When this is not possible, the social worker needs to seek out support resources for the adolescent so they do not become completely isolated and disenfranchised.

Satisfactory negotiation around the issues that accompany teen pregnancy may be complicated in instances where families face long-standing difficulties. Rather than work toward a successful resolution, the family may simply use these issues as a new battleground for playing out chronic family conflicts (Kadushin & Martin, 1988). At the time of the initial contact it would be important to respond to the parents with empathy and positive regard. Regardless of what their attitudes might be with regard to the pregnancy, it is important to communicate a sense of understanding about what they might be going through as well. The pain that they may be experiencing for their daughter is likely to create responses that are largely based on emotion, therefore a genuine, positive approach would be most beneficial to the relationship.

In the initial contact with an adolescent's family it is appropriate to begin the meeting with a brief statement about the agency's purpose and the role of a social worker in working with pregnant adolescents. The information should be presented within the multisystemic framework of practice, emphasizing the social work perspective of working with all the appropriate client systems in an effort to empower an individual to improve their level of functioning. In an effort to engage the family and begin the establishment of a positive working relationship, attempts should be made to encourage honest, open communication of their feelings regarding the pregnancy. As this process is taking place, the worker should focus on the positive aspects of the situation and reinforce the strengths that are observed. Regardless of anger or hurt a family may be experiencing, the social worker must remember that the focus of the helping process is on the strengths, abilities, and capacities of each person rather than on their weaknesses or deficits. Viewing the family and adolescent from a position of admiration and respect helps the worker to validate their feelings and engage them in a collaborative effort in support of the adolescent. In many instances it becomes highly beneficial for both the teenager and her parents to then become involved in a joint planning process.

Phase II: Assess the Situation Briefly and Thoroughly Based on the Following Systems   It is important to emphasize the fact that the reasons for a teenager becoming pregnant are not significant to the assessment or intervention phases of the practice process. Many teenage girls who become pregnant are attempting to fill a sense of emptiness, to resolve a dependency conflict with a parent, to find an excuse to leave home, or to achieve the normal developmental stage of individuation. Nevertheless, it is important to understand that the adolescent's cognitive status influences behavior in that she has a greater difficulty than adults in delaying gratification and controlling her internal processes. Trad (1994) found that pregnant adolescents have higher ratings of external locus of control than nonpregnant adolescents.

A. Adolescent A thorough and accurate assessment of the adolescent and her situation is critical to the development of a contract and intervention plan. The assessment process involves an exploration of problems and barriers, strengths and resources, developmental level and life transitions, and various systems that impinge on her circumstances.

Knowledge of the adolescent's physical and emotional developmental levels, and if they are within the normal range, is an integral part of the assessment process. This knowledge helps to form the basis for the interventions that the social worker formulates with the adolescent and is significant in determining whether or not she might be able to attain realistic goals and objectives. For a social worker to assist an adolescent in establishing goals that she might not have the physical or emotional capacity to attain might exacerbate feelings of inadequacy and failure.

"Beginning where the client is" is particularly important in relation to the prioritization of problems that need to be addressed. Therefore, it would be helpful to ask the teenager to initially list three problems she feels need to be dealt with immediately, and of these three establish a "presenting problem" that seems to be the most pressing at the time. If she has difficulty focusing on three problem areas, the technique of brainstorming can be used, where the social worker and the adolescent mutually focus efforts on generating a broad range of possible problems created by her pregnancy. This technique is discussed more thoroughly in the intervention phase of the model.

When discussing problems that need to be addressed it would also be important to look at the adolescent's pattern of coping and question her about previous methods of coping with problems that she has experienced in the past. The differentiation between dysfunctional coping patterns and those that have been more helpful to the adolescent would be significant information to note during the assessment. Those dysfunctional coping patterns that the adolescent continues to use in her current situation should be targeted for change, and discussing the adaptation of more productive coping methods needs to be part of the goals for intervention.

While adolescents nominally understand the relationship between sexual activity without contraception and the risk of pregnancy, their cognitive orientation often prevents them from grasping the full implications of this behavior. Instead, the adolescent's cognitive disposition is geared to exploration and risk. As a result, many pregnant teens engage in problematic behaviors that reoccur throughout adolescence, and sometimes into adulthood. Therefore, assessment should also focus on the pattern of irrational thoughts and feelings that usually contribute to these behaviors. Teenagers can often engage in dysfunctional and self-defeating thoughts and misconceptions that impair personal functioning. In order for there to be constructive change in problematic behavior it is important for the social worker to assist the adolescent in identifying the pattern of unrealistic thoughts that might have led to her becoming pregnant. Part of the intervention process would focus on assisting her in replacing these unrealistic thoughts with beliefs and behaviors that are aligned with reality and lead to enhanced functioning. Furthermore, this assists the adolescent in developing an internal locus of control which, in turn, helps them to exert more external control over environmental influences that have previously controlled them.

Highlights 8.2 and 8.3 are examples of how irrational beliefs contributed to problematic behavior in the case of Maria.

It is clear that Maria is immobilized by her perceived inability to change the pattern of thinking that contributes to problematic behavior in a number of areas of her life. As a result, she has developed a form of learned helplessness that adolescents often experience when they believe that outcome is independent of their actions. As compared to nonpregnant teenagers who are labeled "resilient" due to their ability to maintain an internal locus of control over environmental influences, pregnant teenagers believe they have no internal controls. Thus, this attitude of learned helplessness, compounded by rapid developmental change and a sense of hopelessness about the future, creates the

---

❖ HIGHLIGHT 8.2   Identifying Irrational Beliefs

Maria has been dating Raphael for 6 months and firmly believes that they are in love. As they have become increasingly involved in communicating affection toward one another, Raphael has put more pressure on Maria to have sexual intercourse. Maria has never had sex before and is somewhat fearful and anxious about the possibility. She begins to think that she might lose Raphael if she does not agree to have sex with him. She also is afraid that he might think she does not love him, or that she is "odd" or "uncool" and completely out of touch with the times. She is embarrassed to mention the use of a condom and believes that it is his responsibility to do so.

❖ HIGHLIGHT 8.3   Irrational Thoughts or Beliefs

1. She is not capable of maintaining Raphael's interest in her without having sex with him.
2. She must be "odd" or "uncool" if she doesn't have sex as it is expected by everyone and everyone is doing it.
3. She is not able to talk with Raphael about the use of condoms as she doesn't know what to say and he might think that she is foolish.

manifestation of a number of deficits (Trad, 1994). The perceived lack of control further exacerbates the pattern of irrational thoughts and beliefs that develop and creates a cyclical pattern of problematic behavior. Maria's involvement in planning and making choices will empower her behavior.

B. Nuclear Family The relationship between parent and adolescent can influence whether the teenager will engage in sexual activity. Parents who are rejecting or neglectful may unknowingly influence the teenager to engage in sexual behavior in search of love and nurturance. Later, after becoming pregnant, the adolescent may separate from the family, both physically and emotionally, due to the underlying feelings of rejection. Adolescents who become pregnant have also been found to come from homes marked by familial discord more frequently than those who do not become pregnant (Hertz, 1977).

The mother-daughter relationship is particularly significant with regard to the teenager's pregnancy. Adaptive maturation requires the teenager to successfully differentiate from her mother; however, this can be problematic when the relationship with the mother is conflicted. This information needs to be considered while formulating an assessment.

In assessing the nuclear family of the adolescent, the focus of the assessment is initially centered on: (1) the material needs of the adolescent combined with the willingness and capacity of the family to assist with these needs; and (2) the emotional needs of the adolescent with regard to the willingness and capacity of the family in helping to provide these needs as well. Should the nuclear family not be available to assist in meeting some or all of the needs, the social worker must look to extended family members or other support systems who have been actively involved in parenting the adolescent to serve as a resource. In this case the worker would follow the same assessment process as she or he would follow in assessing the nuclear family.

In relation to the material needs of a pregnant teenager, these will largely be determined by her decision regarding keeping the baby or placing the baby for adoption. Should she choose to keep and raise the child as a single parent, the level of assistance the family is able or willing to give is of paramount importance. Family members are frequently called upon to provide childcare or financial assistance for a day care program while the young mother works or attends school. Housing and transportation resources may also be needed for mother and child. Assistance with medical care should also be evaluated as a need in view of the extensive amount of medical services young children typically require. Will the child have access to a pediatrician for routine medical follow up? Are there medical problems that will require treatment from a specialist? Will these medical providers accept the financial plan provided by the adolescent, either through her family or through public assistance? All of these factors are integral components of the assessment process.

In relation to the emotional needs, the overall relationship of the family members to the pregnant teen needs to be evaluated. Adolescents typically refer to family members who have held most of the responsibilities for parenting them to provide emotional support. Therefore, it would be important to determine which family member(s) have assumed primary responsibility for this role. Would it be the mother, father, maternal or paternal grandparent, aunt, or uncle? It would also be important to assess their willingness and capacity for continuing to provide support during this extremely difficult time. While they might have assumed much of the responsibility in raising the adolescent and caring for her emotional needs, they might not be supportive of her under the current circumstances. Other questions to ask in assessing emotional support of family members would be: What are the bonds of affection within the family? How is affection communicated to the adolescent? and How is affection communicated to other family members?

Throughout the assessment process it is important for the social worker to use a strengths' approach and identify the strengths within the family system that will need to be considered when setting goals and objectives. While attempting to identify family strengths it is helpful to follow the following tenets:

1. An active role by the family members is extremely beneficial for enabling the adolescent to live a normal life, with or without her child.

2. Society needs to demonstrate concern for the needs of families who are providing assistance to members who are teenage parents.

3. Families themselves are the best informants regarding the needs of their children.

4. Family members have strengths that can be helpful to the social work process.

5. All human beings possess the inherent capacity to learn, grow, and change.

C. Extended Family Systems Several implications for practice with the family follow. These implications serve to guide the child welfare worker throughout the assessment process and beyond.

1. The relationship between the teenager and her family is an important factor in making the helping process work.

2. The family system is used to identify strengths in the adolescents' ability to care for her child, not problems.

3. The family members who want to provide assistance to the teenage parent are able to determine what they need and can communicate these needs to the social worker.

4. Family members providing assistance to a teenage parent should be provided as much information as possible regarding the needs of the adolescent and child.

5. Family and community strengths are used to acquire normal resources to assist in meeting the needs of the adolescent client.

Because the assessment process recognizes that families are systems and, therefore, complex and multifaceted, it is easy to identify strengths in all families. A unique feature of an assessment process from a strengths' approach is that *only* strengths are reinforced. Although problems within the client system are acknowledged, they are emphasized in the intervention process. The primary strengths identified are those that will assist the teenage parent in attaining a normal level of independence in caring for her needs and the needs of her child. It is this list of strengths and identified needs that set the stage for mutual objective setting.

In the case of Maria and Raphael, it would be important for the social worker to discuss the situation openly with both families to assess their level of support and identify strengths within both systems. Let's presume that the families are supportive of Maria keeping the child whether or not they marry. The social worker would focus on offering both teenagers emotional support while, at the same time, determining how the couple may be assisted with other physical needs until the baby is born (i.e., financial assistance for medical care, supplies for the baby, etc.).

The adolescent father's involvement in the process is an important issue to consider. The father can serve as a resource and support for the pregnant mother. We must also recognize that the pregnancy is a part of the father's life and his need for support must be addressed as well as his feelings about the decision.

D. Social Systems During the 1960s there was a rapid development of comprehensive, multiservice, interdisciplinary programs for single white women. These programs initially sought to provide health, educational, and social services for pregnant school-aged girls living at home for the purpose of preventing school dropout. Today these programs are equally concerned about extending services to girls of any racial or ethnic group who have decided to keep their child. They draw on the resources of many community agencies and focus on assisting the teenager in completing necessary developmental tasks while, at the same time, improving overall parenting abilities.

E. Resource Systems It is the role of the social worker to maintain a level of knowledge about community-based programs that provide services to pregnant teens who decide to keep their babies, and those who choose to place them for adoption or in other alternate living situations. As increasing numbers of teenage girls are choosing to raise their children, either independently or with the assistance of others, social workers are typically more involved in providing services for this group following the birth of the child. Their needs primarily center around health issues, housing, and other personal and interpersonal difficulties. In response to these general needs, the social worker will assist the adolescent with primarily supportive and supplemental services. Therefore, community resources should be assessed in terms of their capacity to provide the following services for adolescent mothers:

1. Medical services that provide prenatal, postpartum, and pediatric care
2. Educational or vocational counseling, training, and placement
3. Financial assistance and budget counseling
4. Psychological counseling; group support services
5. Day care assistance and services
6. Family planning services and counseling
7. Parent training services; child development education and counseling
8. Legal counseling and services
9. Transportation services
10. Housing resources

For the unmarried teenage mother living independently, loneliness and isolation become a significant problem in spite of the fact that she may continue to be involved with friends and family members. The need for psychological counseling and mutual aid group support services is particularly important for this group to assist them in dealing with overwhelming feelings of guilt, rejection, and maternal responsibility.

F. Programs and Services Should a teenager choose to place her child for adoption or in an alternate living situation, supportive and supplementary services are also needed in addition to community services. The following services constitute community forms of care:

1. Psychological counseling and support services (before and after placement)
2. Family planning services and counseling
3. Adoption placement services and counseling
4. Medical services that provide prenatal and postpartum care
5. Residential services; maternity home care; adult foster or boarding home care
6. Educational or vocational services and counseling
7. Legal services
8. Transportation services

Clearly, the above-mentioned services cannot provide a comprehensive approach to meeting the needs of the pregnant adolescent; however, the family can play a more central role in assisting the teenager by providing more services, such as economic and childcare. The need and use of informal out of the box services also needs to be addressed. The family as a resource has been virtually untapped by programs that focus on assisting pregnant teens. To the contrary, programs have often designed services that either do not take into account the family's assistance to teenagers, or worse still, undermine the network of familial support. Evidence now suggests that more and more family planning programs have been reaching out to the family system for assistance in providing services (Laird & Hartman, 1985). Therefore, the primary social worker involved in a teen pregnancy case needs to be certain that programs are utilized that promote the involvement of both the nuclear and extended family if possible.

In view of the more strident demands being made by funding sources and administrators for accountability in social work practice, it is becoming increasingly important for child welfare workers to employ evaluation instruments that measure the outcome of their interventions. Therefore, baseline measures need to be taken during the assessment phase that measure the severity of target problems before the change-oriented interventions are implemented. These baseline measures provide a baseline against which measures of progress and measures at termination can be compared. The data provided helps to evaluate the efficacy of the social worker's involvement with the adolescent.

At the beginning of the assessment phase it is suggested that the social worker have the adolescent complete a self-administered scale that is easy to administer, score, and interpret. Another advantage of these scales is that they are a reliable and valid means of quantifying the measurement of a particular target population. The Walmyr Assessment Scales (Hudson, 1992) are particularly useful for child welfare workers, as they involve many of the issues relevant to social work. The following scales, developed by Walter Hudson and fellow social workers, would be appropriate for assessment of problems typically experienced by pregnant adolescents:

- Index of Self-Esteem
- Index of Peer Relations
- Sexual Attitude Scale
- Index of Family Relations
- Index of Parental Attitudes
- Child's Attitude Toward Mother
- Child's Attitude Toward Father
- Index of Brother Relations
- Index of Sister Relations
- Generalized Contentment Scale

Phase III: Plan and Contract for Intervention with All Systems

A. Case Review and Coordination Meeting Planning is the process by which the pregnant teenager, the family (if involved), and the child welfare worker decide which goals to work on and the specific objectives needed to accomplish those goals. All goals need to be mutually agreed upon by the adolescent, the social worker, and the family if possible. They should specify what the adolescent wants to accomplish and provide direction, as well as continuity, in the helping process. Goals must be explicitly stated and meet the following standards:

- Realistic and achievable
- Stated in specific, positive terms
- Measurable and observable
- Focused on resource acquisition or behavioral change
- Emphasize and reinforce strengths

Objectives are the building blocks that are set up to accomplish a specific goal. For example, in the case of Maria, a social worker might establish certain goals and objectives with her and the family based on their desired outcomes. Let's assume that in this case Maria would like to keep her baby and would like the support of her family in doing so. The goals and objectives listed in Highlight 8.4 might be stipulated in the form of a written contract as a means of providing structure and direction in the intervention phase.

❖ HIGHLIGHT 8.4   Example of Contract

Goals	Objectives
1. Learn effective parenting skills	1.1 Attend parenting class sponsored by community agency.
	1.2 Contract with a parent trainer through juvenile family services department.
2. Obtain high school diploma	2.1 Attend teenage parent program sponspored by local school board.
	2.2 Establish a schedule for studying and personal time with the baby.
3. Obtain suitable childcare	3.1 Discuss feasibility of family members providing childcare.
	3.2 Talk with director of teenage parent classes about childcare program.

These are only a few of the goals and objectives that might be negotiated in this case. Others can be added as previously established goals are accomplished, and additional objectives can be substituted to meet corresponding goals as well. The goals mentioned above relate primarily to resource acquisition rather than behavioral change on the part of the adolescent. With regard to the case of Maria, a goal might be to assist her in identifying dysfunctional thought patterns or beliefs that contribute to low self esteem and replacing them with more functional thoughts, as shown in Highlight 8.5.

B. Involve Family in Planning Process It is important to remember that in order for adolescents to be motivated to make a substantive change in their situation, they must believe that the goals selected will improve their lives by

---

❖ HIGHLIGHT 8.5   Example of Cognitive Process

DYSFUNCTIONAL BELIEF	THEMES	MORE FUNCTIONAL THOUGHTS
I am not capable of main-training a relationship with Raphael without having sex with him.	inadequacy worthlessness fear	The fact that I choose not to have sex does not mean that I am not a worthwhile individual. With guidance, I can communicate how I feel about this issue to Raphael in a way that he will understand and a way that will not jeopardize our relationship.
I must be "odd" or "un-cool" if I don't have sex. It's expected by everyone and everyone is doing it.	inferiority self-blame criticism of others	There are many people who have not had sex at age 16. I have many friends who value me as a person regardless of the fact that I have not had sex, and they will continue to be my friends.
I don't want to talk with Raphael about using con-doms. I don't know what to say and he might think I'm foolish.	embarrassment fear inferiority inadequacy	I've not had experience in talking to boys about sex and using condoms, however, this does not mean that I am not ade-quate. With guidance I can talk with him about any-thing and he will not think I'm foolish. We are to talk openly about a lot of things.

---

resolving or diminishing their problems. For adolescents who are somewhat reluctant to pursue a particular goal that the social worker and family believe to be critical to the change process, it might be necessary to frame the goal in a way that adequately addresses the problem as the adolescent defines it. For example, parents may see continuing education as an important issue, but not the adolescent. Framing for the pregnant adolescent how continuing educa-tion may meet her goals will help her in processing decisions, not simply reacting to them. In negotiating goals and objectives, the social worker focuses to the adolescent's level of discomfort in dealing with the problematic situa-tion and her desire to come to some resolution of it; however, it is extremely important for the adolescent to feel that she has established major goals with the assistance of the social worker and family. This process is consis-tent with the social work value of client self-determination.

C. Contract with Family and Support Services for Their Roles in Implementing Plan
Developing a contract or working agreement with the adolescent and other

systems is the primary purpose of contract negotiation. The contract defines what will happen between the adolescent, the social worker, and another system. It is determined by joint agreement and is a major tool in the social worker's contacts with the other systems. It is in these contacts that the other systems are encouraged to become involved in the change effort. It is evident that people are likely to continue in the change process when there is agreement between the social worker and an individual, family, or group on core problems to be worked on, specific goals, and methods to reach these goals.

As stated previously, protocol 5 in the SWPIP model refers to the fact that in order to effectively utilize formal community-based services, the social worker needs to understand: (1) what services are available, (2) the quality of those services, and (3) the building of relationships with individuals who provide these services. This knowledge is imperative in the contract phase of the model and critical to the intervention phase as well.

In the case of Maria, it would be important to involve the family in the contracting process. The social worker might even consider establishing a separate contract for the family in order to establish structure to their involvement, in addition to keeping them on task during the intervention phase. Highlight 8.6 is an example of an appropriate contract established with Maria.

The completion of a contract signifies the end of this phase of the change process. It must be recognized, however, that even the most carefully developed plan of action may not be sufficient when the implementation is attempted. The social worker and adolescent must always be open to renegotiating the contract in light of the experience of actually working to achieve change.

Phase IV: Implementation of Plan   *A. Continued Implementation of Interviewing Skills and Practice Techniques* The major task of the primary social worker during this phase of the model would be to continue to engage the adolescent and support members and maintain the relationship while assisting in the provision of required services that help to meet the goals of the contract. The plan designed to change behavior and/or the situation can now be implemented. It is the responsibility of the social worker to carry out his or her part of the plan, help the adolescent perform the agreed upon tasks, bring necessary resources to bear on the situation, monitor the progress of the change activity, and help to stabilize positive changes that occur.

As in the establishment of the goals of the contract, the interventions used to attain those goals must reflect the desires of the adolescent and make sense to her. They will flow from the assessment process and address each of the problem areas identified by the adolescent. The interventions must also be consistent with the developmental level of the adolescent and must take into account the teenager's level of skill, in addition to the degree of emotional maturity, in accomplishing certain tasks. Knowledge of the adolescent's ethno-cultural group is also critical to the intervention process. It would be

---

❖ **HIGHLIGHT 8.6   Example of Agreement**

Agreement for Services
Name of client:

_____

Address:

_____

Other parties involved:

_____

I. I have established specific goals and tasks to accomplish these goals with
_____ which will enable me to improve my current situation.
I realize that the accomplishment of these goals is necessary in order to resolve major problems in my life and enhance my current situation. During
the course of working on these goals, I will discuss with _____
any major obstacles or dilemmas I might encounter, in addition to any other
information that might be pertinent to the attainment of these goals.
　　Furthermore, I will agree to working actively in the planning and implementation of the specified tasks for the purpose of achieving these goals,
which are as follows:
1. _____
2. _____
3. _____
4. _____
5. _____

II. I agree to meet with my social worker _____ at least (weekly,
bi-weekly) for the duration of this contract. Furthermore, I agree to be on
time for those meetings and if, for any reason, I am not able to meet the
appointment time, I will notify her/him at least _____ (hours, days)
in advance.

III. I agree to participate in the evaluation of my progress by:
a. completing the _____ measurement scale(s) at specific intervals of time designated by the social worker,
b. discussing the results of the scale(s) with the social worker in addition to
any reactions I might have.

IV. I understand that the terms of this agreement can be renegotiated at any
time.

V. I am in agreement with the terms of this agreement and do hereby agree to
abide by them.

_____　　　_____
　　　　Client's Signature　　　　　　　　　　　　Date

VI. I have read the terms of this agreement and agree with them. I also agree
to work collaboratively with _____ and provide my professional
assistance to the best of my ability to assist the client in achieving the goals
listed and any others that we might subsequently agree upon.

_____　　　_____
　　　Social Worker's Signature　　　　　　　　　　Date

---

important to discuss the adolescent's views of what needs to be done, particularly in relation to the role of the family in the interventions. For example,
with Hispanic adolescents the family can be an enormous source of strength

and resources. Strong ties are often maintained with extended family, who usually provide identity and support for the adolescent. The church can also play a vital role in assisting Hispanic adolescents during periods of crisis. All of these factors need to be taken into consideration by the social worker during the intervention phase of the model.

The child welfare worker utilizing the SWPIP model will structure interventions for the pregnant adolescent that primarily fall into two categories: case management services and interventions that address psychosocial, cognitive, and familial factors. In addition, the protocols of the model reflect the need for the child welfare worker to assist in efforts to improve services to adolescents that include community education; interagency training; and networking, case conferences, and coalition building.

B. Continuing Coordination of Services Case management services that are typically needed by pregnant teenagers are (Borgford-Parnell, Hope, & Deisher, 1994):

- Outreach
- Education
- Crisis intervention counseling
- Drug treatment and mental health referral
- Assistance in accessing medical care and social services
- Assistance with financial and housing resources
- General physical assessment of mother and baby
- Individual intervention strategies
- Family intervention strategies
- Referral to and coordination of other community services

C. Support and Empowerment of Child and Family The second category of interventions, those that address psycho-social, cognitive, and familial factors, are:

- Cognitive restructuring
- Previewing
- Communication skills training
- Behavior-analysis skills training
- Task-centered interventions
- Problem-solving skills training
- Parenting skill training
- Relationship enhancement training
- Assertiveness training
- Crisis intervention
- Family interventions

Using the case example of Maria, we will look at several interventions the social worker might employ. As a matter of informed consent, it is always important to explain to the adolescent in great detail everything that is involved in the intervention plan and to obtain her consent, either written or oral, prior to implementation. It is equally important to explain the expected outcomes of the interventions, both positive and negative, in order for the adolescent to be able to consent after having considered all the relevant information. In this chapter we will focus on a few of the interventions previously mentioned; others will be discussed in chapter 9, relating to juvenile delinquency.

Cognitive Restructuring

The primary function of cognitive restructuring is to teach adolescents more adaptive thought patterns by helping them detect their negative and distorted thought patterns, recognize their deleterious impact, and replace dysfunctional cognitions with more accurate and adaptive thought patterns. Cognitions are deemed dysfunctional when they appear to be unrealistic or inaccurate, and when they contribute to unwanted behavioral and emotional responses. Cognitive restructuring techniques are based on the premise that if adolescents can be taught to recognize and correct their own distortions of reality, they will then be in a better position to alter their related dysfunctional behavioral and emotional responses. It is important for the social worker to keep in mind, however, that these techniques are designed to modify inaccurate cognitions. When adolescents discuss negative cognitions that appear to be accurate, cognitive restructuring techniques would not be used.

The social worker, through the use of cognitive restructuring, wants to get across the notion that unwanted feelings and self-defeating behaviors, such as engaging in sexual activity, can be related to negative or distorted automatic thoughts and beliefs. Highlight 8.7 illustrates how the cognitive restructuring process is begun.

In this interaction the social worker has been able to get the adolescent to: (1) identify the distorted belief, (2) identify the unpleasant emotional and behavioral reactions to the distorted belief, and (3) distinguish between the objective observation of the situation and the subjective interpretation of what occurred. Maria was not able to give any evidence that Raphael liked Amy more, only that it was an immediate thought or belief that she had. She was then able to see the irrational nature of her emotional response and the relationship to the dysfunctional behavior. It is important for the social worker to help the adolescent to understand this connection in order to motivate her to alter these beliefs, and thus eliminate the dysfunctional behavior.

Examples of irrational beliefs or irrational thinking habits that teenagers often have include: (1) overreactions, (2) unrealistic expectations, and (3) the habit of jumping to conclusions (Zarb, 1992). An exercise that helps the adolescent to understand what is meant by irrational beliefs, while providing

---

❖ HIGHLIGHT 8.7   Cognitive Restructuring Process

Ellen: Maria, I would like for you to describe for me a situation involving Raphael that was very upsetting to you.

Maria: Well, there was the time that he was flirting with my best friend, Amy, and I got real angry with him.

Ellen: I see, so what did he say to Amy that made you think he was flirting?

Maria: He said, "Amy, that's a really cool sweater you're wearing. I like the way it clings to your body."

Ellen: And what thoughts immediately entered your mind when he said that to Amy?

Maria: I thought that he liked the way Amy looked better than he liked me.

Ellen: How did you reach this conclusion exactly? What evidence did you have that he liked the way Amy looked better than he liked you? Did he ever tell you that, or has anyone else told you?

Maria: No, it's just a feeling I had.

Ellen: Okay, let's suppose for a moment that he really did like the way Amy looked better than he liked the way you looked. Does this necessarily mean that he must like Amy better than he likes you?

Maria: No, I guess not. I don't believe he likes Amy better than he likes me.

Ellen: True, so there really is no relationship between his remark and how he feels about you, is there?

Maria: No.

Ellen: Therefore, this was really a distorted thought that you were having, wasn't it?

Maria: Yes, I believe so.

Ellen: So, when you were thinking this about Raphael and Amy, how did it make you feel?

Maria: Sad, inferior.

Ellen: Which then caused you to argue with Raphael?

Maria: Yes. He really couldn't understand what the big deal was.

---

the adolescent with practical experience in identifying irrational beliefs, is shown in Highlight 8.8.

Previewing

Previewing is an intervention and early prevention strategy to assist teenagers in predicting or anticipating the outcome of certain behaviors. Thus, before the behavior is enacted the adolescent becomes aware of its likely consequences. Previewing is an intervention protocol to deter sexual activity without effective birth control, and it addresses the psychosocial, cognitive, and familial dimensions of adolescence (Trad, 1994).

Many teenagers fail to reflect upon the long-term outcomes of their actions and become pregnant without realizing the ultimate consequences—the responsibility for another life. The tendency to ignore the possible outcome and react impulsively is typical of an adolescent's developmental level.

❖ HIGHLIGHT 8.8   Example of Exercise

Ask the adolescent to discuss a particular situation that occurs quite often and causes unpleasant emotional responses for her. Then, ask her to list under a column labeled *Observations* the activating event that occurred. Now, compare the way you interpreted the same events. Look at the negative automatic thoughts and themes that came into your head and write them down in another column labeled *Interpretations*. Ask the adolescent to write down their *Distorted Belief* in another column, then ask her to give evidence for or against her belief under the *Evidence For* or *Evidence Against* columns. In a final column labeled *Functional Beliefs* assist her in listing more realistic responses to the activating event.

OBSERVATIONS	INTERPRETATIONS	DISTORTED BELIEF
Raphael said he liked Amy's sweater and the way it clung to her body.	Raphael should be saying things like that to me and not to Amy.	Since Raphael told Amy he liked her sweater and how it looks on her body, he must not like me as much as he likes her.

EVIDENCE "FOR" BELIEF	EVIDENCE "AGAINST" BELIEF
No evidence	Raphael often says he cares for me a great deal. Although he likes Amy, he has often said that he could not have her for a girlfriend because she gets on his nerves.

Previewing helps the adolescent predict the probable outcomes of her behavior and heightens her sense of mastery in being able to control future events that can have life-altering consequences.

In the case of Maria, she was too embarrassed to discuss the use of a condom with Raphael and did not consider the possible consequences of such when she decided to have sex with him. She was fully aware of the fact that the failure to do so could, in fact, cause her to become pregnant; however, she chose to ignore this at the time she decided to have sex with him and was unwilling to focus on the effects of having a baby.

In previewing, the teenager is asked to envision a situation in which she has engaged in self-defeating behaviors (i.e., engaging in sexual relations without discussing the use of a condom). Then, she is asked to anticipate how her life would be transformed if she were to have a baby. Because motherhood might be so remote from her experience, supplementary techniques might be used to enhance her previewing skills. For example, she might be shown a videotape of teenage mothers caring for their infants, then she would be asked to share her opinions. The social worker would then ask her to predict scenarios involving the infant's daily care. Another group of representations could focus on the more long-term variables, such as the effect of early motherhood on her educational opportunities.

The technique of previewing can also be used with pregnant teens who have chosen to keep their babies by helping them to predict the implications of caring for a young infant and the realities of motherhood. Based on the perceptions she has described during the pregnancy, she observes the infant's precursory manifestations and predicts which developmental skills are likely to emerge next. As a result, she is able to provide appropriate support and encouragement for the infant. During this key period, when mother and infant are establishing a bond, she is encouraged to observe the infant closely and become sensitive to the developmental phenomena that the infant is experiencing (Trad, 1994).

D. Identification of Barriers and Resolution As in all child welfare situations, the identification of barriers and their resolution is an important part of carrying through on a plan. In a case of teenage pregnancy, it becomes even more important as the teenager may need direct skills to offset any obstacles. Often, the teenager can feel so overwhelmed that carrying through on their plan may prove very difficult.

Task-Centered Interventions

Task-centered interventions are based on the task-centered approach to attaining goals, which are defined after the conclusion of the assessment phase of the model. The task-centered method of social work practice is characterized by highly specified tasks consisting of discrete actions to be taken by the adolescent in an effort to accomplish a particular goal (Hepworth, Rooney, & Larsen, 1997). The tasks may include dismissing inaccurate cognitions that cause maladaptive behavior or attending a parenting class at a local community agency.

Even goals stipulated in clear, simple terms can be overwhelming to an adolescent and difficult to accomplish. Therefore, it might be necessary to break them down into subgoals which require the accomplishment of specific tasks for each subgoal before the primary goal is achieved. For example, in cases involving teenage parents the primary goal might be the development of good parenting skills. Subgoals established for this very broad primary goal would be: (1) attend a parenting class, (2) read material on parenting, and (3) learn about developmental stages of infants and problems normally manifested during these stages. Specific tasks could be identified for the adolescent to complete for each specific goal. In the first goal, attend a parenting class, a task might be to contact a local agency to inquire about parenting classes. Another might be to attend a group with the local teenage parent program in which parenting issues are frequently discussed.

The social worker needs to first ask the adolescent which tasks she would agree to follow up on and in what order. It might be necessary to assist her in developing tasks; however, she must be in complete agreement with them in order for her to be empowered to accomplish goals independently. If the adolescent is unable to come up with specific tasks for each goal or subgoal, the social worker might engage her in the technique of brainstorming. This is a process in which the social worker and adolescent generate a broad range of possible tasks from which the adolescent is able to choose. If she overlooks significant options, the social worker would suggest additional ones to ensure that she has a broad range of possibilities to consider.

After the tasks are developed, the social worker would then help to prepare the adolescent for the implementation of each task. Hepworth, Rooney, and Larsen (1997) describe this systematic approach, termed the Task Implementation Sequence (TIS), as involving a sequence of discrete steps that encompass major ingredients generally associated with successful change efforts. The TIS involves the following steps:

1. Enhance client's commitment to carry out a specific task.
2. Plan the details of carrying out the task.
3. Analyze and resolve obstacles that may be encountered.
4. Have client rehearse or practice the behaviors involved in carrying out the task.
5. Summarize the plan of task implementation and convey both encouragement and an expectation that the client will carry out the task.

It is important in working toward the accomplishment of ongoing goals to plan tasks that involve incremental changes and build on one another. Planning tasks that are graded in difficulty enhances the chances that the adolescent will accomplish them successfully; thus, this can increase the adolescent's motivation to exert greater efforts in the change process.

E. Monitoring of Services and Plan The continued monitoring of services and the plan of intervention takes on more relevance when the adolescent is involved in the process. Issues of control are very prevalent for adolescents and their involvement in the monitoring can bring a sense of control to their situation.

Phase V: Evaluate Outcomes and Terminate Services   *A. Evaluate Outcomes* In evaluating outcomes, the social worker would readminister the same scales to the adolescent that were administered during the assessment process (post-test) to determine the degree of change that has occurred in problem areas. The scales could also be administered at various points during the intervention process as well. Then during the termination phase the social worker would design a chart that indicates the various scores and the progress made by the adolescent throughout. Noting a positive level of change in the end provides much incentive for the adolescent to continue in her efforts to accomplish ongoing goals by enhancing her self-esteem and degree of efficacy. Qualitative evaluation is equally important in working with an adolescent. As scales may not reflect the full growth or process outcomes in the intervention, the use of descriptive materials can help you and the adolescent to understand.

B. Terminate Services The task of terminating with an adolescent can present a number of issues for both the social worker and the adolescent; therefore, the termination process should be planned from the beginning of the relationship. It should be handled with extreme skill and sensitivity in order for the outcome to have a positive impact on the adolescent's ongoing progress. In view of the fact that the social worker has maintained a close, consistent relationship with the adolescent for a significant period of time, it is likely that both will experience a level of grief with the ending of the relationship. The discussion of the feelings commonly associated with grief help to normalize the process for the adolescent and not perceive the termination as a form of abandonment. It would also be helpful to discuss with her a plan for follow up, which might also include "leaving a crack in the door" whereby the adolescent will feel free to call should the need arise.

Phase VI: Follow Up from a Multisystemic Perspective   *A. Family* In cases where pregnant teenagers elect to keep their babies and live alone or with their families, a plan for following up with the adolescent is critical to the ongoing process of change and stability. Prior to and during the termination process, the social worker should explain to the adolescent that there will be follow-up contacts on an informal level to determine if the adolescent is in need of any further assistance. This reduces the level of anxiety for the adolescent about ending her involvement with the social worker, and it also provides an opportunity for the social worker to maintain an interest in the adolescent's progress. During a follow-up contact the social worker is able to assess the ongoing change efforts and provide assistance for further difficulties. It would be particularly important to determine if the child is receiving adequate care and if any new problems might have developed in this area.

Follow-up contact is equally important with the family of the adolescent to "check on" their continued involvement and support of the adolescent, or the lack thereof. Reinforcement should be given to the family who has maintained support and encouragement of the adolescent, and the social worker should assist them in viewing themselves as having played a significant role in the teenager's progress. Further assistance might be needed by the family in allowing the teenager to make ongoing decisions concerning her child, with which they may disagree. Regardless, the family remains a stabilizing force in the lives of the adolescent and her child, therefore every effort should be made to support their continued involvement.

B. Community Community focus in this area is crucial to offset as much as possible the continuation of the increasing numbers of adolescent pregnancies. Additionally, the involvement of teenage mothers in sharing their experiences with other teenagers is likely to have a greater impact than the involvement of adults in lecturing on these issues. Prevention in this area needs to be thought of as not only preventing pregnancies, but also preventing child neglect and maltreatment. Programs that focus on care during pregnancy and childcare following the birth are important prevention programs for children as well as their teenage mothers.

C. Programs and Services With regard to programs and services, the child welfare worker consistently maintains contact with community agencies that provide services to pregnant adolescents. In addition, the social worker has the responsibility of developing a relationship with the individuals in these programs who have direct contact with the adolescents. It is imperative for there to be ongoing communication between professionals who work with pregnant teens in order for the coordination of services to occur in an effective, timely manner. This also facilitates the development of a level of knowledge about the variety of community resources that need to be utilized based on the specific needs of the adolescent.

D. Policy As noted, a major role of the child welfare social worker involved in teen pregnancy is the involvement in programs that focus on teen pregnancy prevention efforts. These programs are largely based in educational and health settings that are accessed by teens, and they predominately focus on sex education and contraceptive practice. While a number of states encourage the development of sex education courses in the schools, a large number provide extremely limited education or none at all. Sex education is also provided under nonacademic auspices through social service organizations, religious agencies, and other health-related programs. In large part, the task of the social worker in these situations involves the provision of essential information about contraceptive options, pregnancy, and childbirth. Little discussion of more complex issues occurs in these settings, and there is an enormous need for the further development of the counseling component of the programs. Additional components recommended would include more indepth counseling to identify problems and assist teens with their concerns about contraception, sexuality, and their lives in general, and to strengthen teenagers' decision-making skills in preventing and resolving their problems.

SUMMARY

This chapter has identified many of the different intervention aspects in situations related to teenage pregnancy. While the chapter notes different causes of teenage pregnancy, perhaps the most important factor to consider is that teen pregnancy is caused by the lack of interest by adolescents in using precautions. The result of this overt decision is children raising children and a new generation of children affected by poverty and immature parenting. Preventive programs that focus on the importance of adolescents recognizing the reality of possible pregnancy may be the most successful approach. Utilizing all support systems available to the adolescent is a process that will aid the teenager in being comfortable with her decisions. The adolescent father must not be forgotten in this intervention. New programs that utilize family support in both preventive education and residual aid can provide an informal approach to working with adolescent pregnancies.

QUESTIONS FOR DISCUSSION

1. Discuss whether or not teenage pregnancy is on the rise and the reasons why.

2. What is the major reason adolescents become pregnant?

3. Discuss the importance of the involvement of the teenage father in the social work intervention.

4. What role do the parents of the pregnant adolescent have in aiding the adolescent with her decision?

5. Give three examples of macro prevention of teenage pregnancy.

6. What are your personal feelings regarding supplying a teenage pregnant women with abortion information?

9

■

Behavioral and Delinquency Issues

Marvin, age 15, is a Native-American male who has lived in an urban housing project with his mother and four younger siblings since birth. His mother, Mrs. Simpson, age 30, is employed during the evenings at a local restaurant, and he is often left at home to supervise his brothers and sisters. Marvin has recently begun to hang out with several members of a gang in the area and is becoming increasingly more involved in criminal activities. He has a conflictual relationship with his mother which is characterized by frequent outbursts of anger, physical fighting, and verbal abuse. He has begun to use drugs and alcohol in addition to participating in other gang-related activities in order to be accepted by his peers. Marvin is quite intelligent and demonstrates a great deal of academic potential; however, he is now skipping school to hang out with his friends, most of whom have dropped out and are unemployed. Recently Marvin was arrested with two of his friends for stealing cellular phones from a local retail store and has been placed under the court-ordered supervision of a social worker with the Department of Juvenile Justice.

INTRODUCTION

The numbers of children with behavioral and delinquency issues is increasing yearly in the United States. According to Sicklund (1992), some 82,000 juveniles are arrested for status offenses a year and approximately 1.5 million juveniles are dealt with in delinquency cases through the courts. Although it is important to recognize that there is a significant difference between status offenses and criminal offenses, the overwhelming majority of cases can be directly related to drug and alcohol abuse (Hawkins, Jenson, Catalano, & Lishner, 1988). Winters, Slenchfield, and Fulkerson (1993) found in their study of juvenile detainees that there was a 52.3 percent severity rate in drug usage compared to an 18.3 percent severity rate for high school students and an 84 percent severity rate for adolescents within a drug clinic. These findings clearly indicate a connection between the use of drugs and juvenile detention rates. Which occurs first, however, is difficult to determine. A study by Barone, Weissberg, and Kasprow Voyce, Arthur, and Shriver (1995) notes that communities with high rates of teenage offenses also appear to have higher rates of substance abuse, poverty, inadequate housing, and single parent households. Whether drugs or environmental conditions are more related to teenage offenses is difficult to determine, but both appear to impact on these behaviors.

The majority of adolescents charged with delinquency offenses are male (80 percent) and Caucasian. The involvement of the court in a case tends to be much higher for visible minorities than for Caucasians (U.S. Department of Justice, 1992). This fact supports the belief of the unusual proportion of adolescent males and minorities detained for legal proceedings. While arrests rates favor males over females, it is also important to note that females once in the system are just as likely to receive similar penalities.

Like the adult courts, minority juveniles are more likely to be arrested and tried for a crime than are Caucasian males. In particular, African-Americans, Hispanics, and Native-Americans share the brunt of this unwanted attention by legal authorities (Mauer, 1990). The Indian Child Welfare Act of 1978, whose purpose was to protect the rights of Native-American children from a disproportional number being placed in foster or adoptive homes and limit the placement of Native-American children for reasons of status offenses, has yet to achieve its original goals. The Act allows Native-American children living on a reservation to be handled through the tribal system of authority and those children of Native-American descent who do not live on a reservation may request to have their case heard by tribal council through their parents, guardians, or the court. While this would seem beneficial at times the consequences of the Act can fall short of providing appropriate interventions.

DEFINING BEHAVIORAL
AND DELINQUENCY ISSUES

There are clearly defined differences between what is considered behavioral and delinquency issues. Very often these definitions can overlap. Acting out behaviors can escalate as children become older and move into their adolescent years. Stealing, fighting, lying, truancy, and destruction of property are all behaviors that can escalate over time and become defined as delinquent and illegal.

Although it is sometimes questionable to utilize a medical diagnosis in situations where familial and environmental factors play such a major role, recognizing some common behaviors can aid you in understanding situations and knowing which inventive methods to undertake. Conduct and/or behavior disorders have also been associated with other diagnostic disorders, such as Attention Deficit Hyperactivity Disorder (ADHD) (American Psychiatric Association, 1994). The child with ADHD has symptoms of overactive motor response, short attention spans, and impulsivity. Often, these early characteristics set the stage for later acting out behaviors. Preventive approaches to dealing with behavioral and delinquency issues may clearly lay in early intervention of children at risk due to biological and/or environmental factors.

Causes of Behavioral and Delinquency Issues

The causes of delinquency and behavioral issues have frustrated social work practitioners and researchers for years. The multiple theories of causal factors include inherent predisposition, biological factors, early childhood development, and community and family influence, to name a few. With little agreement on causal factors, treatment and prevention have become just as difficult to discern as the etiology; however, the primary focus of research and intervention has more recently been on the family environment and adolescent development (Scherer & Brondino, 1994). Other studies have found family structure, poor parent-child bonding and affection, poor parental monitoring, and family discord to have high correlations with delinquent behavior. These correlations clearly encourage the development of preventive types of programs which address at-risk children in at-risk families with educational interventions.

POLICIES

The major policies and laws that have significantly affected children within the juvenile justice system were established by the United States Supreme Court. The Supreme Court has often overturned many laws and policies created by the different states. Two of the most significant cases included Kent v. United States, 1966, and In re Gault 1967, which focused on the establishment of constitutional rights for juveniles. These rights included due process to hearings on the matter of a waiver to a criminal court, entitlement to counsel, written notice of a scheduled hearing to the child and their parents or guardians, right to confront and cross-examine witnesses, and the privilege against self-incrimination. The Juvenile Justice and Delinquency Prevention Act of 1974 was initiated to provide federal funds for prevention of delinquency and alternative programs for detaining juveniles. Amendments to this Act in 1992 provided additional funding for more preventive programs and for a reduction of minority youth being placed in detention.

PROCESSES AND PROCEDURES

Key in behavioral and delinquent cases are the processes and procedures the child welfare social worker must undertake between two significant societal institutions, the child welfare system and the court system. While many behavioral issues will remain within a family and not be handled by a court system, there are those children whose behavioral issues are a beginning sign of the delinquent acts. Without preventive programs, the numbers of children with behavioral problems will continue to increase the numbers within the juvenile justice system.

Much of the contemporary child welfare literature tends to address needs and services for pre-adolescent dependent children and leaves those adolescents involved in the juvenile justice system to youth specialists. Nevertheless, the initial processing for all dependent, neglected, delinquent, and abused children usually begins in the juvenile court system. The juvenile court controls entry of juveniles into the justice system because it has been allocated the power and discretion to determine when the state will intervene in the lives of individual youth and their families. It is generally at this point that social workers initially become involved in delinquency cases and are given the responsibility for assisting the client during and immediately following the court disposition. If the juvenile is confined to detention or another residential facility on a temporary basis, the social worker may be involved in assisting the court in developing a long-term plan for the juvenile. This plan may consist of a recommendation for either further incarceration in a secured facility, or possibly confinement to a community-based program either in the adolescent's home or in an alternate living situation. This decision would ultimately be made by the court, based upon recommendations provided by juvenile justice professionals. Ideally, it would be more beneficial to the adolescent if the primary social worker assigned to work with the juvenile offender is not the individual who would be providing recommendations directly to the court, thus requiring him or her to possibly testify against the client in court. Rather, the social worker would be responsible for providing information to the juvenile justice department on the adolescent's progress, which would be given high priority in the department's final recommendations to the court.

When working with the confined adolescent, the social worker may be involved in assisting in the development of a plan for the juvenile's release which would likely include follow-up services and supervision. An assessment of the community resources that the client would need to access for positive support would be an integral component of this plan and would be structured to address specific problems within the adolescent's environmental system. In addition, an assessment of the informal resources (e.g., extended family members, friends, other professionals needed, etc.) might also be incorporated into the plan to aid in preventing future problems.

SERVICES AND PROGRAMS

A strong juvenile justice system is one that provides a continuum of services for juveniles who come into the system for a variety of reasons, such as truancy, homelessness, drug abuse, mental illness, or delinquent offenses. Social workers employed within the system will need training that enables them to assess the risk the juvenile offender poses to the community, determine rehabilitative needs, and provide graduated sanctions and treatment commensurate with both conduct and needs.

The utilization of the SWPIP model in working with conduct disorder in juveniles provides for a primary social worker to efficiently perform functions that meet the treatment or rehabilitative needs of the young offender. In doing such, the social worker coordinates services that target the identified adolescent and family problems within and between the multiple systems in which family members are embedded. These services are best delivered in the natural environment (e.g., home, school, community) to optimize their effectiveness. A good treatment or case plan is designed in collaboration with family members and is, therefore, family-driven. Emphasis is best placed on family empowerment and the mobilization of child, family, and community resources by the primary social worker. Interventions which are based on the strengths within the client's system and other systems involved, as well as the "fit" between these systems and the identified problems are most likely to succeed.

There are many different kinds of programs for adolescents experiencing delinquent and behavioral problems. Community-focused interventions that involve the whole community, as well as the institutions with which adolescents are the most familiar, are becoming methods of choice for supporting adolescents and families through difficulties. Such programs include house arrest models of intervention with mentors and caseworkers and have proven valuable in preventing incarceration (Borduin, Mann, Cone, Henggeler, Fucci, Blaske & Williams, 1995). These types of programs, along with aftercare interventions, have validated lower recidivism (Barton & Butts, 1990). The Florida Department of Juvenile Justice (1995) defines some of this state's programs as follows:

Host Home: Provides safe housing, care, and surrogate parental supervision in a neighborhood family dwelling to one (1) or two (2) male or female youths who have committed minor offenses and need alternate living arrangements in order to participate in nonresidential day treatment.

Group Treatment Home: Provides custody, care and 24 hour a day awake supervision to a committed population of approximately six (6) to nine (9) all male or all female youths in a therapeutic residential environment which offers opportunities for personal growth, social development, and responsible behavior. This program typically serves younger adolescents who have committed minor offenses, and is most likely the youth's first residential commitment placement.

Family Development: Provides care and supervision in a structured treatment environment for male or female youths committed for minor offenses. This model provides an array of services, including a residential hub for assessment purposes, alternate home placement, in-home counseling services, and family counseling. Therapeutic services are offered to each youth in order to promote prosocial behavior, personal growth, family reunification, school attendance, mental health and substance abuse counseling services, recreation, and community involvement.

Boot Camp: Provides custody, care, and 24 hour a day awake supervision to a population of approximately thirty (30) all male or all female youths at least 14 years of age, but less than 18 years of age at the time of adjudication. This program generally serves youth who have committed third-degree felonies or second-degree felonies that have been mitigated. The program employs a highly structured impact incarceration approach that emphasizes paramilitary training, physical and mental discipline, and prosocial activities.

Halfway House: Provides custody, care, and supervision to a population of approximately fifteen (15) to thirty (30) all male or all female youths, aged 14 to 18 years, who have typically committed first-degree misdemeanors, felonies, or similar offenses and are classified as moderate risks to public safety. The program provides an intentional therapeutic community based on control theory, structured learning, and behavior management techniques which emphasize social skills, academics, pre-vocational and/or vocational training, and life skills.

Clinical Psychiatric Program: Provides custody, care, and supervision to a population of approximately twenty (20) to thirty-five (35) all male or all female youths, ranging in age from 14 to 18 years, who have generally committed serious felony offenses and usually have significant offense histories. This program provides traditional services characteristics of a halfway house model, as well as on-site psychiatric, psychological, physical health care, and mental health and substance abuse treatment. These services are provided by appropriately licensed and certified professionals through a multidisciplinary approach.

Training School: Provides custody, care, and supervision to one hundred (100) or more male felons or violent misdemeanants, typically ranging in age from 14 to 18 years. Provides services through a multidisciplinary approach within an institutional setting, including services in the areas of behavior management, academics, vocational training, mental health, substance abuse, physical fitness, and health care.

These differing programs offer a range of services and some of them emphasize continued involvement of the adolescent and community in resolving the problems together.

CULTURAL DIVERSITY

Many of the child welfare programs and services that have affected Native-Americans have been destructive in nature. With a high percentage of out-of-home placements (20 times greater than those of children of European descent), the focus of child welfare services for Native-Americans has not taken into account the particular cultural needs of the Native-American family (Johnson, 1991). Beginning in the 1900s with boarding schools for the socialization of Native-American children into a Caucasian culture, these forms of placement took the native culture away from Native-American children. The impetus of the Indian Child Welfare Act of 1978 was the result of these large numbers of out-of-home placements. As noted, the Act provided for Tribal Councils to make decisions regarding Native-American youth. This allowed for the Native-American community to be involved in the adolescent's development and thus furthered greater cultural consideration.

For the most part, children in Native-American families are raised to be very independent. In many incidences, the definition of family within this culture incorporates the entire community. Parents and adults involved with the child may not see themselves as authority figures, but rather as "guides or role models" (Devore & Schlesinger, 1987, p. 67).

In the case of Marvin, his mother may have seen the independence of Marvin as positive, but without the support of an entire community she may not know how to guide him. Her beliefs in allowing Marvin to be independent is contradicted by the fact that they do not live in a community that supports the extended family system of tribal members. Marvin's behaviors and actions are not necessarily ones he can afford to continue for the risk of his own safety or that of others. Understanding and accepting that the family context of Marvin's situation is affected by his culture will aid in guiding your approach to working with Marvin's mother in parenting skills.

Identify Protocols in the Following Case Example

SWPIP PRACTICE MODEL

Zigler, Taussig, and Black (1992) note very that few programs have been effective in preventing or reducing delinquency issues. They theorize the causes of the problem are multifaceted and based on a number of social, cultural, and/or familial issues. In a review of four studies that had shown reduction of delinquency in children who received early intervention services, they found that an ecological perspective, which considers multiple factors that impact delinquent behavior, to be the most effective. Some early childhood intervention programs that have primarily focused on improving educational achievement by building more adequate social skills and helping parents provide for their children's basic physical and emotional needs, have shown the unexpected benefit of reducing later delinquency and criminal activity. An ecological perspective, or one that considers multiple factors as impacting delinquent behavior appears to be what is needed (Struck, 1995).

The underlying assumptions of early intervention programs are such that if a family is able to provide for itself in a socially acceptable manner and is able to embrace effective social skills and emotional coping, then the family unit as well as its individual members will be able to maximize their function (Mills, Dunham, & Alpert, 1988). Several studies have shown that delinquency is linked directly or indirectly with key characteristics of youths and the family, peer, school, and neighborhood systems in which they are embedded (Borduin, Cone, Mann, Henggeler, Fucci, Blake, & Williams, 1995). Effective interventions then need to address the multiple causes of antisocial behavior and be delivered within the ecological system. The use of a primary social worker to direct and coordinate interventions has enormous value in addressing three primary concerns: (1) the need for integrated services to overcome the fragmentation of service delivery systems, (2) the need for continuity of care as needs change, and (3) the need for individualized treatment to meet individuals' different constellations of need. The value of addressing these needs will become more evident as we progress through the model and apply its protocols to the juvenile offender.

Phase I: Establish an Immediate Relationship with the Child and Family Based on Warmth, Genuineness, Empathy, Positive Regard, and Empowerment   As in the case of working with a pregnant teenager (chapter 8), a working relationship needs to be established with the juvenile and his or her family that is based on a level of mutual respect and trust. This can be an extremely difficult task in situations involving delinquency. First, there is usually an enormous amount of anger and dysfunction within the family system, and the social worker often encounters this at the time of the initial contact. In addition, a number of other problems reflecting the adolescent's developmental stage can interfere. These may consist of problems of time distortion, exaggerated sense of peer loyalties, mistrust of adults, periodic suspension of logic, and insufficient motivation for change; and finally, adolescents are often unable to look back and see the need for change. At times they mistakenly believe that their problems will suddenly disappear without effort on their part (Zarb, 1992). Therefore, this type of situation initially calls for a much more directive approach with considerable reliance on structured interview techniques.

In the beginning stage of establishing a relationship with the adolescent, the social worker needs to find out how they are perceived by the client. Does the adolescent perceive the social worker as an advocate of the parent, school, or court system, thus embodying qualities that they may be rebelling against? The juvenile offender is typically viewed as being idealistic, in conflict with parents or other adults over authority issues, fiercely attached to peers, seeking conformity within their peer group, and desperately trying to develop a sense of identity apart from their family. An overt attitude of distrust is often projected immediately upon the social worker, who may represent a position of authority. While these are common characteristics of the nonoffending juvenile as well, they are not usually as heavily masked by a hostile, angry persona. Regardless, in working with the juvenile offender it is extremely important to be oneself and to be genuine. Adolescents, in particular, are highly sensitive to any hint of phoniness or artificiality in others, even though they themselves often pretend to be someone they are not. It is also important to be alert to the fact that when we work with adolescent offenders, our own adolescent struggles can rise to the surface and we may project them onto our clients. Our own unresolved authority issues and parent-child conflicts are especially likely to be reactivated by the juvenile client.

Berg (1994) suggests the following ways to build cooperation and decrease resistance in adolescent clients and their families (pp. 58–59):

1. Have an open mind about the client and be prepared to give him or her "the benefit of the doubt."

2. Put yourself in the client's shoes and look at everything from that point of view.

3. Figure out what is important to your client at this time, and see this view as a valuable asset that has served him or her well over the years, although this point of view may get him or her into trouble now and then. Maybe as the client begins to develop more insight, he or she will be willing to change.

4. Do not argue or debate with the client. You are not likely to change his or her mind through reasoning.

5. Evaluate how realistic your expectations for the client are, given his or her limitations and circumstances.

6. Look for the client's past successes, however small, ordinary, or insignificant. Ask how they were achieved. This question alone becomes an indirect compliment.

7. Look for any small *current* successes and ask how he or she accomplishes them; what would it take for the client to repeat or expand these to other parts of his or her life? This indicates your confidence in his or her ability to solve problems.

8. Look for positive motivation behind the client's behavior and comment on it. He or she will begin to believe in himself/herself.

9. Be willing to apologize to the client for any mistakes or misunderstandings. It takes strength, self-confidence, and professional integrity to be willing to apologize but, paradoxically, it gives you credibility and power in the relationship.

10. Always frame information in a positive manner and refrain from using negative, threatening communication.

Essential to the establishment of a relationship is a sensitivity and understanding on the part of the social worker of his or her own multicultural issues and those of his or her clients. Gender issues also need to be considered in relation to particular ethnic groups, in addition to issues of economics, education, religion, generation, race, and minority/majority status. This is not only critical to the development of a relationship, but it is also an integral component of the assessment and intervention processes as well.

The communication of empathy, warmth, and positive regard are important with the juvenile offender who is likely to be resistant to what they may perceive to be intrusion on the part of a social worker. Of equal importance is the social worker's ability to empower the child to believe in his or her ability to change the situation. Usually this antisocial behavior fits the child's social-ecological context. They have merely learned to adapt to and survive in this type of environment to the best of their ability through delinquent activity generated by feelings of confusion, anger, and an overall sense of hopelessness (Robinson, 1994). Parents are at times unable to provide the monitoring and natural consequences to the adolescent's need to negotiate a change in peer groups, as well as in criminal and substance abuse activities. The well-trained social worker can offer other alternatives to juveniles that can provide them a sense of control in dealing with the adversities of their situations following the establishment of a meaningful, trusted relationship.

Concurrently, while working with the juvenile, the social worker must also establish a working relationship with the family based on trust, warmth, and genuineness. It is important for the social worker to communicate a level of understanding about the stresses that the parent might be experiencing and empower him or her to change the situation as well. Initially, however, it is important to determine what the parent wants for themselves and if they are invested in changing the situation. Keep in mind that the worker-client relationship is fluid, ever-changing, and dynamic; however, it is first necessary for the parents to perceive that there is a problem and be able to acknowledge the level of pain or discomfort that the problem has created in their life. Once this is accomplished, the social worker can then communicate a desire to help the parents find solutions and regain a reasonable measure of control.

In cases of juvenile delinquency, the parents may view their relationship with the social worker as being limited to providing information on the juvenile's problems. Although affected by the problem, the parents do not yet see themselves as having a part in its solution. However, parents usually perceive their role as giving detailed and accurate accounts of patterns of behavior exhibited by their child, historical narratives, speculations about causes, and possible solutions to the problem that someone else might perform (Greenwood, 1994). Because the parents described here may not see themselves as involved in solution finding, the social worker needs to be empathetic and thank the parents for the helpful information they have provided. The social worker needs to acknowledge the parent's suffering and applaud them for hanging in there despite the difficulty of the situation.

Highlight 9.1 relates to the case at the beginning of the chapter and indicates how Marvin's mother might conceptualize her difficulty in terms of perceiving herself as having no control over the solution to her son's problems.

Because Mrs. Simpson is not willing to take responsibility for improving communication with Marvin, but sees the problem as belonging to someone else, it is premature to begin talking with her about what she needs to change. For now, the most important approach is for the social worker to empathize with her difficulty and to initially agree with the goal of seeking help for her son.

Conversely, the parent might indicate, both verbally and nonverbally, an interest in and committment to solving his or her problems and helping the child solve theirs, regardless of whether or not the parent feels responsible for them. When the parent reaches the point of verbalizing that he or she cannot handle the situation anymore and is in need of assistance, a fairly positive, cooperative working relationship can usually be developed with a social worker. However, even when parents are highly motivated, it is important to assist them in staying focused on the goals of change and provide encouragement when they are faced with difficult encounters.

Phase II: Assess the Situation Briefly and Thoroughly Based on the Following Systems   In working with the juvenile offender, the primary social worker has the responsibility for assessing the child's overall situation from an ecosystemic perspective. The primary objective is to insure a comprehensive assessment of major areas of the adolescent's functioning through a behavioral analysis of presenting problems, in addition to an analysis of cognitive variables, family variables, peer-relationship variables, and

---

❖ HIGHLIGHT 9.1   Social Worker-Parent Dialogue

Social Worker: What do you think will help you get along with your son?

Mrs. Simpson: It's not me. Marvin will have to get it into his head that he's gonna have to behave or else he's gonna spend the rest of his life in jail!

Social Worker: Sounds like you have a big problem on your hands. So, what would it take for Marvin to start listening to you?

Mrs. Simpson: That child will have to start listening to me and stop saying things like I beat him. I didn't threaten to kill him! He runs around and tells everybody I mistreat him. He lies and steals. He refuses to go to school and everybody at that school thinks it's my fault. I didn't do anything wrong.

Social Worker: It's pretty tough raising a teenager alone. So, what do you think it will take for Marvin to start listening to you so that you don't have to get mad at him?

Mrs. Simpson: He will have to find out how good he has it before he will start to listen to me. I keep telling him what will happen to him if he doesn't listen, that he's going to end up in detention or some correctional home. I think he has to get good and scared before he realizes how good he's got it here.

Social Worker: What do you think Marvin would say would be helpful to him?

Mrs. Simpson: I don't know; he never talks to me. He has this attitude that he knows everything and that he can do anything he wants to do when he wants to do it. I'm just not going to take it anymore.

---

school performance variables. Data is collected from a variety of sources, including the adolescent client, parents, school personnel, and the social worker's own observations of the adolescent interacting with family members.

A. Adolescent The assessment process is ongoing so that fresh information about the adolescent's overall situation and the consequences of his or her adaptive and maladaptive behaviors in home, peer, and school environments will be evaluated repeatedly throughout the social worker's involvement. Initially, however, the focus is on the presenting problem as it is communicated by all of the individuals involved in the client's systems, as well as the adolescent. Basically, the adolescent is asked to provide information about major complaints and problems. They are asked to describe their own behavioral interactions with significant others, as well as their performance in home, peer, and school environments. Parents are asked to present their views of the adolescent's description of their typical daily activities, school behavior, and problem coping styles.

Due to the fact that many juvenile offenders come from impoverished, single-parent families, it is important to extend the assessment to include environmental factors that might be contributing to, or causing, the presenting problems (Hazel, 1982). Is the adolescent living in substandard housing? Are physical needs being met and how? What is the socioeconomic level of the parents and how is that affecting the problems? Are there any medical problems that are not being addressed? What is the level of interest on the part of the parents? Are there factors within the adolescent's neighborhood that might be impacting the situation? What is the level of peer involvement in the problems? These are only a few of the systemic factors that need to be addressed when working with juvenile offenders. Of equal importance is the assessment of ethnic and cultural issues. In the case of Marvin, these may play an important role in his jurisdiction as well as the intervention.

Highlight 9.2 is a suggested format for conducting an assessment interview with the adolescent client. The primary purpose of the interview is to gain as much information as possible on the client's perspective of his or her family, peers, school, and behavioral problems. This information is then considered with data obtained from significant others (i.e., parents, peers, teachers, counselors and other professionals).

Not only is it important to determine the adolescent's perceptions of the areas listed in Highlight 9.2, but it is also important to discuss these areas with the primary parent or caretaker. Oftentimes their perceptions are somewhat different, as are their suggestions for problem solving. Therefore, it is the responsibility of the social worker to compare both perspectives in each individual area and negotiate the differences with both the adolescent and parent or caretaker. In order for interventions to be structured for each of the problem areas, there needs to be mutual agreement on the part of the parties involved on what the real problem is and how it should be resolved. In negotiating the definition of the problem to be solved with the client, it is important to stay close to the client's own definition whenever possible, since he or she will have to make the necessary changes. In addition, it is vital to negotiate a problem that can be solved given the client's current situation and resources.

B. Nuclear Family It is easy to become overwhelmed by the scope of problems of juvenile offenders and their families. At times, these families may lack even simple problem-solving skills, which further contributes to the family's feelings of helplessness. Keep in mind that families can be extremely resourceful and have an enormous degree of strength and resiliency. Their problem-solving methods may be different from those of the mainstream culture, but a solution perspective allows the social worker to see the potential strengths and resources in these unique and diverse situations. Identifying strengths and successes are much more respectful of the client and less exhaustive for the social worker than focusing on weaknesses. For example, in the case of Marvin's mother who is a single parent, she has had to raise several children while maintaining steady employment. This has required her to solve hundreds of major and minor problems of daily living at a very young age. This

---

❖ **HIGHLIGHT 9.2   Asssessment Interview
with Adolescent Client**

I. Adolescent's Perception of the Presenting Problem
The social worker should encourage the adolescent to talk freely about the problems he or she is experiencing. A beginning question might be, "What do you see as the major problem?" This part of the interview would then focus on the following areas:
1. Specific examples stated by the client of each of the problems he or she is experiencing.
2. Information concerning the frequency, intensity, and duration of each of the problems.
3. The client's beliefs or attitudes about what causes the problem, why it occurs, and what is he or she is thinking about when it occurs.

II. Influence of Significant Others on Adolescent and Problems
In this section it is important to glean information from the client concerning feelings toward significant others involved in his or her life, in addition to perceptions of their influence over the problems he or she is experiencing. The following questions might be asked by the social worker:
1. How would you describe your mother? father? siblings? (Should focus on descriptions of personality factors rather than physical appearance)
2. How do you think this person would describe you?
3. What would you most like to change about this individual and your relationship with them?
4. How do you typically deal with upsetting situations involving your mother? father?
   a. Describe an upsetting situation.
   b. What was your response?
   c. What were the consequences following your response?
   d. What were your thoughts at the time? Your feelings?

---

perception reframes her as being a competent woman rather than an irresponsible parent.

An excellent tool for assessing family patterns and strengths is the genogram, which has been described earlier in the text. The genogram is an attempt to map out family coalitions, alliances, historically significant events, life change events, family myths and rules, and other significant issues that may have an impact on the client (Berg, 1994). Detailing such events helps to place the current problems within the context of the family history as well as the social context of the family. In the case of an adolescent, it might be helpful to develop the genogram with them and their primary parent. This can reveal a number of dynamics between the two regarding long-standing family issues. It can also help the adolescent develop insight into these issues and how they might be exacerbating the problems the family is currently experiencing. Nonetheless, it is important to have some knowledge of the adolescent's developmental level and the parent's ability to see the relevance of the genogram exercise before using this technique. Otherwise, it might be viewed

---

❖ **HIGHLIGHT 9.2** *Continued*

---

e. What could you have done differently and what would the consequences have been then? What would you imagine your reactions would be? Your feelings?

Other significant information to obtain would include:

1. Information on the reactions of significant others when the problem behavior occurs (e.g., mother, father, peers, etc.).
2. The client's feelings about the reactions of significant others.
3. Information on the client's pattern of coping when problems arise and are his or her coping skills helpful or harmful to the situation.
4. Information on how ineffective coping skills contribute to his or her problematic behavior with significant others.
5. The client's level of willingness and ability to change problematic behaviors creating conflict in relationships with others.
6. The level of commitment on the part of significant others to engage in the change process.

III. Adolescent's Perception of School Behavior

In this section the social worker would try to obtain information on the adolescent's experiences with school. If he or she has dropped out, it would be important to learn about the problems which precipitated dropping out from the client's perspective. The following questions could be asked to determine how he or she would describe his or her academic performance in school, attendance record, and interpersonal relationships:

1. How are (were) things at school? Describe what school life is (was) like.
2. What subjects do (did) you do the best in? The worst?
3. How do (did) you get along with your classmates? Your teachers?
4. Do (did) you attend school regularly? If not, why?

---

as superfluous and, potentially, could cause the family and/or adolescent to discredit the social worker's professional expertise.

Problems involving substance abuse are often encountered when assessing the juvenile offender and his or her family. The extent of the juvenile's involvement in alcohol or drug abuse needs to be closely monitored in order to determine if residential treatment is needed. Furthermore, the pattern of drug or alcohol use would be important to know in structuring other interventions for the client. This information might be extremely difficult to accurately assess, however, the parents would likely be able to report on the adolescent's pattern of behavioral symptoms indicative of substance abuse.

As noted by Borduin et al. (1995), large numbers of juveniles with conduct disorders grow up in families in which alcoholism is a problem on the part of one or both parents. Alcoholism manifests itself in many different ways and has different effects on family members. For the child of an alcoholic parent, it can have traumatic effects and directly contribute to the development of delinquent behavior. Alcoholism plays a central role in the functioning and dysfunctioning of the family and of its individual members, particularly the adolescent; therefore, it is imperative for the social worker to learn to recognize substance abuse when it exists in a family and to what degree it is affecting the adolescent. It is also imperative to learn how to work with these families in collaboration with substance abuse treatment programs.

C. Extended Family Systems In assessing alcoholic families the social worker will often observe that there are unspoken family attitudes and rules that maintain the parent's pattern of drinking. The family will frequently adopt dysfunctional patterns and roles in order to cope with stress caused by the parent's drunkenness (Combrinck-Graham, 1989). As a result, adolescents may begin acting out both in school and at home as a manifestation of their reactions to the stress and gradually become involved in criminal and other forms of maladaptive behavior. The social worker will need to accurately determine to what extent the adolescent's problems are directly linked to, or resulting from, the parent's alcoholism. Although the ongoing goal should be to involve the alcoholic parent in individual and family treatment programs, few alcoholic parents will actually go to treatment, or the parent's recovery comes too late in the adolescent's formative developmental years to prevent maladjustment. As a result, the social worker is often forced to work with the adolescent alone or with family members alone, excluding the alcoholic parent.

Cognitive Distortions and Juvenile Offenders

As discussed in the previous chapter, cognitive distortions are defined as errors in the process of collecting and using information independent of the particular content of that information. Throughout the ongoing assessment process the social worker will identify both the adolescent and the parents' cognitive distortions and negative maladaptive cognition contributing to dysfunctional behavioral and emotional patterns. They will subsequently be made aware of the part played by these cognitions in maintaining unwanted emotional and behavioral responses, and interventions will then focus on altering these identified dysfunctional cognitions. In assessing cognitive distortions, the social worker focuses on the adolescent's self-statements, beliefs, attitudes, attributions, and self-efficacy expectations accompanying stressful situations and conditions. This information is often contained in client reports of emotional responses, evaluations, plans, and personal historical facts. It is suggested that the social worker assess both the functional and dysfunctional cognition and the role both play in the adolescent's maladaptive behavior.

Studies have suggested that central symptoms of adolescent depression are similar, if not identical, to those of adult depression and that cognitive distortions, automatic thoughts, and schemata of adolescent clients are quite similar to those observed in adult clients (Clark-Lempers, Lempers, & Netusil, 1990). Distorted thinking often accompanies depression, therefore, it would be important to consider this factor when completing the assessment. Substance abuse in a parent may mask problems with depression, and it is likely that the adolescent will also be experiencing difficulties in this area. Depression in adolescents frequently manifests itself in maladaptive or delinquent behavior (Bunyan, 1987). Depression must be dealt with by the social worker immediately in order for the juvenile to make any substantial change in his or her situation.

When assessing distorted thinking patterns in juvenile offenders, the social worker will evaluate the thinking in terms of its appropriateness in relation to two criteria: (1) how valid it is as a representation of objective reality, and (2) how reasonable it is as a standard or as an explanation for certain events that occur when there are no clear objective criteria available for determining reality. These beliefs tend to be dysfunctional when they are inflexible, unattainable, or so extreme that the individual is unable to meet them and their level of functioning is affected. In determining the pattern of distorted thoughts, it would be significant for the social worker to evaluate the frequency with which they occur, or the degree to which the validity of the thoughts is tested by the individual.

Generally, there are several themes that characterize self-statements of the depressed client that provide a useful reference for cognitive assessment of adolescent clients: (1) low self-esteem, (2) self-criticism and self-blame, (3) negative expectations for the future, (4) perception of responsibilities as overwhelming, (5) sense of hopelessness, and (6) anger and blame against individual or agency (Beck, Steen, & Kovach, 1985). Keeping in mind that cognitive distortions are normal to a certain degree, the social worker still needs to note negative cognitions that seem to be contributing to dysfunctional behavior.

Social Skills Deficits in Adolescents

According to Friesen and Poertner (1995), adolescents who experience maladaptive behavior and become involved in delinquent acts can lack the necessary skills to function effectively in their current environment and in anticipated role relationships and lifecycle stages. They frequently have failed to receive adequate socialization during childhood, thus depriving them of learning certain vital social skills that prevent them from experiencing a variety of personal and interpersonal difficulties. Social dysfunction may be commonly associated with a lack of social skills essential to achieving self-esteem, forming satisfying interpersonal relationships, and performing various social roles effectively. Limited social skills contribute to difficulties involving loneliness and depression, parent-child problems, family breakdown, various mental health problems, in addition to other difficulties (Hepworth et al., 1997).

Adolescents who are easily provoked to anger and discharge anger in violent, destructive ways usually lack skills in coping with provocation and controlling anger, therefore, the social worker needs to assess those coping skills that are commonly utilized by the client when encountering difficult situations in which impulsive, aggressive behavior is exhibited. It would also be significant to evaluate the deficits in social skills that need to be targeted for possible Social Skills Training (SST) during the intervention phase.

D. Social Systems Assessment of the concerns of an adolescent and family system requires extensive knowledge about that system, as well as consideration of the diverse systems (e.g., economic, legal, educational, religious, social, etc.) that impinge upon the client. When the social worker assesses the various aspects of an adolescent's level of functioning, she or he must also consider the dynamics of the client's interactions with the formal social systems within their environment and, to what extent, these interactions are problematic for them. Although all of these systems might not play significant roles in the problems of the adolescent a comprehensive assessment of all areas is critical to the intervention process.

As human service brokers, social workers need to assess the various resources available to meet the needs of the juvenile offender. They must be familiar with the programs offered, the quality of staff, the general eligibility requirements, and the costs of services provided. The social worker must also know the best way to help clients gain access to those resources. The formal systems with which a juvenile offender will typically interact are the juvenile justice system, the court system, the educational system, social agencies, medical programs, and so forth.

E. Resource Systems Most juvenile offenders have experienced difficulty in school and have a history of unsuccessful experiences in educational institutions. As the result of problems associated with being part of a dysfunctional family system, they often have received little encouragement or positive reinforcement for educational achievements (Zigler et al., 1992). Therefore, they frequently are truant from school or do not attend at all. The social worker needs to work with school personnel on determining the adolescent's status in school and if there are resources within the educational system that might be beneficial. If the adolescent has a remote desire to remain in or return to school, the linking of them to these resources would be highly advantageous. Many communities provide alternative schools for juveniles with behavior and/or academic problems in which there are more intensive services provided to address not only academic issues, but psychosocial issues as well. A comprehensive assessment of these services would include evaluating the quality of staff providing them, the problems they are designed to address, the eligibility requirements, the referral process, and whether or not they address the individual needs of the client.

With regard to employment services, the issue of unemployment of juveniles is a serious one as the problems associated with this promote deviance among unemployed youth (Sullivan & Wilson, 1995). Career-oriented apprentice training programs and other vocational opportunities should be explored by the social worker based on the adolescent's areas of interest and identified vocational goals. In communities without these types of programs, social workers need to be helping develop ways to obtain these resources to prevent further lack of opportunities for the adolescent.

F. Programs and Services For those juveniles whose crimes or records are not very serious, and whose family is sufficiently supportive that the youth can continue to reside in the home, there are a variety of programs, such as informal or formal probation, intensive supervision, tracking in-home supervision by private agencies, or after-school and all-day programs in which a youth reports to the program site for part of the day and then returns home to sleep at night. For those youth who must be placed out of their homes, but do not represent such a risk that they must be removed from the community, some jurisdictions provide or contract for a wide variety of group homes and other community living situations (Petersilia, 1995). The majority of these programs offer a counseling component and a variety of intervention strategies aimed at reducing recidivism rates.

According to an evaluation of 80 programs by Andrews, Zinger, Hoge, Bonta, Gendreau, & Cullen (1996), appropriate correctional services can reduce recidivism by as much as 50 percent. They defined appropriate services as those that: target high-risk individuals; address criminogenic needs, such as substance abuse or anger management; and use styles and modes of treatment (e.g., cognitive and behavioral) that are matched with client needs and learning styles. In addition, a meta-analysis of more than 400 juvenile program evaluations by Durlak and Lipsey (1991) found that behavioral, skill-oriented, and multimodal methods produced the greatest effects and that these positive effects were larger in community programs rather than institutional settings.

One role of the social worker in locating services for the juvenile offender would be to assess the community-based services that provide intensive counseling for the adolescent by qualified professionals who are receptive to the social worker's involvement. Programs that use cognitive-behavioral and multimodal approaches to address crime-related factors (such as anger management, dispute resolution skills, and substance abuse resistance training) are preferable to simple educational, vocational, or undirected counseling approaches that do not focus on criminogenic needs (Robinson, 1994). Furthermore, programs that are permitted to use these approaches in community settings are more effective than those that use them in institutional settings (Corbet & Petersilia, 1994).

Phase III: Plan and Contract for Intervention with All Systems *A. Case Review and Coordination Meeting* Throughout the assessment process the social worker is focusing on the strengths of the various complex and multifaceted systems in the client's environment. As problems and needs are identified, the social worker emphasizes the strengths of the adolescent, the family, or care giver in developing a plan to deal with these issues. As discussed in chapter 8, planning is the process by which youths, their care givers, and the social worker decide which objectives to work on. With regard to the case of Marvin, the following objectives might be developed by him with the social worker based on a strength's perspective:

- Find five possible part-time jobs in the classified ads.
- Refer to the social worker for alternative ways to handle anger.
- Consult with a vocational counselor concerning entrance into a vocational training program.

The involvement of Marvin in this process adds to the possibility of success.

It is important for the social worker to understand the adolescent's resistance to change and deal with it after a positive working relationship has been developed. A positive relationship is critical to the change process and the social worker must be perceived by the adolescent as having his or her best interests at heart. Although the adolescent might not agree with the social worker's perception of his or her need to change, he or she will likely be able to identify specific areas in life that are causing pain. Getting the adolescent to take responsibility for some of the pain and discomfort in his or her life is a first step toward dealing effectively with the resistance. For example, in dealing with resistance in Marvin, the social worker could assist him in communicating his feelings about experiencing anger from his mother. If Marvin is able to understand and take responsibility for his part in contributing to the anger, then he and the social worker could look at alternative ways of behaving that might not produce angry reactions from his mother. Of course, it would be equally important for his mother to take part in this process by accepting responsibility for her own negative behavior and agree to alternative ways of dealing with Marvin.

When working with resistant or involuntary clients, understanding that these clients may need to develop some voluntary aspect to their contracts will aid the social worker in progressing further. Even adolescents who meet with the social worker because of a court order do not really have to do so; they have the option of taking the consequences for refusing to do so. All adolescents hope to attain some type of goal through their contacts with a social worker, even if it is only to "get social services and my parents off my back." In order to achieve this goal, which is quite reasonable, the adolescent will have to make certain changes, such as getting up in the morning, going to work or school, cleaning the house, and so forth.

Referring to the case of Marvin at the beginning of the chapter, Highlight 9.3 is an example of questions that can be used in the beginning phase of contract negotiation.

In this exchange between the social worker and the adolescent, the worker sets a positive tone by assuming that Marvin wants to stay out of trouble and explaining that she wants the same thing. Having put herself on

---

❖ **HIGHLIGHT 9.3   Contract Negotiation with an Adolescent Client**

Social Worker: I know that coming here is not your idea of how to spend an afternoon. Any idea of what you would like to get out of coming here that will make it worthwhile for you?

Marvin: I really don't need your help. My life is a pretty big mess right now and I don't know what you can possibly do about that.

Social Worker: You say your life is a mess. That must feel pretty bad.

Marvin: Yeah, I just need to get everyone off my back.

Social Worker: Yes, I can understand why you must feel that way. It must be very difficult for you right now.

Marvin: Yeah, I guess. I just don't want people messing with my life.

Social Worker: You know, Marvin, that's exactly what I want too. I want to get out of your life as soon as possible. What do you suppose you have to do so that I stay out of your life and leave you alone?

Marvin: I guess I need to stop getting into trouble.

Social Worker: I agree. How do you suppose you can do that?

Marvin's side immediately, the social worker proceeds to negotiate what the client wants in order to achieve his goal of staying out of trouble. Expressing empathy with the client's situation does not mean the social worker is condoning their behavior; it only means that they are being open-minded and attempting to communicate a sense of fairness to the client.

B. Involve Family in Planning Process Because of the fact that social work services target identified adolescent and family problems in the multiple systems within the client's environment, the service or treatment plan and contract are designed in collaboration with family members. Both would emphasize family empowerment and the mobilization of indigenous child, family, and community resources. Goals and objectives would be based on the strengths of the involved systems and the "fit" between these systems and the identified problems. For example, Marvin's engagement in multiple thefts and extensive alcohol use during all-night street behavior with friends undoubtedly involves parent, peer, school, and neighborhood systems. The neighborhood may offer few recreational outlets for adolescents and harbor a significant criminal subculture. Likewise, the peer group may be predominately engaged in antisocial behavior. The school, where Marvin experiences significant academic and behavioral difficulties, will also be a system which needs intervention.

C. Contract with Family and Support Services for Their Roles in Implementing Plan Although Marvin's mother is socially isolated, lacks some parenting techniques, and feels powerless and overwhelmed; she is a hard worker, is seriously concerned about her son's behavior, and truly wants him to stay out of trouble and complete his education. Because of several barriers that affect her level of functioning as a parent (e.g., lack of knowledge about parenting, fear of son's reprisal, low social support) she is not able to provide the monitoring and natural consequences her son needs to negotiate a change in peer groups and to attenuate criminal and substance abuse activities.

In view of the fact that the probability of favorable long-term outcome may be determined by Mrs. Simpson's strength and competence, the case plan would initially focus on eliminating the barriers to effective parenting. Thus, the social worker could provide individualized skills training in parenting, and considerable attention might be devoted to developing a reliable support system in Mrs. Simpson's natural environment (e.g., tribal elders, extended family, neighbors). These goals would be enumerated in the contract, and specific objectives relating to *how* and *what* Mrs. Simpson would do to accomplish the goals would be delineated as well. As Marvin's family is Native-American, the possibility of involvement of the Native-American community in the contract needs to be addressed. As noted, Marvin's mother did not choose to utilize this option; however, the resources and supports could be helpful in a variety of other ways.

Phase IV: Implementation of Plan   *A. Continued Implementation of Interviewing Skills and Practice Techniques* Serious juvenile offenders are, by far, at the greatest risk for committing additional serious crimes. Unfortunately, interventions with serious juvenile offenders historically have had little success. However, Kazdin (1987) has described several empirically driven interventions as "promising" (e.g., behavioral parent training, cognitive-behavioral therapy), and Lipsey (1984) has argued that such structured, skill-oriented interventions have demonstrated the largest effects on juvenile offenders in general. However, in some clinical trials with serious juvenile offenders, such interventions have failed to produce favorable long-term effects (Borduin et al., 1995).

Overwhelming evidence supports a social-ecological view in which antisocial behavior in youths is conceptualized as multi-determined (Henggeler, 1989). Since several sophisticated causal modeling studies have shown that delinquency is linked directly or indirectly with key characteristics of youths and the family, peer, school, and neighborhood systems in which youths are embedded (Borduin et al., 1995), the primary interventions by social workers with juvenile offenders need to focus on the multiple determinants of antisocial behavior and provide services in the youths' natural environments. Using interventions that are present-focused and action-oriented, the social worker can directly address intrapersonal (e.g., cognitive) and systemic (i.e., family, peer, school) factors that are known to be associated with adolescent antisocial behavior. Because different combinations of these factors are relevant for different adolescents, the interventions are individualized and highly flexible. An overriding goal is to empower parents with the skills and resources needed to independently address the difficulties that arise in parenting adolescents.

The primary social worker working with the juvenile offender will undoubtedly need to provide individual counseling that focuses on personal, family, and academic issues. The social worker should be prepared to offer support, feedback, and encouragement for behavioral change. Individual theoretical orientations that would be most effective in working with juveniles would be a blend of psychodynamic (e.g., promoting insight and expression of feelings), client-centered (e.g., building a close relationship, providing empathy and warmth), behavioral (e.g., providing social approval for school attendance and other positive behaviors), and cognitive-behavioral (e.g., understanding how dysfunctional behavior [aggressiveness, etc.] results from distorted cognitive processes). If the primary social worker does not have the knowledge or training to implement interventions based on these theoretical frameworks, it would be necessary to refer the adolescent to a counselor who can provide these services while, at the same time, coordinating and collaborating with the social worker during the execution of the case plan. As a social worker who will need to develop these skills, every opportunity needs to be taken to seek out continuing education.

B. Continuing Coordination of Services In addition, it is important to reiterate that all professionals collaborating in a case involving a juvenile should have an understanding of their own multicultural issues and those of the client. When using a broad definition of culture, these issues would relate to economics, education, ethnicity, religion, gender, generation, race, and minority/majority status. When developing a network of resources to refer to, the primary social worker needs to determine if the referral source would be able to appropriately address these issues with the client and support the cultural diversity.

Although the literature reflects a variety of programs and models of practice that are used in working with juveniles with conduct disorders, we will address only those interventions that have demonstrated a significant degree of success based on empirical findings. Those would include cognitive-behavioral interventions, social skills training, family-based interventions, case management, and multisystemic therapy.

Cognitive-Behavioral Interventions

Cognitive-behavioral interventions have been demonstrated to be highly effective in helping adolescents in the areas of assertiveness training, anger management, communication skills training, coping skills training, problem-solving skills training, and relationship enhancement training (Sundel & Sundel, 1993). As discussed in the previous chapter, cognitive-behavioral interventions would address the adolescent's self-statements, beliefs, attitudes, attributions, and self-efficacy expectations accompanying stressful situations and conditions. Hence, the social worker would look at the client's reports of emotional responses, plans, evaluations, and personal historical facts to assess both functional and dysfunctional cognitions and the role these cognitions play in the adolescent's particular behaviors. The adolescent's automatic thoughts accompanying reports of stressful situations or conditions are an important source of cognitive data. Those thoughts that occur instantaneously or habitually, and are plausible to the individual, will be found to contain data about their present perceptions of situations, past memories, affective responses, and deeper beliefs. In addition, automatic thoughts often contain self-evaluations, and elements of this self-evaluation process in turn encompass past memories, present perceptions, and related affect (Zarb, 1992).

C. Support and Empowerment of Child and Family Cognitive restructuring is an excellent intervention to use with adolescent offenders and has been described in Chapter 8. Cognitive self-control techniques are cognitive-restructuring approaches designed to teach clients to give themselves covert instructions for controlling problem behavior such as angry outbursts, cognitive impulsivity, and anxiety. In addition, cognitive self training has also been applied to other adolescent acting out behaviors.

According to Zarb (1992), most cognitive self-control interventions share the same basic format. First, the conceptual framework is explained to the adolescent by the social worker in simple terms. Then the concept of speaking privately to oneself and the effect this has on behavior is introduced to the client. In order to illustrate this point further, the social worker could use the analogy of how athletes talk to themselves and repeat instructions over and over again while learning a new sport. Information about the adolescent's private discussions with themselves, or verbalizations that accompany dysfunctional target behaviors, is then elicited using the following format:

Situation	Maladaptive Verbalization	Behavior	Consequences
Peer threatening	"I have to hit him."	Hit peer	Suspension from school

In the next phase, the self-defeating nature of the adolescent's verbalizations accompanying target behaviors is explored with the client and more adaptive self-verbalizations are suggested and modeled by the social worker. These may include a statement of contingencies, statements about the demands of the task, or self-reinforcement for success for completion of a difficult task.

Situation	Verbalization	Behavior	Consequences
Peer threatening	"If I hit him I'll be suspended. It's not worth it."	Walk away calmly	Feel good about myself

The adolescent is then asked to rehearse these adaptive verbalizations and to rephrase them in his or her own language. The adolescent is also instructed to rehearse the new verbalizations while role playing difficult situations. Later, he or she is asked to independently identify their own dysfunctional self-verbalizations and to generate more adaptive statements. In the final phase, the adolescent is asked to apply these cognitive self-instructional skills to daily situations and to discuss their consequences.

Cognitive self-control techniques are helpful when applied to problems of anger and anxiety in adolescents. They can also be applied to the family as well in an effort to promote social competence within the family and child. By doing such as a part of an early intervention effort, it will very likely result not only in increased educational achievement, improved behavioral control, and ultimately decreased delinquency for the juvenile, but also will promote improved interactions and a higher level of independent functioning for the family unit as well (Robinson, 1994).

Programs that use cognitive-behavioral and multimodal approaches to address crime-related risk factors (such as anger management, dispute resolution skills, and substance abuse resistance training) are preferable to simple educational, vocational, or undirected counseling approaches that do not focus on criminogenic needs.

Social Skills Training (SST)

Cognitive-behavioral techniques along with social skills training (SST) contribute further to the social competency of the adolescent client and help to further reduce delinquency. A rationale for using SST in preventive programs is that efforts to prevent social dysfunction by equipping people with coping skills reduces the possibilities of later maladjustment, unhappiness, failure to develop potentials, and loss of productivity. Many research studies document the importance of adequate socialization during childhood and adolescence to facilitate adequate adjustment (Garbarino, 1992). Children who are deprived of adequate socialization fail to learn vital social skills and are at risk of experiencing a variety of personal and interpersonal difficulties. Social dysfunction is commonly associated with a lack of social skills essential to achieving self-esteem, forming satisfying interpersonal relationships, and performing various social roles effectively.

Adolescents who are easily provoked to anger and discharge anger in violent and destructive ways, often lack skills in coping with provocation. Social skills training is also helpful in dealing with parent-child difficulties. The first step in this process would be for the social worker and adolescent to identify a specific skill deficit in the client that he or she might want to address first. Secondly, they would break the skill into its discrete components or subskills. Also considered would be the specific cognitive and emotional components of the problematic behavior, as certain fears and uncertainties associated with new behavior must be mastered before the client can perform requisite actions. The adolescent could then be encouraged to practice these new skills with their parent(s).

Hepworth et al. (1997) describe a format for SST that can be conducted in individual sessions with the client or in a group context utilizing the following steps. The word adolescent has been integrated into this discussion.

1. *Discuss the rationale and describe the skill.*
   This step is critical in helping the adolescent client to believe that developing the skill will benefit him or her. This is done by briefly introducing the skill, alluding in general to situations in which it is applicable, and then eliciting from participants specific relevant social situations that have posed difficulties for them and have led to adverse outcomes because of ineffectual coping.
   Example: Learning to say "No!" with firmness and not giving in to pressure from others helps adolescents avoid things that they really do not want to do that can get them into trouble.

2. *Identify the components of the skill.*
   Explain that the skill has a number of different components and list them for the client. Also, encourage the adolescent to discuss any difficulties associated with the components.

3. *Model the skill.*
   The social worker can model the component of the skill, or ask a member of the group to volunteer to model it. A discussion by the adolescent can be helpful in highlighting aspects of the component that contribute to effective or ineffective performance.

4. *Role play use of each component.*
   The social worker would set the stage by prescribing a role to adolescent. They would be asked to practice each component and give feedback to the social worker. The worker would further explain that the most effective way of learning a skill is to practice until one feels confident in applying the skill.

5. *Evaluate the role play.*
   Adolescents participating in the role play can then be encouraged to evaluate their own performance and share feelings that inhibit them in the role play. This can help to identify specific barriers that prevent them from implementing the skill effectively.

6. *Combine the components in role-play.*
   After the adolescent has role played and demonstrated adequate mastery of the various components of the skill, move on to the next skill and continually give positive feedback.

7. *Apply the skill to real-life situations.*
   Helping the adolescent prepare for applying the skill in real-life situations involves reviewing components of the skill and practicing applications of them. Maximum preparation is further enhanced by anticipating difficulties that will likely arise for them, and preparing him or her to surmount them through rehearsing appropriate thoughts and behaviors. A debriefing session

should follow the application of the skill to an actual situation in which the adolescent is given the opportunity to discuss and analyze the experience.

Family-Based Interventions

Conduct disorders are often conceptualized as strategies of adjustment which the adolescent has learned to his or her own disadvantage (and to the disadvantage of others) in the attempt to cope with the demands of life. Many research studies have indicated that the families of conduct disordered children are characterized by a high rate of coercive interactions among family members. Children seemingly engage in excessive rates of behaviors aversive to parents (e.g., noncompliance, demands, aggression, and temper tantrums) and parents often retaliate with equally excessive aversive responses (e.g., threatening demands and criticism) designed to "turn off" their children's negative behavior (Bunyan, 1987). Effective assessment and treatment of conduct disorders requires observation and intervention in the natural environment of the juvenile and, in particular, the systematic involvement of parents and the extended family.

Behavioral interventions and techniques are often effective if used consistently by the parents and in a systematic fashion. To reinforce this, it is recommended that the social worker initially provide a high level of input by visiting the home two to three times per week in order to sufficiently advise and support parents in administering a specified behavioral scheme. These visits should decrease rapidly once the scheme is established and is consistently carried out.

D. Identification of Barriers and Resolution In structuring a behavioral program with the family, using the case of Marvin as an example, the social worker might assist Mrs. Simpson and Marvin in reducing the frequency of his demanding, defiant, aggressive, and destructive behavior. In doing such, the social worker might engage in behavioral rehearsal with Mrs. Simpson, which is a technique drawn from behavioral therapy that teaches a client how to handle a specific interpersonal exchange for which she or he might be unprepared. As implied by its name, the individual rehearses or practices a specific behavior to be performed in an upcoming situation. It helps to reduce anxiety and builds self-confidence about being able to handle a problematic situation. The social worker might demonstrate or model the behavior so it can be imitated. Again, using the case of Marvin, the following steps would be followed by the social worker and Mrs. Simpson (Sheafor et al., 1998):

1. The client would identify the problem or concern and then describe or demonstrate how she would usually behave in that situation.
   For example, Mrs. Simpson tries to enforce a curfew with Marvin; however he fails to abide by it and comes home an hour or two late. Mrs. Simpson becomes extremely angry, demanding to know where he has been, and Marvin responds back by yelling, "Leave me alone, I'm old enough to come home when I want to!"

2. The social worker makes suggestions on how the situation might be handled more effectively.
   The social worker might suggest that Mrs. Simpson try a different approach, rather than responding with anger. She or he would then discuss with her several different responses and suggest to Mrs. Simpson that she try the response that would be most appropriate for this particular situation.

3. The client is given an opportunity to provide additional information about the problem or concern and also is able to ask the social worker to further explain the response suggested.
   Mrs. Simpson should be encouraged to discuss her reactions to the alternate response and share her concerns about its feasibility. She should have the opportunity to express her feelings about how Marvin is likely to respond to it.

4. A role play is used to demonstrate the behavioral changes suggested to the client.
   Initially, the social worker would play the role of Mrs. Simpson, and Mrs. Simpson would enact the role of Marvin. The social worker would demonstrate the appropriate response while Mrs. Simpson demonstrates how Marvin is likely to respond. Then the roles are reversed and Mrs. Simpson tries the new behavior if she feels ready and understands the changes being suggested.

5. After the role play, the social worker first identifies the positive aspects of the performance then makes additional suggestions for improvement. If necessary, the role play is repeated to further illustrate the preferred way of responding.
   The social worker should encourage Mrs. Simpson to practice the new behavior until she is satisfied with the performance and feels confident that she can follow through with it.

A major limitation of behavioral rehearsal is that the client may successfully learn what to do in the presence of the social worker but may not be able to generalize it to the real world. Sometimes the real situation poses problems that cannot be anticipated during a practice session.

Family therapy interventions consistent with a cognitive-behavioral approach are considered to be very effective in work with parents and adolescents. These interventions would be directed toward (1) the family's dysfunctional interaction styles, and (2) the family skill deficits in the areas of family communication, family problem solving, and parental child-rearing styles. Various family interventions that would follow this approach are behavior analysis skill training, cognitive restructuring in parent and family sessions, communication skills training, conflict negotiation skills training, discipline effectiveness training, problem-solving training, and relationship enhancement training. A few of the interventions mentioned here can be easily incorporated into the social worker's repertoire of skills in order to be more effective in working with juvenile offenders and their families.

E. Monitoring of Services and Plan This type of monitoring aids the child welfare social worker in understanding the adolescent's environment and the supports and pressures that they experience. Having a good relationship with members of the adolescent's environment is important in monitoring the services and plan. The monitoring of services in a public place such as the school, community center, or neighborhood requires a respect for the adolescent's dignity and confidentiality. While some members of the school staff must be informed of your meetings with the adolescent, particular attention needs to be paid to maintaining their confidentiality.

When working with adolescents and their families around issues of delinquency and behavior, it is critical for the social worker to maintain an ongoing relationship with the family and adolescent through a monitoring of services and plan. This monitoring will most likely occur in those environments in which the adolescent finds himself or herself (home, school, neighborhood). This monitoring is most effectively done when the adolescent is part of the monitoring. Allowing them to give feedback on services also places the adolescent in a partnership role in their treatment.

Phase V: Evaluate Outcomes and Terminate Services   *A. Evaluate Outcomes* As discussed in chapter 8, an evaluation of the effectiveness of the interventions employed by the social worker is a necessary component of the casework process. An intervention needs to be effective and efficient in order to achieve its goals and objectives, therefore the social worker must be able to utilize different methods to assess effectiveness of direct practice activities. The single-subject case design, such as those mentioned in chapter 8 by Walter Hudson, is especially useful when intervention focuses on a discrete behavior that is fairly easy to measure in terms of frequency, intensity, or duration.

When social work activities primarily center around making referrals, brokering, coordinating services, and advocating, the most appropriate methods to use might be goal-achievement scaling and task-achievement scaling. Self-anchored and rating scales are additional ways of individualizing the measurements used in an evaluation of client change. A goal checklist can be used to combine certain case planning and evaluation activities, thus reducing the time needed to complete evaluation-related paperwork. Sometimes the use of a post-intervention survey of client satisfaction is the only feasible way of gathering information about the probable impact of the intervention (Sheafor et al., 1998). Basically, evaluation always involves some type of measurement. Its importance cannot be overemphasized in terms of trying to observe and measure those things that are relevant and central to the provision of services to clients.

B. Terminate Services Termination with the juvenile offender and their family is likely to occur for one of two reasons: (1) either the length of time designated for the social worker to be involved in the case has lapsed, or (2) the goal(s) has been accomplished. Regardless, the termination process is one which the social worker must plan for from the beginning of her or his involvement in the case and must be discussed openly with the client during the contracting phase of the helping process. Ideally, termination is a mutual decision by social worker and client that occurs when the goals and objectives have been achieved; however, many situations are far from ideal, such as those involving juvenile delinquents, and the adolescent occasionally decides to end the relationship before reaching the agreed upon objectives.

If the social worker has been ordered by the court to work with the juvenile, the client might want to terminate the relationship but the social worker may believe there is need to continue. It must first be decided if all the terms of the order have been met before terminating service. If so, the social worker needs to explain to the adolescent her or his reasons for wanting to continue her or his involvement and also explain any possible consequences of terminating. If the adolescent still wishes to terminate, this should be discussed with the individual who has the authority to terminate the worker's involvement, in the adolescent's presence, and a mutual decision should be made in this regard.

The social worker must also anticipate how the termination might affect other persons in the adolescent's family and social network. In situations where a termination may place the client or others at risk of harm, it is appropriate to notify others of the termination if this process is consistent with the law and ethics concerning confidentiality and the release of client information.

In situations where the social worker has had a positive relationship with the adolescent and has assisted him or her in the accomplishment of objectives, the termination process can be difficult for both the juvenile and the worker. Therefore, as it approaches, it is desirable to gradually decrease the frequency of contact. If the adolescent has become somewhat dependent on the social worker, this weaning process should be accompanied by efforts to connect the client with natural helpers and informal resources within his or her neighborhood or social network. The feelings of loss and anger that often accompany the end of any important relationship should be discussed by the social worker and normalized for the adolescent.

Phase VI: Follow Up from a Multisystemic Perspective   *A. Family* One of the important factors to consider in follow up of an adolescent with delinquent or behavioral issues is the need of the family to have a sounding board for some time to come. One of the most effective resources for families in these situations is the mutual support of other families with similar circumstances. Programs that administer wrap-around types of services can be an effective base for the organizing of mutual aid groups for parents aiding families in forming neighborhood community groups who can respond together in reaching out to all their children has been found to be a very positive resource. The development of wrap-around programs for adolescents in a community has become an exciting type of program that lends itself to preventive techniques in working with adolescents with delinquent or behavioral issues.

B. Community Community follow ups in cases of delinquency are important in not only one case, but also in preventive services for many different adolescents and their families. One way that follow up becomes preventive is in the establishment of programs and systems that can offset the development of delinquency problems. Programs that attempt to network community institutions and services into a safety net by which the community working together can identify difficulties early and prevent their development are ones which place prevention as a priority.

C. Programs and Services If your community is not one that has resources and alternatives for families and adolescents with problems, it is important to ensure that these programs are developed for the types of case situations which you are encountering. As mentioned, programs and services require a preventive focus that can help identify at-risk youths and supply them with resources to offset their behaviors. A study by Quinn, Epstein, and Cumblad (1995) examined a program that attempted to create a public system of comprehensive, community-based care and individualized wrap-around services to children and adolescents with EBD (Emotional and Behavioral Disorders). The evaluation of the program demonstrated positive results for families and their children in a majority of the situations.

D. Policy Policies that affect delinquent and behavioral problems are often reflective of the general attitude toward criminal behavior regardless of the age of the offender. It is important to keep policymakers aware of and involved in the needs of parents and adolescents and in the outcomes of specific rehabilitative services through information and education that describes the programs. The methods for improving policies for juveniles will involve the social workers educating their community regarding the positive outcomes of programs and policies that help the juvenile and provide a sense of safety in the community.

SUMMARY

This chapter has provided an overview of some of the issues associated with adolescent delinquency and behavioral problems. The chapter example describes a Native-American family situation that has unique implications from the Indian Child Welfare Act. Different theoretical views of working with adolescents have noted unique techniques for use by the child welfare social worker. The chapter further emphasizes the importance of preventive programs and policies that impact on the family's and child's environment before the onset of delinquent or behavioral difficulties. Involvement in the community in terms of not only developing resources but as a network of support aids you in helping the adolescent achieve their goals. Community programs such as mentoring and wrap-around can provide such preventive measures.

QUESTIONS FOR DISCUSSION

1. Describe the difference between status offenses and delinquency cases.

2. What special services does the Indian Child Welfare Act provide for Native-American children?

3. Discuss the term "wrap-around" and how this macro program is utilized for juveniles.

4. Describe two different theoretical interventions to be used with juvenile delinquents.

5. Describe the behavioral rehearsal process and how it can be applied.

6. Describe how you might set up an evaluation tool for Marvin's situation.

10

■

Divorce and Loss

Jen Fungh has experienced enormous change in her five years of life: her family immigrated to this country from China when she was 1 year-old; her mother developed breast cancer approximately 1 year ago; her father recently moved out of the home and wants a divorce; and her maternal grandmother, who has lived with the family for several years, died of congestive heart failure 3 months ago. Jen has two younger siblings, a 4-year-old sister and a 3-year-old brother. Since their father's departure, the family has experienced extreme hardship both emotionally and financially. Jen's mother has applied for Temporary Assistance for Needy Families (TANF). The children have reacted to the dramatic changes that have taken place within the family in a variety of ways. Jen's younger brother has begun wetting the bed again, her sister cries a great deal and has withdrawn from playing with friends, and Jen is having difficulty in school, both socially and academically. Mrs. Fungh has considered the temporary foster home placement of the children until her husband is ordered to provide child support and until her physical health improves after the chemotherapy is completed. A child welfare worker has been assigned to the case by the Family Court for the purpose of assisting the family and assessing the need for temporary placement of the children.

INTRODUCTION

In the wake of a generation of high rates of divorce and the deprivation of parental support or care due to the absence of a parent from the home, there is an accumulating subgroup of single, separated and divorced families in our communities that are being designated as "high conflict" by mental health and legal professionals (Johnston & Roseby, 1997). This fast-growing group of families with 26 percent of the child population poses serious social policy problems (Garbarino, 1992). Many issues from these families clog the family court systems and require an inordinate amount of time and resources. Many of the children in these families are suffering emotional problems of clinically significant levels and, consequently, consume a disproportionate share of the community's mental health services (Wolchik, Ruehlman, Braver, & Sandler, 1989). Oftentimes the plight of these children is thrust into the background as the parents become embroiled in extreme conflict. Of paramount concern to child welfare specialists is the damage being done to the children's capacity to form trusting, authentic, emotionally gratifying relationships as they grow older. Thus, the strategies and policies for prevention or early intervention assumed by child welfare workers become critical to the ongoing development of the child who has experienced divorce or loss of parents.

While recognizing that divorce and parental loss is a crucial time for children affected by it, little attention has been given to a model for counseling children who, generally, are not responsible for what has occurred. These children frequently harbor guilt and feelings of responsibility, therefore it becomes the task of the social worker to be supportive of the child while, at the same time, maintaining a nonjudgmental attitude toward either parent. Although many children differ widely in their reactions to this life transition some other common themes observed in children of divorce and loss are:

- feelings of unworthiness
- divided loyalties and feeling "torn"
- love/hate feelings toward one or both parents
- a perceived lack of control over what is happening in their lives
- unrealistic feelings about a possible reunification of their parents
- a denial of the reality of the situation leading to social isolationism

DEFINING DIVORCE AND
LOSS CONCERNS

Perhaps one of the greatest concerns of divorce and loss is the way in which children seem to become caught in the middle. Regardless of custody outcomes, the loss of a parent can strongly affect the child's sense of self and their own developmental issues.

As the child begins to deal with the separation from parent or parents, they experience differing emotions regarding their bonding relationship. In many cases, children will move toward an estrangement with their parent or parents in order to adjust to their loss. Bowlby (1969, 1980) studied the effects of child/parental attachment and found that there were specific phases small children moved through following separation. Among these, the interaction with mothers as strangers was a phase seen as a copy mechanism for parental deprivation.

Causes of Divorce

While there have been discussions in the preceding chapters about the causes of loss related to a child being placed in foster care, adopted, or re-unified with a family, the causes of these situation tend to be predicated on the protection of a child from a dangerous situation. The changes in the marital patterns in the United States can be accounted for by many factors. Furstenberg (1994) notes that the following issues have attributed to these changes:

1. a change in the gender-based division of labor (women no longer focus on domestic activity and men no longer in the workforce)
2. the fact that most individuals, especially women, are no longer willing to settle for marriages which are "okay"
3. the sexual revolution
4. more liberal divorce laws

Many of the changes reflect the independence and the support of individ-ualization in America. The effect of divorce and the changing family system, however, has led to changes in children's welfare. While the vast majority of children raised in single-parent families do well (Amato, 1993), there are effects on children in regard to economics, instability of parental figures, and the issues of new family arrangements (Furstenberg, 1994).

POLICIES

Policies that affect issues of loss generally are set by the courts in that the courts most often serve as the *parens patriae*. This doctrine allows the court to serve as the parents of a child or adolescent in order to serve the best interests of the child. This can occur most often in divorce, child protection, and delin-quency cases. Beyond state policies and laws mandating custody rules, foster care, adoption, and the termination of parental rights are a few that are more preventive in nature. One such policy often enacted in many states is what is called *guardian ad litem*. This policy was initially attached to the Child Abuse Prevention and Treatment Act of 1974. As part of this Act, states were required to appoint a *guardian ad litem* for children whose best interests were not necessarily being served by their parents. Often, these guardians are asked to recommend to the court what family situations are in the best interest of the child.

Other policies that developed included those issues of financial support to families and children, as well as no-fault divorce laws. Proposals have included policies that (1) increase welfare support to single mothers, (2) increase child support from the absent parent, and (3) provide a combination of governmental policies that would provide a guaranteed standard of living for all families. These policies have yet to occur, however, and the child welfare social worker will need to work toward enacting policies that work toward these objectives.

PROCESSES AND PROCEDURES

Most children who suffer parental loss from the process of divorce do not move through this situation without being affected by the legal procedures. In general, children are included in the procedures through the court system. Sadly, the process within a divorce situation is set to be adversarial rather than collegial as in most legal proceedings. Before the 1970s, the divorce process was more difficult in most states. Prior to this decade, no-fault divorce laws did not exist. Without these laws, many families were left to fight over support, alimony, and custody for many years.

Now children move through this process by decision within the court system. Often there are family courts that will deal specifically with the cases of divorce. These family court systems tend to pay more attention to the well being of the children by attempting to help parents negotiate what are the best arrangements for a child. Social workers often fill the role of the family negotiator within the family court system and provide mediation for the parents.

SERVICES AND PROGRAMS

Perhaps more than any other situation, preventive types of programs have been developed for families in regards to handling difficulties and resolving divorce situations. Among these are groups developed for children to help them in their adjustment to a changing family system, programs that work with the entire family in supporting children through this process, and mediation programs where parents can work out their differences regarding the children before the children are affected by their disagreements. Preventive programs which aid in preventing divorce vary. Among these are programs provided by marriage counselors, intensive workshops to heal relationships, and premarital counseling. The prevention of divorce, however, often depends on the two individuals in the marriage, the issues, and the commitment to the relationship.

CULTURAL DIVERSITY

In the case of Jen and her brother and sister, the losses of the family and the possible placement of the children in a foster care situation places a very unusual strain upon this family. Their cultural background, which is fundamentally founded on the idea that loyalty in a family is of primary importance, is experiencing very strong attacks on this value base. Your understanding and sensitivity to the family's difficulties and concerns is very important to the long-term outcome for the family. In a case such as this, the maintenance of the children within the home would be in their best interest as it would reduce the addition of another loss.

The losses in this family have been overwhelming. The breast cancer of the mother has brought forward underlying loss issues. The death of the maternal grandmother will have caused great anxiety within the family due to the support most extended family members play within the community. Additionally, the pending divorce will have brought embarrassment and shame to all members of the family as issues of privacy and family unity are of utmost importance (Lum, 1996). The role of the child welfare social worker will be difficult in this family situation as aid from people outside the family is generally not wanted in Asian–American families. Your entrance into this family must be respectful of their privacy and their need to build trust. Many children in Asian–American families have a difficult time in speaking about their emotions as they have been taught to keep these to themselves. In many cases, difficulties for these children will be seen in acting out behaviors such as the brother's bed wetting and Jen's difficulties in school. Your work with the family will involve all members as the focus will be on empowering the family and mediating through the support issues so the children may stay within the home.

Identify Protocols in the Following Case Example

SWPIP PRACTICE MODEL

The use of a primary social worker to form a close relationship with the children and family is particularly important in cases of divorce. Working with children who have experienced the loss of the family unit that has provided them with a sense of security throughout their lives can be a significant challenge to the child welfare worker who has limited knowledge of the dynamics of the underlying problems. The issue of trust becomes of paramount concern for these children and must be dealt with immediately by the social worker and other professionals involved in the child's system (Webb, 1993). This critical issue will be discussed more thoroughly as we progress through the tenets and protocols of the model, using the case of Jen as an example of how to establish a practice continuum.

Phase I: Establish an Immediate Relationship with the Child and Family Based on Warmth, Genuineness, Empathy, Positive Regard, and Empowerment   In their study of 104 children of divorce, Wolchik, Ruehlman, Braver, and Sandler (1989) found that the lower the level of support the children received, the stronger the positive relationship between stress and adjustment problems. In addition, they found that children with high support from nonfamily and family adults during periods of high levels of stress, reported fewer adjustment problems than did children with low support. The results of the study further indicated that the relationship between support and adjustment among children of divorce are complex and depend on both the level of stress experienced by the child and the source of support. The researchers also suggest that the value of support from nonparental adults can be beneficial to the child experiencing divorce in the following ways (p. 489):

1. by buffering the negative impact of divorce events
2. by allaying fears of abandonment or who will take care of the child's basic needs
3. by helping children accurately interpret aspects of the divorce, such as who is responsible or why their parents spend less time with them

The supportive relationship of a child welfare worker can help to diminish the loss of self-esteem that children often experience during and after divorce. Just as in cases involving abuse or neglect, a primary task of a social worker is to establish a level of trust and mutual respect with the family that will set the stage for further involvement. This is initially accomplished by explaining to the parent and child your role as a child welfare worker and the functions of the agency you represent. It is also helpful to explain the nature of the helping process and the fact that, as a social worker, you are involved for the purpose of assisting them in seeking a solution to their difficulties.

Just as we have reiterated in previous chapters, it is also important for the social worker to normalize some of the feelings the parent and child might be experiencing. Because many children experiencing divorce often identify with the feelings and perceptions of the custodial parent, it can be advantageous to the establishment of a relationship with the child if, at first, you are able to establish a warm, trusting relationship with the custodial parent. This can be initially accomplished through the use of empathic communication skills in which you reflect sensitively the inner feelings of the client and communicate empathy regarding these feelings on a level that the client will understand. In addition, it is useful to discuss with the parent the normal behaviors and feelings typically manifested by children who are experiencing divorce and a sense of loss. This will enable the parent to normalize some of their own possible feelings of guilt over what they might perceive to be their role in contributing to the breakup of the family unit.

With regard to the case of Jen, it would be important to have a significant level of knowledge about the social and cultural norms and values shared by the Chinese culture with regard to divorce and the communication of feelings to professionals outside the family unit. Many cultures view the sharing of personal and private information about marital or family issues as prohibitive, therefore the social worker needs to communicate with the family a level of knowledge and understanding of these cultural attitudes early in this phase of the working relationship.

In view of the fact that children frequently feel a loss of control over their environment as the result of what is happening in their lives, the social worker can further enhance the relationship by allowing the child to guide the interview process and assume responsibility for making decisions whenever it might be appropriate to do so. For example, in the case of Jen, the social worker could begin the interview as shown in Highlight 10.1.

❖ HIGHLIGHT 10.1   Initial Interview

Social Worker: Hello Jen. My name is Mrs. Trantham and I am a social worker with the Family Court. Do you know what a social worker with the Family Court does?

Jen: No.

Social Worker: Well, we have a lot of parents and children who come to the court to speak to the judge about some problems they are having. The parents of some of these children are going through a divorce, just like your parents, and they need help with a lot of different things. So the judge asks a social worker, like me, to visit the family and provide any help that I can. But before I can help, I need to spend a little time with the family, especially the children, so I can see how they are doing and what type of help they might need. Are you beginning to understand now what a social worker does?

Jen: Sort of, I guess

Social Worker: I know it probably seems a little confusing now. Would you like me to help you understand a little better?

Jen: (nods her head)

Social Worker: Well, most children whose parents are going through divorce are feeling a lot of different things that they don't understand. They usually feel very sad and even a little angry about what is happening to them. They feel sometimes that they have done something wrong, and that is why Daddy has left. They also might feel angry with Mom for not being able to make things better. These are things that you

Continued

❖ **HIGHLIGHT 10.1**   *Continued*

---

might feel uncomfortable talking
about right now, and you don't
have to, but you might want to
later on. I've talked with a lot of
children who have gone through

what your family is going
through, and it's very normal for
you to feel a lot of different
things right now.

While the social worker's task in this case is to establish a working relationship with Jen and her family, it is also necessary to normalize her feelings
and communicate a level of understanding about the fact that she might not
feel comfortable talking about these issues so early in the relationship. Furthermore, by allowing Jen to make the decision about when an appropriate
time might be to communicate on a deeper level, the social worker communicates respect for her feelings as well as her cultural norms. It is important to
note here that a denial of the reality of the situation frequently occurs with
children of divorce, often leading to physical or psychological isolationism. As
a result, they internalize such self-statements as: "I will build a wall around
myself so that I will not be hurt anymore," or "No one understands how bad I
feel and how ashamed I am to come from a broken home."

During this phase of the model it might be beneficial to administer a brief
assessment scale with the child that would measure the level of depression or
sadness she might be experiencing. Scales from Hudson's Clinical Assessment
Package, Reynold's Child Depression Scale, or Burleson's Self-Rating Scale
(Corcoran & Fischer, 1987) would be helpful in planning for the intervention
phase of your work with the family. Not only do measurement instruments
validate your observations of the child, they can also add credibility to your
professional recommendations to the parent(s) concerning other resources or
interventions that might be needed.

**Phase II: Assess the Situation Briefly and Thoroughly Based on the
Following Systems**   *A. Child* It is the theory of many clinical practitioners and child welfare specialists that children who experience divorce in the
family progress through the same basic stages as individuals experiencing a
loss through death (Webb, 1993). Oftentimes the psychological reactions to
the loss of the parent who leaves the home, and the loss of the family unit in
general, strongly resemble the psychological reactions of the child who has
lost a parent or caretaker to death. The professional literature indicates that
the mourning of losses associated with divorce parallels in many ways that of
grief following death (Webb, 1993). For the social worker involved in working with families experiencing divorce, it is recommended that the stages of a
standard loss model, such as that of Elizabeth Kubler-Ross (1969), be utilized

in assessing the child and family systems. Basically, the Kubler-Ross model includes five stages, each of which present varying emotional reactions of children as they struggle to come to terms with the reality of the situation. Highlight 10.2 is a brief overview of the five stages of the model as it relates to divorce and children (Modified in part from Hozman & Froiland, 1976, pp. 271–276).

❖ HIGHLIGHT 10.2   Stages of Loss Model

1. *Stage One: Denial*
   This stage must be overcome by the child before further progress can be made. In an attempt to reject the reality of separation, children often try to eliminate the thought from their minds and show no signs of reacting to the situation. Unfortunately, parents often model this same inappropriate behavior for their children by hiding any indication of a possible separation. Denial in preadolescents often manifests itself through isolation types of behavior. The child may isolate himself from peers, teachers, and his environment. He or she may then learn withdrawal types of behaviors and exhibit a lack of interpersonal skills (Hozman & Froiland, 1976). For example, children who normally have not had difficulty interacting with friends may appear shy, not wishing to play with peers or talk to adults. The normally quiet child may exhibit loud, tantrum types of behavior in an effort to keep others away. As a result of this, the child's self-concept begins to evolve into that of an isolate.

2. *Stage Two: Anger*
   During the anger phase of accepting a loss due to divorce, the child frequently attempts to strike out at those who are involved in the situation. At times the attacks may be directed toward those who take the place of the parents, such as school personnel. The underlying dynamics in this occurrence have to do with the child's feelings of guilt because of the divorce. He or she may exhibit unusual assertive or aggressive behaviors: refusing to cooperate with school assignments or home chores, sullenness and withdrawal, or overt hostility toward peers. Anger exhibited toward the social worker might also be experienced initially in the relationship (Hozman & Froiland, 1976).

   It is extremely important, at this phase of the social worker's involvement, to be in touch with his or her own feelings about loss and if, whether or not, he or she might have some unresolved issues in that area due to his or her own past experiences with death or divorce.

3. *Stage Three: Bargaining*
   The child frequently attempts to bring the parents back together during this phase of the loss model. In doing such, he or she might become caught up in a gaming type of behavior, attempting to renegotiate the parents' relationship by means of the child's own behavior. The child may appear to be unable to focus on the academic material presented in school, or might be perceived as being in another world. On the

Continued

❖ **HIGHLIGHT 10.2** *Continued*

---

other hand, he or she might attempt to overplease one or both parents whenever any specific requests are made. If the child feels that the parents did not respond to angry demands or temper tantrums exhibited previously, he or she may then believe that by being very good the parents will come back together again. Often he will verbalize this in an attempt to negotiate a deal (Hozman & Froiland, 1976).

Another area of bargaining that the child might go through has to do with the debate within himself or herself of the choice of rightness or wrongness attributed to one of the parents. The child may reason, "How can my father be made to see how my mother was wrong (or vice versa)?" An attempt may be made to try to decide which parent is actually to blame for the "evil" of the separation.

4. *Stage Four: Depression*
As the child comes to realize that a bargain cannot be reached with parents, a depression will frequently set in. The child may regret past "evil" behaviors directed toward one of the parents, or may feel badly about some missed opportunities and experiences that did or did not occur within the family unit. Eventually, however, the child begins to prepare for the impending loss of the parental re-

lationship. A type of mourning will usually occur at this time (Hozman & Froiland, 1976). The child may be observed to withdraw from activities, from academics, or from social experiences. Here he or she may be seeking attention in other ways, such as through temper tantrums, or through more passive acting-out behaviors.

5. *Stage Five: Acceptance*
The final stage through which a child progresses in experiencing a loss is the acceptance stage. The child has now come to realize that although the original security of his or her world is presently gone, individual worth is determined intrinsically and not by external forces. During this phase the child comes to a more mature understanding of the love/hate relationship that he or she holds toward her parents. He or she also comes to the realization that future reconciliation is not a distinct possibility and begins to accept the probability of interacting with one parent and another adult in an interpersonal relationship. The child has then, with the assistance of the social worker, learned to accept the support of external resources. He or she has developed a new knowledge of himself or herself and, in addition, both self-confidence and self-esteem have begun to expand (Hozman & Froiland, 1976).

A major difference in mourning loss through divorce versus mourning the loss of a parent through death is the intensity of the anger response following divorce, which is often more pronounced because of the conflicts that precipitated the break-up and the underlying sense of blame and guilt about the failed marriage (Webb, 1993). Obviously, through divorce the bereaved must mourn someone who has not died. Children must also mourn the loss of their intact family, and their mourning is especially complicated because of the possible reversibility of the court's decision. In addition, it is further complicated by the omnipresent wish and fantasy about parental reunion. Intense and prolonged grief should be expected in situations where the parent is considered to be a central personal in the child's life.

Not every child will go through every stage of the loss model, nor will all individuals experience the stages in the order indicated; however, generally speaking, most children may go through the majority of these stages in somewhat the same order. It is possible to pick out a given theme, for example, "guilt," and to follow it through the various stages of denial, anger, depression, and so forth. The social worker, in being aware of the model, can then help to facilitate the progress directly to the culmination in the acceptance stage.

A thorough assessment of Jen in terms of her particular developmental level is of extreme importance when evaluating children involved in divorce in order for the social worker to adequately address the developmental needs of these children during the intervention phase of the model. Developmental information is also important in order for the social worker to determine if the child is progressing through the phases of the divorce normally, or if she or he might be experiencing some disabling adjustment reactions to the crisis. It would be significant to obtain information from others on how Jen has adjusted to various forms of crisis in the past and what, if any, coping skills she might have used. If her manner of coping in the past was adequate, however, and those previously learning skills are not working in the current situation, the social worker should identify the malfunctioning skills for use in structuring an intervention that is consistent with the developmental level of the child.

Black and Cantor (1993) suggest the information listed in Highlight 10.3 be obtained when assessing children experiencing divorce (pp. 130–141).

A parent with whom a child is positively identified can greatly influence and support the child's attempts to cope with anxiety, meet expectations, risk failure and rejection in the pursuit of success, and to negotiate friendships and heterosexual peer attachments. On the other hand, a child may identify with the parent's negative qualities: feelings, attitudes, convictions, or traits. A common means of detecting to what extent a parent is the object of a child's identification is through the use of fantasy. Children may display in their stories a perception of one parent as strong, powerful, or resourceful, thus aspiring them to acquire the same qualities (positive identification). On the other hand, they may identify with negative qualities that may be apparent in the boy who sees himself as inadequate because his father failed, a girl who feels rejected because her mother was self-absorbed, or a child who feels doomed to an impulse-ridden existence because of the precedent set by an alcoholic parent. It is the responsibility of the social worker to discriminate between healthy and unhealthy identification.

A thorough assessment of the child experiencing divorce and loss is extremely important, regardless of the role of the child welfare worker in his or her involvement with the child and their family. The impact of unresolved issues of loss, either through divorce or death, can render life-altering consequences for a child. In order to determine how the social worker and the

---

❖ HIGHLIGHT 10.3   Assessment in a Divorce Situation

1. *General Size and Appearance*
   A child's physical characteristics, gestures, and mannerisms may bear a striking resemblance to those of one of the parents and, as a result, may be favored by the other parent. Likewise, the child favoring a parent could also be a target of hostility or animosity by the other (displacement). As a marital relationship deteriorates, the parents frequently displace their anger toward the other partner onto the children in the family, particularly the child who resembles the other parent.

2. *Hyperactivity or Decreased Activity*
   Either hyperactivity or decreased activity are significant clues to a child's emotional state. Slowed motor movements may indicate depression, which commonly occurs in children whose parents are divorcing. However, the social worker must search further to determine if a depression exists for some other reason: rejection by a parent, school failure, medical illness, etc. Hyperactivity, along with an inability to concentrate and impulsive behavior, are common characteristics of Attention Deficit Hyperactivity Disorder (ADHD) in children. Although hyperactivity may be psychologically caused, it may also have a neurological source. As a result, one must be careful not to universally ascribe behavioral characteristics to flaws in parenting.

3. *Intellectual Function*
   The ability to grasp the significance of the family breakdown will to an extent depend on the child's intelligence. Brighter children with a greater capacity for abstract thinking will think through the possible consequences of a divorce on their future, and their ability to recognize parental manipulation could create less ambivalence in dealing with such a parent. Creative talent or some other manifestations of substantial intellectual ability may cause a child to be the object of parental favoritism. On the other hand, the child's intellectual competence may threaten a parent. Mental retardation can also trigger parental rejection or overprotection, either subtle or overt.

4. *Modes of Thinking and Perception*
   Impaired reality testing in the child may suggest the influence of a family member who is similarly handicapped. The capacity to make reality-based differentiations should be appropriate to the child's age. For example, by age 3 or 4, the child should display some ability to discriminate between fact and fantasy. By 6 or 7 most children should possess that skill. The social worker should carefully

---

parents can help children cope successfully with these issues, it is essential to understand the major factors influencing the child's reactions and adjustment to the loss.

B. Nuclear Family The primary social worker involved in cases of divorce might be required to assess the family system for a number of different reasons. Many child welfare workers are called upon by juvenile and family courts to conduct evaluation studies for the court and make recommendations concerning custody disputes. In some cases where children are involved in

❖ HIGHLIGHT 10.3   *Continued*

analyze the children's perceptions to determine their accuracy. Caught up in a flood of emotions for having witnessed scenes involving charges and countercharges, children of divorce are often taxed by mixed loyalties, fears of rejection and abandonment, rage, and feelings of protectiveness. One common result is a tendency on the part of very young children to distort events and issues. Their interpretation of an incident may change, consciously or unconsciously, to match the perception of their favored parent. Careful scrutiny on the part of the social worker may be necessary to determine the extent to which, and the means by which, parents reinforce an impaired view of reality.

5. *Emotional Reactions*
Children experiencing divorce usually harbor extremely mixed feelings about their parents during, and sometimes long after, the divorce process. While they usually love both of their parents, they might experience disappointment and anger with one or both of them. These emotions often coexist with fear, affection, and love. As a consequence, they are fearful of injuring one or both parents by their actions, thoughts, and feelings.

   When interviewing the child, it is important for the social worker to be creative in order to get him or her to overcome their anxiety sufficiently to generate sincere responses and provide useful information. Therefore, the social worker should clearly transmit the message that the interview is being conducted for the purpose of getting to know them as persons and provide assistance to them, not simply to extract information.

6. *Attachment and Identification Factors*
Identifying a preferred attachment figure is important in cases involving infants, toddlers, and very young children. In the presence of the parents, the social worker would observe the child displaying his or her preference for an attachment figure, often but not necessarily the mother, through attachment behaviors such as smiling, crying, crawling forward, following, and, perhaps more importantly, clinging and sucking. By observing these behaviors, the social worker can get some indication of to whom the child is more tied. For instance, a small child may specifically crawl to one parent, whereas an older child may choose to sit on the preferred parent's lap. This information helps the social worker determine to whom the very young child is most bonded.

heavily contested custody challenges, the court may consider an alternative placement for the child, either indefinitely or until the matter is no longer considered to be injurious to his or her well-being. This might involve placement with a close family member, deemed by the social worker and family to be an appropriate option, or foster care placement for those situations in which a suitable family member is not willing or able to provide adequate care. Regardless of what the role of the social worker might be, it would be important to assess nuclear and extended families as integral components of the client system.

Severe stress and disorganization are frequently experienced by families during the divorce process and in the first post-divorce year (Sandler, West, Baca, Pellow, Gerster, Rogosch, Vidu, Beals, Reynolds, Kallgren, Tein, Kriege, Colege & Ramirez, 1992). Mothers and fathers are often found to possess feelings of incompetency, loneliness, alienation, and depression. Behaviorally, they are less likely to make necessary demands on children, be consistent in discipline, reason with children, communicate effectively with them, or be affectionate with them. From this arises the observation that certain lifestyle changes that impact the emotional status of the custodial parent are manifested behaviorally in the parent–child relationship.

Two elements contribute to the satisfactory adjustment of children who have experienced divorce: (1) the ability of the parents to make the transition from a conflictual spousal relationship to a cooperative coparenting arrangement, and (2) the ability of the children to have free access to both parents. Several studies have found a strong correlation between poor adjustment in children and parental conflict, and the results of many studies indicate that the post-divorce relationship between the parents is the most critical factor in the functioning of the family (Peck, 1989). It is important for spouses to be able to separate the parental role from the marital role following divorce, in an effort to restabilize the family system. In a functional coparenting relationship, a combination of positive and negative feelings usually coexist, though neither to an extreme. Most discussions center around issues of parenting, with the major areas of disagreement revolving around finances and child-rearing practices. Some former spouses get together as a family for children's birthdays, school plays, graduations, and other such events; however, the most important characteristic of a successful coparenting relationship is mutual respect. This seems to insure the flexibility required for the ongoing negotiation of child-related issues.

With regard to the child's access to both parents, a joint custody arrangement can be superior to sole custody, if parents have been sufficiently able to resolve their hostility and support the child in maintaining a qualitative relationship with the other parent. Many children are dissatisfied with traditional, every-other-weekend visitations and often feel cut off from the noncustodial parent. Yet the success of a joint custody arrangement largely depends on the degree to which the parents are able to maintain positive communication and structure the arrangement based on the best interests of the child. Furthermore, it depends on the age and the developmental needs of the child as well. Physical joint custody may be ideal for adolescents, yet be wholly inappropriate for an infant. The social worker needs to consider this information strongly when called upon to make recommendations to the court concerning custody arrangements.

While an assessment of the degree of flexibility on the part of divorced parents in allowing the child free access to the other parent is important, it is equally important for the social worker to assess the degree of structure in the child's environment. All children have a need for structure and feel more secure in this type of environment; however, structure can mean different things at different developmental stages. For example, an adolescent might need to play a more active role in choosing when he or she will visit a noncustodial parent, yet teens need a clear set of limits about parental expectations in each household. With younger children, a set routine of visitation can often be best and reassures the child that he or she will be loved. This does not place them in a decision making position.

B. Extended Family Each and every member of the child's nuclear and extended family is affected by the divorce in ways that influence the process for everyone, depending in part on the lifecycle phase of the family (Peck, 1989). For example, there is evidence that close grandparent/grandchild contact is of value to all three generations following a divorce. However, there is the tendency for the families of origin to blame the other party and become as embroiled in the dynamics of the divorce as the two partners. Assessment of the degree of restabilization the extended family has achieved following the divorce process is important information for the social worker to consider. Many times this is achieved when a new person is brought into the family system (i.e., extended family member, babysitter, lover); however, the restabilization of a family unit depends on many factors, such as the economic and sociocultural factors affecting the entire family, or the distress associated with ongoing parental conflict (Peck, 1989).

As discussed previously, the use of a three-generational family genogram is an excellent tool to use in assessing the nuclear and extended family systems with regard to the issues being discussed here. It creates a graphic record of family membership, ethnic background, gender and occupational roles, significant events, and patterns of closeness and distance. By keeping the entire cast of characters in mind through the genogram, the social worker is able to extend his or her view of the family to those members who may exert considerable influence on the current situation. Nonfamily members, such as a parent's present or former lover, or other individuals who play an important role in family functioning can be added when appropriate. Additionally, the sequence of births, deaths, and other family events and crises occurring before or after the divorce may offer further insight into the family's difficulties. For example, in the case of the Fungh family, the immigration of the family from China, the death of the maternal grandmother, and Mrs. Fungh's development of breast cancer might provide valuable information.

A family's connections with extended family and social networks before the divorce are significant to note. Grandparents, aunts, uncles, and cousins involved with the child prior to the divorce often assume a supportive role and facilitate the adjustment process. Their involvement can provide a sense of continuity and safety during this tumultuous period, as long as the involvement is from a position of neutrality and reflects an attitude of respect for the child's feelings toward both parents.

Ethnic issues surrounding the morality of divorce can play a major role in the adjustment of the child and family members to the divorce itself (Perez & Pasternack, 1991). The ethnic origins of the family often shape patterns of handling a divorce. Different ethnic groups express their grief in the loss of the family unit in different ways. The social worker needs to have a significant level of knowledge concerning the values of a child's ethnic group in relation to divorce issues during the assessment and intervention phases of casework activities. Knowledge of religious factors associated with divorce would be equally important. For example, if a child has been raised in a religious environment in which divorce has been perceived as sinful or unacceptable according to the standards of the religion, then the social worker would need to assess the child's feelings in this area and the degree to which they might be affecting his or her adjustment.

D. Social Systems Divorce can entail major structural realignments in family, household, and kinship systems. With the rise in single-parent families, cohabitation, and homosexual unions, large numbers of the population do not live in what was once considered traditional family forms. Presently, there are no identified organizing principles for such family organization and dissolution; rather choices of kin and the quality of relationships appear to be discretionary and varied (Weston, Klee, & Halfon, 1989). Oftentimes the boundaries of family systems become somewhat blurred with the inclusion of other close relationships outside the family unit. These informal social systems are critical to the future adjustment of the child experiencing divorce. An assessment of the various informal social systems would be performed by the social worker and would include:

1. Stepfamilies, family friends, or neighbors who have maintained a close relationship with the child.
2. Peers of the child who have provided, or are able to provide, a supportive relationship.
3. Teachers and other professional individuals who have been involved with the child on a close interpersonal level.

The emotional needs of a child of divorce are, to a large degree, determined by the support they have received from these various informal social systems. The lower the level of social support, the stronger the positive relation between stress and adjustment problems (Wolchik et al., 1989). The social worker must first of all determine what support is forthcoming and, if that support is not from a person within the family system, will it continue? If support has not been initiated by these significant individuals, then it will be the responsibility of the social worker to set mechanisms in motion to include such people.

E. Resource Systems The formal social systems would include the child's school, church, family court system, public and private agencies, social service agencies, and so forth that might provide relevant services to the child or family in relation to the divorce process. A through assessment of these systems is needed in terms of the specific individualized services that they could provide that would address the particular needs of the client. For example, with increasing frequency the view is expressed that schools should provide services to the needs of this specialized population of children. More and more school districts are training teachers to deal effectively with the problems of children from divorced or single-parent families (Perez & Pasternack, 1991). Many schools are providing school counseling personnel during the evening hours for parents who work during the day, in addition to after school activities so that children may avoid going home to an empty house. School-based intervention strategies are beginning to appear, such as divorce groups for children, bereavement groups, and individualized counseling by school guidance personnel. Research has shown that support groups for children of divorce may serve an important function in lessening the negative effects of divorce processes on children (Farmer & Galaris, 1993).

Family court systems in many areas also provide services to children experiencing divorce in an effort to minimize the traumatic experience of the adversarial nature of the court process. Court counselors and those representing the private sector are often utilized to provide mediation services to families embroiled in divorce issues. *Guardian ad litem* programs are established under the auspices of court systems to represent children involved in heavily disputed child custody cases. Supervised visitation projects are frequently contracted through the courts to provide supervision over noncustodial parents who are involved in heated custody battles while they visit their children on a regular basis. It is extremely important for the child welfare worker who is involved with children of divorce to be familiar with the various court-related services in the community and how they might be able to address the particular needs of their clients. Additionally, the development of these services is necessary when there are none.

F. Programs and Services Programs and services for children experiencing loss will need in large part to be developed on a formal basis by the courts. On a more informal basis, programs and services which make use of the natural environments (schools, religious organizations, extended families) can provide a safe support for the child during difficult periods.

Phase III: Plan and Contract for Intervention with All Systems   The child welfare worker involved in cases involving divorce and issues of loss will develop a repertoire of skills and intervention strategies primarily aimed at two ultimate goals: (1) stabilizing the environmental influences that might be affecting the child(ren); and (2) enhancing the level of functioning on the part of the child and his or her family system. Utilizing a social work perspective in terms of targeting the interventions to include all the relevant systems in the child's environment is the major focus of the primary social worker.

Referring to the case of Jen Fungh at the beginning of the chapter, the intervention phase of the model will begin with the social worker assisting the parents in receding from a position of ongoing conflict and, as a result, focusing on the specific needs of the children. Throughout this process the social worker will interface with a variety of systems and will utilize a number of techniques aimed at specific goals developed with the involvement of the child and family.

In the remainder of this phase of the model, we will look at the various interventions provided by the following individuals and systems. It is the responsibility of the social worker to coordinate these interventions to insure that mutual goals are developed and achieved by involved professionals, thus preventing a fragmentation in services due to competing demands from individuals with different agendas. Of particular importance is the need for professionals who work in private, confidential settings with families of divorce to make sure they are working with the other helping professionals involved by sharing their various perspectives and reaching consensus about goals, prognosis, and intervention strategies.

A. Case Review and Coordination Meeting Making family separation and divorce less painful for children and parents require a fundamental redefinition of the role of the court. Furthermore, it requires new multidisciplinary partnerships between the court and attorneys, mediators, and mental health professionals to arrive at viable solutions. The role of the family court should be one of leadership in bringing the issues, the parties, and their helpers to the table to determine the following (Johnston and Roseby, 1997):

1. How fractured families can coordinate their resources and care for their children after the parents' separation.

2. How families can be helped to protect, preserve, and reconstitute the positive aspects of the parent-child and other family relationships, wherever possible.

3. How parents can resolve their ongoing disputes and deal flexibly with subsequent child-rearing issues in a timely manner, during the years that follow the divorce.

4. How the community can help these families while they are raising their children.

B. Involve Family in Planning Process Within a framework of collaboration, social workers and other mental health professionals cannot work with parents and children involved in divorce in isolation from the legal decision-making process. Some triage and coordination with court-related resources and services is imperative and often must be assumed by the primary social worker assigned to the case. The following court-related services should be considered as possible resources for families involved in divorce, whether disputed custody is an issue or not:

1. *Parenting Education*
   Parenting education may be provided within the court by community agencies in a separate setting, or by collaborative efforts between the two. Such programs serve as preventive measures and are designed for the broadest population of families involved in conflictual divorce issues primarily centering around child custody matters. Several studies note that

divorcing couples with children are frequently ordered by the court to attend parent education classes to learn about the needs of their children, how to minimize the stress of their own divorce transition, how to problem solve and make decisions together, and how to provide a post-divorce family environment that will protect and promote their children's development (Lehner, 1994; Shepard, 1993). Some jurisdictions have mandated parent education for all parents filing for divorce; some require it only when parents register a disagreement about the custody and care of their children at the time of filing. For other jurisdictions, it is still voluntary.

2. *Mediation*
The majority of court jurisdictions now have some provision for mediation of custody disputes by statute, court rule, or judicial referral (Black, 1989). Mediation as originally conceived is the use of a neutral, professionally trained third party (i.e., family law attorneys, clinical social workers, other mental health practitioners) in a confidential setting to help disputing parents clearly define the issues, generate options, order priorities, and then negotiate and bargain differences and alternatives about the custody and care of their children after divorce (Johnston & Rosbey, 1997). Mediation empowers parents to make their own decision, which increases satisfaction and compliance with agreements reached. Parents involved in the mediation process are encouraged to contain their emotional distress and focus on the children's issues. It is an effective preventive measure, as well as the intervention of choice for tailoring visitation schedules to fit the needs of the child and family.

3. *Therapeutic Mediation*
Impasse-directed mediation is a therapeutic approach to custody disputes involving high-conflict, bitterly litigating families, all of whom are re-ferred by family courts after failing brief issue-focused mediation or following custody evaluations and judicial orders. It is a confidential service provided outside the court in a private setting. It is designed to assist parents in dealing with the underlying emotional factors that have converged to create an impasse between the parents in developing a psy-chologically sound agreement based on the needs of their children. The goals of impasse-directed mediation are to develop sound child access plans, to help the family through its divorce transition, and to build a structure that can support the parents' and children's continued growth and development.

4. *Custody Evaluation and Recommendations*
When attorney negotiations, mediation, and therapeutic interventions cannot resolve disputes over custody and care of children, mental health professionals (frequently social workers) are called upon to offer expert opinions to the court as to how these disputes should be resolved accord-ing to the current legal standard, which is "the best interests of the child." Evaluators should serve as impartial experts appointed by the court, or by

stipulation of both parties, and are usually provided access to all parties. Basically, the role of the evaluator is to provide an in-depth assessment of the situation by interviewing the parties and other significant individuals, checking appropriate records and documentation, and then providing a recommendation to the court on custody and other relevant issues.

5. *Supervised Visitation*

    Rapidly growing programs in this area have been developed in response to some types of highly conflictual divorce disputes. They are staffed largely by volunteers or social work interns and their aim is to provide a protective setting for visitation to occur between children and the non-custodial parent. In the most extreme cases, the supervision may be part of a therapeutic intervention into the parent-child relationship and is undertaken by a trained clinical social worker or counselor. When children are at high risk (because of a parent's psychological disturbance, substance abuse problems, history of emotional or physical abuse, molestation, serious domestic violence, or child abduction), visitation may occur only under the continual supervision of a neutral third person in a closed setting. In other situations, it may be performed in a more open setting by family members or friends.

The primary social worker assigned to a case involving children of divorce needs to coordinate and collaborate with pertinent school personnel to insure that appropriate school-based resources are being utilized to meet the child's needs, and that interventions are being carried through with a degree of consistency. After having involved the child's teacher in the assessment process, the social worker would also involve him or her in structuring interventions within the school environment that would be consistent with services being provided through other client systems.

1. *Support Groups for Children of Divorce*

    Counseling groups within the school setting that focus on assisting children through the divorce process and dealing with bereavement issues that occur can be extremely beneficial. Children may be referred to groups by teachers, guidance counselors, school psychologists, or social workers. In order for the group process to be effective it needs to focus on the development of coping skills during the crisis period, stress-management skills, facing and dealing with losses, facilitating self-disclosure, and the development of positive communication skills.

2. *Direct Services*

    Direct services can be provided to children of divorce through individual as well as group counseling. Individual counseling provided by school guidance personnel or school social workers should be child-focused and systematically oriented. A mediation approach that focuses on obtaining parental cooperation and involvement is effective; it works to enhance communication between the parents with the counselor or social worker assuming the role of a "mouthpiece" for the child.

3. *Indirect Services*

In addition to more obvious direct services, schools are in a unique position to provide indirect services that may be helpful to children. These would include training programs or the structuring of teacher in-services that would be directed toward increasing the sensitivity of school personnel to the needs of children of divorce. Mental health personnel and other related professionals could be instrumental in teaching guidance counselors to work with children individually and in groups. Necessary skills and knowledge would include the ability to recognize and address typical and atypical effects of divorce upon children, associated behavioral manifestations, factors that affect the degree of trauma experienced by the child, and appropriate and useful methods of assessment and psychometric tools. Restoration of hopefulness and optimism in the client population should be emphasized (Hutchenson & Spangler-Hirsch, 1989).

Modifications in school curriculum could effectively address the issues associated with divorce in an indirect manner as well. Suggested possibilities might include courses at the secondary level in child development and effective parenting, or social studies courses that address family dynamics as influenced by societal changes. Such curriculum changes can facilitate the ability of children to understand change in their lives and to develop coping mechanisms that are useful in preparing them for changes in their own lives and in the lives of others.

With regard to the case of Jen Fungh, the primary social worker assigned to the case would need to develop interventions that would flow from the process of assessing the child along with her nuclear and extended family systems. The interventions structured in these areas would need to take into consideration the ethnic and cultural values of the Fungh family, and reflect a sensitivity to the relevant issues involved. Within this context, it would be important for the social worker to involve the parties as much as possible in the intervention phase by explaining everything that is being suggested and gaining their consent. This will give them the opportunity to fully consider the pros and cons of the tasks involved, in regard to the "fit" of these tasks with their individual system of cultural values and norms.

The use of family therapy techniques in cases involving divorce and loss warrants careful consideration by the social worker as a potentially effective intervention and, dependent upon assessment and evaluation, in some cases proves to be the intervention of choice. Because of interfering relationship forces within the family system it is often futile to work with the individual child without initially dealing with the family dynamics that might be taking place. However, the majority of child welfare workers have received minimal training in family therapy, if any. Regardless, they are frequently placed in the role of counseling the family to some degree. The social worker's understanding of family systems from a strategic and structural vantage point is essential in working with families of divorce. When problems are conceptualized systemically, an individual's problems cannot be understood in isolation from the context in which they occur (Brandell, 1997). Therefore, a firm grounding in a family system's approach to counseling families is an important aspect of all child welfare.

C. Contract with Family and Support Services for Their Roles in Implementing Plan
During divorce, disturbed family relationships are often characterized by rigidity and repetitive, circular, predictable transactions that often contain several messages where words say one thing, but behavior and intent say another (Mishne, 1983). Parents commonly turn to children for help in maintaining the family equilibrium which, in most cases, places an enormous burden on them. Scapegoating a child may also occur in a family as a way of reachieving homeostasis when the previous family balance included a scapegoat. It is often the responsibility of the social worker to assist the parents in understanding how destructive this can be to the child, and to help them develop a more constructive approach to dealing with the situation through educational methods.

Phase IV: Implementation of Plan   *A.* The first phase of work with the family involves explaining to the parents the need for them to give consent for all information to be held confidential, with the exceptions of any child abuse or threats of violence, for which reporting is mandated. It should be understood that the social worker can exchange information freely between parents in separate interviews, however, the children's confidences will be privileged. The only kind of feedback parents receive about their child should be general clinical impressions, unless the child consents to the release of more specific information. Parents should be told that the child is always the focus of intervention and that they, as adults, are always viewed in their roles as parents.

Secondly, utilizing a family system's approach to working with the family, the social worker would focus on attempting to change the interactional patterns within the family system. This would include the inclusion of an integrative strength-promoting approach that emphasizes each parent's ultimate concern for the welfare of their children. Using the Fungh case as an example, we will discuss an appropriate strategy for counseling the family in this situation, the goals of which are: (1) to improve the coparental relationship between Mr. and Mrs. Fungh through the development of a more positive interaction style, and (2) to address the developmental needs of the children involved.

Based on the assessment, the social worker might conclude that the family needs to deal with the issues surrounding the separation more effectively in order to again achieve a level of homeostasis. In the Fungh family, this might be more effectively accomplished by focusing on changing dysfunctional family interactional patterns to more functional ones, a common characteristic of families experiencing separation and divorce. These dysfunctional patterns of communicating often create double-bind situations for the children, in which there is a discrepancy between overt actions and words and nonverbal communication on the part of one or both parents. For example,

Mr. and Mrs. Fungh would be encouraged to communicate with their children on a feeling level by acknowledging the conflicting feelings they must have surrounding the divorce. It would be helpful to encourage the parents to suspend their own hostility toward each other and talk with the children together. With the assistance of the social worker, they would need to develop a plan in which they would reach a consensus about how to communicate to the children the reasons for the divorce on a level that does not place blame on any particular individual. The social worker might encourage them to talk with each child separately in order to address their individual concerns, after having provided the parents basic educational information on the developmental levels of their children. Many parents are not aware of how children normally perceive and respond to troubling situations based on their particular developmental level as well as their chronological age.

Thirdly, within the system's framework, the social worker would then assist the parents in developing an awareness of how to deal with the individual needs of the children. The Fungh children are all manifesting distressing symptoms pertaining to their difficulties in adjusting to the pending divorce, and each child's needs should be addressed through both parents. For example, with regard to Jen, the social worker might assist the mother in communicating to her a level of empathy concerning the feelings of loss that she might be experiencing and how these feelings might be affecting her interpersonal relationships. Any efforts to normalize feelings on the part of parents can be of considerable comfort to a child and, with the parent's assistance, helps them to more effectively integrate these feelings into their daily repertoire of activities.

It is believed that social workers, in emphasizing the strengths within the family system and within the individual parents themselves, will be able to assist them in making positive changes in their interactional patterns (Friesen & Poertner, 1995). The ultimate results will help the children to progress and grow through the adversity of the divorce, thereby developing a sense of mastery and control over what is happening to them in their environment.

In addition to working extensively with the family during the intervention phase of the model, the social worker must also direct a great deal of attention toward the children. The children frequently are forced to witness highly emotionally charged confrontations between their parents which can be extremely upsetting and frightening to them. The social worker is often put in the position of needing to process the child's feelings and perceptions concerning such incidents with him or her, therefore a strategy of providing emotional support during this process needs to be utilized. In Highlight 10.4 we will demonstrate a supportive interaction between the social worker and Jen Fungh after she had witnessed a violent argument between her parents, during which the police were called to the home.

Utilizing the Kubler-Ross model of loss discussed during the assessment phase, the information obtained would form the basis for structuring interventions that focus on each child separately. Children within the same family often progress through the stages of loss at different intervals of time, depending on

---

❖ **HIGHLIGHT 10.4   Child-Focused Intervention**

Social Worker: Jen, you must have been very scared by all of that.

Jen: Yeah, I thought that my Dad was being arrested.

Social Worker: That must have been awful.

Jen: Yes, and I was afraid that Daddy would hurt Mommy.

Social Worker: Were you ever afraid that Daddy would hurt you, too?

Jen: No, I always go to my room.

Social Worker: You go to your room, when?

Jen: When Daddy and Mommy fight.

Social Worker: Do you get afraid when they fight?

Jen: Yes, but I feel safe in my room.

Social Worker: They can't hurt you in your room.

Jen: No, but . . . *(she begins to cry)*

Social Worker: But what, Jen? *(social worker reaches out for Jen's hand and holds it gently)*

Jen: *(she continues to cry and mumbles something about Daddy hurting Mommy)*

---

their age and developmental level, therefore the different assessment information obtained on each child will be used to structure individual interventions. The techniques used during each stage of the loss model can be applied to other stages as well and are not limited to one particular stage. It is important to keep this in mind as we discuss various interventions based on the stages of loss listed in Highlight 10.5.

B. Continuing Coordination of Services Because so many children suffer the consequences of divorce and loss, the full extent of their needs may be unknown for some time. Maintaining services and the coordination of the programs being offered will enable you as the child welfare social worker to work toward successful outcomes for the child and their family. Coordinating with the court system as well as with the attorneys involved in the case may be difficult but also necessary. Your role in cases such as this will be to work for mediating solutions to issues and to continue to find ways to empower children to take a stand for themselves in these situations.

C. Support and Empowerment of Child and Family As has been noted, of particular significance is the support and empowerment of the child and family during this period of change and restructuring. The child needs to come to an understanding that although he or she may not be able to change the situation that is occurring, they can control their actions and express their emotions in appropriate ways. The methods for empowering a child often depends upon the age of the child and the development level. Helping older children to learn to express their needs to the adults in their lives will aid in these types of loss situations. For younger children, expression of emotion through play therapy allows the child to move forward in the emotional growth and aids in decreasing acting out behavior.

❖ HIGHLIGHT 10.5 Techniques for Stages of Loss

1. *Stage One: Denial*
   During this phase it would be appropriate for the social worker to communicate the ramifications of the child's behavior to the parents so that they might modify their interactions with the child. In working with the child, a direct confrontation of the behavior is suggested. The important concept at this point is to enable the children to legitimize their feelings, whether good or bad, warm or hostile. These feelings must be properly channeled and understood so that the child may come to express them as an acceptable part of his or her personality (Hozman & Froiland, 1976).

   Reality techniques may be used to enable the child to begin to accept the presence of many mixed emotions. Role playing and other forms of behav-ioral rehearsal is one way for him or her to begin testing reality. Various play materials can also be used to help him or her identify various feelings (i.e., doll house and a family of dolls, toy animals, puppets, a play telephone, drawings or paintings). Through the use of these materials, the social worker can encourage the child to express his or her reality by making up stories using dolls or puppets, having pretend conversations over the toy telephone, or complete scenes or situations initiated by the worker.

   The social worker can also use the technique on modeling by demonstrating appropriate coping skills or behavior and encouraging the child to try them out on other significant individuals. Modeling can also take place by encouraging the child to observe individuals (peers, relatives, teachers) who have experienced a divorce and have accepted the reality with appropriate behaviors.

2. *Stage Two: Anger*
   During this stage it is important for the social worker to encourage the child to express feelings of anger in a safe, accepting environment. The worker can assist the child in focusing the anger and to understand its origin (Hozman & Froiland, 1976). This can be done by one-on-one counseling in which the child is allowed the realization of the observed anger. During this process the social worker would provide him or her with unconditional positive regard, even as the anger is being expressed. The worker would then attempt to channel the anger and make certain distinctions to enable the child to understand the sources of the anger and the limits of expressing it appropriately. Finally, the social worker would assist the child in focusing the anger on a visual object in order to work through the feelings successfully. For example, allowing the child to hit a stuffed animal, a box, or blow up a balloon will help legitimize and direct the feelings. The use of toys such as bop bags, play doh or clay, movable puppets, and paints allow the release of angry feelings through aggression.

   In addition to play techniques, the social worker can also use role reversal with the child. In this situation the worker would structure a role playing situation in which she or he might play the parent. The child would then be encouraged to safely express negative feelings, with the social worker responding to the feelings appropriately. It would be important for the parents to be informed of the technique in advance, and advised on how to respond appropriately when negative feelings are expressed to them.

Continued

❖ **HIGHLIGHT 10.5** *Continued*

---

3. *Stage Three: Bargaining*
   During this phase the social worker must be aware that the child's self-perception may be that of an arbitrator.

   She or he should then assist the child in focusing on the lack of personal responsibility for, or control of, the situation (Hozman & Froiland, 1976). This can be done by initiating interactions where the social worker explains to the child that he or she is only responsible for his or her behavior and not that of others, even his parents'. At this point it might be appropriate for the social worker to refer the child to a social interaction or problem-solving group, either at school or at a local mental health agency. A divorce adjustment group in which problem-solving approaches dealing specifically with divorce issues are discussed might be beneficial.

   During the bargaining stage, the social worker might also use toys which could enhance the child's self-concept. It would be important to allow the child to select from a variety of toys that might include lego blocks, puzzles, erector sets, etc. These enable children to achieve a sense of mastery and control by allowing them to solve problems on their own. The social worker would then, through verbal responses, help the child to generalize these concrete successes to real life situations.

4. *Stage Four: Depression*
   When a child begins to withdraw from things going on around him or her, or exhibits temper tantrums that might be viewed as a means of getting attention, it would be important for the social worker to intervene immediately in order to assist him or her in progressing to the acceptance stage. Helping the child verbalize feelings through techniques mentioned previously would be extremely beneficial. He or she should be encouraged to express any emotion that might be observed in the presence of the social worker, followed by statements of empathy and assurance on the part of the worker that normalcy will return to his or her life. Acknowledging the child's feelings of sadness and pain is important, however, efforts should be made to avoid over-assuring remarks such as "everything is okay" (Hozman & Froiland, 1976).

   It would be helpful for the social worker, during this phase, to encourage new relationships and experiences for the child. Planning with the parent(s) a program for initiating new activities, and enlisting the assistance of peers, could draw the child back into a level of social activity. In particular, peers who have experienced divorce, and are now functioning well socially, might be utilized to model desired behaviors for the child.

5. *Stage Five: Acceptance*
   At this stage the child has come to a more mature understanding of the situation, in particular the realization that his or her parents are not going to reconcile. A planned process of terminating with the child will be implemented with the involvement of one or both parents. The child should, at this time, be aware of not only the present status of his or her feelings, but also of anticipated future occurrences and how to deal with them appropriately (Hozman & Froiland, 1976).

D. Identification of Barriers and Resolution Involvement of all the family members early on is a major factor in decreasing the barriers that could develop in your work with the family and child. For example, in Jen's situation she may not feel as if she can express her needs to her parents. Your role will be to identify these cultural issues early and plan your intervention accordingly. If Jen cannot express these verbally, what other ways might she learn to express her needs?

You also need to work toward resolution with the adults in the family in order to support the children. In this case, although the mother has not received support from the father yet, there may be reasons for this lack of financial aid. Working with the father on an individual basis to resolve these issues is a reasonable first step. Being open and empathetic to both parent's needs will enable you to be more successful through your role as a mediator.

E. Monitoring of Services and Plan As has been noted in the majority of chapters, the monitoring of the services and plan are of key importance in bringing about a new healthy family situation. Identifying issues in the services and plan with the family aids you in resolving barriers before they develop. Working with other social workers through networks to resolve the difficulties in these services and programs will prevent additional work in the future.

Phase V: Evaluate Outcomes and Terminate Services   *A. Evaluate Outcomes* A single subject design often consists of an evaluation comparing baseline measures with outcome measures at the time of termination of a case. In order for the social worker to be assured that the interventions utilized have been effective, a baseline measure is obtained at the beginning of the assessment phase through the administration of scales mentioned previously in the chapter. The scales are also administered after each intervention, and then finally are administered again at termination. This provides the social worker with a systematic method of not only determining the effectiveness of the intervention, but it also allows him or her to chart and view the degree of progress the client might be making in accomplishing targeted goals. Nurius and Hudson (1993) have described the use of a computerized assessment system that interactively enables workers and their clients to assess client problems and monitor progress over time. According to these authors, computers can eliminate much of the time and effort involved in various aspects of the evaluation process.

Another form of evaluation is through the feedback elicited from the client by the social worker concerning his or her perceptions of various parts of the helping process that he or she found to be useful or detrimental. A child whose age is above the level of cognitive reasoning, or a parent involved in divorce, should be able to provide feedback to the social worker on specific techniques that were utilized by him or her which facilitated progression through the grief process. In addition, written evaluations in the form of client satisfaction surveys can also be completed by clients following termination to provide feedback on their perceptions of the quality of services provided.

B. Terminate Services Many child welfare workers involved with families of divorce will likely be employed in agencies or organizations whose function involves providing services according to fixed time intervals, thus requiring termination to be planned at the point of initial contact with the client. Under such circumstances, particularly in cases involving divorce, a number of emotional reactions are frequently experienced by the client and the social worker as well. With the issue of loss being a predominate one for the child of divorce, the feelings relating to loss issues are commonly exacerbated by early termination with the social worker. This sense of loss can be a deeply moving experience involving a form of sorrow generally associated with the task of separating from a person whom the client may have learned to value. However, during the course of working with a family experiencing divorce, a form of excessive dependency on the social worker may develop and, as a result, separation may be viewed as the loss of an irreplaceable person and cause negative reactions to termination (Mishne, 1983). Such reactions can include, but not be limited to, the following in children of divorce:

1. *Displays of anger through emotional outbursts, passive-aggressive behavior, or defiance*
   The child may experience the termination process as a form of rejection by the social worker and, as a result, may exhibit an intense anger toward him or her or other significant individuals in the child's system. The anger might come out in a variety of different forms, ranging from emotional outbursts when challenged by authority figures, to the display of passive-aggressive or defiant behavior in which he or she refuses to follow through on required tasks. The social worker should discuss these reactions in relation to the termination by normalizing the child's feelings and providing some reassurance that he or she is not abandoning the child. Furthermore, it would be important to affirm the fact that the child will receive support through significant others in his or her life to help adjust to the losses experienced.

2. *The reoccurrence of old problems or the development of new ones*
   As the final termination date approaches, children may experience a certain amount of anxiety or fear of separating from the social worker and may create a new problem, or reexperience an old one, for the purpose of keeping the worker involved. The child might also be testing the loyalty of the social worker through this process as well, anticipating that he or she will not leave if he or she truly cares about the child and, therefore, will remain involved through the problem resolution period. While it is important for the social worker not to minimize the importance of the problem, it is equally important not to delay the termination by assisting the client in solving the problem without first exploring feelings about termination. When placed in appropriate context, new problems that might arise are generally insignificant.

3. *Increasing dependency needs on social worker*
   Throughout the intervention phase, it is important for the social worker to stress a client's strengths and abilities in dealing effectively with the divorce,

thereby enhancing their self-efficacy and their ability to function satisfactorily outside the worker/client relationship. However, a social worker's lack of focus on client strengths by reinforcing weaknesses and deficiencies can increase dependency and severely limit the client's opportunities for growth.

Despite persistent efforts by the social worker, termination prior to the attainment of goals specified in the beginning can cause the helping process to end unsuccessfully and can create frustration and anger on the part of the social worker as well as the client. In such cases it is imperative that the social worker refer the client elsewhere for additional services. The social worker needs to communicate information about unmet goals to the referral source, with the consent of the client, and receive assurance that there will be some consistency in further casework activities. It is also important for the social worker to discuss with the client directly: (1) factors that prevented the accomplishment of goals, and (2) how the client might feel about seeking additional help in the future. Furthermore, the social worker will be able to gain a better understanding of clients' emotional reactions to termination, and be more effective in assisting them through these reactions, by considering their reactions to their feelings of loss associated with the divorce and their pattern of coping with these feelings. If clients can be made more aware of their previous negative patterns of coping with separation and loss, and develop more positive patterns of coping during the intervention phase, this will enhance their ability to successfully work through the termination process.

Phase VI: Follow Up from a Multisystemic Perspective   *A. Family* In most family situations that suffer from a divorce or loss, there comes a point in which the family restructures to function as a different kind of family. One way to ensure that the family moves in this direction is to help them identify what they want to look like in 2 months, in 6 months, and in a year. By setting goals for the family to become a functioning unit in a different form, you have aided them in learning to cope with a new family structure. Contacting the family at these points to see where they are and to lend support will help in the ongoing change process.

B. Community Following up in your community to ensure that there are preventive types of services for divorce and loss issues is a precursor to reducing your time spent on individual cases. Ensuring that there are programs that educate couples before they marry will help prevent some issues from occurring. Preparation of young adults about the realities of marriage and the importance of a stable environment can begin early. Working with junior and senior high schools on developing family lifestyle courses is one method for advancing change within the system.

C. Programs and Services If there are programs or services within your community that are not family friendly, such as companies that do not support family care and responsibility, it is important that you, as a child welfare social worker, find ways to educate these services or programs about the advantages to maintaining strong family environments for both children and adults. This type of preventive work will help in reducing the numbers of cases seen in child welfare and even, if the reduction is only one case, it will be well worth the effort.

D. Policy Those policies that affect the divorce case will always affect the children. Policies that focus on custody and support issues being handled through family courts with counselors have been shown to aid children best in their adjustment to the new family situation. Continued advocation for more mediating approaches to family loss through divorce, rather than adversarial approaches, will produce less children in need of outside support or guardianship.

SUMMARY

In this chapter we have examined the issues which affect children experiencing loss, particularly as it relates to divorce. The focus of the chapter has been on divorce and the effects of divorce on children. Specific methods for intervention have been presented from both a preventive and residual focus. Your ability to focus on preventive programs and mediating processes in the court systems will reduce the pressures on children and the cases needing residual services.

As a child welfare social worker, your responsibilities extend beyond the family into innovative and out of the box ideas. Working with companies to promote family friendly policies is part of your responsibilities. Developing mediation skills and programs that prepare children for loss can reduce the pain for many children and families.

QUESTIONS FOR DISCUSSION

1. How do the loss stages by Kubler-Ross fit with children in divorcing families?

2. What findings in studies about children of divorce are common?

3. Describe the elements that aid the child to make a satisfactory transition in divorce.

4. Discuss the indirect services that can be instituted for families experiencing divorce.

5. Discuss how contracting with a family going through divorce can have increased difficulty.

6. How can policies affect change for children of divorce?

11

■

Children with
Special Needs

Amanda is a 21-month-old toddler currently living in a foster home. Amanda was born with AIDS and must be tested on a regular basis for the illness. Amanda is the only child of Mary and John Hill. John, who was diagnosed with AIDS following Amanda's birth, died of complications from pneumonia only 10 months after his daughter was born. Mary, who was also diagnosed as having the AIDS virus before the birth of Amanda is currently living with her parents. Although Mary's parents attempted to care for both Amanda and their daughter, due to their age and lack of other family support, Mary decided in the end to give Amanda over to child welfare services for care and possible adoption. Amanda, although born with the virus, has not yet shown any signs of the illness. With new medical interventions, there is every possibility that Amanda may fully recover. Recently, Amanda's foster family has expressed an interest in adopting her.

INTRODUCTION

AIDS is not the only special need with which child welfare social workers work. It is, however, a very serious issue and the number of children born with the disease has until recently increased yearly. In this chapter we will be examining the specialized needs of children who come into contact with child welfare services because of mental or physical challenges, as well as those related to illnesses such as AIDS and drug addiction. These situations have far-reaching effects on our society as these are the children who experience isolation and at times deprivation from basic developmental needs.

DEFINING THE ISSUES

Children with AIDS

In 1993, 4,906 cases of AIDS in children were reported in the United States. These numbers saw steady increases over the next few years with over 8,000 cases reported by 1995 (Centers for Disease Control and Prevention, 1995). More recently, births of children with AIDS has begun to decrease (McCarthy, 1999). Lockhart and Wodarsky (1989) note that social workers must be able to address many different issues affecting children with AIDS. Among these the legal, social, and medical issues continue to challenge both the child welfare worker and the family. The treatment of HIV positive pregnant women during their pregnancy has helped reduce the number of HIV positive children. However, mandatory testing of pregnant women raises privacy concerns for many people and has yet to become a mandatory process.

AIDS has numerous impacts on both the child and the family. The threat of death is an overarching fear for the family manifested in overprotectiveness of the child or in their isolation. Results of these behaviors can intensify a child or adolescent's feelings of rebellion and rejection (Lockhart & Wodarsky, 1989). Issues associated with isolation or rejection can also affect the family, thus, social workers need to develop a variety of community services that address these issues. Mutual aid types of programs in communities may offset some of these concerns (Goldstein, McGowan, Antle, Brownstone, Donoghue, James, Rodger, & Sloane, 1996) as people in communities become more comfortable with the AIDS issue and take steps to offer support.

Children Born with Drug Addictions

Children born with drug addictions are behind their counterparts, even prior to birth. The National Association for Perinatal Addictions Research and Education estimated that some 11 percent of all newborns suffer severe health issues because of their mother's use of illegal drugs in utero (Chasnoff, 1988). These children may suffer from irritability, lower birth weight, growth retardation, developmental delays, and gross motor delays (Chasnoff, 1988). With such a large percentage of children ill, society is affected by the higher costs of medical care and the preparation of education for the drug exposed child beginning school (Miller & Fisher, 1992). Significant costs both financially and emotionally occur in the child welfare field as many of these children need to be placed in specialized foster homes to meet their needs and yet these homes are not available. Mundal, VanDerWeele, Berger, and Fitsimmons (1991) found higher numbers of separations at birth and more attachment issues in substance-abusing mothers than nonusing mothers. Building a relationship with substance-abusing expectant mothers to work through their drug addiction gives them the fullest opportunity to build attachment with and to care for their own children. Gustavsson (1992) notes the need for non-judgmental attitudes and sensitivity to pregnant chemical-using mothers in order to engage and build trust with the child welfare social worker.

Research on innovative programs suggests that bridging projects such as T.E.A.M.S. (Training, Education, and Management Skills), have found their greatest success in the education of the child welfare social worker. The focus of these programs is to educate professionals about drug effects on infants and the methods best utilized for dealing with these problems. The positive results of programs such as these suggest there are many ways to improve not only child welfare services but prevent futher difficulties for this growing population (Edelsten, Kropenske, & Howard, 1990).

Children with Mental and Physical Challenges

Children with special challenges (both physical and mental) are often a forgotten and overlooked population in our society. Due in part to the discomfort many people feel around disabilities; services and programs for this population have not received widespread attention. Morris (1997) suggests this is due in part to the isolation of these groups from the rest of the population. The prevalence of these challenges vary but are estimated to be between 1 and 3 percent of the childhood population. The importance of bringing these children more into the activities of the rest of society lays with the belief that it is by this method that children become more adjusted and society assumes a greater comfort around those with special challenges. It is also important so that we as a society will recognize their needs as individuals to self-actualize and support their growth.

The families of these children are also in need of support and counseling to deal with their special issues. Parental stress and a lack of resources can lead to situations where these children are abused within their own families (Baladerion, 1994). These situations, along with foster care and adoption (Lightburn & Pine, 1996), are a few of the more common problems which need to be addressed.

Causes of Special Challenges

Children who have special challenges span a wide range of areas. Children who are born with physical and mental challenges at birth can generally trace the cause to genetic and/or prenatal factors. When we define newborns with special needs, there are the obvious physical differences which can be seen in children born with illnesses such as Spina Bifida or Down's Syndrome, or congenital physical challenges; however, there are also those children whose needs are not as visible. One such challenge is autism. Autism affects some 3.3 to 16 per 10,000 children (Wing, 1993). These figures emphasize the complexity of the problem and its diagnosis. The major symptoms in autism relate to the child's lack of socializability to others and the lack of motivation to learn to relate. Communication skills are also a problem with limited verbal and nonverbal gestures used to communicate. There is general agreement that autism is a development disorder from neurological causes.

While many of these special needs situations might be prevented through genetic counseling and prenatal care, many cannot. As science focuses on prevention, the role of the child welfare social worker will be to support these children to achieve their highest potential and to encourage parents to seek out appropriate medical care before and after counseling.

POLICIES

Possibly one of the most significant policies passed in the last two decades regarding children with disabilities was the Adoption Assistance and Child Welfare Act of 1980. This Act legislated the concept of permanency planning and reasonable effort being put into the stability of a family life for a child (Maluccio, Fein, & Olmstead, 1986). The act was to also include those with special needs. Yet despite this, many children with special needs are still being placed at an alarming rate in out-of-home placements with no adoption actions occurring. According to Petr and Barney (1993), the placement rate is 20.5 percent of all children in out-of-home placements having special needs. These alarming statistics alert you as the child welfare social worker to the serious need for families and children to have intensive supports and resources for themselves and their children.

Policies and funding that affect children with AIDS, autism, physical and mental disabilities, and infant drug addictions are generally handled by state block grants with little consistency in their implementation. Therefore policies affecting children with these types of special needs differ from state to state in terms of financial support and social services; however, the large numbers of children in need of services in the child welfare system requires that we begin to look at different alternatives to the prevention of their placement. The study by Petr and Barney examined the support systems of families with special needs children (mental, physical, emotional, and medical) and found that the major support vehicle they had were other parents in the same situation. From a mutual aid perspective, these findings indicate the importance of child welfare social workers bringing families together for this support.

Despite the Education of All Handicapped Children Act (P 194-142) initiated in 1975 and Amendments of 1986, which mandated the equal accessibility of children with special needs into the education system, many of the families in these situations do not believe that the education of their children is being adequately handled. Most families felt that the individual educational plans for their children did not take in to account their individual needs. In 1990, the Individuals with Disabilities Education Act attempted to provide parents with a method of expressing concern over their child's plan through an appeal process (Harvey, 1995). This act also expanded the antidiscrimination processes for adults and children with special needs. These policies have slowly begun to make a difference but children with special needs and their families still have much more to secure for themselves through other policy changes.

PROCESSES AND PROCEDURES

There are numerous processes involved in working with children with special needs. Some of these involve child protective services and foster care. Protective services most often becomes involved when there is an identified at-risk child. Children born with drug-addictions, AIDS, and other special needs are often considered at risk because their families do not have the resources or supports available to care for the child. Additionally, children with special needs have been found to be more often neglected or abused due to the stress the family experiences in caring for them (NCCAN, 1993). The identification of abuse in children with special needs is at times difficult, due in part to the denial of the abuse and the attributing of the abuse signs to the child's disability.

Child welfare social workers are often notified of a possible child at risk case through a hospital, health worker, or therapist. Once identified, the process of assisting the family as soon as possible is key. Support and concrete services to these families can often bring quick and positive results. In situations where the child is in immediate danger, such as a drug-addicted infant with a mother who refuses to seek treatment, foster care may be the only alternative until a plan is worked out. What becomes crucial is the timing of the intervention to prevent futher difficulties.

SERVICES AND PROGRAMS

There are a variety of services that have been developed in the child welfare field for children with special needs. Among these programs, as noted, are those which identify at-risk situations in order to provide a preventive and effective method for dealing with concerns. Additionally, programs that bridge between micro and macro social work interventions have been shown to be the most successful. Among these, mutual aid support groups, educational and legislative groups, and government-backed task forces have helped to produce changes in many of these areas of special needs. As a child welfare social worker, you will have the opportunity to be not only a part of but a leader in groups and programs that can bring about dramatic change. Being able to think outside the box and develop services that are both responsive and involve the families and their children will have the most success.

Identify Protocols in the Following Case Example

SWPIP PRACTICE MODEL

Because the SWPIP model is based on prevention as well as intervention, dealing with those circumstances that can negatively affect a child before birth is crucial to the ongoing prevention of children with illnesses such as AIDS, drug addictions, and particular types of genetic birth challenges as in Down's Syndrome, Spina Bifida, and retardation. Prevention in the area of prenatal care accounts for many of the ways social workers can help children before they are born.

Just as important to remember are the prevention of special circumstances that can occur following the birth of a child. Among these, accidents create situations where children will develop special needs. A major condition created by accidents is brain injury. These injuries can manifest themselves through mood disturbances, learning disabilities, speech defects, and sense-related difficulties that may not be easily spotted from physical appearance. An overdose of drugs, whether intended or accidental, is another leading factor in the development of special needs in children and adolescents. Situations that occur after birth have many similarities and at the same time many differences. The SWPIP model provides a framework in both cases.

Phase I: Establish an Immediate Relationship with the Child and Family Based on Warmth, Genuineness, Empathy, Positive Regard, and Empowerment   Often when you are working with families and children with special needs, you may be working with more than just one agency, and in some cases with more than just one family. As in the case of Amanda, there is Amanda's natural biological family, her biological extended family, and her foster family, as well as the health professionals who work with both her and her family. It is important to build relationships with all individuals involved with the child. In Amanda's case, the relationships between the natural parent, extended family, and foster family, will be equally important.

Although Amanda's mother has placed her in foster care, the reality of what will happen with Amanda has yet to be decided by her natural mother and extended family. Additionally, those already established relationships with other professionals involved in the case will influence the outcome of care and family life for Amanda. In a case such as this, the interests of other professionals may conflict with one another. What may be seen as good for Amanda's mother may not be good for Amanda or her grandparents. The ability to coordinate and negotiate in the best interest of Amanda and her family will be important to the process in which decisions will be made.

Children with special needs require not only special services but very often special amounts of time to work through the issues that encompass their families and themselves. Most situations in which you provide services for families and children with special needs will be on a voluntary basis. For this reason, the development of your relationship with the child and family may occur through a much easier and more natural process. However, in some cases, for example a child born with a drug addiction, these situations are often not only nonvoluntary, but difficult to monitor if the drug addiction is not known before the birth of the child. For this reason, early response by hospital and medical personnel to at-risk situations may require you to set up meetings and involve yourself more in working closely with hospital staff.

Phase II: Assess the Situation Briefly and Thoroughly Based on the Following Systems

A. Child The child's situation must be thoroughly assessed based on a full biopsychosocial level. In the case of children with special needs, the physical and mental challenges these children face are at times overwhelming. It is important to clearly assess what strengths and limitations the child and their family are experiencing. In Amanda's situation, as she is not currently exhibiting signs of the virus, it is not as necessary to assess what is happening for her physically; however, the basic fact that she has the AIDS virus in many ways may be affecting how she is interacted with and how this knowledge may be affecting her own sense of self and her development. Although there are hopeful signs of cures for all AIDS victims, positive results for children are just beginning. This reality creates special circumstances for Amanda and the family who will care for her. The strengths that a family can provide Amanda if the illness becomes active are critical for the planning of her home situation.

B. Nuclear Family Part of understanding the nuclear family's role is in gathering information on how the special needs situation came about. One of the most common reactions of parents to the birth of a child with special needs is their feelings of guilt and responsibility for the situation. In Amanda's case, her parents' illness may certainly have affected their feelings towards themselves and Amanda. Ultimately the final decision her mother may make about her upbringing will also be affected by these feelings. While Amanda's natural mother has placed her in the care of a foster family to protect her and to ease the burden experienced by the maternal grandparents, this does not mean her mother will not still hope to return her to herself and/or the maternal grandparents even though she has talked of adoption. Close attention should be paid toward the mother's desires and those fears she may not be discussing (her own illness, as well as the illness Amanda may experience). This will be important in aiding the mother to make her decisions about what is in the best interest of Amanda.

C. Extended Family Systems The maternal grandparents and their desires are also important. As the only extended family members and as the grandparents their rights are upheld by most courts in the United States. Although they may initially recognize that their ability to care for Amanda and her mother are not realistic, they may possibly begin to feel guilty themselves about not having Amanda with them. Their involvement in the decision making process is needed for the success of the intervention. Their support and continued relationship with Amanda is important to maintain even if she is adopted, as these natural helping networks can often form the foundation for the child's future.

D. Social Systems The existence and use of informal social systems to support the family often become more of a difficult issue when there are special needs involved. Because many individuals are uncomfortable around physical and mental challenges, as well as chronic and terminal illnesses, the availability of informal social support systems may be minimal; however, there are social systems that can be developed through more formal means. Mutual support groups that focus on families who have similar circumstances in their lives can make up for a lack of natural helping networks. These can often be developed through the agency.

E. Resource Systems While there are many different types of formal resource systems available to families and children with special needs, it is important to recognize that to a large degree the types of services available are dependent upon the state and local community in which the family lives. This expands your involvement in taking a leadership role to bring about positive and comprehensive services in your community if they do not exist.

F. Programs and Services Let's assume in Amanda's case that there are very few services being offered in her community for families and children with AIDS. This is when you will have an opportunity to think outside the box. You decide to work with your case management team to develop resources in the community for families with AIDS's members. One of the actions you decide to take is to jointly apply for a grant with other team members to produce or support programs at the local hospital. Your ability to bring together different organizations and individuals to focus on needed resources also brings about positive relationships between different members of the community.

Phase III: Plan and Contract for Intervention with All Systems   *A. Case Review and Coordination Meeting* In a case review and coordination meeting, the professionals who may be involved in special needs cases will often include health personnel. Health personnel are sometimes not as familiar with the workings of the child welfare system. It is the social worker's responsibility to not only educate families and children as to the process of utilizing services, but also to educate those other areas of the community that will be involved in the activities. A true community-based focus for Amanda would include the involvement of child welfare services, health personnel, and all resources relevant to meeting Amanda's needs as well as her family's.

B. Involve Family in Planning Process Involving Amanda's natural and extended family in the planning process will help forestall any miscommunications, as shown in Highlight 11.1.

C. Contract with Family and Support Services for Their Roles in Implementing Plan As you can note from the preceding example, contracting with all those involved in the case will build support and empower them to come to decisions. Also, remember that the child's interests regardless of age take precedence over other considerations. As part of your role, you will need to ensure that the community services provided are meeting the family's needs and be able to monitor these processes.

❖ HIGHLIGHT 11.1 Planning and Contracting with Family Members

Meeting with Mother, Grandparents, and Foster Parents

Social Worker: I thought it would be good for all of us to come together and talk about what our desires are for Amanda.

Mother: I am glad we are getting together. I have been very nervous over this meeting but I wanted to talk with you about Amanda.

Foster Mother: We've been very nervous too—hoping you will let us adopt her and yet knowing how unfair this has been for you.

Grandfather: It is hard on all of us.

Social Worker: I know it is, Mr. Levy. Let's talk about ways to make it less hard, especially for Amanda.

Mother: Well, I want Amanda to have a loving family, but I'm frightened that she might develop the illness and then you would regret adopting her.

Grandmother: Amanda and my daughter are all we have. We are scared of losing her even though I know we are not well enough to care for her.

Social Worker: Why don't we start here about our plan for Amanda and each list what we would like to see happen and how working together we can do that.

❖ **HIGHLIGHT 11.2   Dealing with Chronic Grief**

Social Worker: I thought your part in the planning last week was very good. I know it was difficult.

Mother: It was difficult in many ways. I feel guilty about her illness and about her having to go live with another family although I thought they were very nice. I feel like I've lost her already.

Social Worker: That's the hard part, isn't it, to feel like you've lost her? Although she's here and you can see her, you feel like she's gone.

Mother: It's more than that. I feel like I've hurt and lost her twice. It's my fault. (*begins to cry*)

Social Worker: (*reaches over and touches hand*)

Mother: She will hate me. Thank God there is a family who will love her as long as they can.

Social Worker: It is hard for me not to say things to make you feel better because that is what I want to do, but I also know that to resolve many of the feelings you are having, I must let you feel them. (*touching Mother's arm*) However, let's not forget that she does not have the active illness now and many treatments have recently been developed to cut down her risks. You are right that the foster parents do love her, but as we talked last week part of what they will do if you decide that Amanda will be adopted is to let her know how much you loved her and how hard it was for you to leave her.

Phase IV: Implementation of Plan   *A. Continued Implementation of Interviewing Skills and Practice Techniques* Your continued work with Amanda's mother in allowing her to express her fears and hesitations will enable her to make her decisions feeling supported and understood. Very often in special needs situations there is a sense of grieving for the child and their possible loss. Grief signifies the pain many parents continue to suffer when they think of their own child's chronic special needs. Helping parents to understand that these feelings are normal enables them to move past more difficult issues.

B. Continuing Coordination of Services Another major role you will have in special needs cases will be the ongoing coordination of services. Because special needs families and children tend to utilize services for longer periods of time due to the chronic conditions in the family, your role will be to maintain the level of support and coordination needed to achieve their goals. The establishment of groups of concerned parents is also a very practical way to aid in the continuing coordination of services. As parents are empowered they move beyond the needs of their children and can focus with other families to monitor and create changes to affect their situation in a positive way.

C. Support and Empowerment of Child and Family One of the major issues in the case of Amanda will be the empowerment of both her families (biological and foster) to work through whether an adoption is a viable alternative. Support is strongly needed for those who care for Amanda. Symptoms such as failure to thrive, chronic respiratory infections, and malnutrition are only a few of the physical responses that Amanda might experience if she develops the virus in an active state. These medical factors, as well as the reactions of the families to the possible adoption process, will require the support and empowerment of all members in the family. Of vital concern is maintaining a relationship between the mother and foster parents. If their goals become very different, negotiating between these differences can be done on a non-adversarial basis. As the family succeeds in each step they will feel empowered to move beyond these issues and to work toward issues that are more preventive in nature. Each step becomes a gain to the overall goals of the family and their overall confidence in handling situations.

D. Identification of Barriers and Resolution In cases of special needs there are many factors that can serve as barriers to a family and child succeeding in the implementation of their contract. Aside from individual interpersonal factors, there are those issues that are most likely to affect the ongoing support that a family and child need to access over time. These tend to be the policies and resources that can be given to the child and family. In special needs cases, as we have mentioned, there are generally extended periods of time in which outside services and resources are needed. Ensuring that policies offer not only the best resources for families with special needs children but also offer them for extended periods is an important consideration.

E. Monitoring of Services and Plan When you are monitoring the services and plan for a family and child in a special needs case, it is important to be aware and sensitive to the perceptions of the family and child. Services which on the surface appear to be very supportive for some families may in fact be ineffectual if not harmful for others. As we have noted, there are a multitude of emotional issues that are infused throughout most special needs cases. Among these are the parents' and child's feelings toward the condition. Depending upon who is involved in your community for supportive resources and services, it is important to be aware that the method by which service providers and individual families handle these special needs may be quite different. What approach might be good for one child and family may not be good for another. There will be cases, especially in special needs, where there are issues which you or members of the interventive team may not understand. It is especially important in these circumstances to allow the family to determine the priorities of their issues to be resolved.

Phase V: Evaluate Outcomes and Terminate Services The evaluation of outcomes and the termination of service in a special needs case must depend upon the contract that is set. As noted, many children and families will be in continuing need of services for longer periods than other cases in child welfare. Your role will be to empower the family and child to move forward and deal with additional issues as they come. It is important to understand that the policies and services that aid special needs families cannot be done by yourself alone. Families need to be able to aid themselves and stand up for their child's rights. It is your role to help educate and facilitate them in their activities.

A. Evaluate Outcomes In special needs cases we need to evaluate outcomes on a plan that sees even small successes. In many ways these cases are very different from other child welfare situations in that the child may never completely recover to what is considered the traditional development in childhood; however, their development may be right on target or even ahead according to what their special need requires. Establishing what is considered a gain for each child individually will aid in maintaining the successes and morale of the family and child.

B. Terminate Services Treatment in special needs cases allows you as the child welfare social worker to focus on what are both short-term and long-term goals of the family. While your work in the specific role you hold within an agency may be limited, the role you play as a case manager for the child may continue for a longer period of time than your specific responsibilities. This often occurs when plans that are made with the family require some continued involvement on your part.

Ending sessions with a family and child with special needs can also be very draining when the child is unable to understand or comprehend the reason you will no longer be involved. Attempting to clarify this with both the family and child early on will benefit both, however, there may be those circumstances that do not allow for this. Remember that very often children with special needs have experienced many losses in their lives and your gradual ending of this relationship will be the most productive method for termination.

Phase VI: Follow Up from a Multisystemic Perspective   *A. Family* Because resources and services are needed in a special needs family on a more extended basis, the issues that often emerge as part of family follow up are likely to be different. One of the major responsibilities for you will be to continue to follow up on the programs and services that are being provided by other agencies and the advocating activities the families are undertaking themselves. Time can also be a major barrier for many family members. Their desires to advocate for their children may be limited by the amount of time they have to spend caring for their child. This is where respite care and other forms of family support cannot only alleviate the stress of a situation, but also help family members to create changes for themselves as well as their children.

B. Community As we have discussed, the role of advocacy is very important in empowering a family, but just as important is the need for the community in which they live to be responsive to their needs. Recognize that your role in the follow up of these cases is to ensure not only the education of the community in the prevention of special needs, but also in the education of how a community can gain from knowing these families and children and helping them reach their goals.

C. Programs and Services The programs and services related to special needs are often limited in many communities. Issues of transportation, respite care, day programs, home health nursing, and volunteer homemakers are all areas that will require your attention. Indyk, Belville, Lachapelle, Gordon, and Dewart (1993) reported the use of a community-based approach to HIV case management proved to be the most beneficial for families needing continuing coordination.

D. Policy As noted, families of children with special needs are important to the success of policies being enacted to resolve their difficulties and to prevent the continuation of problems within services and programs. Networking families with similar issues and empowering them to continue working toward successful solutions will affect changes in services.

SUMMARY

This chapter has focused on the issues of children with special challenges. While there are a variety of types of special needs, there are many similarities between the difficulties parents and children experience in dealing with these differing needs. While specific methods for handling different types of situations varies with the issue, it is important to remember that the best people to resolve issues for the family is the family themselves. Their empowerment is what will protect the child and help to produce well-being for the entire family. Groups of these families serving as mutual aid support can also bring about policy changes with the appropriate support.

Specific areas of service have also been addressed in this chapter. In particular, issues related to foster care and adoption have been raised. Foster care and permanency planning as it affects children and their futures is an area of child welfare that needs further research and program evaluations. While the adoption process can lead to an independent living situation, the ability of many children to reach this point can be sadly hampered by their age, race, and/or physical condition.

QUESTIONS FOR DISCUSSION

1. Discuss the importance of building the relationship between foster and biological parents.

2. Describe different etiologies of genetic disabilities.

3. Failure to thrive is a term used for infants who often lack nurturing. How might this occur in the case of a child born with a drug addiction?

4. Services for families with special needs children require a longer length of intervention. What types of policies would aid in this?

5. Discuss methods for best integrating special needs children into the community.

6. Describe how a mutual aid group could be facilitated for families of special needs children and what goals it might set.

12

■

Conclusions: Leadership and Learning

INTRODUCTION

The field of child welfare depends upon the beliefs and values that future social workers have in the profession and how they will work with and for children and their families. The focus of this book has been to expose you to a unifying model of practice and to empower you as a social work professional to lend the leadership needed in the child welfare practice arena to implement different models. Your role in thinking outside of the box and taking steps toward a more macro focus of equality for all families will lead to better prevention as well as intervention. The practice and outcomes from different unifying models will in many ways depend upon the leadership available in the child welfare field, as well as in society. As a professionally trained social worker, you will have the opportunity to not only share your thoughts and ideas, but also move into leadership roles that allow you to implement your values and beliefs.

Leadership

The role of leadership is not always an easy one in child welfare, as you will recognize. The responsibilities of performing your job as a child welfare social worker often leaves little time for advocating and lending leadership in creating changes in national policies for children and families. The importance of child welfare practice that focuses on equality and the advancement of all families and children as a priority in this country is a responsibility the child welfare social worker cannot ignore. It is important to remember that social work is about change and that the best way to bring about the change in practice the book is suggesting is to find the opportunities to create challenges to promote the change. Leadership in the social work profession is about the ability to be comfortable with change and to look for opportunities to make situations better for all individuals.

Leadership has been described by Weinbach (1998) as a way to influence and shape behaviors of others. Although this definition clearly acknowledges the role of leadership in the management of individuals, it needs further definition when considered outside the context of the agency in which the person works. In a profession the word leadership means much more than influencing and shaping the behaviors of others. It calls for the person to seek out issues within the profession and examine ways in which these issues can be resolved or improved. In the profession of social work, leadership calls for a person to constantly seek out better methods for preventing hardships on oppressed groups, as well as improving the resources available to all. Because leadership in professions calls for more investment in thought and actions, it is important for all these factors to be recognized by those who seek leadership positions.

All social workers are leaders by the definition of the role a professional must play in helping create changes for the betterment of all people. The ability to recognize this as a part of your professional responsibilities and to develop the skills that can help in achieving these leadership characteristics will aid not only in your own development, but also in your comfort in being part of the profession.

There are many different theories about how leadership develops and what values and skills are needed. Probably one of the most well-known theories is based on personality traits. This theory suggests that there are different qualities in leaders that are similar among individuals. Contingency theory suggests that leadership is created by the situation and the needs of the time. The "person in environment" philosophy of social work fits well within this definition as it takes in both the personality of the individual as well as the context of the situation. From these theories of leadership, it is possible that at any given point in time, any one could serve in a leadership position dependent upon the current situation as it exists at the moment. In the case of social workers within a child welfare agency, an approach to team work and the development of leadership qualities in all members of the team may be the most appropriate.

The ability to be a leader may be open to everyone, but the ability to be a successful leader requires more than being in the right place at the right time. There are several conditions that a leader must attempt to create to be successful. These conditions include: (1) an environment that values professional values and skills, (2) an environment in which teamwork is appreciated and respect is held between professionals, (3) an environment that values each person's position and function, and (4) an environment in which individuals feel comfortable in voicing their opinions and making suggestions (Weinbach, 1998).

Highlight 12.1 looks at an example of a child welfare situation in which leadership is needed. How should Tom go about providing this leadership and in what manner? What are the macro and micro issues that need to be addressed?

The ability to lead in changing policies and creating preventive programs for families and children may require you to spend more than what is considered an 8-hour day. Social work is a profession rather than a career and when you are a part of a profession your values and beliefs affect your life. Therefore, the changes you hope to make in your role are affected by the value system of the profession and your ability to adhere to these values in your personal life.

Because realistic change occurs through a step-by-step process in most situations, it is unrealistic to think of major changes in national policies occurring in one giant leap. Changes, therefore, can occur within the child welfare setting itself which produces more preventive and universal strategies than residual if there is a step-by-step process that can be laid out, implemented and then dispersed. As you read through the protocols in chapter 3, you found a process by which community intervention leading to prevention was introduced. Although many of the protocols listed in chapter 3 are part of the current child welfare system in some ways, some are not. There are also those

---

❖ HIGHLIGHT 12.1   Leadership Opportunity

Tom had been working in the Children's Aid Society for approximately 8 months. During that period, there had been numerous cases of drug-addicted newborns added to his case load. The issues surrounding these situations, which generally came from information from the hospitals, had not been addressed in the agency. No specialized placements or intensive services had been initiated for this population. Additionally, Tom recognized that education in the community was needed to prevent these situations. The number of cases on his workload as well as those on other social workers in the agency appears to preclude other actions than those in dealing with each individual case.

protocols which while written down and taught are seldom implemented because of time constraints and residual types of service requirements that exist in most child welfare agencies. Therefore, going about change through a step-by-step process may be the only alternative that exists for those who care about children and families. This process can be implemented through the leadership of not only child welfare managers and administrators, but as noted, also through frontline workers. Part of your role as a child welfare social worker will be to have the ability to be flexible, to be alert to opportunities, and to create change, while at the same time respecting and carrying out those practices that have been proven to be the most effective intervention for families and children.

Questions you may want to ask yourself regarding your ability to be a leader in the field of child welfare center around your capacity to interact well with others, communicate your ideas effectively, be flexible, and have the ability to transfer learning. As well, your ability to be open to criticism and to make changes as appropriate reflects the social workers' potential for leading and working with others in difficult situations.

Learning

In being an effective change agent and leader in a child welfare setting, it is important to recognize the difference between what is represented in a training environment and a learning environment. The training environments that now exist in child welfare agencies look very much like the organizational training that has been developed through the business approaches of industries. These types of training environments often focus on job behavior and skill implementation rather than on the critical thinking process. This is very true in child welfare settings where "caseworker" jobs are made up of many tasks and the roles can extend and cross with other positions with common tasks and behaviors. For example, a protective service worker may also be a "child abuse investigator" because some of these be tasks overlap. However, as you may have learned, this limited focus on task training does not necessarily address the processes needed in each of these roles. Therefore, the environment in which child welfare is learned needs to be one that focuses more on the ability to process solutions with different skills.

There are several issues about developing learning environments within child welfare settings. Learning environments require time for ongoing education, transferring of knowledge, and understanding of all components of a role; few states have regulated educational competencies for the hiring of child welfare caseworkers or continuing their learning and although the Child Welfare League of America (1991) produced a number of core competencies for child welfare workers, the implementation of these competencies across the country has not mandated as states make their own decisions about training and the skills needed to implement child welfare services and policies.

Many different models of skills and competencies for child welfare workers have been developed (Wells, Stein, Fluke, & Downing, 1989; Stevenson,

Leung, & Cheung, 1992) and many of these programs and training methods have proven invaluable to child welfare social workers in going beyond basic tasks and behaviors. Regardless of the model of learning, however, the transferability of this learning into actual implementation within the field is an area of great concern in child welfare. One of the major causes for the loss of the transference into the field has been the lack of involvement of supervisors in the learning and the continued transference of competencies into field cases (Mather, 1998). Birmingham, Berry, and Bussey (1996) examined a method for developing certification of child protective services in Texas by employing a process that trained and certified supervisors of child welfare workers. This program demonstrated an improvement in the implementation of learning in the field through the active role of supervisors.

Placing this information together enables us to understand that for learning to occur in child welfare there must exist a learning environment that goes beyond tasks and behaviors and involves supervisors to ensure the transference of knowledge and the consistency of competencies and standards within all states and their child welfare agencies. Additionally, in order to produce learning environments and create change in the field of child welfare, we must embrace our role as a change agent. This requires implementing unifying models of practice and gathering families and communities to take part in bringing about the change through a step by step process.

CONCLUSIONS

Leadership and learning are two components that will move the field of child welfare forward. Professional social workers need to seek leadership and ensure that learning is implemented in an appropriate way. Through the utilization of unifying models of practice, which can be learned within both the academic and working environment of child welfare, the programs and services offered can provide preventive as well as interventive treatments.

Appendix: Code of Ethics of the National Association of Social Workers

As Adopted by the Delegate Assembly of August 1996

OVERVIEW

The National Association of Social Workers Code of Ethics is intended to serve as a guide to the everyday professional conduct of social workers. This code includes four sections.

- Section one, "Preamble," summarizes the social work profession's mission and core values.
- Section two, "Purpose of the Code of Ethics," provides an overview of the Code's main functions and a brief guide for dealing with ethical issues or dilemmas in social work practice.
- Section three, "Ethical Principles," presents broad ethical principles, based on social work's core values, that inform social work practice.
  - Service
  - Social Justice
  - Dignity and Worth of the Person
  - Importance of Human Relationships
  - Integrity
  - Competence
- The final section, "Ethical Standards," includes specific ethical standards to guide social workers' conduct and to provide a basis for adjudication.
  - social workers' ethical responsibilities to clients,

- social workers' ethical responsibilities to colleagues,
- social workers' ethical responsibilities in practice settings,
- social workers' ethical responsibilities as professionals,
- social workers' ethical responsibilities to the social work profession, and
- social workers' ethical responsibilities to the broader society.

PREAMBLE

The primary mission of the social work profession is to enhance human well-being and help meet the basic human needs of all people, with particular attention to the needs and empowerment of people who are vulnerable, oppressed, and living in poverty. A historic and defining feature of social work is the profession's focus on individual well-being in a social context and the well-being of society. Fundamental to social work is attention to the environmental forces that create, contribute to, and address problems in living.

Social workers promote social justice and social change with and on behalf of clients. 'Clients' is used inclusively to refer to individuals, families, groups, organizations, and communities. Social workers are sensitive to cultural and ethnic diversity and strive to end discrimination, oppression, poverty, and other forms of social injustice. These activities may be in the form of direct practice, community organizing, supervision, consultation, administration, advocacy, social and political action, policy development and implementation, education, and research and evaluation. Social workers seek to enhance the capacity of people to address their own needs. Social workers also seek to promote the responsiveness of organizations, communities, and other social institutions to individuals' needs and social problems.

The mission of the social work profession is rooted in a set of core values. These core values, embraced by social workers throughout the profession's history, are the foundation of social work's unique purpose and perspective:

- Service
- Social justice
- Dignity and worth of the person
- Importance of human relationships
- Integrity
- Competence

This constellation of core values reflects what is unique to the social work profession. Core values, and the principles that flow from them, must be balanced within the context and complexity of the human experience.

PURPOSE OF THE NASW CODE OF ETHICS

Professional ethics are at the core of social work. The profession has an obligation to articulate its basic values, ethical principles, and ethical standards. The *NASW Code of Ethics* sets forth these values, principles, and standards to guide social workers' conduct.

The *Code* is relevant to all social workers and social work students, regardless of their professional functions, the settings in which they work, or the populations they serve.

The *NASW Code of Ethics* serves six purposes:

- The *Code* identifies core values on which social work's mission is based.

- The *Code* summarizes broad ethical principles that reflect the professions core values and establishes a set of specific ethical standards that should be used to guide social work practice.

- The *Code* provides ethical standards to which the general public can hold the social work profession accountable.

- The *Code* socializes practitioners new to the field to social work's mission, values, ethical principles, and ethical standards.

- The *Code* articulates standards that the social work profession itself can use to assess whether social workers have engaged in unethical conduct. NASW has formal procedures to adjudicate ethics complaints filed against its members. In subscribing to this *Code*, social workers are required to cooperate in its implementation, participate in NASW adjudication proceedings, and abide by any NASW disciplinary rulings or sanctions based on it.

- The *Code* offers a set of values, principles, and standards to guide decision making and conduct when ethical issues arise. It does not provide a set of rules that prescribe how social workers should act in all situations. Specific applications of the *Code* must take into account the context in which it is being considered and the possibility of conflicts among the *Code's* values, principles, and standards. Ethical responsibilities flow from all human relationships, from the personal and familial to the social and professional.

Further, the *NASW Code of Ethics* does not specify which values, principles, and standards are most important and ought to outweigh others in instances when they conflict. Reasonable differences of opinion can and do exist among social workers with respect to the ways in which values, ethical principles, and ethical standards should be rank ordered when they conflict. Ethical decision making in a given situation must apply the informed judgment of the individual social worker and should also consider how the issues would be judged in a peer review process where the ethical standards of the profession would be applied.

Ethical decision making is a process. There are many instances in social work where simple answers are not available to resolve complex ethical issues.

Social workers should take into consideration all the values, principles, and standards in this *Code* that are relevant to any situation in which ethical judgment is warranted. Social workers' decisions and actions should be consistent with the spirit as well as the letter of this *Code*.

In addition to this *Code*, there are many other sources of information about ethical thinking that may be useful. Social workers should consider ethical theory and principles generally, social work theory and research, laws, regulations, agency policies, and other relevant codes of ethics, recognizing that among codes of ethics social workers should consider the *NASW Code of Ethics* as their primary source. Social workers also should be aware of the impact on ethical decision making of their clients and their own personal values and cultural and religious beliefs and practices. They should be aware of any conflicts between personal and professional values and deal with them responsibly. For additional guidance social workers should consult the relevant literature on professional ethics and ethical decision making and seek appropriate consultation when faced with ethical dilemmas. This may involve consultation with an agency-based or social work organization's ethics committee, a regulatory body, knowledgeable colleagues, supervisors, or legal counsel.

Instances may arise when social workers' ethical obligations conflict with agency policies or relevant laws or regulations. When such conflicts occur, social workers must make a responsible effort to resolve the conflict in a manner that is consistent with the values, principles, and standards expressed in this *Code*. If a reasonable resolution of the conflict does not appear possible, social workers should seek proper consultation before making a decision.

The *NASW Code of Ethics* is to be used by NASW and by individuals, agencies, organizations, and bodies (such as licensing and regulatory boards, professional liability insurance providers, courts of law, agency boards of directors, government agencies, and other professional groups) that choose to adopt it or use it as a frame of reference. Violation of standards in this *Code* does not automatically imply legal liability or violation of the law. Such determination can only be made in the context of legal and judicial proceedings. Alleged violations of the *Code* would be subject to a peer review process. Such processes are generally separate from legal or administrative procedures and insulated from legal review or proceedings to allow the profession to counsel and discipline its own members.

A code of ethics cannot guarantee ethical behavior. Moreover, a code of ethics cannot resolve all ethical issues or disputes or capture the richness and complexity involved in striving to make responsible choices within a moral community. Rather, a code of ethics sets forth values, ethical principles, and ethical standards to which professionals aspire and by which their actions can be judged. Social workers' ethical behavior should result from their personal commitment to engage in ethical practice. The *NASW Code of Ethics* reflects the commitment of all social workers to uphold the profession's values and to act ethically. Principles and standards must be applied by individuals of good character who discern moral questions and, in good faith, seek to make reliable ethical judgments.

ETHICAL PRINCIPLES

The following broad ethical principles are based on social work's core values of service, social justice, dignity and worth of the person, importance of human relationships, integrity, and competence. These principles set forth ideals to which all social workers should aspire.

1. Service
2. Social Justice
3. Dignity and Worth of the Person
4. Importance of Human Relationships
5. Integrity
6. Competence

VALUE: *Service*
Ethical Principle: *Social workers' primary goal is to help people in need and to address social problems.*

Social workers elevate service to others above self-interest. Social workers draw on their knowledge, values, and skills to help people in need and to address social problems. Social workers are encouraged to volunteer some portion of their professional skills with no expectation of significant financial return (pro bono service).

VALUE: *Social Justice*
Ethical Principle: *Social workers challenge social injustice.*

Social workers pursue social change, particularly with and on behalf of vulnerable and oppressed individuals and groups of people. Social workers' social change efforts are focused primarily on issues of poverty, unemployment, discrimination, and other forms of social injustice. These activities seek to promote sensitivity to and knowledge about oppression and cultural and ethnic diversity. Social workers strive to ensure access to needed information, services, and resources; equality of opportunity; and meaningful participation in decision making for all people.

VALUE: *Dignity and Worth of the Person*
Ethical Principle: *Social workers respect the inherent dignity and worth of the person.*

Social workers treat each person in a caring and respectful fashion, mindful of individual differences and cultural and ethnic diversity. Social workers promote clients' socially responsible self-determination. Social workers seek to enhance clients' capacity and opportunity to change and to address their own needs. Social workers are cognizant of their dual responsibility to clients and to the broader society. They seek to resolve conflicts between clients' interests and the broader society's interests in a socially responsible manner consistent with the values, ethical principles, and ethical standards of the profession.

VALUE: *Importance of Human Relationships*
Ethical Principle: *Social workers recognize the central importance of human relationships.*

Social workers understand that relationships between and among people are an important vehicle for change. Social workers engage people as partners in the helping process. Social workers seek to strengthen relationships among people in a purposeful effort to promote, restore, maintain, and enhance the well-being of individuals, families, social groups, organizations, and communities.

VALUE: *Integrity*
Ethical Principle: *Social workers behave in a trustworthy manner.*

Social workers are continually aware of the profession's mission, values, ethical principles, and ethical standards and practice in a manner consistent with them. Social workers act honestly and responsibly and promote ethical practices on the part of the organizations with which they are affiliated.

VALUE: *Competence*
Ethical Principle: *Social workers practice within their areas of competence and develop and enhance their professional expertise.*

Social workers continually strive to increase their professional knowledge and skills and to apply them in practice. Social workers should aspire to contribute to the knowledge base of the profession.

ETHICAL STANDARDS

The following ethical standards are relevant to the professional activities of all social workers. These standards concern:

1. social workers' ethical responsibilities to clients,
   a. 1.01 Commitment to Clients
   b. 1.02 Self-Determination
   c. 1.03 Informed Consent
   d. 1.04 Competence
   e. 1.05 Cultural Competence and Social Diversity
   f. 1.06 Conflicts of Interest
   g. 1.07 Privacy and Confidentiality: Clients
   h. 1.08 Access to Records
   i. 1.09 Sexual Relationships
   j. 1.10 Physical Contact
   k. 1.11 Sexual Harassment
   l. 1.12 Derogatory Language
   m. 1.13 Payment for Services
   n. 1.14 Clients Who Lack Decision-Making Capacity
   o. 1.15 Interruption of Services
   p. 1.16 Termination of Services

2. social workers' ethical responsibilities to colleagues,
   a.2.01   Respect
   b.2.02   Confidentiality: Colleagues
   c.2.03   Interdisciplinary Collaboration
   d.2.04   Disputes Involving Colleagues
   e.2.05   Consultation
   f.2.06   Referral for Services
   g.2.07   Sexual Relationships
   h.2.08   Sexual Harassment
   i.2.09   Impairment of Colleagues
   j.2.10   Incompetence of Colleagues
   k.2.11   Unethical Conduct of Colleagues
3. social workers' ethical responsibilities in practice settings,
   a.3.01   Supervision and Consultation
   b.3.02   Education and Training
   c.3.03   Performance Evaluation
   d.3.04   Client Records
   e.3.05   Billing
   f.3.06   Client Transfer
   g.3.07   Administration
   h.3.08   Continuing Education and Staff Development
   i.3.09   Commitments to Employers
   j.3.10   Labor-Management Disputes
4. social workers' ethical responsibilities as professionals,
   a.4.01   Competence
   b.4.02   Discrimination
   c.4.03   Private Conduct
   d.4.04   Dishonesty, Fraud, and Deception
   e.4.05   Impairment
   f.4.06   Misrepresentation
   g.4.07   Solicitations
   h.4.08   Acknowledging Credit
5. social workers' ethical responsibilities to the social work profession,
   a.5.01   Integrity of the Profession
   b.5.02   Evaluation and Research
and
6. social workers' ethical responsibilities to the broader society.
   a.6.01   Social Welfare
   b.6.02   Public Participation
   c.6.03   Public Emergencies
   d.6.04   Social and Political Action

Some of the standards that follow are enforceable guidelines for professional conduct, and some are aspirational. The extent to which each standard is enforceable is a matter of professional judgment to be exercised by those responsible for reviewing alleged violations of ethical standards.

1. SOCIAL WORKERS' ETHICAL RESPONSIBILITIES TO CLIENTS

- 1.01 Commitment to Clients
- 1.02 Self-Determination
- 1.03 Informed Consent
- 1.04 Competence
- 1.05 Cultural Competence and Social Diversity
- 1.06 Conflicts of Interest
- 1.07 Privacy and Confidentiality: Clients
- 1.08 Access to Records
- 1.09 Sexual Relationships
- 1.10 Physical Contact
- 1.11 Sexual Harassment
- 1.12 Derogatory Language
- 1.13 Payment for Services
- 1.14 Clients Who Lack Decision-Making Capacity
- 1.15 Interruption of Services
- 1.16 Termination of Services

1.01 Commitment to Clients

Social workers' primary responsibility is to promote the well-being of clients. In general, clients' interests are primary. However, social workers' responsibility to the larger society or specific legal obligations may on limited occasions supersede the loyalty owed clients, and clients should be so advised. (Examples include when a social worker is required by law to report that a client has abused a child or has threatened to harm self or others.)

1.02 Self-Determination

Social workers respect and promote the right of clients to self-determination and assist clients in their efforts to identify and clarify their goals. Social workers may limit clients' right to self-determination when, in the social workers' professional judgment, clients' actions or potential actions pose a serious, foreseeable, and imminent risk to themselves or others.

1.03 Informed Consent

(a) Social workers should provide services to clients only in the context of a professional relationship based, when appropriate, on valid informed consent. Social workers should use clear and understandable language to inform clients of the purpose of the services, risks related to the services, limits to services because of the requirements of a third-party payer, relevant costs, reasonable alternatives, clients' right to refuse or withdraw consent, and the time frame covered by the consent. Social workers should provide clients with an opportunity to ask questions.

(b) In instances when clients are not literate or have difficulty understanding the primary language used in the practice setting, social workers should take steps to ensure clients' comprehension. This may include providing clients with a detailed verbal explanation or arranging for a qualified interpreter or translator whenever possible.

(c) In instances when clients lack the capacity to provide informed consent, social workers should protect clients' interests by seeking permission from an appropriate third party, informing clients consistent with the clients' level of understanding. In such instances social workers should seek to ensure that the third party acts in a manner consistent with clients' wishes and interests. Social workers should take reasonable steps to enhance such clients' ability to give informed consent.

(d) In instances when clients are receiving services involuntarily, social workers should provide information about the nature and extent of services and about the extent of clients' right to refuse service.

(e) Social workers who provide services via electronic media (such as computer, telephone, radio, and television) should inform recipients of the limitations and risks associated with such services.

(f) Social workers should obtain clients' informed consent before audiotaping or videotaping clients or permitting observation of services to clients by a third party.

1.04 Competence

(a) Social workers should provide services and represent themselves as competent only within the boundaries of their education, training, license, certification, consultation received, supervised experience, or other relevant professional experience.

(b) Social workers should provide services in substantive areas or use intervention techniques or approaches that are new to them only after engaging in appropriate study, training, consultation, and supervision from people who are competent in those interventions or techniques.

(c) When generally recognized standards do not exist with respect to an emerging area of practice, social workers should exercise careful judgment and take responsible steps (including appropriate education, research, training, consultation, and supervision) to ensure the competence of their work and to protect clients from harm.

1.05 Cultural Competence and Social Diversity

(a) Social workers should understand culture and its function in human behavior and society, recognizing the strengths that exist in all cultures.

(b) Social workers should have a knowledge base of their clients' cultures and be able to demonstrate competence in the provision of services that are sensitive to clients' culture and to differences among people and cultural groups.

(c) Social workers should obtain education about and seek to understand the nature of social diversity and oppression with respect to race, ethnicity, national origin, color, sex, sexual orientation, age, marital status, political belief, religion and mental or physical disability.

1.06 Conflicts of Interest

(a) Social workers should be alert to and avoid conflicts of interest that interfere with the exercise of professional discretion and impartial judgment. Social workers should inform clients when a real or potential conflict of interest arises and take reasonable steps to resolve the issue in a manner that makes the clients' interests primary and protects clients' interests to the greatest extent possible. Occasionally, protecting clients' interests may require termination of the professional relationship with proper referral of the client.

(b) Social workers should not take unfair advantage of any professional relationship or exploit others to further their personal, political or business interests.

(c) Social workers should not engage in dual or multiple relationships with clients or former clients in which there is a risk of exploitation or potential harm to the client. In instances when dual or multiple relationships are unavoidable, social workers should take steps to protect clients and are responsible for setting clear, appropriate, and culturally sensitive boundaries. (Dual or multiple relationships occur when social workers relate to clients in more than one relationship, whether professional, social, or business. Dual or multiple relationships can occur simultaneously or consecutively.)

(d) When social workers provide services to two or more people who have a relationship with each other (for example, couples, family members), social workers should clarify with all parties which individuals will be considered clients and the nature of social workers professional obligations to the various individuals who are receiving services. Social workers who anticipate a conflict of interest among the individuals receiving services or who anticipate having to perform in potentially conflicting roles (for example, when a social worker is asked to testify in a child custody dispute or divorce proceedings involving clients) should clarify their role with the parties involved and take appropriate action to minimize any conflict of interest.

1.07 Privacy and Confidentiality

(a) Social workers should respect clients' right to privacy. Social workers should not solicit private information from clients unless it is essential to providing service or conducting social work evaluation or research. Once private information is shared, standards of confidentiality apply.

(b) Social workers may disclose confidential information when appropriate with a valid consent from a client, or a person legally authorized to consent on behalf of a client.

(c)   Social workers should protect the confidentiality of all information obtained in the course of professional service, except for compelling professional reasons. The general expectation that social workers will keep information confidential does not apply when disclosure is necessary to prevent serious, foreseeable, and imminent harm to a client or other identifiable person or when laws or regulations require disclosure without a client's consent. In all instances, social workers should disclose the least amount of confidential information necessary to achieve the desired purpose; only information that is directly relevant to the purpose for which the disclosure is made should be revealed.

(d)   Social workers should inform clients, to the extent possible, about the disclosure of confidential information and, when feasible, before the disclosure is made. This applies whether social workers disclose confidential information as a result of a legal requirement or based on client consent.

(e)   Social workers should discuss with clients and other interested parties the nature of confidentiality and limitations of clients' right to confidentiality. Social workers should review with clients circumstances where confidential information may be requested and where disclosure of confidential information may be legally required. This discussion should occur as soon as possible in the social worker–client relationship and as needed throughout the course of the relationship.

(f)   When social workers provide counseling services to families, couples, or groups, social workers should seek agreement among the parties involved concerning each individual's right to confidentiality and obligation to preserve the confidentiality of information shared by others. Social workers should inform participants in family, couples, or group counseling that social workers cannot guarantee that all participants will honor such agreements.

(g)   Social workers should inform clients involved in family, couples, marital, or group counseling of the social worker's, employer's, and agency's policy concerning the social worker's disclosure of confidential information among the parties involved in the counseling.

(h)   Social workers should not disclose confidential information to third-party payers unless clients have authorized such disclosure.

(i)   Social workers should not discuss confidential information in any setting unless privacy can be ensured. Social workers should not discuss confidential information in public or semipublic areas such as hallways, waiting rooms, elevators, and restaurants.

(j)   Social workers should protect the confidentiality of clients during legal proceedings to the extent permitted by law. When a court of law or other legally authorized body orders social workers to disclose confidential or privileged information without a client's consent and such disclosure could cause harm to the client, social workers should request that the court withdraw the order or limit the order as narrowly as possible or maintain the records under seal, unavailable for public inspection.

(k)   Social workers should protect the confidentiality of clients when responding to requests from members of the media.

(l) Social workers should protect the confidentiality of clients' written and electronic records and other sensitive information. Social workers should take reasonable steps to ensure that clients' records are stored in a secure location and that clients' records are not available to others who are not authorized to have access.

(m) Social workers should take precautions to ensure and maintain the confidentiality of information transmitted to other parties through the use of computers, electronic mail, facsimile machines, telephones and telephone answering machines, and other electronic or computer technology. Disclosure of identifying information should be avoided whenever possible.

(n) Social workers should transfer or dispose of clients' records in a manner that protects clients' confidentiality and is consistent with state statutes governing records and social work licensure.

(o) Social workers should take reasonable precautions to protect client confidentiality in the event of the social worker's termination of practice, incapacitation, or death.

(p) Social workers should not disclose identifying information when discussing clients for teaching or training purposes unless the client has consented to disclosure of confidential information.

(q) Social workers should not disclose identifying information when discussing clients with consultants unless the client has consented to disclosure of confidential information or there is a compelling need for such disclosure.

(r) Social workers should protect the confidentiality of deceased clients consistent with the preceding standards.

1.08 Access to Records

(a) Social workers should provide clients with reasonable access to records concerning the clients. Social workers who are concerned that clients' access to their records could cause serious misunderstanding or harm to the client should provide assistance in interpreting the records and consultation with the client regarding the records. Social workers should limit clients' access to their records, or portions of their records, only in exceptional circumstances when there is compelling evidence that such access would cause serious harm to the client. Both clients' requests and the rationale for withholding some or all of the record should be documented in clients' files.

(b) When providing clients with access to their records, social workers should take steps to protect the confidentiality of other individuals identified or discussed in such records.

1.09 Sexual Relationships

(a) Social workers should under no circumstances engage in sexual activities or sexual contact with current clients, whether such contact is consensual or forced.

(b) Social workers should not engage in sexual activities or sexual contact with clients' relatives or other individuals with whom clients maintain a close personal relationship when there is a risk of exploitation or potential harm to the client. Sexual activity or sexual contact with clients' relatives or other individuals with whom clients maintain a personal relationship has the potential to be harmful to the client and may make it difficult for the social worker and client to maintain appropriate professional boundaries. Social workers—not their clients, their clients' relatives, or other individuals with whom the client maintains a personal relationship—assume the full burden for setting clear, appropriate, and culturally sensitive boundaries.

(c) Social workers should not engage in sexual activities or sexual contact with former clients because of the potential for harm to the client. If social workers engage in conduct contrary to this prohibition or claim that an exception to this prohibition is warranted because of extraordinary circumstances, it is social workers—not their clients—who assume the full burden of demonstrating that the former client has not been exploited, coerced, or manipulated, intentionally or unintentionally.

(d) Social workers should not provide clinical services to individuals with whom they have had a prior sexual relationship. Providing clinical services to a former sexual partner has the potential to be harmful to the individual and is likely to make it difficult for the social worker and individual to maintain appropriate professional boundaries.

1.10 Physical Contact

Social workers should not engage in physical contact with clients when there is a possibility of psychological harm to the client as a result of the contact (such as cradling or caressing clients). Social workers who engage in appropriate physical contact with clients are responsible for setting clear, appropriate, and culturally sensitive boundaries that govern such physical contact.

1.11 Sexual Harassment

Social workers should not sexually harass clients. Sexual harassment includes advances, sexual solicitation, requests for sexual favors, and other verbal or physical conduct of a sexual nature.

1.12 Derogatory Language

Social workers should not use derogatory language in their written or verbal communications to or about clients. Social workers should use accurate and respectful language in all communications to and about clients.

1.13 Payment for Services

(a) When setting fees, social workers should ensure that the fees are fair, reasonable, and commensurate with the service performed. Consideration should be given to the client's ability to pay.

(b) Social workers should avoid accepting goods or services from clients as payment for professional services. Bartering arrangements, particularly involving services, create the potential for conflicts of interest, exploitation, and inappropriate boundaries in social workers' relationships with clients. Social workers should explore and may participate in bartering only in very limited circumstances when it can be demonstrated that such arrangements are an accepted practice among professionals in the local community, considered to be essential for the provision of services, negotiated without coercion, and entered into at the client's initiative and with the client's informed consent. Social workers who accept goods or services from clients as payment for professional services assume the full burden of demonstrating that this arrangement will not be detrimental to the client or the professional relationship.

(c) Social workers should not solicit a private fee or other remuneration for providing services to clients who are entitled to such available services through the social workers' employer or agency.

1.14 Clients Who Lack Decision-Making Capacity

When social workers act on behalf of clients who lack the capacity to make informed decisions, social workers should take reasonable steps to safeguard the interests and rights of those clients.

1.15 Interruption of Services

Social workers should make reasonable efforts to ensure continuity of services in the event that services are interrupted by factors such as unavailability, relocation, illness, disability, or death.

1.16 Termination of Services

(a) Social workers should terminate services to clients, and professional relationships with them, when such services and relationships are no longer required or no longer serve the clients' needs or interests.

(b) Social workers should take reasonable steps to avoid abandoning clients who are still in need of services. Social workers should withdraw services precipitously only under unusual circumstances, giving careful consideration to all factors in the situation and taking care to minimize possible adverse effects. Social workers should assist in making appropriate arrangements for continuation of services when necessary.

(c) Social workers in fee-for-service settings may terminate services to clients who are not paying an overdue balance if the financial contractual arrangements have been made clear to the client, if the client does not pose an imminent danger to self or others, and if the clinical and other consequences of the current nonpayment have been addressed and discussed with the client.

(d) Social workers should not terminate services to pursue a social, financial, or sexual relationship with a client.

(e) Social workers who anticipate the termination or interruption of services to clients should notify clients promptly and seek the transfer, referral, or continuation of services in relation to the clients' needs and preferences.

(f) Social workers who are leaving an employment setting should inform clients of all available options for the continuation of service and their benefits and risks.

2. SOCIAL WORKERS' ETHICAL RESPONSIBILITIES TO COLLEAGUES

- 2.01 Respect
- 2.02 Confidentiality: Colleagues
- 2.03 Interdisciplinary Collaboration
- 2.04 Disputes Involving Colleagues
- 2.05 Consultation
- 2.06 Referral for Services
- 2.07 Sexual Relationships
- 2.08 Sexual Harassment
- 2.09 Impairment of Colleagues
- 2.10 Incompetence of Colleagues
- 2.11 Unethical Conduct of Colleagues

2.01 Respect

(a) Social workers should treat colleagues with respect and represent accurately and fairly the qualifications, views, and obligations of colleagues.

(b) Social workers should avoid unwarranted negative criticism of colleagues with clients or with other professionals. Unwarranted negative criticism may include demeaning comments that refer to colleagues' level of competence or to individuals' attributes such as race, ethnicity, national origin, color, age, religion, sex, sexual orientation, marital status, political belief, mental or physical disability, or any other preference, personal characteristic, or status.

(c) Social workers should cooperate with social work colleagues and with colleagues of other professions when it serves the well-being of clients.

2.02 Confidentiality with Colleagues

Social workers should respect confidential information shared by colleagues in the course of their professional relationships and transactions. Social workers should ensure that such colleagues understand social workers' obligation to respect confidentiality and any exceptions related to it.

2.03 Interdisciplinary Collaboration

(a) Social workers who are members of an interdisciplinary team should participate in and contribute to decisions that affect the well-being of clients by drawing on the perspectives, values, and experiences of the social work profession. Professional and ethical obligations of the interdisciplinary team as a whole and of its individual members should be clearly established.

(b)   Social workers for whom a team decision raises ethical concerns should attempt to resolve the disagreement through appropriate channels. If the disagreement cannot be resolved social workers should pursue other avenues to address their concerns, consistent with client well-being.

2.04 Disputes Involving Colleagues

(a)   Social workers should not take advantage of a dispute between a colleague and employer to obtain a position or otherwise advance the social workers own interests.
(b)   Social workers should not exploit clients in disputes with colleagues or engage clients in any inappropriate discussion of conflicts between social workers and their colleagues.

2.05 Consultation

(a)   Social workers should seek advice and counsel of colleagues whenever such consultation is in the best interests of clients.
(b)   Social workers should keep informed of colleagues' areas of expertise and competencies. Social workers should seek consultation only from colleagues who have demonstrated knowledge, and competence related to the subject of the consultation.
(c)   When consulting with colleagues about clients, social workers should disclose the least amount of information to achieve the purposes of the consultation.

2.06 Referral for Services

(a)   Social workers should refer clients to other professionals when other professionals' specialized knowledge or expertise is needed to serve clients fully, or when social workers believe they are not being effective or making reasonable progress with clients and additional service is required.
(b)   Social workers who refer clients to other professionals should take appropriate steps to facilitate an orderly transfer of responsibility. Social workers who refer clients to other professionals should disclose, with clients' consent, all pertinent information to the new service providers.
(c)   Social workers are prohibited from giving or receiving payment for a referral when no professional service is provided by the referring social worker.

2.07 Sexual Relationships

(a)   Social workers who function as supervisors or educators should not engage in sexual activities or contact with current supervisees, students, trainees, or other colleagues over whom they exercise professional authority.
(b)   Social workers should avoid engaging in sexual relationships with colleagues where there is potential for a conflict of interest. Social workers who

become involved in, or anticipate becoming involved in, a sexual relationship with a colleague have a duty to transfer professional responsibilities, when necessary, in order to avoid a conflict of interest.

2.08 Sexual Harassment

Social workers should not engage in any sexual harassment of supervisees, students, trainees, or colleagues. Sexual harassment includes sexual advances, sexual solicitation, requests for sexual favors, and other verbal or physical conduct of a sexual nature.

2.09 Impairment of Colleagues

(a) Social workers who have direct knowledge of a social work colleague's impairment which is due to personal problems, psychosocial distress, substance abuse, or mental health difficulties, and which interferes with practice effectiveness, should consult with that colleague and assist the colleague in taking remedial action.

(b) Social workers who believe that a social work colleague's impairment interferes with practice effectiveness and that the colleague has not taken adequate steps to address the impairment should take action through appropriate channels established by employers, agencies, NASW, licensing and regulatory bodies, and other professional organizations.

2.10 Incompetence of Colleagues

(a) Social workers who have direct knowledge of a social work colleague's incompetence should consult with that colleague when feasible and assist the colleague in taking remedial action.

(b) Social workers who believe that a social work colleague is incompetent and has not taken adequate steps to address the incompetence should take action through appropriate channels established by employers, agencies, NASW, licensing and regulatory bodies, and other professional organizations.

2.11 Reporting Unethical Conduct

(a) Social workers should take adequate measures to discourage, prevent, expose, and correct the unethical conduct of colleagues.

(b) Social workers should be knowledgeable about established policies and procedures for handling concerns about colleagues' unethical behavior. Social workers should be familiar with national, state, and local procedures for handling ethics complaints. These include policies and procedures created by NASW, licensing and regulatory bodies, employers, agencies, and other professional organizations.

(c) Social workers who believe that a colleague has acted unethically should seek resolution by discussing their concerns with the colleague when feasible and when such discussion is likely to be productive.

(d) Social workers should defend and assist colleagues who are unjustly charged with unethical conduct.

3. SOCIAL WORKERS' ETHICAL RESPONSIBILITIES IN PRACTICE SETTINGS

- 3.01 Supervision and Consultation
- 3.02 Education and Training
- 3.03 Performance Evaluation
- 3.04 Client Records
- 3.05 Billing
- 3.06 Client Transfer
- 3.07 Administration
- 3.08 Continuing Education and Staff Development
- 3.09 Commitments to Employers
- 3.10 Labor-Management Disputes

3.01 Supervision and Consultation

(a) Social workers who provide supervision or consultation should have the necessary knowledge and skill to supervise or consult appropriately and should do so only within their areas of knowledge and competence.
(b) Social workers who provide supervision or consultation are responsible for setting clear, appropriate, and culturally sensitive boundaries.
(c) Social workers should not engage in any dual or multiple relationships with supervisees in which there is a risk of exploitation of or potential harm to the supervisee.
(d) Social workers who provide supervision should evaluate supervisees' performance in a manner that is fair and respectful.

3.02 Education and Training

(a) Social workers who function as educators, field instructors for students, or trainers should provide instruction only within their areas of knowledge and competence and should provide instruction based on the most current information and knowledge available in the profession.
(b) Social workers who function as educators or field instructors for students should evaluate students' performance in a manner that is fair and respectful.
(c) Social workers who function as educators or field instructors for students should take reasonable steps to ensure that clients are routinely informed when services are being provided by students.
(d) Social workers who function as educators or field instructors for students should not engage in any dual or multiple relationships with students in which there is a risk of exploitation or potential harm to the student. Social work educators and field instructors are responsible for setting clear, appropriate, and culturally sensitive boundaries.

3.03 Performance Evaluation

Social workers who have responsibility for evaluating the performance of others should fulfill such responsibility in a fair and considerate manner and on the basis of clearly stated criteria.

3.04 Client Records

(a)   Social workers should take reasonable steps to ensure that documentation in records is accurate and reflects the services provided.

(b)   Social workers should include sufficient and timely documentation in records to facilitate the delivery of services and to ensure continuity of services provided to clients in the future.

(c)   Social workers' documentation should protect clients' privacy to the extent that is possible and appropriate and should include only information that is directly relevant to the delivery of services.

(d)   Social workers should store records following the termination of service to ensure reasonable future access. Records should be maintained for the number of years required by state statutes or relevant contracts.

3.05 Billing

Social workers should establish and maintain billing practices that accurately reflect the nature and extent of services provided, and specifically by whom the service was provided in the practice setting.

3.06 Client Transfer

(a)   When an individual who is receiving services from another agency or colleague contacts a social worker for services, the social worker should carefully consider the client's needs before agreeing to provide services. In order to minimize possible confusion and conflict, social workers should discuss with potential clients the nature of their current relationship with other service providers and the implications, including possible benefits or risks, of entering into a relationship with a new service provider.

(b)   If a new client has been served by another agency or colleague, social workers should discuss whether consultation with the previous service provider is in the client's best interest.

3.07 Administration

(a)   Social work administrators should advocate within and outside their agencies for adequate resources to meet clients' needs.

(b)   Social workers should advocate for resource allocation procedures that are open and fair. When not all clients' needs can be met, an allocation procedure should be developed that is nondiscriminatory and based on appropriate and consistently applied principles.

(c)   Social workers who are administrators should take reasonable steps to ensure that adequate agency or organizational resources are available to provide appropriate staff supervision.

(d)   Social work administrators should take reasonable steps to ensure that the working environment for which they are responsible is consistent with and encourages compliance with the *NASW Code of Ethics*. Social work administrators should take reasonable steps to eliminate any conditions in their organizations that violate, interfere with, or discourage compliance with the *Code of Ethics*.

3.08 Continuing Education and Staff Development

Social work administrators and supervisors should take reasonable steps to provide or arrange for continuing education and staff development for all staff for whom they are responsible. Continuing education and staff development should address current knowledge and emerging developments related to social work practice and ethics.

3.09 Commitments to Employers

(a)   Social workers generally should adhere to commitments made to employers and employing organizations.

(b)   Social workers should work to improve employing agencies' policies and procedures, and the efficiency and effectiveness of their services.

(c)   Social workers should take reasonable steps to ensure that employers are aware of social workers' ethical obligations as set forth in the *NASW Code of Ethics* and of the implications of those obligations for social work practice.

(d)   Social workers should not allow an employing organization's policies, procedures, regulations, or administrative orders to interfere with their ethical practice of social work. Social workers should take reasonable steps to ensure that their employing organizations' practices are consistent with the *NASW Code of Ethics*.

(e)   Social workers should act to prevent and eliminate discrimination in the employing organization's work assignments and in its employment policies and practices.

(f)   Social workers should accept employment or arrange student field placements only in organizations that exercise fair personnel practices.

(g)   Social workers should be diligent stewards of the resources of their employing organizations, wisely conserving funds where appropriate and never misappropriating funds for unintended purposes.

3.10 Labor-Management Disputes

(a)   Social workers may engage in organized action, including the formation of and participation in labor unions, to improve services to clients and working conditions.

(b)   The actions of social workers who are involved in labor-management disputes, job actions, or labor strikes should be guided by the profession's values, ethical principles, and ethical standards. Reasonable differences of opinion exist among social workers concerning their primary obligation as professionals during an actual or threatened labor strike or job action. Social workers should carefully examine relevant issues and their possible impact on clients before deciding on a course of action.

4. SOCIAL WORKERS' ETHICAL RESPONSIBILITIES AS PROFESSIONALS

- 4.01 Competence
- 4.02 Discrimination
- 4.03 Private Conduct
- 4.04 Dishonesty, Fraud, and Deception
- 4.05 Impairment
- 4.06 Misrepresentation
- 4.07 Solicitations
- 4.08 Acknowledging Credit

4.01 Competence

(a)   Social workers should accept responsibility or employment only on the basis of existing competence or the intention to acquire the necessary competence.
(b)   Social workers should strive to become and remain proficient in professional practice and the performance of professional functions. Social workers should critically examine, and keep current with, emerging knowledge relevant to social work. Social workers should routinely review professional literature and participate in continuing education relevant to social work practice and social work ethics.
(c)   Social workers should base practice on recognized knowledge, including empirically based knowledge, relevant to social work and social work ethics.

4.02 Discrimination

Social workers should not practice, condone, facilitate, or collaborate with any form of discrimination on the basis of race, ethnicity, national origin, color, age, religion, sex, sexual orientation, marital status, political belief, or mental or physical disability.

4.03 Private Conduct

Social workers should not permit their private conduct to interfere with their ability to fulfill their professional responsibilities.

4.04 Dishonesty, Fraud, and Deception

Social workers should not participate in, condone, or be associated with dishonesty, fraud, or deception.

4.05 Impairment

(a)   Social workers should not allow their own personal problems, psychosocial distress, legal problems, substance abuse, or mental health difficulties to interfere with their professional judgment and performance or to jeopardize the best interests of people for whom they have a professional responsibility.

(b)   Social workers whose personal problems, psychosocial distress, legal problems, substance abuse, or mental health difficulties interfere with their professional judgment and performance should immediately seek consultation and take appropriate remedial action by seeking professional help, making adjustments in workload, terminating practice, or taking any other steps necessary to protect clients and others.

4.06 Misrepresentation

(a)   Social workers should make clear distinctions between statements made and actions engaged in as a private individual and as a representative of the social work profession, a professional social work organization, or of the social worker's employing agency.

(b)   Social workers who speak on behalf of professional social work organizations should accurately represent the official and authorized positions of the organization.

(c)   Social workers should ensure that their representations to clients, agencies, and the public of professional qualifications, credentials, education, competence, affiliations, services provided, or results to be achieved are accurate. Social workers should claim only those relevant professional credentials they actually possess and take steps to correct any inaccuracies or misrepresentations of their credentials by others.

4.07 Solicitations

(a)   Social workers should not engage in uninvited solicitation of potential clients who, because of their circumstances, are vulnerable to undue influence, manipulation or coercion.

(b)   Social workers should not engage in solicitation of testimonial endorsements (including solicitation of consent to use a client's prior statement as a testimonial endorsement) from current clients or other persons who, because of their particular circumstances are vulnerable to undue influence.

4.08 Acknowledging Credit

(a)   Social workers should take responsibility and credit, including authorship credit, only for work they have actually performed and to which they have contributed.

(b) Social workers should honestly acknowledge the work of and the contributions made by others.

5. SOCIAL WORKERS' ETHICAL RESPONSIBILITIES TO THE SOCIAL WORK PROFESSION

- 5.01 Integrity of the Profession
- 5.02 Evaluation and Research

5.01 Integrity of the Profession

(a) Social workers should work toward the maintenance and promotion of high standards of practice.

(b) Social workers should uphold and advance the values, ethics, knowledge, and mission of the profession. Social workers should protect, enhance, and improve the integrity of the profession through appropriate study and research, active discussion, and responsible criticism of the profession.

(c) Social workers should contribute time and professional expertise to activities that promote respect for the value, integrity, and competence of the social work profession. These activities may include teaching, research, consultations, service, legislative testimony, presentations in the community and participation in their professional organizations.

(d) Social workers should contribute to the knowledge base of social work and share with colleagues their knowledge related to practice, research, and ethics. Social workers should seek to contribute to the profession's literature and to share their knowledge at professional meetings and conferences.

(e) Social workers should act to prevent the unauthorized and unqualified practice of social work.

5.02 Evaluation and Research

(a) Social workers should monitor and evaluate policies, the implementation of programs, and practice interventions.

(b) Social workers should promote and facilitate evaluation and research in order to contribute to the development of knowledge.

(c) Social workers should critically examine and keep current with emerging knowledge relevant to social work and fully utilize evaluation and research evidence in their professional practice.

(d) Social workers engaged in evaluation or research should consider carefully possible consequences and should follow guidelines developed for the protection of evaluation and research participants. Appropriate institutional review boards should be consulted.

(e)   Social workers engaged in evaluation or research should obtain voluntary and written informed consent from participants, when appropriate, without any implied or actual deprivation or penalty for refusal to participate; without undue inducement to participate; and with due regard for participants' well-being, privacy, and dignity. Informed consent should include information about the nature, extent, and duration of the participation requested and disclosure of the risks and benefits of participation in the research.

(f)   When evaluation or research participants are incapable of giving informed consent, social workers should provide an appropriate explanation to the participants, obtain the participants' assent to the extent they are able, and obtain written consent from an appropriate proxy.

(g)   Social workers should never design or conduct evaluation or research that does not use consent procedures, such as certain forms of naturalistic observation and archival research, unless rigorous and responsible review of the research has found it to be justified because of its prospective scientific, educational, or applied value and unless equally effective alternative procedures that do not involve waiver of consent are not feasible.

(h)   Social workers should inform participants of their right to withdraw from evaluation and research at any time without penalty.

(i)   Social workers should take appropriate steps to ensure that participants in evaluation and research have access to appropriate supportive services.

(j)   Social workers engaged in evaluation or research should protect participants from unwarranted physical or mental distress, harm, danger, or deprivation.

(k)   Social workers engaged in the evaluation of services should discuss collected information only for professional purposes and only with people professionally concerned with this information.

(l)   Social workers engaged in evaluation or research should ensure the anonymity or confidentiality of participants and of the data obtained from them. Social workers should inform participants of any limits of confidentiality, the measures that will be taken to ensure confidentiality, and when any records containing research data will be destroyed.

(m)   Social workers who report evaluation and research results should protect participants' confidentiality by omitting identifying information unless proper consent has been obtained authorizing disclosure.

(n)   Social workers should report evaluation and research findings accurately. They should not fabricate or falsify results and should take steps to correct any errors later found in published data using standard publication methods.

(o)   Social workers engaged in evaluation or research should be alert to and avoid conflicts of interest and dual relationships with participants, should inform participants when a real or potential conflict of interest arises, and should take steps to resolve the issue in a manner that makes participants' interests primary.

(p)   Social workers should educate themselves, their students, and their colleagues about responsible research practices.

6. SOCIAL WORKERS' ETHICAL RESPONSIBILITIES TO THE BROADER SOCIETY

- 6.01 General Welfare
- 6.02 Public Participation
- 6.03 Public Emergencies
- 6.04 Social and Political Action

6.01 General Welfare

Social workers should promote the general welfare of society, from local to global levels, and the development of people, their communities, and their environments. Social workers should advocate for living conditions conducive to the fulfillment of basic human needs and should promote social, economic, political, and cultural values and institutions that are compatible with the realization of social justice.

6.02 Public Participation

Social workers should facilitate informed participation by the public in shaping social policies and institutions.

6.03 Public Emergencies

Social workers should provide appropriate professional services in public emergencies, to the greatest extent possible.

6.04 Social and Political Action

(a)   Social workers should engage in social and political action that seeks to ensure that all people have equal access to the resources, employment, services, and opportunities they require to meet their basic human needs and to develop fully. Social workers should be aware of the impact of the political arena on practice and should advocate for changes in policy and legislation to improve social conditions in order to meet basic human needs and promote social justice.

(b)   Social workers should act to expand choice and opportunity for all persons, with special regard for vulnerable, disadvantaged, oppressed, and exploited persons and groups.

(c)   Social workers should promote conditions that encourage respect for cultural and social diversity within the United States and globally. Social workers should promote policies and practices that demonstrate respect for difference, support the expansion of cultural knowledge and resources, advocate for programs and institutions that demonstrate cultural competence, and promote policies that safeguard the rights of and confirm equity and social justice for all people.

(d)   Social workers should act to prevent and eliminate domination of, exploitation of, and discrimination against any person, group, or class on the basis of race, ethnicity, national origin, color, sex, sexual orientation, age, marital status, political belief, religion, or mental or physical disability.

References

Aaronson, M. (1989). The case manager-home visitor. *Child Welfare, 68* (3), 339–346.

Addams, J. (1918). The subjective necessity for social settlements. *Hull House.* Chicago: University of Illinois.

Amato, P. R. (1993). Urban-rural differences in helping friends and family members. *Social Psychology Quarterly, 56* (4), 249–262.

American Psychiatric Association (1994). DSM IV, Washington, DC.

Amer-Hirsch, W. (1989). Educating youth about AIDS: A model program. *Children Today* (Sep/Oct), 16–19.

Anderson, J. D. (1992). Family-centered practice in the 1990s: A multicultural perspective. *Journal of Multicultural Social Work, 1* (4), 17–29.

Andrews, D. Z., Zinger, I., Hoge, R. D., Bonta, J., Gendreau, P., & Cullen, F. T. (1996). Does correctional treatment work? A clinically relevant and psychologically informed metaanalysis. In D. I. Greenburg, (Ed.). *Criminal Careers, Vol II. The International Library of Criminology, Criminal Justice, and Penology.* Aldershot, England: Dartmouth.

Antle, B. J., Wells, L. M., Salter-Goldie, R., DeMatteo, D., & King, S. M. (1997). *The challenges of parenting for families living with HIV/AIDS.* Unpublished manuscript.

Archacki-Stone, C. (1995). *Family-based mental health services: Children in families at risk.* Combrinck, New York: Guilford Press.

Baily, T., & Baily, W. (1986). *Operational definitions of child emotional maltreatment: Final report.* Augusta, ME: National Center for Child Abuse and Neglect.

Baladerian, N. J. (1994). Intervention and treatment of children with severe disabilities who become victims of abuse. *Developmental Disabilities Bulletin, 22* (2), 93–99.

Balgopal, P. R., Patchner, M., & Henderson, C. H. (1988). Home visits: An effective strategy for engaging the involuntary client. *Child and Youth Services, 11* (1), 65–76.

Barone, C., Weissberg, R. P., Kasprow, W. J., Voyce, C. K., Arthur, M. W., & Shriver, T. P. (1995, Spring). Involvement in multiple problem behaviors of young urban adolescents. *The Journal of Primary Prevention, 15* (3), 261–283.

Barton, W., & Butts, J. A. (1990, April). Viable options: Intensive supervision programs for juvenile delinquents. *Crime and Delinquency, 36* (2), 238–256.

Beck, A. T., Steen, R. A., & Kovach, M. (1985). New York Academy of Science. Hopelessness and eventual suicide: A 10-year prospective study of patients hospitalized with suicidal ideation. *142* (5), 559–563.

Berg, I. K. (1994). *Family based services: A solution-focused approach.* New York: W. W. Norton & Co.

Berrick, J., Barth, R., & Needel, B. (1993). A comparison of kinship foster homes and family foster homes. In R. P. Barth, J. D. Berrick, & N. Gilbert (Eds.), *Child welfare research review.* New York: Columbia University Press.

Bicknell-Hentges, L. (1995). The stages of reunification process and the tasks of the therapist. In L. Combrick-Graham (Ed.), *Children in Families at Risk: Maintaining the Connections.* New York: Guilford.

Birmingham, B. M., & Bussey, M. (1996). Certification for child protective services staff members: The Texas initiative. *Child Welfare, 75* (6), 727–740.

Black, D., Wolkin, S., & Hendriks, J. H. (1989). *Child Psychiatry and the Law.* London: Gaskell.

Black, J. C., & Cantor, D. J. (1993). *Child Custody.* New York: Columbia University Press.

Blitsch, T., Mears, S., & Sharma, S. (1995). Child welfare in America through the family preservation movement. *Guru Nanak Journal of Sociology, 16* (1), 31–48.

Borduin, C. M., Mann, B. J., Cone, L. T., Henggeler, S. W., Fucci, B. R., Blaske, D. M., & Williams, R. A. (1995). Multisystemic treatment of serious juvenile offenders: Long-term prevention of criminality and violence. *Journal of Consulting and Clinical Psychology, 63* (4), 569–578.

Borduin, C., & Henggeler, S. (1987, July-Sept.). Post-divorce mother-son relations of delinquent and well-adjusted adolescents. *Journal of Applied Developmental Psychology, 8* (3), 203–288.

Borgford-Parnell, D., Hope, K. R., & Deisher, R. W. (1994). A homeless teen pregnancy project: An intensive team case management model. *American Journal of Public Health, 84* (6), 1029–1030.

Bowlby, J. (1969). *Attachment and Loss, Volume 1 & 2.* New York: Basic Books.

Bowlby, J. (1980). *Loss: Sadness and Depression (Volume 3: Attachment and Loss).* New York: Basic Books.

Brandell, J. R. (1997). *Theory and Practice in Clinical Social Work.* New York: Free Press.

Brown, S. E., Whitehead, K. R., & Braswell, M. C. (1981). Child maltreatment: An empirical examination of selected conventional hypotheses. *Youth and Society, 13*, 77–90.

Bunyan, A. (1987). "Help, I can't cope with my child": A behavioural approach to the treatment of a conduct disordered child within the natural homesetting. *British Journal of Social Work, 17*, 237–256.

Burndoroff, S., & Scherer, D. (1994, June). Wilderness family therapy: An innovative treatment approach for problem youth. *Journal of Child and Family Studies, 3* (2), 175–191.

Byington, D. B., & McCammon, S. (1988, Spring). Networking as an approach to advocacy: A campus sexual assault awareness program. *Response to the Victimization of Women & Children, 11* (1), 11–13.

Cameron, G. (1990). The potential of informal social support strategies in child welfare. In M. Rothery, & G. Cameron (Eds.), *Child maltreatment: Expanding our concept of helping* (pp. 145–168). New York: Lawrence Erlbaum.

Cameron, G., Vanderwoerd, J., & Peirson, L. (1997). *Protecting children and supporting families:* New York: Aldine de Gruyter. Promising programs and organizational realities.

Carlo, P. (1991). Why a parental involvement program leads to family reunification: A dialogue with childcare workers. *Residential Treatment for Children and Youth, 9* (2), 37–48.

Centers for Disease Control and Prevention. (1993). *HIV/AIDS Surveillance Report: Year-end 1993,* Vol. 5, No. 4. Atlanta: Author.

Centers for Disease Control and Prevention. (1995). *HIV/AIDS Surveillance Report: Year-end 1995,* Vol. 7, No. 4. Atlanta: Author.

Centers for Disease Control and Prevention. (1997). *National HIV Prevalence Surveys 1997 Summary.* Atlanta: Author.

Cervera, N. J. (1993). Decision making for pregnant adolescents: Applying reasoned action theory to research and treatment. *Families in Society: The Journal of Contemporary Human Services, 74* (6), 355–365.

Chapman, J. R., & Smith, B. (1987). Response of social service and criminal justice agencies to child sexual abuse complaints. *Response, 10* (3), 7–13.

Chasnoff, I. J. (1988). Drug use in pregnancy. *Pediatric Clinics of North America, 35* (6), 1403–1412.

Children's Defense Fund. (1994). Births to teens. *CDF Reports, 16* (8).

Child Welfare League of America. (1988). *Standards for health care services for children in out-of-home care.* Washington, DC.

Child Welfare League of America. (1990). *Standards for child welfare services.* Washington, DC.

Child Welfare League of America. (1991). *Core training for child welfare caseworkers curriculum.* Washington, DC.

Child Welfare League of America. (1995). *Standards for child welfare services.* Washington, DC.

Child Welfare League of America. (1996). *Standards for child welfare services.* Washington, DC.

Chilman, C. S. (1991). Working poor families: Trends, causes, effects and suggested policies. *Family Relations, 40* (April), 191–198.

Clark-Lempers, D. S., Lempers, J. D., & Netusil, A. (1990, February). Family financial stress, parental support and young adolescent academic achievement and depressive symptoms. *Journal of Early Adolescence, 10* (1), 21–36.

Cohen, N. A. (Ed.). (1992). *Child welfare: A multicultural focus.* Boston MA: Allyn and Bacon.

Colapinto, J. A. (1995). Dilution of family process in social services: Implications for treatment of neglectful families. *Family Process, 34* (1), 59–74.

Cole, E. S. (1987). Adoption. In A. Minahan (Ed.), *Encyclopedia of social work: Vol. 1.* (18th ed.). Silver Spring, MD: National Association of Social Workers.

Combrinck-Graham, L. (1989). *Children in family contexts: Perspectives on treatment.* New York: Guilford Press.

Compton, B. R., & Galaway, B. (1994). *Social work processes* (5th ed.). Pacific Grove, CA: Brooks/Cole.

Cook, K. (1998). Working in Child Welfare. Unpublished manuscript. Wilfrid Laurier University.

Corbett, J., & Petersilia, J. (1994). Up to speed. *Federal Probation, 58* (3), 51–57.

Corcoran, K., & Fischer, J. (1987). *Measures for clinical practice: A sourcebook.* New York: The Free Press.

Corey, M. S., & Corey, G. (1997). *Groups: Process and Practice* (5th ed.). Pacific Grove, CA: Brooks/Cole.

Costin, L., Karger, H. J., & Stoze, D. (1996). *The politics of child abuse in America.* New York: Oxford University Press.

Cowger, C. D. (1994, May). Assessing client strengths: Clinical assessment for client empowerment. *Social Work, 39* (3), 262–267.

Cox, E., & Longres, J. (1981). *Critical practice—curriculum implications.* Paper presented at the Annual Meeting of the Council on Social Work Education, Louisville, KY.

Crewdson, J. (1988). *By silence betrayed: Sexual abuse of children in America.* Boston: Little, Brown.

Curry, J. (1991). Outcome research on residential treatment: Implications and suggested directions. *American Journal of Orthopsychiatry, 61,* 348–358.

Delgado, R. (1992). Generalist child welfare and hispanic families. In N. A. Cohen (Ed.), *Child welfare: A multicultural focus.* Boston: Allyn and Bacon.

Devore, W., & Schlesinger, E. G. (1987). *Ethnic-sensitive social work practice.* Columbus, OH: Merrill.

Dore, M. M., Doris, J. M., & Wright, P. (1995). Identifying substance abuse in maltreating families: A child welfare challenge. *Child Abuse and Neglect, 19* (5), 531–543.

Downs, S., Costin, L. B., & McFadden, E. J. (1996). *Child welfare and family services: Policies and practice* (5th ed.) New York: Longman.

Drake, B. (1994, September). Relationship competencies in child welfare service. *Social Work, 39* (5), 595–602.

Durlak, J., & Lipsey, M. (1991, June). A practitioner's guide to meta-analysis. *American Journal of Community Psychology, 19,* 291–332.

Edelstein, S., Kropenske, V., & Howard, J. (1990). Project training, education and management skills: Meeting the needs of infants prenatally exposed to drugs (T.E.A.M.S.). *Social Work, 35* (4), 313–318.

Egan, G. (1975). *The skilled helper.* Monterey, CA: Brooks/Cole.

English, P. C. (1978). Failure to thrive without organic reason. *Pediatric Annals, 7* (11), 774–781.

Evans, S., Reinhart, J., & Succop, R. (1983). Failure to thrive: A study of 45 children and their families. *Journal of*

American Academy of Child Psychiatry, 11, 440.

Fahlberg, V. (1991). *A child's journey through placement.* Indianapolis, IN: Perspectives Press.

Falicov, C. (1983). *Cultural perspectives in family therapy.* Rockville, MD: Aspen Press.

Faller, K. C. (1988). Criteria for judging the credibility of children's statements about their sexual abuse. *Child Welfare, 67* (5), 389–401.

Faller, K. C. (1991). What happens to sexually abused children identified by child protective services? *Children and Youth Services Review, 13,* 101–111.

Fanshal, D. (1982). *On the road to permanency: An expanded data base for service to children in foster care.* New York: Child Welfare League of America, Columbia University School of Social Work.

Farmer, S., & Galaris, D. (1993). Support groups for children of divorce. *The American Journal of Family Therapy, 21* (1), 40–50.

Feigelman, W., & Silverman, A. R. (1983). *Chosen children: New patterns of adoptive relationships.* New York: Praeger.

Filip, J., McDaniel, N. S., & Schene, P. (Eds.) (1992). Helping in child protective services: A casework handbook. Englewood, CA: The American Humane Association.

Finkelhor, D. (1979). *Sexually victimized children.* New York: Free Press.

Finkelhor, D. (1984). *Child sexual abuse: New theory and research.* New York: Free Press.

Finkelhor, D., Hotaling, G., Lewis, I. A., & Smith, C. (1990). Sexual abuse in a national survey of adult men and women: Prevalence, characteristics, and risk factors. *Child Abuse & Neglect, 14* (1), 19–28.

Fosberg, S. (1981). Family day care in the United States: Summary of findings. Final Report of the National Day Care Home Study, Vol 1. (DHHS Publication No. [OHDS]80-30282). Washington, DC: U.S. Department of

Health & Human Services, Administration for Children, Youth and Families.

Friesen, B. J., & Poertner, J. (Eds.) (1995). *From case management to service coordination for children with emotional, behavioral, or mental disorders*. Baltimore: Brookes.

Furstenberg, F. F. (1994). History and current status of divorce in the United States. *Future of Children, 4* (1), 29–43.

Furstenberg, F. F., Brooks-Gunn, J., & Chase-Lansdale, L. (1989). Teenaged pregnancy and childbearing. *American Psychologist, 44*, 313–320.

Garbarino, J. (1992). *Toward a Sustainable Society: An Economic, Social and Environmental Agenda for Our Children's Future*. Chicago: Noble Press.

Garbarino, J. (1980). Preventing child maltreatment. In R. H. Price, R. F. Ketterer, B. C. Bader, & J. Monahan (Eds.), *Prevention in mental health: Research, policy, and practice* (pp. 63–80). Beverly Hills, CA: Sage.

Garbarino, J., Gutterman, E., & Seeley, J. W. (1986). *The psychologically battered child*. San Francisco: Jossey-Bass.

Gelles, R. (1996). *The Book of David: How Preserving Families Can Cost Children's Lives*. New York: Basic Books.

Germaine, C., & Gitterman, A. (1980). *The life model of social work practice*. New York: Columbia University Press.

Gershenson, C. P. (1990). *Preparing for the future backwards: Characteristics of the ecology for children and youth in long term out of home care*. Unpublished manuscript, prepared for the Casey Family Program Symposium on Long Term Care, Seattle, WA.

Gil, D. G. (1971). Sociocultural perspective on physical child abuse. *Child Welfare, 50* (7), 389–395.

Gil, D. G. (1981). The United States versus child abuse. In L. Pelton (Ed.), *The social context of child abuse and neglect*. New York: Human Services Press.

Gill, M. M., & Amadio, C. M. (1983). Social work and law in a foster care/adoption program. *Child Welfare, 62* (5), 455–467.

Godman, R. (1998). *Child Welfare*. Unpublished manuscript. Wilfrid Laurier University.

Goldstein, A., McGowan, S., Antle, B. J., Brownstone, D., Donoghue, S., James, M., Rodger, M., & Sloane, G. (1996). Leading the way: Innovating support for children, youth, parents and guardians affected by HIV and AIDS. *The Social Worker, 64*, 67–73.

Greenwood, P. W. (1994). What works with juvenile offenders: A synthesis of the literature and experience. In R. P. Corbett & J. Petersilia (Eds.), Up to speed: A review of research for practitioners, *Federal Probation, 58* (4), 63–67.

Grigsby, K. (1994). Maintaining attachment relationships among children in foster care. *Families in Society, 75* (5), 269–276.

Gustavsson, N. S. (1992). Drug exposed infants and their mothers: Facts, myths, and needs. *Social Work in Health Care, 16* (4), 87–100.

Gutierrez, L., Parsons, R., & Cox, E. (1998). *Empowerment in social work practice*. Pacific Grove, CA: Brooks/Cole.

Hartman, A., & Laird, J. (1983). *Family-centered social work practice*. New York: Free Press.

Harvey, V. S. (1995). Interagency collaboration: Providing a system of care for students. *Special Services in the Schools, 10* (1), 165–181.

Hawkins, J. D., Jenkins, J. M., Catalano, R. F., & Lishner, D. M. (1988). Delinquency and drug abuse: Implications for social services: *Social Service Review, 62* (2), 258–284.

Hayes, C. D., Palmer, J. L., Zaslow, M., & National Research Council Panel on Child Care Policy (1990). *Who Care for America's Children? Child Care Policy for the 1990's* Washington, DC: National Academy of Sciences Press.

Hazel, K. N. (1982). New hope for the teenage outcast: The family placement of disturbed and delinquent adolescents. *International Journal of Offender Therapy and Comparative Criminology, 26* (1), 62–71.

Henggeler, S. W. (1989). *Delinquency in Adolescence*. Newbury Park, CA: Sage.

Hepworth, D. H., & Larsen, J. (1993). *Direct social work practice: Theory and skills* (4th ed.). Pacific Grove, CA: Brooks/Cole.

Hepworth, D. H., Rooney, R. H., & Larsen, J. A. (1997). *Direct social work practice: Theory and skills* (5th ed.). Pacific Grove, CA: Brooks/Cole.

Hertz, D. (1977). Psychological implications of adolescent pregnancy patterns of family interaction in adolescent mothers-to-be. *Psychosomatics, 18* (1), 13–16.

Hill, R. (1972). *The strengths of black families*. New York: Emerson Hall.

Hill, B. K., Hayden, M., Lakin, K., Mendke, J., & Amado, A. (1990). State-by-state data on children with handicaps in foster care. *Child Welfare, 69*, 447–462.

Holder, W. M., & Corey, M. (1986). *Child protective services in risk management: A decision making handbook*. Charlotte, NC: Action for Child Protection.

Hooper-Briar, K. (1994). *Framework for action*. Oxford, OH: Institute for Educational Renewal.

Hozman, T. L., & Froiland, D. J. (1976). Families in divorce: A proposed model for counseling the children. *The Family Coordinator, 25* (3), 271–276.

Hudson, J., & Galaway, B. (Eds.) (1995). *Child welfare in Canada: Research and policy implications*. Toronto: Thompson Educational Publishing, Inc.

Hudson, W. (1982). *The clinical measurement package: A field manual*. Homewood, IL: Dorsey Press.

Hudson, W. (1992). *Walmyr assessment scales*. Tempe, AZ: Walmyr.

Hutchinson, R. L., & Spangler-Hirsch, S. L. (1989). Children of divorce and single-parent lifestyles. In *Children of divorce: Developmental and clinical issues* (pp. 5–23). New York: Haworth Press.

Indylr, B., Belville, R., Luchapelle, S., Gordon, G., & Dewart, T. (1993). A Community-based Approach to HIV case management: Systematizing the unmanageable. *Journal of Social Work, 38*, 380–387.

Ivanoff, A. M., Blythe, B. J., & Tripodi, T. (1994). *Involuntary clients in social work practice: A research-based approach*. New York: Aldine de Gruyter.

Jenkins, S., & Norman, E. (1972). *Filial deprivation and foster care*. New York: Columbia University.

Johnson, K. (1991, Fall). Review essay—Black Africans and Native Americans: Color, race and caste in the evolution of red and black peoples. (Review of Forbes, Jack D.) *The Journal of Ethnic Studies, 19* (3), 135–142.

Johnston, J. R., & Roseby, V. (1997). *In the name of the child: A developmental approach to understanding and helping children of conflicted and violent divorce*. New York: Free Press.

Kadushin, A. (1984). *Child welfare services* (4th ed.). New York: Macmillan.

Kadushin, A. (1987). Child welfare services. In A. Minahan (Ed.), *Encyclopedia of social work* (18th ed., pp. 265–275). Washington, DC: National Association of Social Workers.

Kadushin, A., & Martin, J. K. (1988). *Child welfare services* (4th ed.). New York: Macmillan.

Kamerman, S. B., & Kahn, A. J. (1990). Social services for children, youth, and families in the United States. *Children and Youth Services Review, 12* (1–2), i–184.

Kassebaum, G., & Chandler, D. B. (1992). In the shadow of best interest: Negotiating the facts, interests, and interventions in child abuse cases. *Sociological Practice, 10*, 49–66.

Kazdin, A. (1987, September). Treatment of antisocial behavior in children: Current status and future directions. *Psychological-Bulletin, 102*, 187–203.

Keefe, S. E., Padilla, A., & Carlos, M. L. (1978). The Mexican-American extended family as an emotional support system. In M. J. Casas & S. E. Keefe (Eds.), *Family and mental health* in the Mexican-American community (pp. 49–68). Los Angeles: Spanish Speaking Mental Health Research Center, University of California at Los Angeles, Monograph No. 7.

Kempe, C. (1962). The battered child syndrome. *Journal of the American Medical Association, 181,* 17–24.

Kempe, C. H., Silverman, F., Steele, B., Droegmueller, W., & Silver, H. (1962). The Battered Child Syndrome. *Journal of the American Medical Association, 181,* 17–24.

Kirst-Ashman, K. K., & Hull, G. H. (Jr.). (1993). *Understanding generalist practice.* Chicago: Nelson-Hall.

Knudsen, D. D., & Miller, J. L. (Eds.). (1991). *Abused and battered: Social and legal responses to family violence.* Hawthome, NY: Walter de Gruyter.

Kubler-Ross, E. (1969). *On death and dying.* New York: Macmillan.

Laird, J., & Hartman, A. (Eds.). (1985). *A handbook of child welfare: Context, knowledge, and practice.* New York: Free Press.

Lehner, L. (1994). Education for parents divorcing in California. *Family & Conciliation Courts Review, 32* (1), 50–54.

Lightburn, A., & Pine, B. A. (1996). Supporting and enhancing the adoption of children with developmental disabilities. *Children and Youth Services Review, 18* (1/2), 139–162.

Lindholm, K. J. (1983). Child abuse and ethnicity: Patterns of similarities and differences. Los Angeles: Spanish Speaking Mental Health Research Center.

Lindholm, K. J. (1986). Child sexual abuse within the family: CIBA foundation report. *Journal of Interpersonal Violence, 1* (2), 240–242.

Lindsey, D. (1994). *The welfare of children.* New York. Oxford University Press.

Lipsey, M. (1984, November). Is delinquency prevention a cost effective strategy? *Journal of Research in Crime and Delinquency, 21,* 279–302.

Litzenfelner, P., & Petr, C. G. (1997). Case advocacy in child welfare. *Social Work, 42* (4), 392–402.

Lockhart, L. L., & Wodarski, J. S. (1989). Facing the unknown: Children and adolescents with AIDS. *Social Work, 34* (3), 215–221.

Lum, D. (1992). *Social work practice with people of color.* A Process Stage Approach (2nd ed.). Monterey, CA: Brooks/Cole.

Lum, D. (1996). *Social work practice with people of color* (3rd ed.). Monterey, CA: Brooks/Cole.

Macaskill, A., & Ashworth, P. (1995, October). Parental participation in child protection case conferences: The social workers view. *The British Journal of Social Work, 25* (5), 581–597.

Magazino, C. J. (1983). Services to children and families at risk of separation. In B. G. McGowan & W. Meezan (Eds.). *Child welfare: Current dilemmas, future directions* (pp. 211–254). Ilasca, IL: F. E. Peacock.

Maluccio, A. N. (1990). Family preservation services and the social work practice sequence. In J. K. Whittaker, J. Kinney, E. M. Tracy, & C. Booth (Eds.), *Reaching high-risk families: Intensive family preservation in human services* (pp. 113–126). Hawthome, NY: Aldine de Gruyter.

Maluccio, A. N., Fein, E., & Olmstead, K. A. (1986). *Permanancy planning for children: Concepts and methods.* London and New York: Routledge, Chapman and Hall.

Mather, J. (1999). *Training outcomes in Ontario, Draft Report.* Ontario Association of Children's Aid Societies.

Mauer, M. (1990). Young black men and the criminal justice system: A growing national problem. Washington, DC: The Sentencing Project.

McCallum, S. (1995). Safe Families: A Model of Child Protection Intervention. Unpublished doctoral dissertation. Wilfrid Laurier University. Ontario, Canada.

McCarthy, M. (1999). Perinatal AIDS decreasing rapidly in USA. *Lancet, 354,* 573.

McGoldrick, M. (1996). *Ethnicity and family therapy.* Monica McGoldrick, J. Giordano, & J. K. Pearce (Eds.). New York: Guildford Press.

McKenzie, J. K. (1993). Adoption of children with special needs. *The Future of Children, 3* (1), 62–76 (A publication of the Center for the Future of Children, the David and Lucile Packard Foundation).

McPhee, B. (1997). Child Welfare: Out of the Box Services. Unpublished doctoral dissertation: University of Toronto.

Meezan, W. (1983). Child welfare—An overview of the issues. In B. G. McGowan & W. Meezan (Eds.), *Child welfare: Current dilemmas, future directions.* Itasca, IL: F. E. Peacock.

Meyers, M. (1995, November/December). Child day care in welfare reform: Are we targeting too narrowly? *Child Welfare, 74,* 1071–1090.

Middleman, R. R., & Goldberg, G. (1974). *Social service delivery: A structural approach to social work practice.* New York: Columbia University Press.

Miller, L. B., & Fisher, T. (1992). Some obstacles to the effective investigation and registration of children at risk-issues gleaned from a worker's perspective. *Journal of Social Work Practice, 6* (2), 129–140.

Mills, C., & Usher, D. (1996, September-October). A kinship care case management approach. *Child Welfare, 75* (5), 600–618.

Mills, R., Dunham, R., & Alpert, G. (1988). Working with high risk youth in prevention and early intervention programs: Toward a comprehensive wellness model. *Adolescence, 23* (88), 643–60.

Minty, B., & Pattinson, G. (1994, December). The nature of child neglect. *The British Journal of Social Work, 24* (6), 733–797.

Mishne, J. (1983). *Clinical work with children.* New York: Free Press.

Mitchel, L. B., & Savage, C. (1991). The relationship between substance abuse (working paper #854) p. 1, Chicago: The National Committee for the Presenting of Child Abuse (as noted in Pecora et al.).

Morris, J. (1997). Gone missing? Disabled children living away from their families. *Disability & Society, 12* (2), 241–258.

Moss, H., & Engles, R. (Jr.). (1959). Children in need of parents. New York: Columbia University Press.

Mundal, L. D., VanDer Weele, T., Berger, C., & Fitsimmons, J. (1991). Maternal-infant separation at birth among substance using pregnant women: Implications for attachment. *Social Work in Health Care, 16* (1), 133–143.

National Association of Social Workers. (1982). *New Standards for classification of social work practice.*

National Association of Social Workers. (1996). Office of government relations. Washington, DC.

National Center on Child Abuse and Neglect. (1993). Washington, DC.

National Committee for Adoption. (1986). Washington, DC.

Netting, E., Kettner, P., & McMurty, S. (1993). Social Work Macro Practice. White Plains, NY: Longman.

Netting, F. E. (1986, Fall). The religiously affiliated agency: Implications for social work administration. *Social Work and Christianity, 13,* 50.

Nelson, B. (1995). *Making an issue of child abuse:* Political agenda setting for social problems. Chicago: University of Chicago Press.

Nelson, B. J., & Frantz, T. T. (1997). Family interactions of suicide survivors and survivors of non-suicidal death. *Omega, 33* (2), 131–146.

Nelson, B. S., & Harrison, M. (1997). Bridging the politics of identity in a multicultural classroom. *Theory into Practice, 35* (4), 256–263.

New York State Department of Social Services. (1992). *Comprehensive risk assessment — Adapted from the New York state risk assessment and service planning model*. Albany, NY: Division of Administration and Office of Human Resource Development.

Nugent, W. (1992). The affective impact of a clinical social worker's interviewing style: A single-case experiment. *Research on Social Work Practice, 2* (1), 6–27.

Nurius, P. S., & Hudson, W. (1993). *Computer assisted practice: Theory, methods, and software*. Belmont, CA: Wadsworth.

Ontario Children's Aid Society. (1998). Ontario Children's Aid Society. Inquest Finding and Recommendations. Ontario, Canada.

Ooms, T., & Herendeen, L. (1990). Teenage pregnancy programs: What have we learned? *Background briefing report and meeting highlights: Family impact seminar*. May 29, 1989. Washington, DC: American Association for Marriage and Family Therapy.

Ozawa, M. N., & Lum, Y. (1996). How safe is the safety net for poor children? *Social Work Research, 20* (4), 238–254.

Pallone, S. R., & Malkemes, L. C. (1984). *Helping parents who abuse their children: A comprehensive approach for intervention*. Springfield, IL: Charles C. Thomas.

Peck, J. S. (1989). The impact of divorce on children at various stages of the family lifecycle. In *Children of divorce: Developmental and clinical issues* (pp. 81–106). New York: Haworth Press.

Pecora, P. J., Fraser, M. W., & Haapala, D. A. (1991). Intensive home-based family preservation services: Client outcomes and issues for program design. In K. Wells & D. E. Biegel (Eds.), *Family preservation services: Research and evaluation*. Newbury Park, CA: Sage.

Pecora, P. J., Fraser, M., Haapala, D., & Bartholomew, (1987). Defining family preservation services: Three intensive home-based treatment programs (Research Rep. No. 1) Salt Lake City: University of Utah, Social Research Institute.

Pecora, P., Whittaker, J., Maluccio, A., Barth, R., & Plotnick, R. (1992). *The child welfare challenge: Policy, practice and research*. New York: Walter de Gruyter.

Pelton, L. H. (1989). *For reasons of poverty: A critical analysis of the public child welfare system in the United States*. New York: Praeger Publishers.

Pelton, L. H. (1991). Child welfare system. *Social Work, 36* (4), 337–343.

Perez, Y., & Pasternack, R. (1991). To what extent can the school reduce the gaps between children raised by divorced and intact families? *Journal of Divorce and Remarriage, 15* (3/4), 143–157.

Petersen, V., & Steinman, S. B. (1994). Helping children succeed after divorce. *Family and Conciliation Courts Review, 32* (1), 27–39.

Petersilia, J. (1995, Summer). A crime control rationale for reinvesting in community corrections. *Spectrum, 68*, 16–27.

Petr, C. G., & Barney, D. D. (1993). Reasonable efforts for children with disabilities: The parents' perspective. *Social Work, 38* (3), 247–254.

Phillips, M. H., DeChillo, N., Kronenfeld, D., & Middleton-Jeter, V. (1988). Homeless families: Services make a difference. *Social Casework, 69*, 48–53.

Polansky, N. A., Chalmers, M. A., Buttenwieser, E., & Williams, D. P. (1981). *Damage parents: An anatomy of child neglect*. Chicago: University of Chicago Press.

Popple, P. R., & Leighninger, L. (1996). *Social work, social welfare and American society* (3rd ed.). Boston, MA: Allyn and Bacon.

Quinn, K. P., Epstein, M. H., & Cumblad, C. L. (1995). Developing comprehensive, individualized community-based services for children and youth with emotional and behavior disorders: Direct service providers' perspectives. *Journal of Child and Family Studies, 4* (1), 19–42.

Reid, W. J., & Epstein, L. (1977). *Task-centered practice.* New York: Columbia University Press.

Robinson, S. (1994). *Implementation of the cognitive model of offender rehabilitation and delinquency prevention.* Unpublished doctoral dissertation, University of Utah.

Rose, S., & Meezan, W. (1993, June). Defining child neglect: Evolution, influences and issues. *The Social Service Review, 67* (2), 279–293.

Rosenthal, J. A. (1993). Outcomes of adoption of children with special needs. *The Future of Children, 3* (1), 77–88 (a publication of the Center for the Future of Children, the David and Lucile Packard Foundation).

Russell, D. E. (1984). *Sexual exploitation: Rape, child sexual abuse, and workplace harassment.* Beverly Hills, CA: Sage.

Russell, D. (1986). *Secret trauma: Incest in the lives of girls and women.* New York: Basic Books.

Rzepnicki, T. L., Sherman, J. R., & Littell, J. H. (1991). Issues in evaluating intensive family preservation services. In E. M. Srancy, D. A. Haapala, J. M. Kinney, & P. J. Pecora (Eds.), *Intensive family preservation services: An instructional handbook.* Cleveland, OH: Case Western Reserve University, Mandel School of Applied Social Sciences.

Saleebey, D. (1992). *The strengths perspective in social work practice.* New York: Addison-Wesley.

Sallee, A. L., & Lloyd, J. C. (1991) (Eds.). *Family-based services.* Riverdale, IL: National Association for Family-Based Services.

Salter, A. C. (1992). Response to the "abuse of the child sexual abuse accommodation syndrome." *Journal of Child Sexual Abuse, 1* (4), 173–176.

Samantrai, K. (1992). To prevent unnecessary separation of children and families: Public law 96–272, policy and practice. *Social Work, 37* (4), 295–302.

Sandler, I. N., West, S. G., Baca, L., Pillow, D. R., Gersten, J. C., Rogosch, F., Virdin, L., Beals, J., Reynolds, K. D., Kallgren, C., Tein, J. T., Kriege, G.,

Cole, E., & Ramirez, R. (1992). Linking empirically based theory and evaluation: The family bereavement program. *American Journal of Community Psychology, 20* (4), 491–520.

Schacter, R. (1978). Kinetic Psychotherapy. *Family Coordinator, 27* (3), 283–288.

Scherer, D. G., & Brondino, M. J. (1994). Multisystemic family preservation therapy: Preliminary findings from a study of rural and minority serious adolescent offenders. *Journal of Emotional and Behavioral Disorders, 2* (4), 198–206.

Sheafor, B. W., Horejsi, C. R., & Horejsi, G. A. (1998). *Techniques and guidelines for social work practice.* Boston: Allyn & Bacon.

Shepard, M. (1992). Child-visiting and domestic abuse. *Child Welfare, 71* (4), 357–367.

Shulman, L. (1984). *The skills of helping individuals and groups* (2nd ed.). Itasca, IL: Peacock.

Sicklund, M. (1992, February). Offenders in juvenile court. 1988 *OJJDP Update on Statistics,* pp. 1–11.

Simon, B. (1990). Rethinking empowerment. *Journal of Progressive Human Services, 1* (1), 27–40.

Simon, B. L. (1994). *The empowerment tradition in American social work: A History.* New York: Columbia University Press.

Simon, R. J., & Alstein, H. (1987). *Transracial adoptees and their families: A study of identity and commitment.* New York: Praeger.

Staff, I., & Fein, E. (1992). Together or separate: A study of siblings in foster care. *Child Welfare, 71* (3), 257–270.

Stevenson, K. M., Cheung, K. M., & Leung, P. (1992). A new approach to training child protective services workers for ethnically sensitive practice. *Child Welfare, 71* (4), 291–305.

Strauss, S. S., & Clarke, B. A. (1992). Decision-making patterns in adolescent mothers. *Image: Journal of Nursing Scholarship, 24* (1), 69–74.

Struck, C. (1995, Autumn). Prediction and prevention of child and adolescent antisocial behavior: Special sectia. *Journal of Consulting and Clinical Psychology, 63*, 515–584.

Sugland, B., Manlove, J., & Romano, A. (1997). *Perceptions of Opportunity and Adolescent Fertility Operationalizing across Race/Ethnicity and Social Class.* Child Trends. Washington, DC.

Sullivan, R., & Wilson, M. F. (1995). New directions for research in prevention and treatment of delinquency: A review and proposal. *Adolescence, 30* (117), 1–17.

Sundel, S. S., & Sundel, M. (1993). *Behavior modification in the human services: A systematic introduction to concepts and applications*, (3rd ed.). Newbury Park, CA: Sage.

Teare, R. J., & Sheafor, B. W. (1995). *Practice-sensitive social work education: An empirical analysis of social work practice and practitioners.* Alexandria, VA: Council on Social Work Education.

Teram, E. (1988). From self-managed hearts to collective action: Dealing with incompatible demands in the child welfare system. *Children and Youth Services Review, 10*, 305–315.

Terpstra, J. (1992). Foreward in K. H. Briar, V. H. Hanse, & N. Harris (Eds.), New Partnerships: Proceeding from the National Public Child Welfare Training Symposium, 1991 Miami Florida (in Costen).

Teyber, E. (1992). *Helping Children Cope with Divorce.* New York: Lexington Books.

Trad, P. V. (1994). Teenage pregnancy: Seeking patterns that promote family harmony. The *American Journal of Family Therapy, 22* (1), 42–56.

Trasler, G. (1960). *In place of parents.* London: Routledge & Kegan Paul.

U.S. Bureau of the Census. (1998). *Money Income and Poverty Status in the U.S. 1997.* Washington, DC: Department of Commerce.

U.S. Department of Health and Human Services, Administration for Children and Families, Office of Public Affairs.

(1997). *Change in welfare caseloads since enactment of the new welfare law.* Washington, DC: Author.

U.S. Department of Justice. Washington, DC (1992): U.S. Department of Justice Statistic, Office of Juvenile Justice and Delinquency Prevention.

Vann, B. H., & Rofuth, T. W. (1993). Child care needs of welfare recipients in Maryland's Welfare Reform Program. *Journal of Sociology and Social Welfare, 20* (2), 69–88.

Veronico, A. (1983). One church, one child: Placing children with special needs. *Children Today, 12*, 6–10.

Vosler, N. R. (1996). *New approaches to family practice: Confronting economic stress.* Thousand Oaks, CA: Sage.

Vourlekis, B. S., & Greene, R. R. (1992). *Social Work Case Management.* New York: A. de Gruyter.

Webb, N. B. (1993). *Helping bereaved children: A handbook for practitioners.* New York: The Guilford Press.

Weinbach, R. W. (1998). *The social worker as manager: A practical guide to success* (3rd ed.). Boston, MA: Allyn and Bacon.

Wells, K., & Tracey, E. (1996). Reorienting intensive family preservation services in relation to public child welfare practice. *Child Welfare, 75* (6), 667–692.

Wells, S. J., Stein, T. J., Fluke, J., & Downing, J. (1989). Screening in child protective services. *Social Work, 34* (1), 45–48.

Weston, D., Klee, L., & Halfon, N. (1989). Mental Health. In M. W. Kirst (Ed.), Conditions of children in California (pp. 206–224, 359–363).

Whittaker, J. K. (1988). *Family support and group child care* (pp. 29–55). Washington, DC: Child Welfare League of America.

Windle, M., Windle, R., & Scheidt, D. (1995, September). Physical and sexual abuse and associated mental disorders among alcoholic inpatients. *The American Journal of Psychiatry, 152*, 1322–1328.

Winefield, H. R., & Barlow, J. A. (1995). Client and worker satisfaction in a child protection agency. *Child Abuse and Neglect, 19* (8), 897–905.

Wing, L. (1993). The definition and prevalence of autism: a review. *European Child Adolescent Psychiatry, 2,* 61–74.

Winters, K., Slenchfield, R., & Fulkerson, J. (1993, Winter). Patterns and characteristics of adolescent gambling. *Journal of Gambling Studies, 9* (4), 371–386.

Wolchik, S. A., Ruehlman, L. S., Braver, S. L., & Sandler, I. N. (1989). Social support of children of divorce: Direct and stress buffering effects. *American Journal of Community Psychology, 17* (4), 485–499.

Wolf, D. A. (1991). Child care use among welfare mothers—A dynamic analysis. *Journal of Family Issues, 12* (4), 519–536.

Wood, L., Herring, A. E., & Hunt, R. (1989). *On their own: The needs of youth in transition.* Elizabeth, NJ: Association for the Advancement of the Mentally Handicapped.

Yoshikami, R. (1983). Placement of foster children in group care facilities: An analysis of a decision-making system. Unpublished dissertation, Berkeley, California.

Zarb, J. M. (1992). *Cognitive-behavioral assessment and therapy with adolescents.* New York: Brunner/Mazel.

Zigler, E., & Styfco, S. J. (1994). Head Start: Criticisms in a constructive context. *American Psychologist, 49* (2), 127–132.

Zigler, E., Taussig, C., & Black, K. (1992). Early childhood intervention: A promising preventative for juvenile delinquency. *American Psychologist, 47,* 997–1004.

Zill, N., & Coiro, M. J. (1992). Assessing the condition of children. *Children and Youth Services Review, 14* (1–2), 199–136.

Zuckerman, E. (1983). *Child welfare.* New York: Collier Macmillan.

Zuravin, S. J., & DePanfilis, D. (1997). Factors affecting foster care placement of children receiving child protective services. *Social Work Research, 21* (1), 34–42.

Photo Credits

Index

Underlined page numbers indicate boxed material or figures.

TO THE OWNER OF THIS BOOK:

I hope that you have found *Child Welfare: A Unifying Model of Practice* useful. So that this book can be improved in a future edition, would you take the time to complete this sheet and return it? Thank you.

School and address: _____

_____

Department: _____

Instructor's name: _____

1. What I like most about this book is: _____

_____

_____

2. What I like least about this book is: _____

_____

_____

3. My general reaction to this book is: _____

_____

_____

4. The name of the course in which I used this book is:_____

_____

5. Were all of the chapters of the book assigned for you to read? _____

   If not, which ones weren't?_____

6. In the space below, or on a separate sheet of paper, please write specific suggestions for improving this book and anything else you'd care to share about your experience in using this book.

_____

_____

_____

_____

OPTIONAL:

Your name: _____ Date: _____

May we quote you, either in promotion for *Child Welfare: A Unifying Model of Practice*, or in future publishing ventures?

Yes: _____ No: _____

Sincerely yours,

Jannah Hurn-Mather

Patricia B. Lager

FOLD HERE

- -

||||||

BUSINESS REPLY MAIL

FIRST CLASS   PERMIT NO. 358   PACIFIC GROVE, CA

POSTAGE WILL BE PAID BY ADDRESSEE

ATTN: *Lisa Gebo, Social Work Editor*

BROOKS/COLE/THOMSON LEARNING
511 FOREST LODGE ROAD
PACIFIC GROVE, CA   93950-9968

|||...||||.|..|.|.||...|.|.|.|...||.|.|..|.||

- -

FOLD HERE

SWPIP MODEL

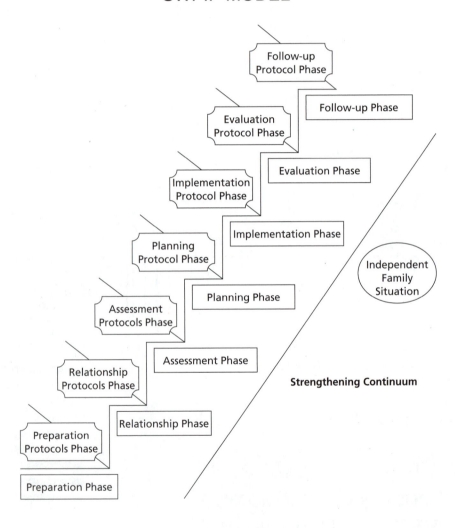